With Special Distinction

A Collection of Recipes
from the
Mississippi College Family

With Special Distinction is a collection of favorite recipes from the Mississippi College family: faculty, staff, alumni, and friends of the institution. We extend our sincere appreciation to the many individuals who submitted recipes; because of space limitations, all recipes could not be used, but those recipes have been retained for possible subsequent editions.

First Printing October 1993 10,000 copies

ISBN 0-9636101-0-4
Library of Congress Catalog Card Number 93-77090

To order additional copies of ***With Special Distinction,*** please use the order form provided at the back of this book or write:

Mississippi College Cookbook
P.O. Box 4041
Mississippi College
Clinton, MS 39058

Dedication

This book is dedicated to ***Joy Nobles****, who for more than twenty-five years graciously served as First Lady of Mississippi College. Her commitment to family, church, and community; her interest and concern in global missions efforts; her dedication to upholding the traditions of Mississippi College; and her unwavering support for Christian higher education have earned her the admiration and respect of all who know her.*

Mississippi College Cookbook Committees

Chairman: Dorothy Ivey Carpenter
Co-Chairmen: Joy Nobles, Bettye Coward
Editor: Janet Lee

Editorial
Neal Brashier
Mary Denson
Mable Gaston
Peggy Lee
Anne Martin
Wanda Mosley
Martha Shepherd
Rachel Smith
Janet Taylor
Janie White

Recipe Collection
*Carnette McMillan
Shelia Carpenter
Mary Catherine Gentry
Jan Hurt
Katty Ireland
Madelyn Lofton
Tina Magers
Maellen McIntire
Dot Parkman
Donna Purvis

Recipe Testing
*Barbara Parks
Laverne Applewhite
Tommie Broome
Carolyn Cannon
Edith Cassibry
Fleta Collins
Cheryl Cox
Joyce Dotson
Ann Eaves
Sarah Folkes
Louise Griffith
Sonia Hancock
Jeannie Lane
Cynthia Leavelle
Dixie Martin
Vicki McCall
Hazel McCarty
Charlotte McMath
Annie Ruth McPhail
Alice Nettles
Kari Norberg
Libby Patterson
Jean Ramsey
Jennifer Ray
Beverly Taylor
Mary Etta Thompson

Cookbook Sections
*Alicia Pittman
Betty Barber
Sadie Carroll
Beverly Coleman
Anne Dial
Diane Hutto
Jewel Merritt
Ed Valente
Alicia Wilbanks

Public Relations and Marketing
*Johnnie Ruth Hudson
*Susie Jordan
Robbie Bell
Jannis Gilstrap
Bill Lytal
Donna Sones
Pam Sultan

Design Format
*Marleen Gough
Ruth Glaze
Kent Mummert

Wordprocessing
Alice Smith
Pat Turner

Photography
Robert Wall

Treasurer & Bookkeeper
Jerold Meadows

* *Committee Chairman*

Introduction

Mississippi College proudly claims numerous faculty and alumni as authors, but the publication of this cookbook may represent the broadest effort yet to utilize the talents of hundreds of individuals who are connected in some manner to the oldest institution of higher learning in Mississippi.

Founded in 1826, Mississippi College has, from its earliest beginnings, exemplified a distinctive spirit in its academic curriculum and in the caliber of its people. Thus, through months of planning, recipe solicitation, testing, and editing, ***With Special Distinction*** evolved as the title which best characterizes the academic excellence of the institution as well as a mark of approval for recipes of outstanding quality.

Response to the request for favorite recipes was overwhelming. Hundreds of neatly-typed forms, dog-eared index cards, and lovingly creased and folded hand-written copies were received. The cookbook steering committee then faced the difficult task of establishing criteria for selection.

Upon receipt, each recipe was assigned a number to ensure a "blind" testing result. If an acceptable rating was indicated by the tester, the recipe was then evaluated in terms of suitability for a particular section, uniqueness, variety in food type, level of difficulty, and availability of ingredients. To prepare and taste the foods, more than 150 different individuals were involved in testing. The number of recipes submitted by any one individual was considered, as well as historical relationship to the College. Compatibility with Mississippi College traditions was also a factor for inclusion.

But deciding which recipes to use still proved to be a challenge. To involve as many people as possible, similar recipes were co-authored, with minor changes in amounts of ingredients or wording of instructions. A basic recipe might also contain a variation or optional ingredients. Occasionally, the name of the original recipe was modified to more accurately reflect the finished product, and brand names were changed to generic descriptions in most cases.

The name of each contributor has been printed as the individual requested. No professional titles were used, as that information was not always available. The year following a donor's name may indicate the date a degree was granted, the last known year of attendance, or the date a student would have graduated with other members of an entering freshman class. A name in parentheses signifies that the spouse, rather than the recipe contributor, is the alumnus. The term "Faculty Wife" is used to mean any member of the Mississippi College Faculty Wives Club: spouses of faculty, staff, administrative staff, and local Baptist ministers.

Particular care has been taken to indicate treasured family recipes which have been "handed-down" from a deceased person. The designation "From the recipes of" was created to acknowledge and give credit to the culinary contributions of earlier generations.

The recipes which were submitted came from an astonishing variety of sources including faculty, staff, students, alumni, and friends. Mississippi College alumni are scattered throughout the United States, and many of them sent recipes which provide a cross-section of regional foods. International cuisine is also a strength of the cookbook, with many such recipes coming from foreign missionaries. Recipes representing five different continents are found in this book.

Proceeds from the sale of the first printing will help to restore and preserve some of the older, historic buildings on campus. Jennings Hall, a charming former dormitory with an open courtyard, has assumed a new role in recent years as classrooms and offices were created. Jennings will be the first beneficiary of the book's sales.

We hope this cookbook will be prominently displayed in bookshelves and on kitchen counters but more importantly, that it will find its way into the hands of both veteran and novice cooks to be used, shared, and enjoyed by generations of those who love Mississippi College.

Table of Contents

Appetizers and Beverages 11
Beverages 11
Dips 17
Sandwiches 24
Hors d'oeuvres 28
Breads 39
Rolls and Biscuits 51
Cornbread 55
Muffins and Breakfast Baking 61
Salads and Soups 73
Vegetables and Fruits 113
Entrees 147
Fish and Shellfish 153
Poultry 172
Meat 192
Eggs, Cheese, and Pasta 223
Desserts 235
Cookies 243
Cakes and Icings 260
Pies 293
Puddings and Custards 311
Candy 318
Ice Cream and Frozen Desserts 324
Miscellaneous 329
Sauces, Pickles, and Herbs 329
Cooking Hints 335
Special Foods and Special People 357
Index 379

JENNINGS HALL

Jennings Hall, named for the Z. D. Jennings family and completed in 1907, is the second oldest building on the main campus. Its three floors have wide porches surrounding an interior courtyard which often serves as the site of art exhibits, dramatic and musical performances, and wedding receptions. Jennings was originally a men's dormitory (1907-1942). With the merger of Mississippi College and Hillman College, Jennings became the women's dormitory and later was designated especially for freshman women. It was last used as a dormitory in 1981-82. Part of the space has now been remodeled for offices and classrooms.

APPETIZERS AND BEVERAGES

50's Open-House Homecoming Punch

2 gallons apple juice
2 (2-liter) bottles ginger ale
2 quarts lemonade (from powdered mix)
12 dozen lemonade ice cubes (1 qt. liquid = 3 doz. cubes)

Chill liquid ingredients and place half of each in large punch bowl. Use cubes to keep chilled. Replenish with remaining liquid ingredients.

Yield: 60 (5-ounce) servings

Alicia Jones Pittman '60, Faculty Wife

This punch has been served since 1976 at the Pittmans' annual Homecoming Open House for alumni, staff, and friends from the era of the 50's.

Wedding and Shower Punch

5 cups water
4 cups sugar
4 (3-ounce) boxes gelatin (any flavor)
1 (12-ounce) can frozen lemonade
1 (12-ounce) can frozen orange juice
1 (46-ounce) can unsweetened pineapple juice
3 Tablespoons almond flavoring
1 gallon water
2 gallons lemon-lime carbonated drink

Mix 5 cups water with sugar in large boiler. Bring to a boil and stir in gelatin until dissolved. Remove from heat. Add lemonade, juices, almond flavoring, and 1 gallon of water. Mix well. Store in freezer containers. Remove from freezer 2 hours before serving. Pour fruit mixture into punch bowl, add carbonated drink. For a yellow punch suitable for golden wedding anniversary celebrations, use 2 packages lemon and 2 packages apricot gelatin. For a rose-colored punch, use strawberry gelatin and add 2 (10-ounce) packages frozen strawberries.

Yield: 65-70 servings

Lisa Cornelson

Mississippi Punch

1 (32-ounce) bottle scuppernong juice (or muscadine juice)
1 (2-liter) bottle lemon-lime carbonated drink
Fruited ice ring (optional)

Mix juice and lemon-lime carbonated drink. Pour into punch bowl. Top with fruited ice ring. This makes a delicious golden punch.

Yield: 20 (5-ounce) servings

Margaret Ann Fortenberry '51

Lemonade Base Punch

5 pounds sugar
2 cups water
12 lemons
2 ounces almond flavoring
2 ounces vanilla
2 Tablespoons citric acid
6 (2-liter) bottles lemon-lime soft drink
Crushed ice

Heat the sugar and water together until the sugar dissolves. Add juice and pulp of lemons, almond flavoring, vanilla, and citric acid to sugar and water to make a base. Use 1½ cups of base to 2 (2-liter) bottles lemon-lime soft drinks. Add enough crushed ice to cover the bottom of a punch bowl. This base will keep in the refrigerator up to a year.

Yield: Approximately 160 (4-ounce) servings with ice

Thelma Bush

Blackberry Punch or Punch Base

12 pounds blackberries
5 ounces tartaric acid
2 quarts warm water
3 cups sugar

Add the tartaric acid dissolved in the warm water to the blackberries. Let stand 24 hours. If commercially frozen blackberries must be used, let fruit mixture stand 48 hours. Strain. To 2 cups juice, add 3 cups sugar. Chill. To serve, fill each cup half full with punch base; finish filling with water.

Yield: 1 gallon punch base

Margaret Germany, Faculty Wife (Archie Germany '39)

Kissimee Punch Slush

6 cups water
4 cups sugar
4 (6-ounce) cans frozen orange juice
1 (46-ounce) can pineapple juice
Juice of 2 lemons
2 oranges, peeled
6 large bananas, mashed well
1 small bottle maraschino cherries, chopped well
3 quarts lemon-lime carbonated drink or ginger ale

Combine water and sugar; boil about 3 minutes to make a syrup. Cool and add juices. Place 1 cup of juice mixture into a blender or food processor, add oranges and blend well. Stir in mashed bananas and cherries. Freeze. Remove from freezer 2-3 hours before serving; thaw and make slushy with a potato masher. Add carbonated drink just before serving.

Yield: 60 servings

Linda Gayle Ganaway Liechty '63

First Baptist Punch

10 cups water, divided
2 cups sugar
1 (46-ounce) can unsweetened orange juice
1 (46-ounce) can unsweetened pineapple juice
1 (8-ounce) bottle lemon juice

Bring 3 cups of water and the sugar to a boil. Cool; then add juices and remaining water. Stir well and chill. Food coloring may be added. This mixture freezes well.

Variation: *Rosamond Parker Rankin* '58 adds 1 (6-ounce) can frozen orange juice and 2 (12-ounce) cans peach or apricot juice.

Yield: 1½ gallons

Kimberly Entrican Henderson '88

This punch is a staple at First Baptist Church, Senatobia, receptions and functions.

Lemon-Pineapple Slush Punch

14 cups water, divided
1 (6-ounce) box lemon gelatin
2 (46-ounce) cans unsweetened pineapple juice
1 (8-ounce) bottle lemon juice
3 cups sugar
1 quart ginger ale (optional)

Bring 4 cups of water to a boil. Remove from heat and mix in gelatin; stir until dissolved. Add juices and sugar. Stir until sugar is dissolved, then add 10 cups of water. Store in a large-mouthed container designed for freezer storage. Remove from freezer 2-3 hours before needed (5-6 hours if frozen hard). Mash until slushy; add ginger ale and serve. To change yellow color of punch, change the flavor of the gelatin.

Yield: 2 gallons punch base

Jackie Earley (Paul Earley '75)

Fruited Mint Julep

2 cups sugar
2½ cups water
½ cup fresh mint leaves, crushed
1 cup lemon juice
1 cup orange juice
Sparkling water
Crushed ice
Mint sprigs

Boil sugar and water until sugar is dissolved. Add mint leaves. Cool and strain. Add fruit juices. Mix with equal parts of sparkling water and serve over crushed ice. Garnish with mint sprigs.

Yield: 12 (6-ounce) servings

Nancy Wright Futral '58

Lemonade Tea

3 quarts water, divided
6 regular tea bags
1 cup sugar (or equivalent sugar substitute)
1 (6-ounce) can frozen lemonade concentrate

Boil 1 quart of water. Add tea bags and steep for 5 minutes. Add sugar, lemonade, and remaining water. Chill and serve.

Yield: 20 (5-ounce) servings

Ann Beckham McCurdy '73

Russian Tea

1 teaspoon whole cloves
1 teaspoon whole allspice
2 sticks cinnamon
11 cups water
3 tea bags
½ cup sugar
1 (6-ounce) can frozen orange juice concentrate
1 (6-ounce) can frozen lemonade concentrate
1 (46-ounce) can unsweetened pineapple juice

Put spices in large boiler; add water and bring to a boil. Simmer covered for 5 minutes. Add tea bags and steep for 1 hour. Remove tea bags and spices. Add sugar and stir well. Mix in orange juice and lemonade until fully dissolved. Stir in pineapple juice. This mixture may be reheated in quantity on rangetop or in individual servings in the microwave. The tea must be stored in the refrigerator; it will keep for 10 days.

Yield: 18 cups

Janet Stampley Lee '74, Faculty Wife

Hot Cherry Punch

1 (.15-ounce) package cherry-flavored drink mix
¾ cup sugar
1¾ ounces red hot candies
1 (46-ounce) can unsweetened pineapple juice
6 cups water
16 cinnamon sticks or peppermint candy canes (optional)

Combine drink mix, sugar, red hot candies, pineapple juice, and water in a large saucepan. Heat on rangetop to dissolve sugar and red hot candies. Serve hot with cinnamon sticks or peppermint candy canes.

Yield: 16 servings

Carnette R. McMillan '50, Faculty Wife

Iced tea requires half as much sugar if sweetened while hot.

Hot Spiced Wassail

Spice mixture:
6 sticks cinnamon
16 whole cloves
1 teaspoon allspice

Juice mixture A:
½ cup sugar
4 cups cranberry juice
12 cups apple juice

Juice mixture B:
1 cup brown sugar
4 cups water
8 cups cranberry juice
1 (46-ounce) can pineapple juice

Choose either juice mixture A or juice mixture B. Tie spices in a cloth bag. Combine sugar and juices in a large container. Add spices and simmer for 10 minutes. Remove spice bag and serve hot. To serve at a buffet pour either juice mixture into a 30-cup percolator and place spices in the basket. Red hot candies or dried apple chips may be added.

Yield: 16-18 cups

Susan S. Slater '76
Trudy Nash Smith (Chris Smith '79)

Fireside Coffee

2 cups non-dairy coffee creamer
1½ cups hot cocoa mix
1½ cups instant coffee crystals
1½ cups sugar
1 teaspoon cinnamon
½ teaspoon ground nutmeg

Mix all ingredients and store in an air-tight container. To serve, stir 3 teaspoons mix into 1 cup boiling water.

Yield: 6½ cups mix

Candy Phillips Anderson '77

Hot Chocolate Mix

1 (8-quart) box non-fat dry milk
1 pound chocolate milk drink mix
1 pound confectioners' sugar
1 (6-ounce) jar non-dairy creamer

Mix all ingredients well. Store in an air-tight container. Use ⅓ cup mix with 1 cup boiling water per serving.

Yield: 4 quarts dry mix or 50 servings

Carolyn Cannon '73, Faculty Wife

Spiced Tea Mix

1 (15-ounce) jar orange flavor instant breakfast drink
1⅓ cups sugar
⅔ cup instant tea
6 Tablespoons lemonade mix
1½ teaspoons nutmeg
1 teaspoon ground cloves

Mix all ingredients together in a large bowl. To serve, use 2-3 heaping teaspoons per 8 ounces of hot water. A small jar of this mix makes an ideal Christmas gift.

Yield: 4-5 (6-ounce) jars

Tamra Potter Helms '81

Almond Fruited Cheese Ball

2 cups almond cereal, crushed fine
1 (8-ounce) package cream cheese, softened
¼ cup raisins
¼ cup flaked coconut (preferably frozen)
1 (8-ounce) can crushed pineapple
½ teaspoon almond flavoring

Set aside one-fourth cup crushed cereal. Mix all remaining ingredients together and shape into a ball. Roll ball in reserved cereal and refrigerate 30 minutes or longer. Serve with assorted crackers or old-fashioned gingersnaps.

Yield: 12 servings

Doug Palmer '58

Choctaw Cheese Ball

1 (8-ounce) package cream cheese, softened
1 (8-ounce) jar pasteurized processed cheese spread
1 (7-ounce) roll cheese n' onion processed cheese food
6 ounces Monterey Jack cheese
8 ounces Colby cheese
2 Tablespoons garlic powder
1 small onion, grated
2 eggs, hard boiled and mashed
¼ cup red bell pepper, chopped fine
½ cup pecans, chopped fine
Paprika

With wooden spoon, combine cream cheese, cheese spread, and cheese food. Shred Monterey Jack and Colby cheeses; add to cream cheese mixture. Add garlic powder, onion, eggs, and red bell pepper to cheese mixture. Mix well and shape into a ball. Refrigerate about 4 hours, the roll ball in pecans; sprinkle with paprika. Serve with choice of crackers or chips. This cheese ball may be prepared in advance.

Yield: 35-40 party-size snacks

Linda Gayle Ganaway Liechty '63

Delicious Cheese Ball

¼ cup bell pepper, chopped fine
2 Tablespoons onion, chopped fine
2 (8-ounce) packages cream cheese, softened
1 (8¼-ounce) can crushed pineapple, drained
1 Tablespoon seasoned salt
2 cups nuts, chopped fine (divided)
½ cup parsley, chopped

Mix pepper, onion, cream cheese, pineapple, seasoned salt, and 1½ cups nuts. Shape into a ball. Roll ball in parsley and remaining chopped nuts. Wrap in foil or plastic wrap and refrigerate.

Yield: 1½ pound ball

Helen Panzica '61
Lynn King

Cheese Ring

1 pound sharp Cheddar cheese, grated
1 Tablespoon onion, grated
1 cup pecans, chopped
1 Tablespoon lemon juice
1 teaspoon salt
1 cup mayonnaise
1 teaspoon Tabasco sauce
1 (16-ounce) jar strawberry jelly or preserves, chilled

Mix cheese, onion, pecans, lemon juice, salt, mayonnaise, and Tabasco sauce. Form into a ring with a hollow center and chill. Fill the middle of the ring with jelly or preserves immediately before serving. Serve with round buttery crackers.

Yield: 12-15 servings

Jeannie Lane '81, Staff

Party Dip for Fruit

1 cup sour cream
¾ cup brown sugar
1 (8-ounce) package cream cheese, softened
1 Tablespoon flavored instant coffee (any flavor)
1 cup frozen whipped topping
¾ cup unsalted peanuts, chopped coarsely
Fresh pears and apples, sliced

Blend sour cream, brown sugar, cream cheese, and flavored coffee with a wooden spoon. Gently fold in the whipped topping and peanuts. Serve with fresh pear and apple slices. The dip keeps well in refrigerator when covered. Mixture will thicken, but may be diluted with 2-3 tablespoons milk.

Variation: For a simple version of this dip, use just the brown sugar and sour cream.

Yield: 20 appetizer servings

Carolyn Breland Ray '56
Donna Powell Diaz '80

Dipping fresh fruit into pineapple juice will keep the fruit from darkening.

Cheesecake Dip

1 (3-ounce) package cream cheese
2 Tablespoons sugar
3 Tablespoons low-fat milk
2 cups frozen lite whipped topping
1 teaspoon vanilla

Beat cream cheese, sugar, and milk until well blended and smooth. Fold in whipped topping and vanilla; store in refrigerator. Use as a dip for cookies, cake cubes, fresh fruit, pretzel sticks, etc. This dip contains 6 calories per teaspoon.

Yield: 2 cups

Marie Gaddis

Jezebel Dip

1 (18-ounce) jar pineapple preserves
1 (18-ounce) jar apple jelly
1 ounce dry mustard
5 ounces horseradish
1 teaspoon cracked pepper
1 (8-ounce) package cream cheese

Mix preserves, jelly, mustard, horseradish, and pepper in blender, then refrigerate overnight. Mixture will appear liquid when blended but will have a preserve-like consistency after refrigeration. Pour Jezebel Dip over room-temperature cream cheese and serve with round buttery crackers. This dip may also be used for boiled shrimp, egg rolls, or sausage biscuits.

Yield: 15 appetizer servings

Jean Pope

Hot Artichoke Dip

1 (14-ounce) can artichoke hearts, drained
2 cups fresh Parmesan cheese, grated
2 cups mayonnaise
¼ teaspoon garlic salt
½ teaspoon lemon juice

Mash artichoke hearts. Combine with remaining ingredients. Bake in a 2-quart baking dish in a preheated 350 degree oven for 10-20 minutes.

Yield: 12 servings

Trudy Nash Smith (Chris Smith '79)

Hot Broccoli Dip

2 ribs celery, chopped fine
1 onion, chopped fine
2 Tablespoons butter
1 (6-ounce) roll garlic cheese
1 can cream of mushroom soup
1 (4-ounce) can chopped mushrooms
1 (10-ounce) package frozen chopped broccoli, cooked and drained

Sauté celery and onion in butter until tender. Add cheese, soup, mushrooms, and broccoli. Heat. Serve hot with crackers. This dip may be used as a topping for baked potatoes, too.

Yield: 12-15 appetizer servings

Carol Marsh Humphrey '70
Jan Simmons Cameron '78

Crabmeat-Shrimp Dip

2 cans small shrimp
2 cans cream of shrimp soup
2 large cans crabmeat
1 (6-ounce) can water-pack tuna
3 Tablespoons onion, grated
Salt
Pepper
2 packages sour cream mix

Heat shrimp soup; add crab, shrimp, and tuna. When mixture is heated, add onion, salt, and pepper. Prepare sour cream mix according to package instructions. Fold in seafood just before serving. Serve with party crackers.

Yield: 20-25 appetizer servings

Carroll Overton Waller '48

Carroll Waller is the wife of former governor, William Waller. She received an honorary Doctor of Letters degree from the College in 1977.

Savory dips may be served in a hollowed-out head of purple cabbage. Serve sweet dips in a hollowed-out pineapple half.

Shrimp Party Dip

1 can cream of shrimp soup
1 (8-ounce) package cream cheese, softened
¼ cup green pepper, chopped fine
1½ teaspoons pimiento, chopped fine
Dash of Tabasco sauce
½ teaspoon chili powder

Gradually blend soup into cream cheese. Beat until just smooth. Add green pepper, pimiento and Tabasco sauce. Chill. When ready to serve, pour into a serving dish and sprinkle with chili powder.

Yield: 2½ cups

Cynthia Barber Evans '87

Layered Nacho Dip

1 (16-ounce) can refried beans
½ package dry taco seasoning mix
1 (6-ounce) carton avocado dip
1 (8-ounce) carton sour cream
1 (4-ounce) can ripe olives, chopped
2 tomatoes, diced
1 onion, chopped
1 (4-ounce) can chopped green chilies
1½ cups Monterey Jack cheese, shredded

Combine beans and taco seasoning mix. Spread in 9x13 Pyrex dish. Layer remaining ingredients in order listed. Serve with large corn chips.

Yield: 16 appetizer servings

Jo Ellen Clark

For a never-fail, delicious hors d'oeuvre, keep a package of cream cheese on hand. Pour Worcestershire sauce, green or red pepper jelly, crab meat, and cocktail sauce (or another favorite) over it and serve with crackers.

Tangy Mild Salsa

2 (14½-ounce) cans stewed tomatoes, drained
1 (8-ounce) can tomato sauce
1 large onion, chopped fine
⅓ cup green pepper, chopped
1 large garlic clove, crushed
1 teaspoon parsley
1 teaspoon cilantro
½ teaspoon cumin
½ teaspoon salt (or to taste)
¼ teaspoon pepper
1 teaspoon olive oil
1 Tablespoon lemon juice
1-2 drops Tabasco sauce

Chop stewed tomatoes in blender until chunky but not pureed. Pour tomatoes into bowl and combine with the remaining ingredients. Chill thoroughly (at least overnight) before serving so that flavors are well blended. Serve with tortilla chips.

Yield: 5 cups

Debra Richmond King '77

Nacho Delight

2 pounds ground beef
1 (30-ounce) jar spaghetti sauce
1 pound Cheddar cheese, grated
Nacho chips or corn tortilla chips
Large jalapeño pepper (optional)

In a large skillet brown the ground beef; drain, add spaghetti sauce and grated cheese. Heat to boiling point. Add chopped pepper to sauce or serve on side. Serve over chips or as a dip.

Variation: Brown 1 pound of sausage; drain. Add 1 pound jalapeño process cheese spread and 1 large can stewed tomatoes. Simmer until cheese melts.

Yield: 25 appetizer servings

Sarah Carolyn Moody Majors '63
Karen G. Pruitt '88

Asparagus Foldovers

1 loaf fresh white sandwich bread
1 (15-ounce) can asparagus spears, drained
Mayonnaise
Margarine, melted
Garlic salt

Trim crusts from bread; flatten slices with a rolling pin. Spread each piece of bread with mayonnaise. Roll up 1 asparagus spear in each slice of bread. Cut into thirds or halves. Secure with toothpicks. Brush with margarine melted with a little garlic salt. Bake until brown in a preheated 350 degree oven. Serve warm.

Yield: 50 appetizer servings

Fleda McElvoy Collins '57

Cucumber Sandwiches

1 large cucumber
3 Tablespoons vinegar
1 Tablespoon lemon juice
1 Tablespoon sugar
¼ teaspoon salt
Dash of pepper
½ teaspoon onion, grated
12 ounces cream cheese, softened
Dash of MSG (monosodium glutamate)
Green food color (optional)
24 slices sandwich bread

Peel cucumber and grate coarsely, removing any large seeds. Mix together the vinegar, lemon juice, sugar, salt, and pepper. Soak cucumber for 15 minutes in liquid (can be soaked longer for more flavor). Drain cucumber well. Blend in other filling ingredients. Mix well. Do not put in blender. Spread on bread. Sandwiches can then be stored in an airtight container. The sandwiches may be refrigerated for 1-2 days.

Yield: 24 sandwiches

Connie B. Evans, Staff

Shrimp Sandwiches

½ cup mayonnaise
1 (8-ounce) package cream cheese, softened
½ teaspoon onion, grated
1 Tablespoon lemon juice
1 (5-ounce) can cocktail shrimp, chopped fine
¼ cup celery, chopped fine
24 slices sandwich bread, trimmed and frozen

Cream mayonnaise and cheese; add onions and lemon juice. Fold in shrimp and celery. Spread on bread. Cut to desired size with electric knife. Refrigerate until ready to serve. These may be frozen for later use. If any mix remains, add sour cream to make a good dip.

Yield: 24 sandwiches

Mae Beth Walsh, Faculty Wife

Shrimp Wheels

1 (5-ounce) can shrimp, drained and mashed
2 Tablespoons stuffed green olives, chopped
2 Tablespoons bottled chili sauce
¼ cup mayonnaise
1 Tablespoon celery, chopped fine
1 (8-ounce) package refrigerated crescent rolls

Combine shrimp, olives, chili sauce, mayonnaise, and celery; set aside. Separate rolls into 4 rectangles. Spread one-fourth mixture on each rectangle and roll in jelly roll fashion. Refrigerate until thoroughly chilled for easier slicing. Slice and place on greased cookie sheet; bake until golden brown in a preheated 375 degree oven for approximately 12 minutes. Crabmeat may be substituted for shrimp.

Yield: 4 dozen

Bessie Hutto

To keep tea sandwiches moist, arrange one layer of sandwiches in an airtight container; cover with a damp white paper towel followed by a piece of wax paper. Layer in this manner to the top of the container. Cover tightly and refrigerate for up to 2 days.

Meatlover's Delight

1 pound hot sausage
1 pound ground beef
1 pound processed cheese spread
1 teaspoon oregano
Party bread or Melba rounds

Preheat oven to 400 degrees. Brown sausage and ground beef together; drain. Melt cheese in microwave and combine with browned meat. Top bread with this mixture and bake for 20 minutes or until slightly browned. The mixture may be prepared ahead and refrigerated until needed.

Yield: 16-18 appetizer servings

Raecheal Bell (Damon Bell '91)

Mississippi Sin

1 loaf round bread (French or Hawaiian)
1½ cups sour cream
2 cups Cheddar cheese, shredded
1 (8-ounce) package cream cheese, softened
⅓ cup green onion, chopped
½ cup ham, chopped
⅓ cup green chilies, chopped
Dash of Worcestershire sauce

Preheat oven to 350 degrees. Slice off top of bread and hollow out inside, reserving chunks of bread. Mix all filling ingredients together. Pour into the bread shell. Replace top on bread and wrap in foil. Place on cookie sheet and bake 1 hour. Use chunks of bread for "dippers" or crackers or chips.

Yield: 1 loaf

Alice Germany Nettles '76, Faculty Wife

Date Sandwich Spread

1 package pitted dates, chopped
¾ cup sugar
⅔ cup milk
Pinch of salt
2 Tablespoons butter
1 cup nuts, chopped fine
1 (8-ounce) package cream cheese, softened
Raisin bread

Combine chopped dates, sugar, milk, salt, and butter. Boil slowly until dates have melted and mixture is thick. Cool. Add nuts and cream cheese. Spread on raisin bread and cut into party sandwiches.

Yield: 60-70 party sandwiches

Emogene Ray Stephenson '47

Hot Cheese Toasties

2 (8-ounce) jars sharp pasteurized processed cheese spread
1 stick margarine, softened
1 egg, well beaten
¼ teaspoon red pepper or Worcestershire sauce
1 Tablespoon onion, grated
Dash of garlic powder
20 slices sandwich bread, trimmed

Mix all filling ingredients together. Assemble sandwiches. Frost with remaining filling. Cut into halves or fourths. These may be frozen for later use. Bake in a preheated 350 degree oven for 10 minutes. Serve hot.

Yield: 20 halves or 40 fourths

Nan M. Sibley '56, Staff

Texas Tortilla Pinwheels

1 (8-ounce) package cream cheese
1 (8-ounce) carton sour cream
1 (4-ounce) can green chilies, chopped
1 (4-ounce) can black olives, chopped
1 teaspoon garlic salt
1½ cups Cheddar cheese, grated
2 Tablespoons onion, minced
6 large flour tortillas

Mix all ingredients except tortillas. Spread mixture on tortillas. Roll and chill. Slice into pinwheels to serve. Use with picante sauce for dipping.

Yield: 48 appetizer servings

Ann Beckham McCurdy '73
Melanie Taylor Widman '79

Shrimp or Smoked Oyster Mousse

2 envelopes unflavored gelatin
½ cup water
1 (8-ounce) package cream cheese
1 cup mayonnaise
2 (6½-ounce) cans shrimp or smoked oysters, chopped
2 Tablespoons Worcestershire sauce
½ teaspoon garlic powder
Dash Tabasco sauce
Lemon slice or black olives for garnish (optional)

Soften gelatin in water and set aside. Combine cream cheese and mayonnaise in saucepan and cook over medium heat or in microwave until cream cheese melts, stirring often. Add other ingredients. Spoon into well-greased fish mold or any 3½ cup mold. Cover and chill overnight. Unmold, garnish with a lemon slice or black olives. Serve with crackers.

Yield: 12-15 appetizer servings

Monica Fioranelli

Sausage Balls

1 pound hot or mild sausage, cooked and crumbled
1 (8-ounce) package cream cheese
3½ cups biscuit baking mix

Combine cream cheese and drained sausage in top of double boiler and heat until cheese melts. Cool. Stir in biscuit mix. Place mixture in the refrigerator for 1 hour or until cool. Remove and mold into bite-sized balls. These freeze well. At serving time, bake for about 20 minutes in a preheated 325 degree oven.

Yield: Approximately 50 balls

Carroll Overton Waller '48

Ham and Cheese Bites

½ pound margarine
3 Tablespoons poppy seed
1 teaspoon Worcestershire sauce
3 Tablespoons mustard
1 medium onion, finely chopped
2 packages 1-inch rolls
Shredded ham
Shredded Swiss cheese

Blend together margarine, poppy seed, Worcestershire sauce, mustard, and onion. Split the packages of rolls. Spread each split side with the blended mixture. Sprinkle the shredded ham and cheese over the mixture. Replace top on rolls. Wrap in foil and bake for 10 minutes in a preheated 400 degree oven. Separate or cut rolls apart to serve.

Yield: 48 appetizer servings

Janice Jones

Marinated Carrot Strips

5 small or 3 large carrots, cut into 2-inch sticks
2 Tablespoons red wine vinegar
2 Tablespoons oil
½ clove garlic, minced
½ teaspoon seasoned salt
¼ teaspoon salt

Mix vinaigrette ingredients and pour over carrots. Chill overnight, turning occasionally. Serve with toothpicks or cocktail forks.

Yield: 6-8 servings

Vicki Furr Derrick '62, Staff

Marinated New Potatoes

1 pound new potatoes

Marinade:
2 (16-ounce) bottles Italian salad dressing
Garlic salt
Worcestershire sauce

Dip:
1 package ranch buttermilk dressing mix
Seasoned salt
Red pepper
Chives
1 package dry Italian salad dressing mix

Boil potatoes until done and leave in skins. Place in a deep pan for marinating. Marinate overnight in the Italian salad dressing mixed with garlic salt and Worcestershire sauce. Remove from marinade and place in a baking pan. Sprinkle again with garlic salt. Bake in a preheated 350-400 degree oven for 20 minutes. Dip: Prepare ranch dressing as directed on package. Add garlic salt, seasoned salt, red pepper, chives, and dry Italian dressing mix. Serve potatoes with dip.

Yield: 6 servings

Cindy Hampton, Staff

Pickled Mushrooms

⅔ cup oil
⅓ cup wine vinegar
1 Tablespoon lemon juice
1 Tablespoon chives, chopped
1 Tablespoon seasoned salt flavor enhancer
1 teaspoon dry tarragon leaves
1 teaspoon black pepper
2 small cloves garlic, finely cut
3 (6-ounce) cans small, whole mushrooms

Mix all ingredients except mushrooms in a quart jar that can be sealed tightly. Add mushrooms then refrigerate. Marinade will become milky. Shake well to mix. Let mixture stand at least 24 hours before serving, turning jar upside down several times while mushrooms are marinating. To serve, drain liquid from mushrooms. Serve with cocktail forks or toothpicks.

Yield: 12-15 appetizers

Ruth Ann Gibson, Faculty

Vegetable Appetizers

2 (8-ounce) cans refrigerated crescent rolls
2 (8-ounce) packages cream cheese, softened
¾ cup margarine
1 package ranch-style salad dressing mix
1 large carrot, shredded
1 cup broccoli, chopped coarsely
1 medium red onion, chopped (optional)
1 cup Cheddar cheese, shredded

Preheat oven to 350 degrees. Unroll crescent rolls and pat flat into jelly roll pan. Press edges and perforations together to line bottom of pan. Bake for 7-8 minutes, then cool. Mix cream cheese, margarine, and salad dressing mix. Spread over cooled roll layer. Sprinkle carrots, broccoli, and red onion over cream cheese mixture. Top with shredded Cheddar cheese. Cover and chill 8 hours. Cut into 1¼-inch squares.

Yield: 8 dozen

Mary Jean Padgett '73, Faculty
Amy Ellen McAlpin '93
Susan Newman, Staff

Curried Chicken Balls

1 (3-ounce) package cream cheese
2 Tablespoons mayonnaise-type salad dressing
1 cup cooked chicken, ground
1 cup almonds, chopped fine
1 Tablespoon chutney
¼ teaspoon curry
½ teaspoon salt
½ cup coconut (optional) *or*
½ cup parsley, chopped (optional)

Mix all ingredients together, except coconut or parsley. Refrigerate 1 hour; shape into bite-size balls. Roll in coconut or parsley. These may be frozen but remove from the freezer 1 hour before serving.

Yield: 30-40 balls

Louella Crawford '24

Tortilla Roll-Ups

2 (8-ounce) packages cream cheese, softened
1 package ranch salad dressing mix (original milk recipe)
2 green onions, minced
4 (12-inch) flour tortillas
8 squares thinly-sliced ham
8 squares thinly-sliced Swiss cheese
½ cup red bell pepper, diced
½ cup celery, diced
1 (4-ounce) can sliced black olives, drained

Mix cream cheese, salad dressing mix, and onions. Spread half of this mixture on tortillas. Place 2 slices of ham side by side on each tortilla. Sprinkle red bell pepper, celery and olives on top of the ham. Place 2 slices of cheese side by side on top of the vegetable mixture. Frost cheese slices with the remainder of the cream cheese mixture. Roll tortilla, wrapping tightly. Chill for 2 hours. Trim roll ends and cut rolls into 1-inch slices. Arrange on plate with vegetable garnishes.

Yield: 3 dozen

Julie Fussell '84

Nannie McLemore's Cheese Straws

½ pound butter or margarine, softened
1 pound sharp cheese, grated
2 cups all-purpose flour
½ teaspoon salt
Red pepper to taste

Preheat oven to 400 degrees. Mix all ingredients together by hand. Use a cookie press to make long strips on ungreased cookie sheet. Cut to 2-inch length straws in pan before baking. Bake for about 8 minutes or until straws begin to brown at bottom edges. Remove quickly from cookie sheet.

Yield: About 60 two-inch cheese straws

Lucy O. Barnett

Mrs. McLemore was the wife of R. A. McLemore, President of Mississippi College, 1957-68.

Mushroom Puffs

1 (4-ounce) can mushroom pieces and stems, chopped
1 (8-ounce) package cream cheese, softened
3-4 shallots, chopped
1 teaspoon seasoned salt
2 (8-ounce) cans refrigerated crescent rolls
1 egg, beaten
Poppy seed

Preheat oven to 350 degrees. Mix mushrooms, cream cheese, shallots, and seasoned salt. Set aside. Pinch diagonal seams in crescent rolls to form rectangles (4 per package). Spread cheese mixture onto dough and roll lengthwise in jelly roll fashion. Cut each log into 5 or 6 pieces. Brush with egg and place on a greased cookie sheet. Sprinkle with poppy seed. Bake for 20-25 minutes or until golden brown.

Yield: 32 bite-size pieces

Charlotte C. Daley '85

MC Bacon-Wrapped Chicken Livers

1 pint chicken livers
Salt and pepper to taste
4 Tablespoons paprika
2 cups all-purpose flour
1 pound bacon, cut into thirds

Preheat oven to 300 degrees. Sprinkle a jelly roll pan with water and line with wax paper. Drain and rinse chicken livers. Cut each liver into 2 pieces. Salt and pepper the chicken livers. Mix paprika and flour together. Roll each liver in flour mixture. Wrap with bacon, secure with a toothpick, and roll in flour again. Place onto a jelly roll pan. Bake until golden brown. Watch closely - they burn easily!

Yield: 12-15 appetizer servings

Melissa C. Wiggins '88, Faculty

Oysters Point Clear

1 pint raw oysters
Oyster half shells
1 box rock salt
1 pint sour cream
1 stick butter, melted
1 package saltine cracker crumbs
1 cup Parmesan cheese, grated

Place one raw oyster on each oyster half shell. Place shells on a bed of rock salt on a cookie sheet. Mix butter, cracker crumbs, and cheese together in a small bowl until crumbly; set aside. On each oyster, place 1 teaspoon of sour cream, then top with 1 tablespoon crumb mixture. Cook until brown in a preheated 350 degree oven for about 20-25 minutes. Serve hot. If oyster shells are not available, cook oysters in a flat dish without rock salt. The quantities may be increased to serve a large party.

Yield: 6-8 servings

Lisa Eichelberger, Faculty

Barbecued Shrimp

2 pounds jumbo shrimp with heads and shells
1 stick margarine, cut into pats
2 lemons
Black pepper, ground fine

Preheat oven to 350 degrees. Place rinsed, drained shrimp and margarine in a 11x13 baking dish. Sprinkle lemon juice over shrimp. Quarter lemon shells and place in pan. Season generously with pepper. Bake for 15-20 minutes. Baste and stir every 5 minutes. Place under broiler 2-3 minutes to brown sauce.

Yield: 10-12 appetizer servings

Linda Merritt Pratt '57

Crabmeat Hors d'oeuvres

1 stick margarine, softened
1 (8-ounce) package pasteurized processed cheese spread, softened
1½ Tablespoons mayonnaise
½ teaspoon garlic salt
¼ teaspoon celery salt
¼ teaspoon pepper
1 teaspoon onion, minced
1 (6½-ounce) can all-white crabmeat, drained
1 (3-ounce) jar pimiento, diced and drained
6 English muffins, halved

Mix together all ingredients and spread on muffin halves. Muffin halves may be frozen, then cut into four pieces. After cutting, place in freezer bags until ready to use. Bake on cookie sheet in a preheated 350 degree oven for 10-15 minutes. Do not overcook

Yield: 48 pieces

Dorothy Ann Morton Beatty '58
Andy Hughes '78

Cocktail Meatballs

Meatballs:
2 pounds ground beef
1 cup corn flake crumbs
⅓ cup dried parsley flakes
2 eggs
2 Tablespoons soy sauce
¼ teaspoon black pepper
½ teaspoon garlic powder
⅓ cup catsup
2 Tablespoons onion, minced

Sauce:
1 (1-pound) can cranberry sauce
1 (12-ounce) bottle of chili sauce
2 Tablespoons brown sugar, firmly packed
1 Tablespoon lemon juice

Preheat oven to 350 degrees. In a large bowl, combine all meatball ingredients. Blend well. Form into small meatballs and place in a deep dish. In a saucepan, combine sauce ingredients and cook over low heat, stirring occasionally. When mixture is smooth and cranberry sauce is melted, pour over the meatballs. Bake uncovered for 30 minutes. Serve in a chafing dish or crockpot to keep warm.

Yield: 60-75 meatballs

Mary Ann Graves '72

Chipped Beef Hors d'oeuvres

1 (8-ounce) package cream cheese, softened
2 Tablespoons milk
2 (3-ounce) packages chipped beef, shredded
¼ cup green pepper, chopped
2 Tablespoons dehydrated onion flakes
½ teaspoon garlic salt
¼ teaspoon pepper
½ cup sour cream

Topping:
½ cup broken pecans
2 Tablespoons margarine
½ teaspoon salt

Preheat oven to 350 degrees. Mix the cream cheese and milk together. Add beef, green pepper, onion flakes, garlic salt, pepper, and sour cream to the cream cheese mixture. For topping sauté pecans in margarine and salt. Sprinkle topping over beef mixture and bake for 20 minutes. Serve hot in chafing dish with crackers or fresh vegetables.

Yield: 2 cups

Bea Snazelle, Faculty Wife

Mari's English Horse Drawers

1 package English muffins
1 cup mayonnaise
6 scallions, chopped fine
1½ cups Cheddar cheese, shredded
1 teaspoon capers, chopped fine

Preheat oven to 350 degrees. Split each muffin in half. Mix mayonnaise, scallions, cheese and capers well. Spread on muffin halves. Quarter muffin halves with sharp knife. Bake on cookie sheet until cheese is melted. These may be frozen on cookie sheets and baked just before serving.

Yield: 48 appetizers

Ruth Ann Gibson, Faculty

The intriguing name of this dish evolved in our family from the more well-known term "hors d'oeuvres."

LOWREY HALL

Lowrey Hall, built in 1914, was named for W. T. Lowrey, President of the College, 1898-1911. It housed the main library until 1959. In 1947, to accommodate the growing collection, a wing was added at the rear of the building. In 1960, after the library had moved to a more modern facility, the building was renovated, and it became the home of the Division of Education and Psychology, reorganized as the School of Education in 1977. Alumni from earlier years may remember the top floor of Lowrey as the assembly area for the Philomathean and Hermenian Literary Societies.

BREADS

Banana Bread

2 cups flour
½ teaspoon salt
1 teaspoon cinnamon
1 stick margarine, melted
1 cup sugar
2 eggs
1 teaspoon vanilla
3 large ripe bananas, mashed
1 teaspoon soda
½ cup nuts, chopped (optional)

Preheat oven to 350 degrees. Grease loaf pan (8x4x2½). In small bowl, combine flour, salt, and cinnamon; set aside. In large bowl, mix together margarine, sugar, eggs, and vanilla. In small bowl, mash bananas and stir in soda. Add flour and bananas to margarine mixture alternately. Stir in nuts. Pour into a loaf pan. Bake about 50 minutes. The bread may be served warm with cream cheese spread that has fruit added.

Yield: 1 loaf

Kristy Lee '92
Johnnie Harper, Faculty Wife

Chocolate Chip Banana Bread

½ cup butter or margarine, softened
1 cup sugar
2 eggs
3 ripe bananas, mashed
2 cups all-purpose flour
1 teaspoon baking powder
½ teaspoon soda
1 teaspoon salt
¾ cup semisweet chocolate mini-morsels
½ cup walnuts, chopped

Preheat oven to 350 degrees. Grease a loaf pan (9x5x3). Cream butter or margarine; gradually add sugar, beating well at medium speed with an electric mixer. Add eggs, one at a time, beating after each addition. Stir in bananas. Combine flour, baking powder, soda and salt and gradually add to creamed mixture, beating until blended. Stir in mini-morsels and walnuts. Spoon batter into a prepared loaf pan. Bake for 1 hour and 10 minutes or until a wooden pick inserted in center comes out clean; shield with aluminum foil after 1 hour if bread is browning too quickly. Cool in pan for 10 minutes; remove from pan and cool completely on a wire rack.

Yield: 1 loaf

Lacey Ann Campbell '91

Pluckin' Bread

6 cups all-purpose flour
½ cup sugar
1 teaspoon salt
2 cups milk
1 package yeast
2 eggs
10 Tablespoons melted butter
Extra sugar, cinnamon, melted butter and chopped pecans

To 3 cups sifted flour, add sugar and salt, and resift. Scald milk and cool to lukewarm. Measure one-half cup milk and stir in yeast. Stir slightly beaten eggs and melted butter into remaining milk. Combine this with flour, sugar, and yeast mixture. Stir well. (Looks like thick syrup.) Cover and let rise 1½ hours. Stir in remaining flour and refrigerate overnight. Grease pans (will make enough for a tube pan and a loaf pan). Turn dough onto floured board and form balls smaller than ping-pong balls. Dip each ball in melted butter, then cinnamon and sugar mixture. Form all balls first; when dough gets sticky, give it a turn on the floured surface. Be generous with the butter, sugar, and cinnamon. It's also easier to work in small amounts, as everything gets "gooey." It will probably take at least 2 sticks of butter and 1 tablespoon cinnamon for each cup of sugar. Form single layer of balls on bottom of pan and cover loosely with pecans. Repeat until 3 layers are formed. Let rise till double. Bake in a preheated 325 degree oven for 1 hour. Remove from pan immediately and leave upside down on plate. This bread is best when served warm. Happy pluckin'!

Yield: 8-12 servings

Nan Laurence Grantham '57

When making yeast breads, dissolve yeast in liquid which has been heated to 105-115 degrees. Higher temperature will kill the yeast.

Easy Sweet Monkey Bread

1 cup granulated sugar
2 teaspoons cinnamon, divided
4 (10-ounce) cans biscuits
1¾ sticks (14 Tablespoons) margarine
1¾ cups brown sugar
½-1 cup pecans, chopped

Preheat oven to 375 degrees. Lightly grease Bundt pan. Mix granulated sugar and 1 teaspoon cinnamon. Cut each biscuit into 4 equal pieces and roll in the sugar and cinnamon mixture. To make the syrup mixture, melt margarine and add brown sugar, 1 teaspoon cinnamon and pecans. Stir until dissolved. Cool before using. Place biscuits in layers in Bundt pan. After each biscuit layer, pour syrup mixture over biscuits. Bake for 35-40 minutes or until golden brown. Turn bread onto a serving plate. Let each person pull off a bite at a time.

Yield: 1 loaf

Tamera Butler Garner '86

Buttermilk-Nut Bread

4 cups all-purpose flour, sifted
2 teaspoons baking powder
2 teaspoons soda
2 teaspoons salt
Pinch of saffron (optional)
¾ teaspoon nutmeg
½ teaspoon cinnamon
2 eggs
2 cups brown sugar, firmly packed
¼ cup butter, melted
2 cups buttermilk
2 cups pecans, coarsely chopped

Preheat oven to 350 degrees. Grease 2 loaf pans (8½x4½x2½). Sift dry ingredients together. Beat eggs; add sugar and mix well. Stir in butter and buttermilk. Blend in dry ingredients quickly, until moistened. Add nuts. Pour batter into 2 loaf pans. Bake for 30 minutes or until a straw or metal skewer inserted in center comes out clean. Remove from pan. Cool on cake racks.

Yield: 2 loaves

Sarah N. Spencer, Staff

Tribesman Pumpkin-Nut Bread

3½ cups all-purpose flour
1½ teaspoons cinnamon
2 teaspoons soda
3 cups sugar
½ teaspoon nutmeg
1½ teaspoons salt
¾ cup water
1 cup oil
4 large eggs
1 (16-ounce) can pumpkin (2 cups)
1 cup pecans, chopped fine
Confectioners' sugar (optional)

Preheat oven to 350 degrees. Grease and flour 3 loaf pans (9x5x3). Sift flour, cinnamon, soda, sugar, nutmeg, and salt into a large mixing bowl. Make a well in the center of the dry ingredients and add water, oil, eggs, and pumpkin. Beat well. Fold in pecans. Pour batter into prepared pans. Bake for 1 hour or until toothpick inserted in center comes out clean. Cool on cake racks. Invert bread and remove. Bread may be sprinkled with confectioners' sugar. This bread freezes well.

Yield: 3 loaves

Linda Gayle Ganaway Liechty '63
Mrs. Julian L. Jones

I gave loaves of this bread for Christmas gifts on third floor of Mary Nelson Dorm. LGL

Cinnamon Bread

Stripe:
½ cup pecans, ground
¼ cup sugar
1½ teaspoons cinnamon

Dough:
2 cups all-purpose flour
1 teaspoon baking powder
½ teaspoon soda
½ teaspoon salt
¼ cup oil
1 egg
1 cup buttermilk
1 cup sugar

Preheat oven to 350 degrees. Grease and flour a loaf pan (9x5x3). Mix stripe ingredients and set aside. Mix dough ingredients for 2 minutes with mixer. Divide into 3 parts (1 cup each). Alternate dough and stripe until all is used (dough on top). Use a knife to swirl into dough. Bake for 55 minutes. Cool 10 minutes before slicing.

Yield: 1 loaf

Ann Fisher Godwin '81

Glazed Raisin Loaf

1 package yeast
¼ cup warm water
¼ cup butter, softened
¼ cup sugar
1½ teaspoons salt
½ cup milk, scalded
3 to 3¼ cups all-purpose flour
1 egg, slightly beaten
1 cup seedless dark or light raisins

Sugar/Cinnamon Mixture:
½ cup sugar
1½ teaspoons cinnamon

Confectioners' Glaze:
1 cup confectioners' sugar, sifted
1½ Tablespoons milk

Soften yeast in warm water. In large mixing bowl, combine butter, sugar, salt, and hot milk. Stir to dissolve sugar and cool to lukewarm. Add 1½ cups of flour; beat well. Add softened yeast and egg; beat. Add raisins. Stir in enough flour to make moderately stiff dough. Turn out on lightly floured surface and knead about 10 minutes or until dough is smooth. Place in lightly greased bowl and turn to grease surface. Cover and let rise until double (about 1½ hours). Punch down. Round into ball, cover and let rest 10 minutes. On lightly floured surface, roll to 8x12 rectangle. Sprinkle with sugar/cinnamon mixture. Roll and place in greased loaf pan (8x4x2). Cover and let rise until almost double (45-60 minutes). Bake in a preheated 375 degree oven (350 degrees if using glass dish) about 35-40 minutes or until bread sounds hollow when tapped with knuckles. Remove bread from pan and cool about 10 minutes. Drizzle with Confectioners' Glaze. Recipe may be quadrupled; this recipe freezes well.

Yield: 1 loaf

Jewel Pittman Merritt '49

To release a stubborn loaf of bread, muffins, cakes, or pies from the pan, place the pan onto a cool, wet cloth, then remove.

Holiday Bread

(Panetone, pronounced "punny-tony")

Dough:
½ cup shortening, softened
½ cup sugar
2 teaspoons salt
½ cup milk
½ cup warm water
2 packages yeast
3 eggs
½ teaspoon vanilla
4½ cups all-purpose flour
½ cup raisins
½ cup almonds, coarsely chopped
½ cup candied fruit

Glaze:
½ cup confectioners' sugar
1½ teaspoons hot water
½ teaspoon lemon juice
½ teaspoon lemon rind, grated
Optional: Tiny decorative candies

In mixer bowl combine shortening, sugar, and salt. Heat milk to boiling and pour over sugar mixture. Dissolve yeast in warm water. When milk-sugar mixture cools to lukewarm, add yeast, eggs, vanilla, and 2 cups flour. Beat 2 minutes at medium speed. At low speed beat in 1 more cup of flour with raisins, almonds, and candied fruit. Remove bowl from mixer stand and with spoon add only enough remaining flour (up to 1½ cups) to handle easily. Turn onto floured board and knead about 3 minutes. In greased bowl let rise until doubled. After dough rises, punch down, knead 5 minutes and divide into 3 balls. Place into 3 well-greased 1 pound metal coffee cans. Cover and let rise until doubled or until dough is slightly above the top of the cans. Depending on room temperature, this may take 4-6 hours. Place a shallow pan with one-fourth inch water on bottom shelf of oven; put cans upright in water to bake. Bake for 35 minutes in a preheated 375 degree oven or until golden brown. Remove from cans and serve hot or cool; store in sealed plastic bags in refrigerator. This bread resembles a baker chef's hat.

Drizzle with confectioners' sugar glaze. For festive occasions tiny decorative candies may be added.

Yield: 3 loaves

Ann Kolb, Faculty Wife (Raymond Kolb '39)

This recipe is popular in southern Brazil for the Christmas and New Year's seasons. The mosque-like shape is characteristic of old Russia's holiday breads.

Holiday Fruit Bread

2 eggs
½ cup water
2 (10-ounce) packages quick bread mix
1 (28-ounce) jar mincemeat
2 cups candied fruit

Preheat oven to 350 degrees. Generously grease and flour a 10-inch Bundt or tube pan. In a large bowl combine eggs and water; add remaining ingredients. Stir by hand until well-mixed and pour into pan. Bake for 80-90 minutes.

Yield: 16-20 servings

Katie G. McPhearson (Mrs. E. L.) '36

Date Nut Loaf

¾ cup nuts, chopped
1 (8-ounce) box dates, chopped
1½ teaspoons soda
½ teaspoon salt
¼ cup shortening
¾ cup boiling water
2 eggs, beaten
1 cup sugar
1 teaspoon vanilla
1½ cups sifted all-purpose flour

Preheat oven to 350 degrees. Grease 1 loaf pan (9x5x3). Combine nuts, dates, soda, salt, shortening, and boiling water; let stand for 15 minutes. Stir in beaten eggs, sugar, vanilla, and flour. Do not overmix. Bake for 1 hour.

Yield: 1 loaf

Mrs. Edward F. McDonald (Edward F. McDonald '48)

Savory French Bread

1 pound butter or margarine
¾ teaspoon cayenne pepper
¾ teaspoon savory salt
1½ teaspoons thyme
¾ teaspoon salt
1 loaf French bread

Preheat oven to 325 degrees. Mix herbs with softened butter. Slice a loaf of French bread without cutting each slice completely apart. Spread the mixture between slices. Place bread on baking sheet; bake for about 20 minutes.

Yield: 12-15 slices

Carole T. Kelly '90

White Nut Loaf

¾ cup sugar
2 Tablespoons shortening
1 egg
1½ cups milk
3 cups all-purpose flour, sifted
3½ teaspoons baking powder
1½ teaspoons salt
¾ cup nuts, chopped

Preheat oven to 350 degrees. Grease a loaf pan (9x5x3). Mix sugar, shortening, and egg. Stir in milk, then add dry ingredients. Add nuts, stirring until nuts are just blended into mixture. Pour into a loaf pan; let stand for 20 minutes before baking. Bake for 1 hour and 10 minutes. Slice very thin to serve.

Yield: 1 loaf

Carnette R. McMillan '50, Faculty Wife

Easy Supper Bread

2 cups biscuit mix
3 teaspoons onion, minced
1 teaspoon dry mustard
¾ cup milk
2 eggs
2 Tablespoons oil
1 cup ham, chopped fine
1½ cups shredded Cheddar cheese, divided
2 Tablespoons sesame seed
3 Tablespoons butter, melted

Preheat oven to 375 degrees. Grease a 10-inch pie pan. Combine biscuit mix, onion, and mustard. Add milk, eggs, and oil. Stir in ham and three-fourths cup cheese. Spread dough in pie pan. Sprinkle seeds and remaining cheese evenly on top of dough. Pour melted butter over the dough. Bake for 30-40 minutes.

Yield: 6 servings

Kathy Kitchings Nowell '73

Kathy Kitchings Nowell is the granddaughter of A. A. Kitchings, chairman of the Department of Foreign Languages at Mississippi College, 1932-60.

Dilly Bread

1 package yeast
¼ cup warm water
1 cup cottage cheese, heated to lukewarm
2 Tablespoons sugar
1 teaspoon minced onion
1 Tablespoon butter or margarine
1 egg, unbeaten
2 Tablespoons dill seed
1 teaspoon salt
¼ teaspoon soda
2½ cups all-purpose flour

Dissolve yeast in warm water. Add cottage cheese, sugar, onion, margarine, egg, dill seed, salt, and soda. Mix well and add flour. Stir to form stiff dough. Cover. Let dough rise in a warm place until it has doubled in size (about 2 hours). Stir the dough down and turn into a well-greased 2-quart glass baking dish. Let dough rise 30-40 minutes. Bake in a preheated 350 degree oven for 40-50 minutes. Brush with melted butter and salt when cooked.

Variation: To make this recipe "low-fat," use fat-free cottage cheese, light margarine, and egg substitute. Spray with non-stick vegetable spray, then sprinkle with salt.

Yield: 10-12 servings

Mot Powell Lyons '65

Zucchini Bread

3 eggs
2 cups sugar
½ cup oil
2 teaspoons vanilla
2 cups zucchini, grated
1 (8-ounce) can crushed pineapple, drained
3 cups self-rising flour
1½ teaspoons cinnamon
¾ cup nuts, chopped

Preheat oven to 350 degrees. Line 2 loaf pans (8x4x2½) with wax paper. Beat eggs, sugar, oil, and vanilla, mixing very well. Stir in grated zucchini and pineapple; sift all dry ingredients together. Stir only until moistened. Add nuts. Bake in loaf pans for 1 hour.

Yield: 2 loaves

Myrtle Curtis, Staff

Sweet Potato Bread

2 cups cooked sweet potatoes, mashed
2 cups sugar
4 eggs
1 cup canola oil
⅔ cup frozen orange juice concentrate
1 Tablespoon vanilla
3½ cups all-purpose flour
1½ teaspoons salt
1½ teaspoons nutmeg
1½ teaspoons cinnamon
1 Tablespoon soda
1 cup pecans, chopped
1 cup raisins (optional)
1 cup candied fruit (optional)

Preheat oven to 350 degrees. Grease 2 loaf pans (9x5x3). Mix potatoes, sugar, eggs, oil, orange juice, and vanilla. Mix remaining ingredients and combine with potato mixture a little at a time. Pour into 2 prepared loaf pans (miniature loaf pans may be used to take care of extra mix if large loaf pans do not hold all the batter); bake for 1 hour. Test for doneness after 50 minutes. This is a nice holiday treat which also freezes well.

Yield: 2 loaves

Ruth Davis (Hemby Davis '38)

Bread Sticks

8 hot dog buns
2 sticks margarine, softened
½ teaspoon thyme
½ teaspoon basil
1 teaspoon rosemary
2 cloves fresh garlic, pressed (or equivalent)
Parmesan cheese to taste

Preheat oven to 200 degrees. With electric knife (not essential, but helpful), slice each bun lengthwise into 4 strips. If desired, cut these long strips in half. Blend thyme, basil, rosemary, and garlic into margarine; spread generously on buns. Place on ungreased cookie sheets and sprinkle with Parmesan cheese. Bake for at least 2 hours until crisp. These freeze well in self-sealing bags.

Yield: 32 long or 64 short bread sticks

Dell Dickins Scoper '56

Mrs. Scoper's father, John W. Dickens, served on the Mississippi College Board of Trustees, 1959-65 and 1968-72.

Sourdough Bread

Starter:
1 package yeast
1 cup warm water (105-115 degrees)
¾ cup sugar
4 Tablespoons instant potato flakes

Starter Food:
¾ cup sugar
3 Tablespoons potato flakes
1 cup warm water (105-115 degrees)

Bread:
⅓ cup sugar
½ cup oil
1 teaspoon salt
1½ cups warm water (105-115 degrees)
1 cup starter
6 cups bread flour
3 Tablespoons margarine, melted (optional)

To make starter, dissolve yeast in one cup of warm water. Add sugar and potato flakes and stir well. Let stand at room temperature for 24 hours, then cover with plastic wrap (do not use tight lid) and refrigerate. On 4th day add starter food ingredients and stir well; let stand at room temperature for 24 hours. Remove 1 cup of starter for bread, give 1 cup to a friend (or discard it), and return remaining cup to refrigerator. Feed starter every 4-7 days; do not let bubbles die between feedings. To make bread, using a wooden or plastic spoon (do not use metal), mix sugar, oil, salt, water, and one cup of starter. Beat in flour 1 cup at a time (knead in last cup if dough is too stiff to stir). Place mixture in a large, well-oiled bowl (do not use metal), turning to be sure top is oiled. Cover with a clean cloth or wax paper and let rise until doubled in bulk (12 to 24 hours). Divide into three loaves and place in greased loaf pans. Let rise 5-7 hours. If desired, brush tops with melted margarine. Bake in a preheated 350 degree oven for about 30 minutes or until loaves sound hollow when tapped.

Yield: 3 loaves

Mildred Thrailkill '56

Remove breads from baking pans immediately to prevent sogginess.

Red's Garlic Bread

3-4 Kaiser or oblong hard French rolls
Margarine
Garlic salt
Oregano
Parmesan or Romano cheese (or both)

Slice rolls in half. Spread margarine on each half of bread. Top with garlic salt, oregano, and cheese to taste. Arrange on baking sheet and place under broiler until toasted.

Yield: 6-8 servings

Peggy Parks Lee '85

Honey Whole Wheat Bread

4 cups whole wheat flour, divided
½ cup dry milk
1 Tablespoon salt
2 packages yeast
3 cups water
½ cup honey
2 Tablespoons oil
3½ - 4½ cups all-purpose flour

Preheat oven to 350 degrees. Grease 2 loaf pans (9x5x3). Combine 3 cups whole wheat flour with the next 3 ingredients in a mixing bowl. Heat next 3 ingredients slightly in saucepan until warm. Pour warm (not hot) liquid over flour mixture. Beat until well mixed. Stir in remaining flours. Knead about 5 minutes using additional all-purpose flour if necessary. Place in greased bowl, turn, cover, and let rise until double in bulk. Punch down, divide dough in half and shape into loaves. Place in 2 loaf pans. Cover and let rise for 40-45 minutes. Bake for 35-45 minutes until bread sounds hollow when tapped.

Variation: Replace 1 cup whole wheat flour with soy flour. Add ¼ cup wheat germ.

Yield: 2 loaves

Charlotte Parkman Shephard '61

Old-Fashioned Yeast Rolls

2 cups milk
½ cup sugar
½ cup shortening
1 package yeast
¼ cup cool water
6 cups all-purpose flour
1½ teaspoons salt
½ teaspoon soda
1 teaspoon baking powder
5 Tablespoons butter

Heat milk, sugar, and shortening just to boiling point. Cool to lukewarm. Dissolve yeast in cool water and add to lukewarm milk mixture. Beat in about 3 cups flour or enough to make a dough the consistency of cake batter. Let rise until double in bulk, about 2 hours. Then sift over this mixture the salt, soda, and baking powder. Work in 2½ or 3 cups of flour or enough to make a moderately stiff dough. Cover and refrigerate until ready to use. Take out as much as desired, knead lightly on a floured surface. Roll out and cut with biscuit cutter. Brush with melted butter. Place in greased pan and let rise about two hours. Bake in a preheated 400 degree oven for 10-12 minutes. For classic cloverleaf rolls, shape dough into 3 small balls for each roll. Place balls in greased muffin cups and brush with butter.

Variation: If whole wheat rolls are desired, add one-fourth cup sugar to the milk, sugar, and shortening mixture in the first step. Then use whole wheat flour in the last application of adding flour. This dough will keep in the refrigerator about a week.

Yield: 4 dozen

Josephine Trotter Spell (Howard Spell '26)

Howard Spell served as Dean of the College 1947-69.

When storing flour and meal, place a bay leaf in container to prevent weevils.

Never-Fail Rolls

1 cup boiling water
1 cup shortening
1 cup sugar
1½ teaspoons salt
2 eggs, beaten
2 packages yeast
1 cup warm water
6 cups unsifted all-purpose flour

Pour boiling water over shortening. Add sugar and salt; blend and cool. Add eggs. Dissolve yeast in warm water. Add to mixture. Add flour, sifted. Blend well. Put into refrigerator in covered bowl. (Will keep in refrigerator for ten days). For Parker House rolls, work extra flour in as needed. Roll out to ½-inch thickness and cut with round cookie cutter; brush with melted butter. Fold over envelope style. Place in greased pan and let rise 3 hours. Bake in preheated oven at 350 degrees for 15-20 minutes. This dough is also good for cinnamon rolls.

Yield: 3½-4 dozen

Jean Horn Ross '45

Ice Box Rolls

¾ cup shortening
½ cup sugar
1½ cups hot milk
1 egg
1 Tablespoon baking powder
2 teaspoons salt
4 cups all-purpose flour
1 package yeast
½ cup warm water

Cream shortening and sugar. Add hot milk and egg. Stir. Add dry ingredients that have been sifted together. Add yeast that has been dissolved in the warm water. Stir. Place in a well-oiled bowl; turn dough to oil the top. Let rise about 3 hours. Punch down dough, cover and place in refrigerator until ready to use. (Dough will stay fresh 5 or 6 days.) Roll out on lightly floured surface. Cut to desired size. Dip into melted butter and place in pan. Let rise until double in size (about 2 hours). Bake in preheated oven at 400 degrees for 6-8 minutes (longer for larger rolls).

Yield: 100-125 bite-size rolls or 4-5 dozen regular size

June East Lofton '50

Rebecca's Easy Yeast Rolls

1 package yeast
½ cup lukewarm water
½ cup sugar
½ cup shortening
½ cup boiling water
½ cup cold water
1 egg
1 teaspoon salt
5 cups unsifted all-purpose flour

Dissolve yeast in one-half cup lukewarm water. Cream sugar and shortening. Add ½ cup boiling water and mix. Next add one-half cup cold water and mix. Blend in egg, yeast mixture, and salt. Add flour. Cover and refrigerate for 24 hours. Roll out 2 hours before baking. Dip each roll in melted butter. Preheat oven to 400 degrees; bake for 10 minutes. Keep unused dough in refrigerator. These rolls are very light and delicious.

Yield: 2-3 dozen

Lisa Vickery Kelly '80

Lisa Vickery Kelly is the daughter of Harry Vickery, who has served on the Mississippi College Board of Trustees, 1974-80, 1981-87, 1988-.

Quick Yeast Rolls

1 package yeast
4 Tablespoons warm water
2 Tablespoons sugar
2 cups milk
¾ cup oil
4 cups self-rising flour

Preheat oven to 400 degrees. Mix yeast, water and sugar. Add milk, oil, and flour, beating by hand with a slotted spoon. Fill greased muffin tins three-fourths full. Bake for 15 minutes. Dough may be stored in tightly covered container in refrigerator for 2 weeks.

Yield: 2 dozen

Dell Fail Mayfield '50
Carol Barrett Kirk, Staff
Mildred Dickey

Mashed Potato Rolls

1 package yeast
1 cup mashed potatoes (not instant mashed potatoes)
1½ cups lukewarm potato water, divided
⅔ cup sugar
1½ teaspoons salt
2 eggs, beaten
⅔ cup shortening
4½ to 5 cups all-purpose flour

Dissolve yeast in one-half cup of the potato water; set aside for 5 minutes. Combine mashed potatoes, sugar, and salt in a large mixing bowl. Add eggs and shortening, mixing well. Stir in yeast mixture and remaining potato water, then add flour. Cover and let rise until doubled in bulk. Punch down dough, cover and put in refrigerator. Fill greased muffin tins half full. Bake in a 450 degree preheated oven for 12-15 minutes. Bake within 24-36 hours of preparing dough or rolls may taste a bit fermented.

Yield: 3 dozen

Mrs. John G. McCall, Faculty Wife

John G. McCall served on the Mississippi College Board Trustees, 1958-64, 1970-76, 1977-83.

All-Bran Rolls

¾ cup sugar
1 cup bran cereal
½ teaspoon salt
1 cup oil
1 cup boiling water
2 eggs
2 packages yeast
1 cup warm water (118 degrees)
6 cups all-purpose flour

Mix sugar, bran, salt, and oil with one cup boiling water. Let stand until lukewarm. Add eggs and beat slightly. Dissolve yeast in one cup warm water; add to mixture. Beat in flour. Cover and refrigerate overnight. Make into rolls and place on greased pan or into greased muffin cups. Brush with melted butter. Let rise. Bake in preheated 375 degree oven for 20 minutes or until brown.

Yield: 2 dozen

A. W. Trusty '25

Buttermilk Biscuits

6 cups unsifted self-rising flour
1 teaspoon soda
3 cups buttermilk
1 cup oil

Preheat oven to 450 degrees. Lightly grease cookie sheets. Add buttermilk to flour and soda. Add oil. Mix well by hand (dough should be sticky but pull away from side of bowl). On floured board, roll out ½-inch thick. Cut with 2½-inch biscuit cutter. Bake for 10-12 minutes. One-third of the recipe makes 12-15 biscuits.

Yield: 40-50 biscuits

Prentiss G. Cox, Faculty

Mayonnaise Biscuits

2 cups self-rising flour
4 Tablespoons mayonnaise (reduced calorie - not fat free)
1 cup milk

Preheat oven to 450 degrees. Mix ingredients together. Spoon into greased muffin cups. Bake for 12-15 minutes.

Yield: 12 biscuits

Dana Masterson '92

Mexican Cornbread

1 cup cream-style corn
1½ cups cornmeal
3 teaspoons baking powder
3 teaspoons bell pepper, diced
⅔ cup oil
2 eggs
2 pods hot pepper, crushed (or 1 teaspoon red pepper)
½ cup green onion, chopped
1 cup sour cream
1 teaspoon salt
1 cup cheese, grated

Preheat oven to 350 degrees. Grease 9x9 pan. Mix all ingredients except cheese. Put half of batter into pan; sprinkle with half of cheese, then put remaining batter, topping with remaining cheese. Bake for approximately 40 minutes.

Yield: 8-10 servings

Mary Johnson Dorsett '30
Loretta Ford

Graham Scones

1 cup all-purpose flour
1 cup graham flour
2 teaspoons baking powder
½ teaspoon salt
⅓ cup sugar
½ cup shortening
1 egg
Water

Preheat oven to 450 degrees. Sift together the dry ingredients. With a pastry blender or two knives, cut in the shortening until crumbly. In a large liquid measuring cup, break the egg; pour off about 1 tablespoon of the egg white into a saucer. Fill the measuring cup to the ⅔-cup mark with water; stir well. Using a fork, stir the liquid into the dry mixture to make a soft, slightly sticky dough. Do not overmix. (Good scones are not handled too much!) Turn the dough out on a lightly floured board and knead gently 8-10 times. Pat out ½-inch thick; cut into circles. Brush tops with the reserved egg white. Bake on ungreased cookie sheet for 12-15 minutes or until golden brown. Serve warm with butter and jam or jelly.

Variation: Add 1 cup currants, raisins, or chopped nuts before adding the liquid.

Yield: 8-10 scones

Carol C. West, Faculty

This recipe is a favorite of the Law School Faculty; the scones have been served at the annual Valentine's "High Tea" for several years.

1-2-3 Spoon Bread

2 cups milk
1 cup yellow cornmeal
3 eggs, separated
2 Tablespoons butter or margarine
1 Tablespoon sugar
¼ teaspoon salt

Preheat oven to 350 degrees. Grease an 8-inch casserole. Heat milk on low heat and slowly add cornmeal, stirring constantly to prevent lumping. Cook until mushy, approximately 10 minutes. Remove from heat; cool. Add egg yolks to cooled mixture. Add butter, sugar, and salt. Beat egg whites until stiff and fold into other ingredients. Pour into greased casserole and bake for 45 minutes. Serve immediately. Dish will fall as it cools.

Yield: 6-8 servings

Betty Merritt '50

Onion Cornbread

1 medium Spanish onion
1 stick margarine
1 (8-ounce) carton sour cream
¼ teaspoon dill weed
¼ teaspoon salt
1 cup sharp cheese, grated
1 (8½-ounce) box cornmeal muffin mix
1 (8½-ounce) can yellow cream-style corn
1 egg beaten with ⅓ cup milk
Few drops Tabasco sauce

Preheat oven to 400 degrees. Grease 8x8 pan. Slice onion into thin rings. Sauté onion rings in margarine; set aside. When cool, add sour cream, dill weed, salt and cheese. In another bowl, stir together cornmeal mix, corn, egg mixture, and Tabasco sauce. Pour into prepared pan. Spoon onion mixture over batter. Bake for 30-35 minutes.

Yield: 12 servings

Mary Allan Smith Willis '56

Sausage Cornbread

1 pound sausage
1 cup onion, chopped
⅓ cup bell pepper, chopped
2 Tablespoons flour
1 (6-ounce) can tomato paste
1 teaspoon salt
1 teaspoon chili powder
⅛ teaspoon pepper
4 ounces Cheddar cheese, grated
2 (8½-ounce) packages cornbread muffin mix

Preheat oven to 375 degrees. Cook sausage, onion, and bell pepper. Drain. Stir in flour, tomato paste, salt, chili powder and pepper. Remove from heat; stir in cheese. Prepare muffin mix according to package directions; stir in sausage mixture. Pour into a 9-inch square glass baking dish; bake for 30-35 minutes.

Yield: 6 servings

Debbie Alderman DePriest '82, Staff

Broccoli Cornbread

2 (8½-ounce) packages cornbread mix
1 (8-ounce) carton sour cream
4 eggs, beaten lightly
1 medium onion, chopped
6 Tablespoons margarine, melted
1 (10-ounce) package chopped broccoli, thawed

Preheat oven to 375-400 degrees. Grease a 9x13 pan. Combine cornbread mix, sour cream, eggs, onion, and margarine. Fold in the broccoli. Place in a baking pan. Bake for 35-40 minutes.

Yield: 20 servings

Christine Byrd (Harrell Byrd '46)

Broccoli-Cheese Cornbread

1 (10-ounce) package frozen chopped broccoli
4 eggs
1 box corn muffin mix
1 medium onion, chopped
2 cups Cheddar cheese, grated
1 stick margarine, melted

Preheat oven to 400 degrees. Grease a 9-inch square dish. Thaw and drain broccoli. Mix eggs and muffin mix together. Add onion, cheese, margarine, and broccoli (the mixture will be thick). Pour into a prepared baking dish. Bake for 30-40 minutes, or until slightly brown.

Yield: 6-8 servings

Bobbie Walden Foster '44
Ann Douglas Majors '62
Authurine Branton

Bobbie Walden Foster served on the Mississippi College Board of Trustees, 1948-54.

Company Cornbread

1½ cups self-rising cornmeal
2 eggs, beaten
1 (16-ounce) can cream-style corn
¾ cup oil
1 (8-ounce) carton sour cream
⅛ teaspoon salt
1 medium onion, chopped (optional)

Preheat oven to 350 degrees. Lightly grease muffin cups. In mixing bowl, combine first six ingredients. Fold in chopped onion. Fill muffin tins three-fourths full. Bake for 45 minutes. Serve immediately or let cool and store in air-tight container for several days.

Yield: 16-18 muffins

Roberta R. Moak '51
Beverly Craig McBride '61
Candy Phillips Anderson '77

Calhoun Cornbread

¾ cup plain white cornmeal (not cornmeal mix)
½ teaspoon salt
½ teaspoon soda
¾ cup buttermilk

Preheat oven to 450 degrees. Spray a 6½-inch or 8-inch black skillet with vegetable cooking spray. Set on rangetop and heat. Mix cornmeal, salt, soda, and buttermilk in small mixing bowl until smooth. Pour into hot skillet and bake for 12-15 minutes or until brown. This cornbread is good for persons on a cholesterol-free diet or those who have heart problems. It is very good with vegetables. The recipe may be doubled if using a larger skillet.

Yield: 4 servings

Myrtilla Burris Kirk '59

Healthy Cornbread

½ cup cream of wheat
½ cup self-rising flour
1 egg substitute
1 cup low-fat buttermilk (½ cup can be skim milk)
¼ teaspoon soda
½ teaspoon salt (optional)
¼ teaspoon baking powder
1 Tablespoon canola oil

Preheat oven to 350 degrees. Put oil into an iron skillet and heat in oven until hot. Mix other ingredients together. Pour cornbread into skillet; bake for 20-25 minutes.

Yield: 6 servings

Betty Robinson '63

Aunt Maggie's Cornbread Dressing

4 cups cornbread, finely crumbled
2 cups breadcrumbs, bread toasted until crisp
1 cup onion, finely chopped
1 cup celery, coarsely chopped
5 cups strong chicken broth
5 eggs, beaten
Salt and pepper
Sage (optional)

Combine the first 5 ingredients, mix well and season to taste. Add eggs and if possible let sit over night in refrigerator. Spoon into 9x13 casserole. Bake in a preheated 350 degree oven for 45-60 minutes until top is brown.

Variation: A similar recipe was submitted by *Brenda S. McMillan '77*. She suggests using crumbled biscuits to make 2 cups breadcrumbs.

Yield: 10-12 servings

Anita Watkins Clinton '29, Hillman

In the days when dormitories were not available, "Aunt Maggie" Watkins ran a boarding house for students in the family home on the site where part of First Baptist Church, Clinton, now stands. This recipe from her menus was submitted by her niece, Anita Watkins Clinton, daughter of Asa Carroll Watkins, an 1886 graduate of Mississippi College, pioneer missionary to Mexico, founder of the first Baptist seminary in Mexico, and Mississippi College professor of Spanish and Bible, 1923-25.

Mississippi College Hushpuppies

Oil for frying
4 cups self-rising cornmeal
2 large onions, chopped fine
2 bell peppers, chopped fine
2 eggs, beaten
1⅞ cups buttermilk
1 Tablespoon crushed red pepper

Mix all ingredients thoroughly. Drop into hot oil using a teaspoon. Cook until golden brown.

Yield: 80 hushpuppies

Lisa Hall Edwards '80

Lisa is the daughter of Sam Hall, Superintendent of Campus and Grounds at Mississippi College. A similar recipe was submitted by Catherine Blackwell, wife of Bernard Blackwell, who served as Director of Alumni Affairs for many years. Coach Blackwell uses less red pepper for a milder taste. Both Sam and Coach Blackwell have made hundreds of these distinctly Southern delicacies for friends and guests of the College.

Favorite Blueberry Muffins

1 egg
½ cup milk
¼ cup oil
1½ cups all-purpose flour
½-¾ cup sugar
2 teaspoons baking powder
½ teaspoon salt
1 cup fresh blueberries (or ¾ cup well-drained frozen berries, thawed)
1 cup pecans, broken (optional)

Preheat oven to 400 degrees. Grease bottoms of 12 medium (2¾-inch) muffin cups. Beat egg; stir in milk and oil. Mix in flour, sugar, baking powder, and salt. Mix just until flour is moistened. Batter should be lumpy. Fold blueberries into batter. Add pecans, if desired. Fill muffin cups two-thirds full and bake for 20-25 minutes or until golden brown. Immediately remove from pan.

Yield: 12 muffins

Lynda Word Smith '69
Phyllis Jenkins Peavy '83
Lisa Ann Arduini '92

Healthy Apple Muffins

1 cup oats, uncooked
½ cup whole wheat flour
½ cup all-purpose flour
½ cup unprocessed bran
¼ cup dark brown sugar, firmly packed
1 Tablespoon baking powder
½ teaspoon salt
1 teaspoon cinnamon
½ cup apple, chopped
¾ cup milk
1 egg
¼ cup oil
¼ cup honey

Preheat oven to 400 degrees. Grease or use paper liners for muffin cups. Mix dry ingredients with apple. Add remaining ingredients, mixing just until moistened. Fill muffin cups two-thirds full. Bake for about 15 minutes or until golden brown. Use 1 cup all-purpose flour instead of whole wheat if desired.

Yield: 1 dozen

Pat Turner, Staff

Bran Muffins

2 cups bran buds
2 cups boiling water
1⅓ cups shortening
2½ cups sugar
4 eggs
5 teaspoons soda
2 teaspoons salt
1 quart buttermilk
6 cups flour
4 cups bran flakes
1 cup pecans, chopped (optional)

Preheat oven to 400 degrees. Grease or use paper liners for muffin cups. In a large mixing bowl, pour water over buds. Cool. Cream sugar with shortening. Add bran buds and mix all together. Add eggs, unbeaten, one at a time. Put soda and salt in buttermilk. Add one cup flour to bran buds mixture, then buttermilk, flour, buttermilk, etc., until all flour and buttermilk are used. With a spatula, stir bran flakes into batter. Mix well. Bake until slightly browned. This mixture may be frozen or kept in the refrigerator for six weeks.

Variation: *Joann Branson Cunningham '84* adds 1 teaspoon each of cloves, nutmeg, and cinnamon; 1 teaspoon vanilla; and 1 cup raisins to the batter.

Yield: 2 dozen large or 60 miniature muffins

Mary Jean Padgett '73, Faculty
Lisa Leavell '80

Honey Bran Muffins

2 cups bran cereal
1¼ cups milk
1 cup whole wheat flour
2 teaspoons baking powder
½ teaspoon soda
⅓ cup honey
¼ cup butter, melted
1 egg, beaten

Preheat oven to 400 degrees. Spray muffin cups with non-stick vegetable spray. Combine bran and milk. Allow to stand 5 minutes. Combine flour, baking powder, and soda. Into bran and milk mixture, stir honey, butter, and egg. Add the dry ingredients to mixture and stir until combined. Bake for 10 minutes.

Yield: 2 dozen muffins

Mrs. Lloyd Roberts '80, Faculty Wife

Sweet Potato Muffins

½ cup butter
1¼ cups sugar
2 eggs
1¼ cups canned sweet potatoes, drained and mashed
1½ cups all-purpose flour
2 teaspoons baking powder
¼ teaspoon salt
1 teaspoon cinnamon
¼ teaspoon nutmeg
1 cup milk
¼ cup pecans, chopped
½ cup raisins, chopped

Preheat oven to 400 degrees. Grease 1½-inch muffin cups. Cream butter and sugar, add eggs and mix well. Blend in the sweet potatoes. Sift the flour with the baking powder, salt, cinnamon, and nutmeg. Add alternately with the milk. Do not overmix. Fold in the nuts and raisins. Fill the greased muffin tins two-thirds full and bake for 25 minutes. Muffins may be frozen and reheated.

Yield: 5 dozen

Jan Simmons Cameron '78

Elegant Orange Muffins

2 cups all-purpose flour, sifted
⅔ cup sugar
1 Tablespoon baking powder
⅔ cup shortening
⅓ cup butter, softened
4 eggs, beaten
½ cup milk
½ cup orange juice
½ cup orange sections, diced
¼ cup almonds, slivered

Preheat oven to 350 degrees. Grease or use paper liners for muffin cups. Mix flour, sugar, and baking powder in large mixing bowl. Add the following ingredients gradually in order, one at a time while stirring: shortening, soft butter, beaten eggs, milk, and orange juice. Put batter into muffin tins, filling each two-thirds full. Top each with diced orange sections and slivered almonds. Bake for 25 minutes or until done. These muffins are sweet and would be ideal for a holiday brunch.

Yield: 16 muffins

Cynthia B. Foster, Staff

Cranberry Crunch Muffins

1 cup nuts, chopped
1 cup cranberries, coarsely chopped
2 cups all-purpose flour
1 Tablespoon baking powder
1 cup light brown sugar, firmly packed
⅔ cup fresh orange juice
3 eggs
⅓ cup oil

Preheat oven to 375 degrees. Line 2 muffin pans with paper liners. In small bowl, mix cranberries and nuts. In large bowl, combine flour with baking powder. With fork, mix in brown sugar; then add remaining ingredients. Stir in cranberries and nuts. Batter will be lumpy. Spoon batter into prepared muffin cups. Fill approximately half full. Bake for 16-18 minutes or until golden brown. Remove from pan. Cool on wire rack. These muffins are even better as they have time to mellow.

Yield: 24 muffins

Susan Sword Thames

Butter Pecan Muffins

1 box butter pecan cake mix
4 eggs
1 (3⅜-ounce) package toasted coconut instant pudding
¼ cup poppy seed
¼ cup oil
1 cup hot water

Preheat oven to 350 degrees. Line 3 muffin pans with paper liners. Mix all ingredients together. Fill muffin cups two-thirds full. Bake for 20 minutes.

Yield: 3 dozen muffins

Beth Lofton Case '75

Whole Wheat Muffins

1 cup whole wheat flour
1 cup all-purpose flour, sifted
½ teaspoon salt
2½ teaspoons baking powder
3 Tablespoons sugar
1 cup milk
½ cup oil
1 egg

Preheat oven to 425 degrees. Grease muffin tins. Sift all dry ingredients together. Add milk, oil, and egg; stir quickly, barely blending. Do not beat. Bake for 15-20 minutes. Dry ingredients may be put together and kept in a container prior to use.

Yield: 18 muffins

Pansy R. Rankin '57

Sour Cream Muffins

1 stick butter, melted
1 (8-ounce) carton sour cream
2 cups biscuit mix or self-rising flour

Preheat oven to 350 degrees. Grease muffin tins. Combine ingredients and blend thoroughly with a fork. Drop into muffin cups and bake for about 15 minutes.

Yield: 12 muffins or 2½-3 dozen miniature muffins

Dorothy McCool Parker '36, Hillman
Connie S. Wadsworth '68

Morning Glory Muffins

1¼ cups sugar
2¼ cups all-purpose flour
1 teaspoon cinnamon
2 teaspoons baking powder
1 teaspoon salt
3 eggs
1 cup oil
1 teaspoon vanilla
1 (8-ounce) can crushed pineapple, drained
2 cups carrots, shredded
½ cup coconut, shredded
½ cup raisins
½ cup pecans, chopped

Preheat oven to 400 degrees. Line 3 muffin tins with paper liners. Sift all dry ingredients together. Beat eggs and oil, then add to flour mixture. Gently stir in remaining ingredients. Fill muffin cups two-thirds full with batter. Bake for about 15 minutes or until brown.

Yield: 36 muffins

Laurie Lofton Davidson '82

Strawberry Jam Coffeecake

¾ cup sugar
1 (8-ounce) package cream cheese, softened
1 stick butter, softened
2 eggs, beaten
¼ cup milk
1 teaspoon vanilla
2 cups all-purpose flour, sifted
1 teaspoon baking powder
½ teaspoon soda
¼ teaspoon salt
1 (18-ounce) jar strawberry preserves
1 Tablespoon lemon juice

Topping:
½ cup pecans, broken
¼ cup brown sugar

Preheat oven to 350 degrees; grease and flour a 9x13 pan. Beat sugar, cream cheese, and butter until fluffy. Mix beaten eggs, milk and vanilla and add to creamed mixture, blending well. Sift dry ingredients together and add to creamed mixture. Spread half of batter evenly over bottom of prepared pan. Mix strawberry preserves and lemon juice; spread over batter. Dot remaining batter on top of the preserve layer. Mix pecans and brown sugar together, sprinkle over top. Bake for 30-40 minutes. Cut into squares and serve warm.

Yield: 15-18 servings

Jeannie Lane '81, Staff

Sour Cream Coffeecake

Cake:

2 cups all-purpose flour
1 teaspoon baking powder
½ teaspoon salt
1 cup margarine
2 cups sugar
2 eggs
1 Tablespoon vanilla
1 cup sour cream

Topping:

1 cup nuts, chopped (pecans or slivered almonds)
4 Tablespoons sugar
2 teaspoons cinnamon

Preheat oven to 325 degrees. Grease and flour one 9x12 pan or 2 loaf pans. Sift flour, baking powder, and salt. Cream margarine, sugar, eggs, and vanilla using mixer on low speed. Add flour mixture and sour cream alternately to creamed mixture. Pour into prepared pans. Add half of batter and sprinkle with half of topping mix; then add rest of batter and sprinkle remaining topping mix. Bake for 1 hour or until toothpick inserted in the center comes out clean. This makes a very moist cake, which needs to be covered tightly when cooled.

Yield: 16-20 servings

Carol Garrett, Staff

For gifts, wrap homemade bread in a colorful cellophane and tie with a pretty ribbon.

Butterscotch Breakfast Ring

1 (6-ounce) package butterscotch morsels
2 Tablespoons butter or margarine
2 Tablespoons all-purpose flour
⅛ teaspoon salt
½ cup pecans, chopped
1 (8-ounce) package refrigerated crescent rolls
7 teaspoons light corn syrup

Preheat oven to 375 degrees. In double boiler, melt one-half cup butterscotch morsels and butter over hot water. Remove from heat and stir in flour, salt and pecans; set aside. Separate the 8 crescent roll triangles. On greased baking sheet, arrange triangles, long pointed ends out and edges overlapping, to form a circle. Spread 2 teaspoons butterscotch mixture on each triangle. Roll up triangles toward center, tucking ends under. Slash inside half of each roll. Bake for 15 minutes. Meanwhile, melt remaining butterscotch morsels with corn syrup. Drizzle over top of baked breakfast ring.

Variation: Rolls may be sliced crosswise and used as cookies. Decorated with finely crushed nuts and red and green cherry tidbits, these make a lovely Christmas treat. This recipe freezes well.

Yield: 8 servings

Pansy R. Rankin '57

Easy Cinnamon-Jelly Rolls

½ cup sugar
2 teaspoons cinnamon
2 cups self-rising flour
2 to 3 teaspoons shortening
¾ cup milk
3 Tablespoons grape jelly or other

Preheat oven to 450 degrees. Grease muffin tins. Mix sugar and cinnamon together; set aside. Cut shortening into flour and add milk, a little at a time, to make soft dough. Turn dough out onto a well-floured board and knead lightly about 30 seconds. Roll out to ¼-inch thickness. Sprinkle generous layer of cinnamon and sugar over dough surface. Roll dough one turn and spread with jelly; then continue to complete the roll. Cut into sections about 2 inches thick. Put into prepared muffin cups. Bake for 10-15 minutes.

Yield: 12 rolls

Robert H. Perry '55

Cinnamon Roll-Ups

Cinnamon and Sugar Mixture:
2 cups sugar
1 Tablespoon cinnamon

Dough:
1 cup butter or margarine
2 (8-ounce) packages cream cheese, softened
2 egg yolks
½ cup sugar
48 slices fresh white bread (trim crusts)
½ cup butter, melted (may require more)

Make a light brown mixture of 2 cups sugar and 1 tablespoon cinnamon. Set aside. Cream together the butter, cream cheese, egg yolks, and one-half cup sugar. Spread mixture on slices of bread and roll up. Brush each roll with melted butter and roll in the cinnamon/sugar mixture. Freeze the roll-ups. This step is essential. When ready to serve, bake for 15 minutes in a preheated 400 degree oven. Do not thaw before baking. Serve warm. These are great for brunches, breakfasts, etc.

Yield: 48 servings

Janie Branyan Peacock '54

Pancakes

delicious

1 cup all-purpose flour
½ teaspoon salt
2¼ teaspoons baking powder
1 Tablespoon sugar
1 egg - used 2
1 cup milk
2 Tablespoons oil

Preheat ungreased griddle. Stir dry ingredients together. In a separate bowl, combine liquid ingredients. Combine the 2 mixtures, stirring just enough to moisten flour (mixture may be lumpy). Drop generous spoonful for each pancake onto ungreased griddle which has been heated slowly. When pancake is full of bubbles, it is ready to be turned. Remove from griddle when pancake rises in the middle slightly and browns on bottom.

Yield: 6-8 pancakes   add 1c. cooked wild rice

Alicia Jones Pittman '60, Faculty Wife

This is a favorite recipe of Doug Hodo, President of Houston Baptist University. He has prepared these pancakes for us on several occasions when we have been guests in his home.

Glazed Doughnuts

Dough:
2 cups milk, scalded
½ cup shortening
1 cup sugar
1½ teaspoons salt
1 teaspoon nutmeg
½ teaspoon soda
2 eggs, beaten
2 packages yeast dissolved in ½ cup warm water
4-5 cups all-purpose flour
Oil for frying

Glaze:
1 pound confectioners' sugar
3 Tablespoons ice water

Add shortening to scalded milk. Cool to lukewarm. Add all remaining dough ingredients except flour and mix well. Add flour until thick (like bread dough). Let rise until triple in size. Punch down and roll ½-inch thick. Cut with doughnut cutter and let rise again until twice the size. Fry in oil or shortening 3 inches deep on medium temperature. When one side is brown, flip and brown the other side. Drain on paper towels and glaze while hot. Freeze all doughnuts not eaten within 24 hours. Warm in microwave or conventional oven before serving.

Yield: 44-48 doughnuts

Martha Ellen Marler '48

Our doughnut-making has been a family tradition since Mississippi College days. Three of our children and their families carry on this delicious tradition.

To make a fruited butter, add jelly or preserves to softened butter and whip to blend.

LIBRARY

LELAND SPEED LIBRARY

Leland Speed Library, built in 1959, was named for Leland Speed, former mayor of Jackson and a generous supporter of Mississippi College. In 1973, a major expansion approximately doubled the size of the building, with one floor designated for a Learning Resources Center. In 1975-1980, the Library shared its space with the newly acquired School of Law, providing faculty and administrative offices and bookstacks for the Law Library. The Speed Library houses the Mississippi Baptist Historical Collection and representative sculpture from the work of Katherine Speed Ettl.

SALADS AND SOUPS

Pasta Salad

1 (12-ounce) package vermicelli
½ cup light olive oil
3 Tablespoons lemon juice
3 Tablespoons seasoned salt
3 Tablespoons mayonnaise
1 (8-ounce) can ripe olives, sliced
1 (4-ounce) jar pimientos, diced
5 or 6 green onions, including tops, chopped
4 ounces feta cheese, crumbled

Cook vermicelli. Mix olive oil, lemon juice, seasoned salt, and mayonnaise. Pour over pasta. Add olives, pimientos, green onions, and feta cheese. Mix well and chill.

Variation: Add 2 medium cucumbers, peeled and chopped, and 2 small chopped bell peppers to the cooked vermicelli. Substitute 1 (16-ounce) bottle Italian salad dressing for olive oil/lemon juice dressing.

Yield: 10-12 servings

Peggy Lee Allen '53
Carolyn V. Hand '65, Staff

Quick Potato Salad

2 pounds small red potatoes, cooked
½ cup green onions, chopped
1 cup prepared ranch salad dressing
Paprika or black pepper
6 slices crisp bacon, crumbled
Chives

Cut slightly cooled potatoes into 1-inch slices. In large bowl, combine potatoes, onions, and salad dressing; toss gently. Dust with paprika or pepper and sprinkle crumbled bacon on top. Garnish with chives. Serve warm or at room temperature.

Yield: 5-6 servings

Bettye Stewart, Staff (Franklin D. '71)

Big Mom's Potato Salad

6 medium red potatoes, peeled, boiled, and cubed
2 eggs, hard-boiled
¾ cup sweet pickles, chopped
½ teaspoon salt
1-2 teaspoons sweet pickle vinegar
½ cup salad dressing or mayonnaise
1 Tablespoon prepared mustard

Cool cooked potatoes. Separate whites and yolks of boiled eggs and set aside yolks. Chop egg whites and pickles and add to potatoes. Mash egg yolks and add salt. Gradually add vinegar until a thin paste is formed. Add salad dressing and mustard gradually, mixing until smooth. Combine all ingredients and chill.

Yield: 8 servings

Danny Faye Sullivan '57

From the recipes of Roberta Ellis Langston '08, Hillman

Hot Potato Salad

6 large white potatoes
2 cups sour cream
1 cup milk
2 cups sharp Cheddar cheese, grated
1 stick margarine, melted
⅔ cup green onions and tops, chopped
Salt and pepper to taste

Boil potatoes in jackets. Chill until firm, peel, and shred with a grater. Mix all ingredients and place in 2 buttered (2-quart) casseroles or 1 large casserole. Bake uncovered in a preheated 350 degree oven for 45 minutes. This recipe freezes well.

Yield: 16 servings

Betty Tullos Legg '58, Faculty Wife

Fresh Cranberry Salad

2 cups fresh cranberries, chopped
3 cups miniature marshmallows
¾ cup sugar
½ cup nuts, chopped
1 large apple, chopped
1 cup seedless grapes, halved
Dash of salt
1 (8-ounce) carton whipped topping

Mix cranberries, marshmallows, and sugar. Refrigerate overnight. Add the nuts, apple, grapes, and salt. Fold the whipped topping into the mixture. Refrigerate.

Yield: 12 servings

Mrs. A. C. Hurst '52

Strawberry Supreme

1 (21-ounce) can strawberry pie filling
1 (20-ounce) can crushed pineapple, drained
1 cup nuts, chopped
1 can sweetened condensed milk
1 (6-ounce) package frozen, grated coconut
1 (8-ounce) carton whipped topping
Juice of 1 lemon
Maraschino cherries (optional)

Combine pie filling, pineapple, nuts, milk, coconut, whipped topping, and lemon juice in large salad bowl. Stir gently. Cover and refrigerate until ready to serve. Garnish with whipped topping and cherries.

Yield: 10-12 servings

Marilyn McLain

Pink Fluff Salad

1 (21-ounce) can cherry pie filling
1 can sweetened condensed milk
1 cup miniature marshmallows
1 (8-ounce) carton whipped topping
1 (16-ounce) can crushed pineapple, drained
½ cup pecans, chopped

Mix all ingredients in a large bowl. Cover and refrigerate. This salad will keep 2-3 days in the refrigerator.

Yield: 8 servings

Mellany McClure Sapp '84

Gooseberry Salad

½ cup sugar
1½ cups water
2 (3-ounce) packages lemon gelatin
1 (6-ounce) can frozen orange juice concentrate
1 (15-ounce) can gooseberries
Green food coloring
2 cups celery, chopped
1 cup pecans, chopped

Bring sugar and water to a boil; add gelatin and dissolve. Add orange juice concentrate to mixture, then add undrained gooseberries and 1-2 drops food coloring. When mixture is partially congealed, add the celery and pecans. Pour into individual molds or a large mold. This tart salad is delicious with any meat dish, especially ham.

Yield: 10-12 servings

Mrs. Jane Johnson (Jean W. '54)

Grease salad molds with mayonnaise before pouring in the gelatin for easier removal and extra flavor.

Vitamin A & C Congealed Salad

1 (3-ounce) package orange gelatin
1 cup hot water
1 (6-ounce) can orange juice concentrate
1 cup carrots, grated
1 cup crushed pineapple, drained
½ cup pecans, chopped

Dissolve gelatin in hot water, cool slightly; add orange juice concentrate, carrots, pineapple, and pecans. Stir until orange juice is melted. Chill until firm.

Yield: 6 servings

Barbara Barnett '90

Dieters' Congealed Salad

1 (16-ounce) can unsweetened crushed pineapple, undrained
1 (6-ounce) package gelatin, any flavor
2 cups buttermilk
1 (12-ounce) carton frozen whipped topping

Place pineapple into a saucepan, add gelatin. Heat and stir until gelatin is dissolved. Remove from heat and cool for 15 minutes. Stir in buttermilk. Fold in whipped topping. Mix well by hand. Place into a 9x13 dish. Chill until firm. Cut into squares to serve.

Yield: 12-15 servings

Indy Whitten (Charles Whitten '43)

A teaspoon of vinegar added to any gelatin recipe will keep molded salads (or desserts) from melting away.

Sunshine Veggie-Fruit Salad

2 packages of unflavored gelatin
1 cup cold water
12 large marshmallows
1 (3-ounce) package cream cheese
1 (14-ounce) can crushed pineapple with juice
½ cup celery, chopped fine
1 large carrot, peeled and grated
Juice of 2 fresh lemons
1 Tablespoon mayonnaise
1 Tablespoon sugar
Dash of salt
½ cup pecans, chopped
1 cup whipping cream, whipped

Mix gelatin with cold water and heat in a saucepan to dissolve. Add marshmallows and cream cheese and blend well. When mixture cools, add all remaining ingredients. Spoon into an oiled mold. Chill overnight. Serve on a lettuce leaf.

Yield: 6-8 servings

Doris Waller (John Waller '43)

Deluxe Tomato Aspic

1 (3-ounce) package lemon gelatin
1 cup boiling water
1 envelope unflavored gelatin
1 can tomato soup
Juice of 1 lemon
½ green pepper, diced
1 small onion, minced
4 large ribs celery, cut fine
¾ cups toasted almonds, chopped fine
½ cup black or green olives, sliced (optional)

Dissolve lemon gelatin in boiling water; add unflavored gelatin. Add this mixture to the tomato soup and lemon juice. Refrigerate; when partially set, add all the remaining ingredients. Pour into a greased mold. Refrigerate until set.

Yield: 10-12 servings

Mrs. S. S. Kety

Chunky Fruit Salad

1 (16-ounce) can sliced peaches
1 (16-ounce) can mixed chunky fruit
1 (16-ounce) can pineapple chunks
1 (3½-ounce) box instant French vanilla pudding
2 cups whole strawberries

Drain peaches, chunky fruit, and pineapple; reserve juices. Gradually add reserved juices to pudding until a sauce consistency is obtained. Add drained fruit and strawberries to pudding mixture. Mix well. Keep refrigerated.

Yield: 8-12 servings

Gerry W. Britt '86

Ambrosia Salad

2 (20-ounce) cans unsweetened pineapple chunks, undrained
8 navel oranges, peeled and sectioned
2 cups fresh grated coconut or 1 (4-ounce) can shredded coconut
1½ cups heavy cream, whipped (optional)
Mint leaves (optional)

Pour pineapple chunks with juice into a 2-quart bowl. Add oranges and coconut. Cover and chill at least 4 hours or overnight. Serve with whipped cream and a mint leaf for garnish. This dish may also be used as a dessert.

Yield: Serves 10-12

Carol Garrett, Staff

Pineapple-Apple Salad

1 (20-ounce) can pineapple tidbits
½ cup sugar
2 Tablespoons cornstarch
2 medium red apples, diced
½ cup pecans, chopped

Drain pineapple tidbits, reserving juice. In a small saucepan, combine sugar and cornstarch; add juice drained from pineapple. Cook over low heat until thick and clear. Cool slightly. Combine apples with pineapple tidbits and pecans. Pour the thickened mixture over fruit and stir. Cover and refrigerate. Serve cold.

Yield: 6-8 servings

Marleen Marie Gough '78, Staff

Jeweled Fruit Salad

1 (21-ounce) can peach pie filling
1 (20-ounce) can pineapple chunks, drained
1 (11-ounce) can mandarin orange sections, drained
3 bananas, sliced (optional)
1 (8-ounce) package frozen, sliced strawberries, thawed
3 (8-ounce) cartons nonfat lemon chiffon yogurt
2 cups fresh fruit in season (cantaloupe, apples, grapes, kiwi, pears)

Combine all ingredients and mix well. Chill.

Yield: 20 servings

Jerri Bennett '62, Faculty

Five Cup Salad

1 cup sour cream
1 cup miniature marshmallows
1 cup mandarin oranges, drained
1 cup coconut
1 cup pineapple chunks, drained
¼ cup maraschino cherries, sliced

Mix all ingredients except cherries. Refrigerate for several hours. Top with cherries just before serving.

Yield: 6-8 servings

Andy Hughes '78

Winter Fruit Salad

1 can sweetened condensed milk
¼ cup lemon juice
1 (12-ounce) carton whipped topping
1 (30-ounce) can fruit cocktail, drained
1 (8-ounce) can crushed pineapple, drained
½ cup sliced strawberries (optional)
1 sliced banana (optional)

Mix condensed milk and lemon juice. Fold in whipped topping and fruit. Mix well. Chill overnight.

Yield: 12 servings

Ray Myers '88

24-Hour Fruit Salad

2 cups pitted canned white or Bing cherries, drained
2 cups pineapple bits or chunks, drained
1 cup mandarin oranges, drained
2-3 cups mini-marshmallows

Old Fashioned Fruit Dressing:
2 eggs
2 Tablespoons sugar
2 Tablespoons vinegar or lemon juice
2 Tablespoons pineapple juice
1 Tablespoon butter
Dash of salt
1 cup heavy whipping cream, whipped

Toss fruits and marshmallows together. Mix all dressing ingredients in a saucepan over low heat, stirring constantly until dressing thickens. Remove from heat. Cool. Fold in whipped cream. Blend fruits and marshmallows into dressing mixture. Chill for several hours.

Yield: 8-10 servings

Mary Pollan Lane

Fruit Salad with Pineapple Pecan Whip Topping

1 (20-ounce) can pineapple chunks, undrained
2 large grapefruits, peeled and sectioned
2 oranges, peeled and sectioned
2 apples, cut into wedges
2 bananas, sliced (added at the last minute)

Pineapple Pecan Whip Topping:
1 (20-ounce) can crushed pineapple, with natural juice
Cold milk
1 (3½-ounce) box instant vanilla pudding
½ cup pecans, chopped
1 teaspoon ground cardamom
½ teaspoon ground ginger
1 cup whipping cream, whipped

Mix all fruits except bananas. Stir well to coat, as the pineapple juice will keep fruit from darkening. Add bananas at serving time. Pineapple Pecan Whip Topping: drain pineapple, reserving juice; add enough milk to make 1 cup liquid. Combine juice mixture and pudding mix. Stir in pineapple, pecans, cardamom, and ginger. Fold whipped cream into fruit mixture. This topping freezes well and makes enough to double the fruit recipe.

Yield: 8-10 servings

Nylon Bassett Hellen '71

Orange Fruit Mélange

2½ cups orange juice
2 Tablespoons quick-cooking tapioca
2 Tablespoons sugar
⅛ teaspoon salt
2 cinnamon sticks
1½ cups orange sections with juice
1 (16-ounce) package frozen peach slices, thawed
1 banana, sliced
Sour cream (optional)

Combine orange juice, tapioca, sugar, and salt in a heavy 3-quart saucepan; let stand for 5 minutes. Add cinnamon sticks. Bring to a boil over medium heat. Remove from heat and cool mixture for 20 minutes. Add orange sections, peaches, and banana. Heat thoroughly. Serve with a dollop of sour cream, if desired.

Yield: 8 servings

Mary Young '71

Classic Strawberry Salad

2 (3-ounce) packages strawberry gelatin
2 cups boiling water
1 (14-ounce) can crushed pineapple
2 (10-ounce) packages frozen strawberries, partially thawed
2 bananas, mashed
12 ounces sour cream

Dissolve gelatin in hot water; add pineapple, strawberries, and bananas. Pour half of mixture into a greased (9-inch) square pan and let set. Spread the sour cream over the congealed mixture; spread the remaining gelatin mixture on top. Cover and refrigerate.

Yield: 15-20 servings

Brian W. Wells '88

Strawberry Pretzel Salad

2 cups crushed pretzels
1 cup plus 3 Tablespoons sugar, divided
¾ cup margarine, melted
1 (8-ounce) package cream cheese, softened
1 (8-ounce) carton whipped topping
1 (6-ounce) package strawberry gelatin
2 cups boiling water
2 (10-ounce) packages frozen strawberries, undrained
1 (8-ounce) can crushed pineapple

Blend pretzels, 3 tablespoons sugar, and margarine; press into 9x13 pan coated with non-stick cooking spray. Bake for 10 minutes in a preheated oven at 400 degrees. Cool thoroughly. Blend 1 cup sugar, cream cheese, and whipped topping. Spread over crust, sealing to edges. Chill. Dissolve gelatin in water. Add strawberries and pineapple to gelatin. Chill until slightly thickened and pour over cream cheese mixture. Refrigerate until completely set.

Yield: 15 servings

Susan Newman, Staff

Congealed Grapefruit Salad

2 (3-ounce) packages lemon gelatin
1½ cups boiling water
1 (16-ounce) can grapefruit sections, drained
1 (11-ounce) can mandarin oranges, drained
1 (20-ounce) can crushed pineapple, undrained
12 maraschino cherries

Mix gelatin and boiling water. Add grapefruit, mandarin oranges, and pineapple. Pour into an 8x11 dish. Arrange cherries on top making three rows of four cherries. Congeal. Cut into 12 squares. Serve on a lettuce leaf.

Yield: 12 servings

Roberta R. Moak '51

Orange Pineapple Salad

1 cup orange juice
1 cup water
2 (3-ounce) packages orange gelatin
1 (8-ounce) package cream cheese, softened
½ cup sugar
½ pint heavy cream, whipped
1 (11-ounce) can mandarin orange sections, drained
1 (20-ounce) can crushed pineapple, undrained
1 cup pecans, chopped

Boil orange juice and water; pour over gelatin. Stir until dissolved; cool gelatin mixture. Add softened cream cheese and sugar to whipped cream. Add this mixture to cooled gelatin. Add mandarin orange sections, crushed pineapple, and chopped pecans and stir thoroughly. Pour into a 13x9x2 dish. Cut into squares when congealed. Serve on lettuce leaf.

Variation: Substitute 2 envelopes unflavored gelatin, 1 cup of pineapple juice for orange juice and 1 cup grated cheese for cream cheese.

Yield: 15-18 squares

Bessie Gilder Fleming '50
Sandra Sandifer Gunn '57

Sandra Gunn is the wife of Frank Gunn '57, who served as a member of the Mississippi College Board of Trustees, 1978-84, 1988-92.

Blueberry Salad

2 (3-ounce) packages blackberry gelatin
2 cups boiling water
1 (15-ounce) can blueberries
1 (8¼-ounce) can crushed pineapple

Topping:
1 (8-ounce) package cream cheese
½ cup sugar
½ teaspoon vanilla
½ pint sour cream
½ cup pecans, chopped

Dissolve gelatin in water. Drain blueberries and pineapple, reserving juice. Measure juice and add enough water to make 1 cup. Add liquid to gelatin. Stir well. Add blueberries and pineapple. Pour into a 2-quart flat dish and cover. Refrigerate until firm.

Topping: Combine cream cheese, sugar, sour cream, and vanilla. Blend well. Spread over congealed salad. Sprinkle with chopped pecans.

Variation: To reduce fat, ¾ cup plain yogurt and ¼ cup sour cream may be used.

Yield: 10-12 servings

Deborah Dillard

Mrs. Bill Causey suggests arranging a purple pansy on each salad plate for an attractive presentation.

Frozen Strawberry Fruit Salad

2 (8-ounce) cartons sour cream
2 Tablespoons lemon juice
¾ cup sugar
⅛ teaspoon salt
1 (20-ounce) can crushed pineapple, drained
1 (16-ounce) package frozen strawberries, sliced
3 bananas, mashed

Place paper liners in muffin cups. Thoroughly mix sour cream, lemon juice, sugar, and salt. Stir in pineapple and strawberries. Carefully fold in bananas. Spoon into lined muffin cups, cover with foil, and freeze.

Yield: 16-18 servings

Sarah King Folkes, Faculty Wife

Frozen Waldorf Salad

2 eggs
½ cup pineapple juice, drained from pineapple tidbits
½ cup sugar
Dash salt
¼ cup lemon juice
1 (20-ounce) can pineapple tidbits, drained
3 medium, firm apples, peeled and chopped
½ cup celery, diced
½ cup nuts, chopped
1 envelope whipped topping mix
½ cup milk

Mix eggs, pineapple juice, sugar, salt, and lemon juice. Cook over medium heat, stirring until slightly thickened. Cool. Stir fruit, celery, and nuts into cooled mixture. Prepare whipped topping with milk according to package instructions. Fold into fruit mixture. Spoon into 9x13 dish and freeze. Cut into squares to serve.

Yield: 20 servings

Mrs. Charlie C. Parks

Cornbread Salad

1 (8-ounce) box cornbread mix
1 small can cream-style corn
1 (4-ounce) can mild chili peppers, chopped
4 tomatoes, chopped
1 bell pepper, chopped
1 medium onion, chopped
1 cup sweet pickle relish
1 cup mayonnaise
¼ cup sweet pickle juice
½ pound mild Cheddar cheese, grated
12 slices crisp bacon, crumbled

Prepare cornbread mix according to package directions; add corn and chili peppers and bake. Crumble cooked bread and set aside to cool. Mix tomatoes, bell pepper, onion, and pickle relish; set aside. In a large bowl, mix the mayonnaise and sweet pickle juice, then add tomato mixture and cooled cornbread; mix well. Pour into a serving bowl; cover and refrigerate overnight. Top with cheese and crumbled bacon before serving.

Variation: A Mexican cornbread mix and chopped jalapeño peppers may be used for a spicier taste.

Yield: 8-10 servings

Julie Fussell '84
Kathleen Spears

Marinated Vegetable Salad

1 (16-ounce) can shoe peg corn, drained
1 (16-ounce) can small English peas, drained
1 (16-ounce) can French-style green beans, drained
1 cup onion, chopped
1 cup celery, chopped
1 green pepper, chopped
1 (4-ounce) jar pimiento, chopped

Marinade:
1 cup sugar
¾ cup vinegar
1 cup oil
1 teaspoon salt
1 teaspoon pepper

Mix all vegetables; set aside. Combine marinade ingredients and bring to a boil. Cool. Pour cooled marinade over vegetables. Mix well. Refrigerate in a covered container for at least 24 hours. This salad will keep up to 2 weeks in the refrigerator.

Yield: 8-10 servings

Hazel Newman Hemphill '53, Retired Faculty

Green Wonder Salad in Marinade

Salad:
1 (14-ounce) can Chinese vegetables
1 can sliced water chestnuts, drained
1½ cups celery, diced
1 medium onion, thinly sliced
1 (16-ounce) can French-style green beans
1 (15-ounce) can small English peas

Marinade:
¾ cup cider vinegar
2 cups sugar
1 teaspoon salt

Thoroughly drain and rinse vegetables; place into a 2½-quart bowl. Mix all marinade ingredients; pour marinade over salad ingredients. Cover and refrigerate several hours or overnight. Drain marinade before serving. This salad will keep for up to 10 days in refrigerator, if covered.

Yield: 12-16 servings

Mary Waller Duckworth '77

Vegetable Bouquet

Vegetables:

1 (16-ounce) can cut green beans, well-drained
1 (16-ounce) can kidney beans, well-drained
1 (7-ounce) can pitted ripe olives, well-drained
1 (15-ounce) can artichoke hearts, well-drained
1 (6-ounce) can whole or sliced mushrooms, drained
1 (4-ounce) jar diced pimiento, drained
1½ cups celery, diagonally sliced
1 onion, thinly sliced

Dressing:

¼ cup tarragon vinegar
1½ teaspoons monosodium glutamate
1¼ teaspoons salt
1 teaspoon sugar
1 Tablespoon finé herbs
¼ teaspoon Tabasco sauce
½ cup oil

Topping:

¼ cup fresh parsley, chopped
2 Tablespoons capers

Combine drained vegetables, celery, and onion. For the dressing, measure vinegar into a container. Add monosodium glutamate, salt and sugar; stir until dissolved. Add herbs, Tabasco sauce, and oil; shake until blended. Pour dressing over vegetables and refrigerate for several hours or overnight. Toss occasionally. Turn into serving bowl and sprinkle with parsley and capers. Flavors blend better if made ahead.

Yield: 12-16 servings

Anne Meydrech, Faculty

Apple-Pineapple Slaw

3 cups cabbage, shredded
1 (8½-ounce) can pineapple chunks, drained
1 cup unpeeled apples, diced
1 cup miniature marshmallows
1 cup celery, chopped
½ cup mayonnaise
½ cup pecans, chopped

Mix all ingredients well and refrigerate.

Yield: 10-12 servings

Anne A. Martin '53, Faculty Wife

Grace's Tomatoes

2 Tablespoons olive oil
2 Tablespoons white wine vinegar
1 Tablespoon green onions, chives, or fresh basil, diced
1 teaspoon sugar
½ teaspoon Dijon mustard
⅛ teaspoon pepper
3 ounces Gorgonzola cheese or blue cheese, crumbled
4 large tomatoes, sliced
Fresh parsley

Combine oil, vinegar, onions, chives, or basil, sugar, Dijon mustard and pepper; shake. Chill the dressing. Sprinkle crumbled cheese on top of sliced tomatoes. Pour dressing over tomatoes and cheese. Snip and sprinkle parsley on top. This recipe may be served over a platter of fresh spinach.

Yield: 8 servings

Lucy Coward Gross '66

Easy Layered Salad

1 head lettuce, shredded
½ head cauliflower, chopped
½ cup onion, chopped
8-ounces Cheddar cheese, shredded
½-¾ pint mayonnaise
2 Tablespoons sugar
Parmesan cheese
Bacon bits

Place lettuce, cauliflower, and onion into a large bowl. Spread Cheddar cheese over the vegetables. Completely cover cheese with mayonnaise. Sprinkle 2 tablespoons sugar over mayonnaise. Sprinkle Parmesan cheese and bacon bits on top. Refrigerate covered for 6 hours.

Variation: Use 1 pound fresh spinach instead of lettuce; add 1 can sliced water chestnuts to layers. Add 1 tablespoon prepared mustard to the mayonnaise.

Yield: 10 servings

Mary Nelle Hooker Townsend '66
Ron L. Sharpless '70

Don't-Stop-At-Seven Layer Salad!

1 head lettuce, shredded
½ pound spinach, torn
3 hard-cooked eggs, chopped
½ cup celery, chopped
½ cup green pepper, chopped
½ cup green onions, chopped
1 can sliced water chestnuts, drained
½ pound crisp bacon, crumbled
1 (10-ounce) package frozen green peas, thawed and drained
1 cup mayonnaise
½ cup sour cream
½ (1-ounce) package buttermilk dressing mix
1 cup New York sharp Cheddar cheese, shredded

Using a 13x9x2 dish or a very large glass salad bowl, arrange the following ingredients in layers: lettuce, spinach, eggs, celery, green pepper, green onions, water chestnuts, bacon, and peas. Combine mayonnaise, sour cream, and dry buttermilk dressing mix; stir well. Spread over top of green peas, sealing to edge; top with shredded cheese. Cover tightly; refrigerate for several hours or overnight. Toss gently before serving salad onto plates.

Variation: Instead of New York sharp Cheddar cheese, top with one-fourth cup grated Parmesan cheese and cracked pepper to taste.

Yield: 6-8 servings

Peggy O'Neill Hewlett, Faculty

Broccoli Salad

2 (10-ounce) packages frozen broccoli, chopped
4 hard-boiled eggs, chopped
⅓ cup red onion, chopped fine
1 teaspoon salt
1 teaspoon monosodium glutamate (optional)
⅓ cup mayonnaise-type salad dressing
Mushrooms (optional)
Olives (optional)

Cook broccoli for about 4-5 minutes or until crisp-tender; drain well. Place warm broccoli into a serving dish. Mix in eggs, onion, salt, monosodium glutamate, and salad dressing. Garnish with mushrooms and olives, if desired; serve warm. When doubling recipe, use less salt and monosodium glutamate.

Yield: 8 servings

Cynthia B. Foster, Staff

Crunchy Broccoli Salad

1 bunch fresh broccoli, chopped
6-12 slices crisp bacon, crumbled
1 medium red onion, diced
1 cup sunflower seeds
1 cup mayonnaise
½ cup sugar
2 Tablespoons cider vinegar

Combine all ingredients. Toss well. Chill before serving. Unflavored yogurt may be substituted for mayonnaise and artificial sweetener for sugar, to taste.

Variation: Add ½ cup each of chopped bell pepper, celery, carrots, and 1 cup each raisins and chopped pecans. Substitute ranch-flavor dressing for mayonnaise. Add another bunch of broccoli, chopped.

Yield: 8 servings, 15-20 with variation

Nina R. L. Compton '74
Martha Tess Ramzy '92
Ernestine M. Daniel, Staff

Garden Salad with Almonds and Oranges

1 head iceberg lettuce
1 head romaine lettuce
6 green onion tops, sliced thin
1 cup almonds, sliced or slivered
½ cup sugar, divided
1 cup oil
¼ cup vinegar
1 teaspoon salt
1 Tablespoon parsley flakes
Dash of black pepper
Dash of red pepper
1 (22-ounce) can mandarin oranges, drained and chilled

Wash and tear lettuce into bite-size pieces. Add onions. Put in large, covered bowl and refrigerate. Combine almonds and one-fourth cup sugar in saucepan, stirring over medium heat until sugar browns. Cool caramelized almonds on an ungreased cookie sheet. Break into tiny pieces and set aside. Combine oil, vinegar, salt, parsley, black pepper, red pepper, and the remaining one-fourth cup sugar in a bowl. Refrigerate. Before serving, combine lettuce and green onions with almonds and oranges. Toss with desired amount of dressing.

Yield: 12-16 servings

Jean Pittman Williams '55

Jean Williams is the wife of J. Kelley Williams, who served as a member of the Mississippi College Board of Trustees, 1975-78, 1980-86.

Easy Tossed Salad

2-3 Tablespoons lemon juice
½ cup olive oil
1½-2 teaspoons garlic, minced
1 teaspoon salt
½ teaspoon pepper
1 head lettuce
1 cup mozzarella cheese, grated
½ cup Romano cheese, grated

Mix lemon juice, oil, garlic, salt, and pepper; refrigerate at least 1 hour before serving. Mix lettuce and cheeses and cover with dressing; stir and serve.

Yield: 8-10 servings

Carol Ann Shamblin Oakman '66

Fresh Spinach Salad

2 packages fresh spinach
8 ounces fresh mushrooms
1 large avocado
2 medium tomatoes
1 bunch green onions (optional)
1 pound crisp bacon, crumbled
1 small bottle Italian dressing

Cut up spinach, mushrooms, avocado, tomatoes, and green onions. Sprinkle bacon on top of vegetables. Heat Italian dressing. Pour over salad mixture and serve.

Yield: 10-12 servings

Audra Rouse

Low-Fat Taco Salad

1 pound ground turkey
1 package taco seasoning mix
Lettuce, chopped
Tomato, chopped
Low-fat cheese, grated
Non-fat sour cream
Taco sauce
5 taco shells

Prepare taco sauce using ground turkey according to directions on taco seasoning package. Make individual salads by layering lettuce, tomato, one-fifth of the meat mixture, cheese, sour cream, and taco sauce. Crumble 1 taco shell over the top of each salad.

Yield: 5 servings

Pat Turner, Staff

Corned Beef Salad

1 (3-ounce) package lemon flavored gelatin
2 beef bouillon cubes
1 cup hot water
1 envelope unflavored gelatin
1 cup cold water
¾ cup celery, chopped
½ cup onions, chopped
1 can water chestnuts, chopped
1 cup mayonnaise
1 teaspoon Worcestershire sauce
1 (12-ounce) can corned beef
Lettuce
Mayonnaise

Dissolve lemon gelatin and bouillon in hot water. Dissolve unflavored gelatin in cold water. Mix celery, onions, water chestnuts, mayonnaise, and Worcestershire sauce in bowl. Rinse excess fat from corned beef and break into bite-size pieces. Combine with celery mixture. Pour dissolved gelatins and bouillon over mixture and stir well. Pour into a 8x12 greased dish and refrigerate overnight. Serve on lettuce with a dab of mayonnaise.

Yield: 12 servings

Effie McDonald Perry '33

Marion W. Perry '32 and his wife, Effie, established in 1983 a series of awards for scholarship achievement at Mississippi College. The Perry Academic Awards, in the form of gold medals, are presented annually at Honors Day ceremonies.

Hot or Cold Chicken Salad

2 cups boiled chicken (4 breasts), diced
2 cups celery, diced
2 teaspoons onion, grated
½ cup toasted almonds, chopped
2 Tablespoons lemon juice
1 cup mayonnaise
½ teaspoon salt
2½ teaspoons tarragon vinegar
1 (8-ounce) can sliced water chestnuts

Topping (for hot chicken salad):
½ cup cheese, grated
1 cup potato chips, crushed

Mix all ingredients, chill and serve. For hot chicken salad, mix basic salad ingredients and place in casserole. Top with cheese and potato chips. Bake 10 minutes at 450 degrees.

Yield: 6 servings

Betty Rasberry Nester '52

Exotic Salad

3 cups chicken, cooked and cubed
1½ cups celery, sliced
1½ cups seedless green grapes, cut in half
3 Tablespoons lemon juice
1 cup toasted almonds, sliced
1 cup fat-free mayonnaise
¼ cup pineapple juice
Salt and pepper to taste
1½ cups cheese, grated
1½ Tablespoons green pepper, diced
1 teaspoon Worcestershire sauce
1 Tablespoon minced onion
½ teaspoon lemon juice

Mix chicken, celery, grapes, 3 tablespoons lemon juice, almonds, mayonnaise, pineapple juice, and salt and pepper together. In a separate bowl, mix cheese, green pepper, Worcestershire sauce, onion and lemon juice together. Sprinkle sauce over the chicken salad. For best results, chill in refrigerator for about an hour before serving.

Variation: *Sue Parker Jackson '67*, suggests serving the chicken salad on croissant halves.

Yield: 6-8 servings

Tamra Potter Helms '81

Curried Chicken and Pecan Salad

2 cups cubed chicken, cooked or canned
1½ cups cooked rice
½ cup crushed pineapple, well drained
1 Tablespoon red wine vinegar
2 Tablespoons salad oil
1 teaspoon salt
¾ teaspoon curry powder (scant)
1 cup celery, diced
¼ cup pecans, broken
½ to ¾ cup mayonnaise
Lettuce and pecan halves

Combine chicken, rice, pineapple, vinegar, salad oil, salt, and curry powder. Chill 2 hours or longer. Fold in celery, green pepper, broken pecans, and enough mayonnaise to moisten. To serve, pile on crisp lettuce and garnish with pecan halves.

Yield: 12-15 servings

Danie Robbins, Staff

Cantaloupe/Chicken Salad

½ head green lettuce (iceberg, greenleaf, Boston, etc.)
1 rib celery, chopped
2 green onions, chopped
¼ cup zucchini, julienned
1 cup cooked chicken cut into bite-size pieces
½ cantaloupe, cut into bite-size pieces
2 kiwis, peeled and sliced
Poppy Seed Dressing

Tear lettuce into bite-size pieces and place into large salad bowl. Sprinkle celery, onions, and zucchini over lettuce. Add layers of chicken, cantaloupe, and kiwi over green vegetables. Serve with a favorite dressing or with Poppy Seed Dressing. This makes a delicious light lunch or dinner.

Variation: Smoked chicken is especially good in this recipe.

Yield: 6 servings

Donna Powell Diaz '80

Poppy Seed Dressing

⅔ cup sugar
1 teaspoon dry mustard
1 teaspoon salt
⅓ cup vinegar
1½ teaspoons onion juice
1 cup oil
1½ Tablespoons poppy seed

Place sugar, mustard, salt, vinegar, and onion juice into a food processor cylinder or blender. Gradually add oil, beating until the mixture is thickened. Add poppy seed. Stir until well blended. Cover and store in refrigerator.

Yield: 1½ cups

Lucy O. Barnett

Thousand Island Salad Dressing

1½ cups mayonnaise
½ cup chili sauce
1 Tablespoon sweet pickle relish
Sprinkle of garlic powder

Mix all ingredients and refrigerate.

Judy Hand Daws '74

I found this simple recipe in my husband's Bachelor Survival File.

Cool-As-A-Cucumber Dressing

1 large cucumber, peeled
Juice of 2 lemons
1 medium white onion
1 small clove garlic
1 quart mayonnaise
1 teaspoon seasoned salt flavor enhancer
Dash of Worcestershire sauce
Salt
Few drops green food coloring

Process all ingredients in a blender. Pour into a storage container and cover; refrigerate and allow to chill. This dressing will keep well for several days.

Yield: 2 quarts

Jackie Fara

French Country Dressing

½ cup sugar
½ cup white vinegar
1 can cream of tomato soup
2 Tablespoons prepared mustard
1 large onion, finely grated
1 clove garlic, minced
1 cup oil
1 Tablespoon pepper
Salt to taste

Thoroughly mix ingredients in bowl. Cover and store in refrigerator for 2 days to improve flavor. Serve on favorite green salad. This dressing keeps well in the refrigerator for up to a week.

Yield: 3 cups

Laura L. Parkman

French Vinaigrette

2 Tablespoons vinegar or lemon juice
½ cup oil
1 large clove garlic, whole
1 teaspoon salt
Pepper to taste
1 teaspoon Dijon mustard

Combine all ingredients in a jar. Shake well. Let stand for a few minutes before using for flavors to blend. This dressing may be prepared in advance and stored in the refrigerator for a week. It is delicious poured over lettuce, sliced tomatoes, grated carrots, grated/seeded cucumbers, or warm asparagus; it's the Dijon mustard that makes this dressing distinctive.

Yield: ⅔ cup

Florence Blush Frederick '60

Blue Cheese Dressing

1 quart mayonnaise
4-6 ounces blue cheese, crumbled
1 small white onion, minced
1 clove garlic, minced
1 pint light cream
1 Tablespoon parsley, optional

Blend blue cheese into mayonnaise. Add onion, garlic, and parsley. Stir in the cream. Whisk until all ingredients are blended. Refrigerate. Serve over tossed green salad or use as a dip for fresh raw cauliflower, celery, or carrots.

Variation: For a "pink roquefort," add 2 tablespoons catsup.

Yield: 6½ cups

Carolyn Webb '58
Linda Beal Cloud '59

Citrus Salad Dressing

2 lemons, seeded and quartered
2 medium oranges, seeded and quartered
1 teaspoon pepper
½ teaspoon salt
½-¾ cup sugar
2 cloves garlic, finely chopped
1 cup fresh or frozen lemon juice
2 cups oil

Finely process lemons and oranges, including rinds. Add pepper, salt, sugar, and garlic. Add lemon juice and oil. The thickened mixture may be thinned by adding extra lemon or orange juice. This dressing will keep for several days in the refrigerator, covered. Serve with crisp salad greens.

Yield: 3-4 cups

Carolyn Breland Ray '56

Celery and lettuce will keep longer if stored in paper bags.

Quick Gazpacho

1 cup breadcrumbs
2 Tablespoons red wine vinegar
2 cloves garlic
2 cucumbers
1 green pepper
1 onion
⅓ cup oil
½ cup water
1 cup tomato juice
Salt
1 teaspoon pepper
1 cup croutons

Soak breadcrumbs in vinegar. Chop vegetables coarsely and process in blender with oil and water; process in two portions. Stir in breadcrumbs and tomato juice. Season with salt and pepper. Chill and serve with croutons on top.

Yield: 4-6 servings

Anita Gowin, Faculty

Spicy Gazpacho

2½ cups tomatoes (canned or fresh), chopped
½ cup cocktail vegetable juice
Juice of 3 lemons
1½ cups tomato cocktail mix
2 cups cucumbers, chopped fine
½ cup onions, chopped fine
½ cup green peppers, seeded, chopped fine
¼ cup fresh parsley, minced
2 teaspoons salt (optional)
1 teaspoon Tabasco sauce
⅓ cup olive oil

Combine ingredients and chill overnight. Serve cold.

Variation: Boiled shrimp may be added for a main course.

Yield: 6-8 servings

Jimmy Gartin, Jr. '58

When cutting up vegetables for soups or stews, cut each type of vegetable into a different shape or size. This adds variety to the appearance of your dish.

Caquela De Ave

(Chicken Soup)

1 whole chicken, cut up
3 quarts water
1 large onion, chopped
1 carrot, cut into thin strips
½ cup French-style green beans
8 small whole, peeled potatoes
2 ears of corn, cut in 3 sections each
Salt and pepper
Celery leaves, fresh parsley (optional)
½ cup cooked rice

Cook the first 5 ingredients for 30 minutes in a stockpot. Then add whole potatoes, corn, and seasonings. Cook on medium heat until potatoes are tender. Add rice. To serve place a piece of chicken, corn, and a potato in each bowl; finish filling bowls with remaining mixture. Sprinkle with chopped parsley.

Yield: 8 servings

Marilyn Lewis Graves '75

Mrs. Graves, a missionary to Chile, reports that this soup is a typical Chilean dish.

Crabmeat Soup

1 cup celery, chopped
1 large onion, chopped
1 stick butter
2 cans cream of mushroom soup
2 soup cans milk
Salt and pepper
1 pound white crabmeat

Sauté celery and onion in butter in a medium saucepan. Stir in other ingredients except crabmeat. Heat thoroughly but do not boil. Just before serving, add crabmeat.

Yield: 6-8 servings

Martha B. Lee '50

Teacher's Soup

2 Tablespoons oil
1 onion, chopped
1 pound ground beef
3 cans minestrone soup
2 (14½-ounce) cans Mexican tomatoes, cut up
1 can water
2 (15-ounce) cans ranch beans
1 (15¼-ounce) can whole-kernel corn
2 Tablespoons chili powder

Sauté onion in oil until tender. Add ground beef and brown. Add all other ingredients and simmer.

Yield: 8-10 servings

Hazel McCarty, Former Faculty Wife

This soup is quick and easy and may be prepared when a tired teacher comes in from school!

Cabbage Beef Soup

2 (14½-ounce) cans beef broth
1 (16-ounce) can tomatoes
4 beef bouillon cubes
3 (14½-ounce) cans water
1 cup onion, diced
1 pound ground beef, browned and drained
2 cups cabbage, chopped into 1-inch pieces
1 (16-ounce) can pinto beans, drained
Salt, pepper and Creole seasoning

In a 4½-quart stockpot combine broth, tomatoes, bouillon cubes, water, and onions. Cook over medium-high heat for 35 minutes. Add remaining ingredients, cover, and cook for 30 more minutes. Turn off heat; let stand covered for 15-20 minutes before serving.

Yield: 8-10 servings

Melissa C. Wiggins '88, Faculty

Sirloin Vegetable Soup

1 pound sirloin steak
3 carrots, sliced thin
2 ribs celery, chopped
1 onion, chopped
1 can stewed tomatoes
6 beef bouillon cubes
6 cups hot water
½ teaspoon thyme
¼ teaspoon pepper
1 (6-ounce) can mushrooms
Dried parsley
5 or 6 medium potatoes, cubed

Broil the steak to medium-well and cut into small cubes. Combine ingredients except parsley and potatoes and place into a 5-quart slow cooker. Cook on High for 6-7 hours. Add potatoes and parsley during the last 1½ hours of cooking. More water may be added to increase stock.

Yield: 8-10 servings

Nylon Bassett Hellen '71

Norm's Broccoli-Cheese Soup

½ stick butter, melted
4 Tablespoons all-purpose flour
6 cups milk, divided
1 teaspoon seasoned salt
1 teaspoon beef bouillon granules
Pinches of monosodium glutamate, Creole seasoning, herbs to taste
4 broccoli stalks, diced and steamed until tender
1 pound pasteurized processed cheese spread, diced

Combine melted butter and flour in a stockpot to make white sauce. Gradually add 3 cups of milk and seasonings, stirring to prevent sticking. In a blender puree 1½ cups of milk and cooked broccoli; stir into the white sauce. Blend 1½ cups milk and diced cheese together and stir into soup. Heat until cheese is melted. This soup freezes well.

Variation: Add 1 onion and/or 3 ribs celery, steamed and diced. Cauliflower or celery may be substituted for broccoli.

Yield: 10 cups

Norman S. Deaton '54

Oaty Vegetable Soup

1 Tablespoon butter, melted
1 medium onion, chopped
1 medium carrot, chopped
1 small turnip, diced
1 leek, white and pale green part, chopped
2 Tablespoons old-fashioned oatmeal
2½ cups stock (beef or chicken)
Salt and freshly ground pepper
1 teaspoon parsley, chopped
2 cups milk

Combine melted butter and vegetables in a saucepan and stir gently. Cover and steam vegetables for 2-3 minutes. Add oatmeal and heat for 3-4 minutes. Add stock, reduce heat, and simmer covered for 45 minutes. Season to taste and add parsley. Heat milk in another saucepan to just below boiling point. Stir milk into soup. Serve piping hot.

Yield: 4-6 servings

Doug Palmer '58

Artichoke Soup

1 onion, chopped
3 cloves garlic, minced
1 stick margarine
3 (15-ounce) cans artichoke hearts
2 cans cream of mushroom soup
2 cans cream of celery soup
2 cups milk
½ teaspoon pepper

Sauté onion and garlic in margarine in a Dutch oven. Drain, rinse, and quarter artichokes. Add remaining ingredients to sautéed onion and garlic. Heat to just below boiling point. Reduce heat and simmer until ready to serve.

Yield: 8-10 servings

Bettie Posey Bullard '59

Light Zucchini Soup

8 cups zucchini, sliced
4 cups onion, chopped
6 cups water
7½ teaspoons chicken bouillon granules
2 cups instant mashed potato flakes
3 cups skim milk
½ teaspoon black pepper

Combine in a stockpot zucchini, onion, water, and chicken bouillon granules; boil for about 15 minutes until the zucchini and onion are very tender. Add potato flakes. Puree this mixture in batches in food processor or blender and return to stockpot. Add the milk and pepper. Heat on Low for 2-3 minutes. This recipe makes a thick, fluffy soup; for a thinner consistency, add more milk. This soup freezes well or will keep in the refrigerator for 4-5 days.

Variation: Yellow squash, carrots, or English peas may be substituted for the zucchini.

Yield: 12 cups

Katty Ireland, Faculty Wife

Ten Bean Soup

Dried Bean Mixture:
1 pound each: black-eyed peas, small limas, large limas, black beans, pinto beans, kidney beans, navy beans, great northern beans, pink beans; ½ pound lentils, ½ pound split peas

Soup:
2 cups Dried Bean Mixture
1 onion, chopped
1 can stewed tomatoes
Salt and pepper
1 ham bone
1 clove garlic
1 jalapeño pepper, optional

Soak beans overnight. Drain water. Add all ingredients and cover with fresh water. Simmer 2 hours. Add water as needed.

Yield: 6-10 servings

Fleda McElvoy Collins '57

Cheese and Potato Chowder

3 cups water
3 chicken bouillon cubes
4 medium potatoes, peeled and cubed
1 medium onion, chopped
1 cup carrots, sliced thin
½ cup green pepper, diced
⅓ cup butter or margarine
½ cup all-purpose flour
3½ cups milk
4 cups Cheddar cheese, shredded
¼ teaspoon Tabasco sauce (optional)

Combine water and bouillon cubes in a Dutch oven; bring to a boil. Add all vegetables, cover, and simmer for 12 minutes or until tender. Melt butter or margarine in a heavy saucepan; blend in flour and cook for 1 minute. Gradually add milk. Cook over medium heat until thickened, stirring constantly. Add shredded cheese, stirring until melted. Stir cheese mixture and hot sauce into vegetable mixture. Cook on low heat until both mixtures are thoroughly combined.

Yield: 8-10 servings

Janet Stampley Lee '74, Faculty Wife

Five-Hour Stew

1½ pounds beef stewmeat, cubed (chuck preferred)
2-3 potatoes, quartered
4 carrots, sliced
2 ribs celery, cut
1-2 onions, sliced
Garlic to taste
1 (16-ounce) can tomatoes
1 Tablespoon sugar
1 Tablespoon tapioca
2 teaspoons salt
Pepper

Mix all ingredients without browning meat. Bake in a covered casserole at 250 degrees for 4-5 hours.

Yield: 6-8 servings

Mrs. S. S. Kety

Mackinac Island Potato Soup

2 large carrots, peeled, diced
3 ribs celery, chopped fine
1 white onion, chopped fine or 4 green onions, chopped
3 large potatoes, peeled, cubed
3 quarts water
2 teaspoons salt
6 Tablespoons all-purpose flour
1 pint light cream
1 cup finely diced baked ham (optional)

Boil carrots, celery, and onion in a small saucepan. Cook potatoes in 3 quarts water for about 45 minutes; add other cooked vegetables and salt. Reduce heat. Place flour in measuring cup slowly stir in one-half cup cold water. Gradually add enough hot soup to fill the cup, stirring constantly. Slowly stir this flour mixture into the soup. Bring soup to a boil for 2 minutes. Reduce heat; slowly stir in cream.

Variation: For a thicker soup, *Anna Simmons* substitutes 1 can each of cream of onion and cream of celery soups for 2 cups of the water. Substitute one-half pound pasteurized processed cheese and one-fourth pound jalapeño pasteurized processed cheese, melted with 2 cups of milk, for the light cream.

Yield: 12 servings

Ovin Ray '48

Cowboy Stew

2 pounds ground beef
1 onion, chopped
1 clove garlic, chopped fine
1 bell pepper, chopped
2 (17-ounce) cans whole kernel corn
2 (15-ounce) cans kidney beans
2 (16-ounce) cans tomatoes
1 teaspoon salt
1 teaspoon chili powder

Brown beef, onion, garlic, and bell pepper in a large saucepan. Pour juice from corn, beans, and tomatoes into meat and cook for 30 minutes on low heat. Add corn, beans, salt, and chili powder and cook for 30 more minutes. This stew may be prepared ahead; it freezes well.

Yield: 6-8 servings

Tracy Fouché '90

No-Peep Stew

2 pounds lean stew meat
1 cup potatoes, peeled and cubed
1 cup celery, chopped
1 cup onions, chopped
1 cup carrots, sliced
2 dashes Tabasco sauce
Salt and pepper
2 (12-ounce) cans cocktail vegetable juice
2 Tablespoons cornstarch

Brown the stew meat in a small amount of oil. Mix meat and vegetables in a large pot or Dutch oven. Add salt, pepper, and Tabasco sauce. Dissolve cornstarch in cocktail vegetable juice and pour over mixture. Bake for 5 hours at 250 degrees or in a slow cooker. Do not peep! Serve with cornbread sticks.

Yield: 6-8 servings

J. Richard Hurt '75, Faculty

Brunswick Stew

1 large stewing hen
4 cups potatoes, diced
2 cups carrots, diced
1 cup green pepper, chopped
1 cup celery, chopped
2 cups frozen lima beans
2 cups frozen blackeye peas
2 cups frozen butterbeans
1 large can stewed tomatoes
2 large onions, diced
1 medium bottle catsup
¾ cup Worcestershire sauce
Tabasco sauce to taste
Salt and pepper
2 cups frozen corn

Boil hen until meat falls off bones. Remove hen from broth and cut into bite-size pieces. Add raw vegetables to the broth and cook for about 10-12 minutes. When vegetables are tender, add the meat and other ingredients except for corn. Simmer for 2-5 hours, stirring occasionally to prevent sticking. Add corn near the end of cooking time to thicken stew.

Yield: 10-12 servings

Sherry Bobo, Staff

Spanish Mama's Red Hot Chili

2 pounds ground beef
2 cups onions, chopped
¼ cup chili powder
2 teaspoons garlic, minced
2 (15-ounce) cans tomato sauce
2 (8-ounce) jars taco sauce
2 (15-ounce) cans kidney beans, drained and rinsed
Shredded Cheddar cheese (optional)
Tortilla chips (optional)

Brown ground beef; add onions and cook for about 2 minutes. Drain excess fat. Stir in chili powder and garlic. Cook for 1 minute. Stir in tomato sauce and taco sauce. Bring to a boil; reduce heat and simmer uncovered for 10 minutes. Stir in kidney beans and heat thoroughly. Serve with cheese and chips for garnish.

Yield: 10 servings

Beth Stapleton '92

Maggie's Easy Gumbo

2-3 pounds small shrimp
¼ pound pork (chops, bacon, or sausage)
2 Tablespoons oil
1 onion, chopped
1½ cups celery, chopped
3 cups hot water
1 (16-ounce) can tomatoes
1 (16-ounce) can tomato sauce
1 (10-ounce) package frozen, cut okra
1 Tablespoon Worcestershire sauce
1 teaspoon liquid crab boil
1 bay leaf
Dash of cayenne
Salt and pepper
Hot cooked rice

Peel and refrigerate uncooked shrimp. Cook pork in oil with celery and onion until lightly browned and tender. In a stockpot combine water, tomatoes, and tomato sauce. Bring to a boil and add all other ingredients except for shrimp and rice. Simmer 45 minutes. Add shrimp and cook on low heat for 15 minutes. Allow the gumbo to stand for a few minutes and then serve over rice.

Yield: 8-10 servings

Dorothy Price Nixon '68, Staff

Chicken and Sausage Gumbo

Stock:

3½ - 4 pound chicken
3 quarts water
2 ribs celery with leaves, chopped
1 carrot, sliced
1 onion, quartered
1 bay leaf
1 teaspoon salt

Bring to a boil and simmer until chicken is done. When cool, bone, and chop.

Gumbo:

⅓ cup oil
½ cup all-purpose flour
½-1 pound okra cut into ¼-inch pieces
1 cup onion, chopped
¾ cup celery, chopped
½ cup green pepper, chopped
½ cup green onions, chopped
2 cloves garlic, minced
¼ cup fresh parsley, chopped
1 bay leaf
½ teaspoon thyme
½ teaspoon basil
1 (16-ounce) can whole tomatoes with juice
½ pound ham, cubed
½ pound link sausage sliced, or andouille sausage
1 teaspoon Worcestershire sauce
Salt, pepper, cayenne, Tabasco sauce, to taste
Hot cooked rice

In a stockpot make a medium brown roux with oil and flour. Add okra, onion, celery, and green pepper. Cook, stirring, until okra is tender. Add green onions, garlic, parsley, bay leaf, thyme, basil, tomatoes with juice, ham, and chicken meat. Strain stock and slowly stir into gumbo. Cook sausage, drain well, and add to gumbo. Simmer for 1½ hours, stirring occasionally. Season with Worcestershire sauce, salt, pepper, cayenne, and Tabasco sauce. Serve over rice.

Yield: 1½ gallons

Mickey Landrum, Former Faculty (DeWitt Landrum '47)
Carolyn Buckner Hall '72

If you oversalt your soup, add cut raw potatoes. Discard them once they have cooked and absorbed the extra salt.

Best Gumbo Ever

3 Tablespoons oil
3 Tablespoons all-purpose flour
3 cups okra, sliced
1¼ cups onions, chopped
1 clove garlic, minced
2 Tablespoons fresh parsley, minced
1½ teaspoons salt
Pepper
1 cup chicken stock
2 teaspoons Worcestershire sauce
8 drops Tabasco sauce or cayenne to taste
¼ cup fresh lemon juice
Pinch of thyme
2 bay leaves
Chopped ham (optional)
2 pounds raw shrimp
1 pound crabmeat
Hot cooked rice
Gumbo filé

Heat oil and flour in a large Dutch oven over medium heat. Stir until browned to make a roux. Add all other ingredients except for seafood, filé, and rice; simmer for 30 minutes. Add shrimp and crabmeat. Stir, cover the Dutch oven, and cook for 10-20 minutes. Uncover, stir well, and adjust seasonings. Serve gumbo over the rice. Sprinkle filé powder over gumbo.

Variation: One pint of oysters and/or 1 pound of white chicken may be added with the shrimp and crab.

Yield: 8-10 servings

Mrs. W. E. Hannah
Sylvia Meeks '63
Dot Parkman (James E. Parkman '48, Former Faculty)

A lettuce leaf dropped in a pot of soup will absorb the grease from the top.

NELSON HALL

NELSON HALL

Nelson Hall, named for Dotson M. Nelson, President of the College, 1932-57, was completed in 1948. It contains central administrative offices, some academic departments and classrooms, and Swor Auditorium. For decades the chimes of the clock tower informed both campus and community of the time of day as well as the beginning and ending of class periods. Although chimes still ring the hour, the school-bell function has been assumed by digital watches. "Nellie Bell," as the clock tower has been fondly called by hundreds of students, is the visual focal point of the campus.

VEGETABLES AND FRUITS

Granny's Baked Tomatoes

4 cups cut-up canned tomatoes, undrained
3 cups day-old breadcrumbs
1 cup sugar
½ stick butter
Salt to taste

Mix tomatoes, breadcrumbs, and sugar together. Dot with butter, sprinkle salt to taste. Bake for 30 minutes in a preheated 350 degree oven.

Yield: 6 servings

Kathy Kitchings Nowell '73

From the recipes of Mrs. A. A. Kitchings

Fried Green Tomatoes

2 medium green tomatoes
1 cup cornmeal
½ teaspoon salt
½ teaspoon black pepper
Oil for frying

Slice tomatoes ¼-inch thick. Season cornmeal with salt and pepper. Dredge tomatoes in cornmeal. Fry immediately in hot oil until golden brown. Drain on paper towels.

Yield: 2 servings

Christa Boykin Powell '92

Stewed Okra and Tomatoes

1 stick margarine, melted
1 large onion, chopped
3 cups sliced okra
2 (16-ounce) cans tomatoes
2 Tablespoons sugar
Salt and pepper to taste

In a 3-quart saucepan, combine margarine, onion, and okra. Add tomatoes, sugar, and seasonings. Mix well, then cook covered until vegetables are tender. Remove cover and continue cooking until mixture thickens. Stir frequently.

Yield: 6-8 servings

Mary Etta Thompson, Faculty Wife

Fried Okra

Fresh okra, cut into ¾-inch pieces
Cornmeal
All-purpose flour
Salt and pepper
Buttermilk
Oil

Mix together equal amounts of cornmeal and flour; add salt and pepper to taste. Dip cut okra into buttermilk, then roll in the cornmeal mixture. Let dry and recoat, if necessary. Fry in hot, deep oil until golden brown. Drain and serve hot.

Variation: This coating may also be used on pre-boiled cauliflower before frying.

Yield: Variable

Carolyn Webb '58, Former Faculty

Harvard Beets

½ cup sugar
1½ Tablespoons cornstarch
¼ cup vinegar
¼ cup liquid from beets
1 quart beets, fresh cooked or canned
Salt to taste
2 Tablespoons butter

Mix sugar and cornstarch. Add vinegar and beet liquid. Boil for 5 minutes. Cut beets into desired size pieces and add to sauce. Salt to taste. Let stand at least 30 minutes. Before serving, heat well and add butter.

Yield: 6 servings

Sue Epting Lee '39
Mrs. W. E. Hannah

Sue Epting Lee is the wife of Judge Roy Noble Lee '38, who has served on the Mississippi College Board of Trustees, 1967-73, 1974-80, 1984-90, 1991-.

Bohemian Creamed Cabbage

4 cups cabbage, chopped
1 teaspoon salt
1 Tablespoon sugar
½ teaspoon caraway seed
1 cup light cream
1 Tablespoon flour

Boil cabbage in as little water as possible with salt, sugar, and caraway seed. When cabbage is cooked clear, add cream blended with flour. The amount of salt may be reduced and skimmed milk substituted for cream.

Yield: 4 servings

Hugh Brown '39

From the recipes of Joan Keller

Eggplant Pyramids

1 (1¼-pound) eggplant, cut into ½-inch slices
2 medium fresh tomatoes, sliced
1 large red onion, sliced thin
¾ cup butter, melted (divided)
½ teaspoon salt
½ teaspoon dried basil leaves
¼ pound mozzarella cheese, sliced
½ cup Italian breadcrumbs
2 Tablespoons Parmesan cheese, grated

Coat pan with non-stick vegetable spray. In a medium-size casserole, arrange eggplant slices; stack a tomato slice and an onion slice on top of each eggplant slice. Drizzle with one-fourth cup butter. Sprinkle with salt and basil. Bake uncovered in a preheated 450 degree oven for 20 minutes. Cut mozzarella cheese into four pieces. Arrange on top of eggplant pyramids. Stir crumbs into remaining butter; top each pyramid with crumbs. Sprinkle with Parmesan cheese. Bake uncovered for 10 minutes or until cheese is bubbly.

Yield: 4 servings

Jean A. Jones '53

Buckwheat with Roasted Eggplant and Pepper

1 small eggplant, halved vertically
1 sweet red pepper, cored and halved vertically
2 teaspoons olive oil
1 cup buckwheat
2 cloves garlic, minced
2 cups chicken stock
1 bay leaf
1 lemon
2 teaspoons butter
1 teaspoon dried sage
1 teaspoon dried thyme
½ cup fresh basil, minced

Blanch eggplant in boiling water for about 10 minutes or until tender. Place eggplant and pepper halves cut side down on a baking sheet and broil for about 6-7 minutes or until charred. Place vegetables into a brown paper bag, fold to seal, and set aside. In a large non-stick skillet sauté buckwheat in oil for about 5 minutes or until fragrant and roasted. Add garlic, stock, and bay leaf. Cover and simmer for about 8 minutes or until all liquid is absorbed. Add lemon juice and pulp, butter, sage, thyme, and basil to buckwheat and stir well. Remove eggplant and pepper from the bag and peel the charred skins. Chop the vegetables; add to the buckwheat and stir well. Remove bay leaf and place mixture into a serving dish. Serve warm or at room temperature.

Yield: 4 servings

Nell Middleton '54

Carrot Soufflé

2 pounds carrots, peeled and sliced
3 cups sugar (less if desired)
2 teaspoons baking powder
4 Tablespoons all-purpose flour
½ teaspoon cinnamon
6 eggs, beaten (or equivalent egg substitute)
2 cups milk

Cook carrots in water until tender; drain and mash well. Mix together sugar, baking powder, flour, and cinnamon. Add mashed carrots. In mixing bowl, combine eggs and milk. Add to carrot mixture. Blend well. Pour into a 9x13 greased baking dish. Bake in a preheated 350 degree oven for 45-50 minutes. This soufflé freezes well.

Yield: 10-12 servings

Betty Robinson '63

Horseradish Carrot Casserole

2 cups carrots, cooked and diced
½ cup mayonnaise
¼ cup onion, grated
¼ cup horseradish
Round buttery crackers, crushed
Butter or margarine, melted

Combine carrots, mayonnaise, onions, and horseradish. Spoon into a buttered 1-quart baking dish. The mixture may be refrigerated for 1-2 days, if desired. When ready to bake, preheat oven to 350 degrees. Sprinkle cracker crumbs over top of casserole; drizzle with melted butter. Bake for 30 minutes.

Yield: 4 servings

Barbara Irby Thrash '71

Baked Celery

2 bunches of celery hearts, sliced very thin
1 cup almonds, chopped
4 ounces sharp Cheddar cheese, shredded
¼ teaspoon salt, optional
⅛ teaspoon pepper
1 teaspoon paprika
2 cans cream of celery soup
2 Tablespoons margarine, melted
1 cup breadcrumbs

Coat an 8x8 casserole with non-stick vegetable spray. Place thinly sliced celery in the prepared casserole. Sprinkle with almonds, then cheese. Combine all seasonings with celery soup and pour over celery. Mix melted margarine and breadcrumbs. Sprinkle on top. Bake uncovered in a preheated 350 degree oven for 45 minutes.

Yield: 10 servings

Janie James Gore '50

Most of the vitamins in vegetables are close to the skin. So if you must peel them, pare thinly.

Vegetable Garden Casserole

1 (16-ounce) package frozen green beans, slightly cooked
1 cup celery, chopped
1 cup pepper, chopped
¾ cup onions, chopped
1 (16-ounce) can tomatoes, diced
1½ cups carrots, sliced
4 Tablespoons butter
1 Tablespoon sugar
1 teaspoon each salt and pepper
4 Tablespoons tomato sauce
1 (2.8-ounce) can French-fried onions, optional

Mix all ingredients. Put into a 1½-quart casserole. If desired, sprinkle with French-fried onions. Cover and bake 1½ hours in a preheated 350 degree oven.

Yield: 8 servings

Fannie H. Peeples (Widow of Sam Peeples '35)

Mama Bell's Mixed Vegetable Casserole

1 (10-ounce) box frozen mixed vegetables
½ stick margarine
⅓ cup onion, chopped
1 cup celery, chopped
1 cup mayonnaise
1 cup sharp cheese, grated
1 can sliced water chestnuts, drained (optional)
Butter-flavored crackers, crushed

Cook mixed vegetables according to directions; drain well. Sauté onion and celery in margarine. Add mayonnaise and cheese. Mix with vegetables and pour into greased casserole. Cover with butter-flavored cracker crumbs. Bake in a preheated 350 degree oven for 20-30 minutes or until browned.

Yield: 6-8 servings

Paul Douglas Shirley, II '92

Boil vegetables that grow above the ground without a cover and vegetables that grow below the ground with a cover.

Viva Veggie Casserole

4 large tomatoes, sliced
2 green peppers, diced
1 large potato, diced
2 small carrots, sliced thin
1 onion, chopped
1 zucchini, chopped
3 Tablespoons parsley, chopped
1 cup rice (uncooked)
3 teaspoons salt
1 teaspoon pepper
¾ cup chicken broth
¼ cup margarine, melted
2 teaspoons vinegar
1 teaspoon Tabasco sauce
1 cup cheese, grated

Line bottom of 9x13 greased baking dish with half of tomato slices. Cover with half of prepared vegetables, then sprinkle with rice and layer the remaining vegetables; top with tomato slices. In a small bowl mix together salt, pepper, broth, margarine, vinegar and Tabasco sauce. Pour over veggies. Cover and bake 1½ hours in a preheated 350 degree oven. Uncover; sprinkle cheese over top. Put back into oven until cheese melts or brown under broiler. The casserole may be prepared ahead of time and refrigerated until ready to bake.

Yield: 6-8 servings

Linda Gayle Ganaway Liechty '63

Parmesan Vegetable Casserole

1 (10-ounce) package frozen baby limas
1 (10-ounce) package frozen French-style green beans
1 (10-ounce) package frozen English peas
2 bell peppers
1½ cups sour cream
¾ cup mayonnaise
1 (3-ounce) can grated Parmesan cheese

Cook vegetables separately following package directions and drain. Cut bell peppers into strips, boil, and drain. Layer all vegetables in 2-quart casserole. Mix sour cream, mayonnaise, and Parmesan cheese; spoon over layered vegetables. Bake for 30 minutes in a preheated 325 degree oven.

Yield: 8 servings

Mary Evelyn Dorsett Evans '57

Hobo Platter

3 potatoes, sliced
3 carrots, cleaned and sliced
1 large onion, sliced
1 small bell pepper, sliced
2 ribs celery, sliced
1 teaspoon seasoned salt
Salt and pepper
½ stick margarine, sliced

Layer vegetable slices in a 2-quart casserole. Sprinkle with seasonings and pats of margarine. Cover and bake in a preheated 350 degree oven for 25-30 minutes.

Yield: 5 servings

Charlene Gray '90

Mother's Holiday Sweet Potato Bake

1 (40-ounce) can sweet potatoes, drained and mashed
1½ cups sugar
¾ stick margarine, softened
2 eggs
1 (5-ounce) can evaporated milk
1 teaspoon vanilla
½ teaspoon cinnamon
½ teaspoon nutmeg

Topping:
3 cups corn flakes, crushed coarsely
½ cup pecan pieces
½ cup brown sugar, packed
¾ stick margarine, melted

Spray a 2-quart square Pyrex dish generously with non-stick vegetable spray. Beat potatoes until they are smooth. Cream sugar, margarine, eggs, milk, vanilla, and spices. Add gradually to the potatoes. Pour potato mixture evenly into dish and bake for 45 minutes in a preheated 350 degree oven. Prepare topping while potatoes cook. Mix topping ingredients thoroughly. Spread evenly over potato mixture and bake for 20 additional minutes.

Variation: Omit cinnamon and nutmeg, add 1 teaspoon lemon flavoring. Fresh sweet potatoes may also be used.

Yield: 6-8 servings

Beverly Barber '92
Lorell Bailey Coleman

Sweet Potato Casserole

this is really good!

3 cups cooked or canned sweet potatoes, mashed
½ teaspoon salt (optional)
½ stick margarine, melted
1 teaspoon vanilla
½ cup sugar
2 eggs, beaten
½ cup milk or 1 (5-ounce) can evaporated milk

Topping:
1 cup brown sugar
⅓ cup all-purpose flour
1 cup nuts, chopped — pecans (cashews weren't the best)
⅓ stick margarine, melted

Coat a 1½-quart dish with non-stick vegetable spray. Combine casserole ingredients and put into dish. Mix topping ingredients and spoon on top of casserole. Bake for 30 minutes in a preheated 350 degree oven.

Yield: 8-10 servings

Evelyn Stigler Harvey '52
Martha Nell Wilson Cotten '58
Penny Brown Adams '69
Nina R. C. Compton '74
Sheila Robertson Carpenter '87, Staff

Skewered Grilled Potatoes

2 pounds red potatoes, quartered
½ cup water
½ cup mayonnaise-type salad dressing
¼ cup chicken broth
2 teaspoons dried oregano leaves
1 teaspoon garlic powder
½ teaspoon onion powder

Place potatoes and water in a 2-quart casserole; cover. Microwave on high 12-15 minutes, stirring after 8 minutes. Drain. Mix remaining ingredients and stir into potatoes; cover. Refrigerate 1 hour. Drain, reserving salad dressing mixture. Arrange potatoes on skewers and place on grill over hot coals. Grill covered for 4 minutes. Rotate skewers; brush with reserved salad dressing mixture. Continue grilling 4 minutes more. The potatoes may be cooked under a broiler in the oven.

Yield: 4-6 servings

Peggy Parks Lee '85

Potato Casserole

10 average size potatoes, peeled and diced
1 green pepper, chopped
1 (2-ounce) jar pimiento
4 dill pickles, chopped

Sauce:
1 stick margarine
3 Tablespoons all-purpose flour
2 cups milk
4 teaspoons prepared mustard
1 Tablespoon salt
1 Tablespoon Worcestershire sauce
½ cup cheese, grated

Boil potatoes just until tender. Drain well. Combine potatoes with pepper and pimiento. Mix ingredients for sauce and cook on low heat until sauce thickens. Pour sauce over potatoes. Spoon dill pickles over potatoes. Bake in a large casserole in a preheated 350 degree oven for 45 minutes or until lightly browned. This dish freezes well.

Yield: 10 servings

Ann T. Hall '63, Faculty Wife

Venetian Potatoes

9 red potatoes
6 Tablespoons butter
3 cups sharp Cheddar cheese, shredded
3 cups sour cream
½ cup green onions, chopped, tender tops included
Salt and pepper to taste

Boil potatoes until tender; chill, peel, and grate into a large bowl. In medium saucepan over low heat, combine butter and cheese and stir until melted. Remove from heat and blend in sour cream, onions and seasonings. Pour over potatoes and mix well. Place mixture in a greased 3-quart casserole and dot with additional butter. Bake for 45 minutes in a preheated 350 degree oven.

Yield: 12 servings

Beverly Ferrell Alman '50

Giant's Potato Fingers

3 Tablespoons margarine
¼ cup Parmesan cheese, grated
2 Tablespoons dried parsley flakes
¼ cup flour
¾ teaspoon salt
⅛ teaspoon pepper
6 medium potatoes, well-scrubbed, unpeeled

Melt margarine and spread evenly in 13x9x2 casserole. Mix Parmesan cheese, parsley, flour, salt, and pepper in large plastic bag. Slice each potato lengthwise into 8 pieces. Coat potatoes, dropping about 6 slices at a time into bag and shaking gently. Place potatoes in a single layer in dish; bake for 1 hour in a preheated 375 degree oven. This is a recipe with which children may help.

Yield: 8 servings

Claudia Wilkinson

Hash Brown Potato Casserole

1 (32-ounce) package frozen hash brown potatoes, thawed
1 (16-ounce) carton sour cream
1 can cream of mushroom soup
½ teaspoon salt
1 small onion, diced
2 cups pasteurized process cheese spread, cubed
1 cup shredded mozzarella cheese
2 cups corn flakes, crushed
½ cup butter, melted

Mix first 6 ingredients and spoon into a greased 9x13 baking dish. Top with mozzarella cheese. Combine corn flakes and butter and sprinkle over cheese. Bake for 1 hour in a 350 degree preheated oven. This casserole may be frozen and reheated in the microwave.

Yield: 8-10 servings

Ann Polk (Daniel Polk '52)

Granny's Rice Casserole

1 cup rice
1 teaspoon Worcestershire sauce
1 can chicken broth
1 can consommé
Salt and pepper to taste
1 stick margarine
1 onion, chopped

Mix together rice, Worcestershire sauce, chicken broth, consommé, salt, and pepper in a medium casserole. Sauté onion in melted margarine. Add to rice mixture. Cook covered for 1 hour in a preheated 350 degree oven. Do not add water.

Yield: 6 servings

Robin Harvey Thompson '89

Green Rice

¾ cup green onion, minced
3 Tablespoons oil
2 cups chicken broth
1 cup uncooked rice
½ cup green pepper, minced
¼ cup parsley, minced
1 teaspoon salt
¼ teaspoon pepper

Cook onion in oil until soft. Combine with all other ingredients and pour into a 2-quart casserole. Bake for 30-40 minutes in a preheated 350 degree oven until rice is tender. Stir rice several times while cooking.

Yield: 4-6 servings

Anne A. Martin '53, Faculty Wife

From the recipes of Nannie Pitts McLemore

To prevent tears, place onions in freezer four to five minutes before peeling and cut the root end off last.

Broccoli-Rice Casserole

1 cup rice, cooked
1 (10-ounce) package frozen chopped broccoli
3/4 stick margarine
1 onion, chopped
1 (8-ounce) package pasteurized process cheese spread, cubed
1 can cream of chicken soup
Canned French-fried onions (optional)

Cook rice according to package directions. Cook broccoli according to package directions. Do not drain. Sauté onion in margarine until tender. Mix all ingredients together; bake in a greased casserole for about 40 minutes in a preheated 350 degree oven. French-fried onions may be added on top for the last 10 minutes of baking.

Yield: 6-8 servings

Jean Hollis Nall '70

Black-eyed Peas with Rice

2 slices bacon
1 medium onion, chopped
1 (15-ounce) can black-eyed peas, drained
1 (14½-ounce) can stewed tomatoes, undrained
1 cup rice, cooked
1/4 teaspoon salt
1/4 teaspoon pepper

Cook bacon in skillet until crisp. Remove bacon, reserving 2 tablespoons bacon drippings in skillet. Crumble bacon, set aside. Sauté onions in drippings until tender. Add peas, tomatoes, rice, salt, and pepper, stirring well. Spoon the mixture into a 1½-quart greased casserole. Bake for 30 minutes in a preheated 350 degree oven. Garnish with bacon.

Yield: 6 servings

Mrs. Luke Roberts

Fried Rice with Almonds

2 Tablespoons oil
1 small onion, chopped
½ medium green pepper, chopped
¼ teaspoon garlic salt
¼ teaspoon black pepper
2 cups cold, cooked white rice
2 Tablespoons soy sauce
½ cup blanched sliced almonds

Sauté onion, green pepper, garlic salt, and black pepper in oil for 5 minutes. Add rice, soy sauce, and almonds. Mix well. Cover and cook on low heat for 10 minutes or until thoroughly heated. This is a good side dish with sweet and sour spareribs and may be prepared ahead and reheated.

Yield: 4 servings

Alicia Jones Pittman '60, Faculty Wife

Western Style Beans

1 pound ground round steak
1 medium onion, chopped
2 (16-ounce) cans pork and beans
1 Tablespoon prepared mustard
1 Tablespoon Worcestershire sauce
½ cup catsup
½ cup brown sugar (light or dark)
Salt and pepper to taste

Brown meat and onions; add salt and pepper. Mix with remaining ingredients. Spoon bean mixture into a 2-quart casserole and cover. Bake for 30 minutes in a preheated 300 degree oven. Stir halfway through baking time.

Yield: 12 servings

Syble Anne Brown Dial '65, Staff

Deluxe Baked Bean Casserole

2 (28-ounce) cans baked beans
1 (18-ounce) bottle barbecue sauce
1⅓ pounds ground chuck, cooked and drained
7 slices bacon, cooked and crumbled
3 ribs celery, sliced
½ (1-pound) box brown sugar (light or dark)

Layer ingredients in order given in a 9x13 baking dish. Bake for 2 hours in a preheated 250 degree oven. Ground turkey may be substituted for ground chuck.

Yield: 12 servings

June Campbell (Mrs. Richard)

Zucchini Casserole

4 Tablespoons butter
4 cups zucchini, sliced
1 cup potatoes, diced
½ cup green pepper, chopped
1½ cups tomatoes, chopped
1½ cups cheese, grated
1½ teaspoons salt
¼ teaspoon black pepper
1 teaspoon oregano (or to taste)
1½ cups cheese crackers, crumbled

Melt butter in a skillet; add zucchini, potatoes, and green pepper, and cook for 12-15 minutes. Add tomatoes, grated cheese, salt, black pepper, and oregano. Cook 10 minutes more or until cheese melts. Pour into a greased casserole and top with crumbled cheese crackers. Bake uncovered in a preheated 350 degree oven for 30 minutes.

Yield: 6 servings

Anita Gowin, Faculty

Cut vegetables into small pieces and cook quickly for maximum flavor.

Butternut Squash Casserole with Crunchy Topping

2 cups butternut squash, cooked
1 cup sugar
½ stick margarine, melted
½ cup evaporated milk
1 teaspoon vanilla
¼ cup all-purpose flour
2 eggs, beaten

Topping:
2 cups corn flakes, crushed
½ cup brown sugar
½ cup margarine
½ cup nuts, chopped

In a large mixing bowl, blend squash and sugar. Add remaining casserole ingredients. Mix until smooth. Pour into a 2-quart baking dish and bake in a preheated 325 degree oven for 45 minutes or until center is done. Mix topping ingredients and spread over hot casserole. Return to oven for 10-15 minutes until margarine and sugar melt and topping is crisp.

Variation: Omit topping. Add 1 (8-ounce) can crushed pineapple and 1 cup grated coconut to casserole mixture before pouring it into baking dish. Top with maraschino cherries and toasted coconut if desired.

Yield: 6-8 servings

Mrs. Samuel Gore '54, Faculty Wife

Squash Delight

1 pound yellow squash, sliced
½ cup onion, chopped
2 Tablespoons green pepper, chopped
½ stick margarine
1 Tablespoon sugar
½ cup mayonnaise
1 egg
½ cup Cheddar cheese, grated
Salt and pepper to taste
Round buttery crackers, crushed

Cook squash in lightly salted water until tender; drain. Sauté onion and green pepper in margarine. Combine all ingredients. Pour into a greased 9x13 baking dish and top with buttery cracker crumbs. Bake for 30 to 40 minutes in a preheated 350 degree oven. For a creamier texture, stir in 1 can cream of mushroom soup.

Yield: 6-8 servings

Mable Gaston, Faculty
Annie L. Browning, Staff

Creamy Squash Casserole

3 pounds yellow squash, sliced (fresh or frozen)
1 large onion, chopped
2 teaspoons salt
2 Tablespoons butter (divided)
2 Tablespoons cornstarch
1 cup whipping cream
1 (8-ounce) package pasteurized process cheese spread, melted
1 roll butter-flavored crackers, crushed

Boil squash, onion, salt, and 1 tablespoon butter until tender. Drain. Combine cornstarch, whipping cream, and cheese. Cook over low heat, stirring constantly until sauce thickens. Mix squash and cheese mixture and place in a 9x13 casserole. Top with crackers and dot with 1 tablespoon butter. Cook for 30 minutes in a preheated 350 degree oven.

Yield: 6-8 servings

Beth Lofton Case '75

Squash Dressing

1 medium onion, chopped
¼ pound margarine
2 cups squash, cooked
2 eggs, slightly beaten
1 can cream of chicken soup
2 cups cornbread, crumbled
Salt and pepper to taste

Grease a 1½-quart casserole. Sauté onion lightly in margarine. Mash squash with fork. Combine sautéed onion with eggs. Add squash, chicken soup, cornbread, salt, and pepper. Mix well and pour into a greased casserole. Bake for 20 to 25 minutes in a preheated 350 degree oven.

Yield: 6 servings

Mary Frances Ingram

Substitute chicken bouillon cubes or granules for the high fat bacon drippings often used in Southern cooking.

Souped-Up Asparagus

3 (10½-ounce) cans asparagus tips, drained
3 eggs, boiled and sliced
½ stick margarine
2 Tablespoons cream of mushroom soup
2 (10½-ounce) cans chicken à la king
1 teaspoon salt
¼ teaspoon black pepper
1 (2-ounce) jar diced pimiento
2 cups mild Cheddar cheese, grated
¾ (6-ounce) bag onion/sour cream potato chips, crushed

Mix mushroom soup with chicken à la king. Arrange 1½ cans of asparagus in a layer in a buttered shallow 1½-quart casserole. Top with a layer of half the sliced eggs. Cover with thin pats of margarine. Spread with half of chicken à la king mixture. Mix salt, pepper, diced pimiento, grated cheese, and crushed potato chips. Sprinkle half of this mixture over chicken à la king. Repeat the procedure for a second layer. Bake uncovered for 20 minutes in a preheated 325 degree oven.

Yield: 8 servings

Kathleen Bush Stovall '73

Classic Asparagus Casserole

2 (15-ounce) cans asparagus, drained
1 can cream of mushroom soup
½ soup can water
Salt to taste
¼ teaspoon pepper
1 cup Cheddar cheese, grated
1 cup breadcrumbs
½ cup sliced almonds
4 Tablespoons butter

Arrange asparagus on bottom of 8x8-inch casserole. Mix soup, water, salt, and pepper and pour over asparagus. Sprinkle cheese over asparagus mixture; top with breadcrumbs, almonds, and butter. Bake until bubbly in a preheated 350 degree oven.

Yield: 6-8 servings

Alice Ann McCann Smith '63, Staff

Easy Asparagus Casserole

1 (15-ounce) can cut asparagus, drained
½ teaspoon salt
1 teaspoon white pepper
1 (4-ounce) jar pimiento, diced and drained
2 eggs, beaten
1 cup buttery cracker crumbs
1 cup milk
4 ounces Cheddar cheese, shredded
¼ cup butter or margarine, melted

Combine ingredients and spoon into a greased 8-inch square baking dish. Bake uncovered for 30 minutes in a preheated 400 degree oven.

Yield: 6 servings

Mrs. Bruce K. Harris

Spinach Casserole with Crumb Topping

2 (10-ounce) packages frozen chopped spinach
4 Tablespoons butter or margarine
2 Tablespoons all-purpose flour
3 Tablespoons onion, chopped
½ cup evaporated milk
½ cup spinach liquid
1 teaspoon Worcestershire sauce
½ teaspoon black pepper
¾ teaspoon celery salt
¾ teaspoon garlic salt
1 (6-ounce) roll jalapeño cheese, cubed
1 cup breadcrumbs, mixed with 2 Tablespoons melted butter or margarine

Cook spinach according to package directions; drain and retain liquid. Melt butter in saucepan over low heat; add flour, stirring until smooth but not brown. Add onion and cook until soft. Pour in liquid slowly, stirring constantly and cook until smooth and thick. Add seasonings and cheese, stirring until melted. Add spinach. Pour into a 1½-quart casserole; cover with breadcrumbs and bake in a preheated 325 degree oven for 30-40 minutes or until bubbly. The flavor is improved if made a day ahead. This casserole may be frozen.

Yield: 6-8 servings

Nona Gillis Fortenberry '40

Spinach-Cheese Casserole

3 eggs, beaten
6 Tablespoons all-purpose flour
1 (16-ounce) package frozen chopped spinach, thawed
2 cups Cheddar cheese, grated
2 cups cottage cheese
1 teaspoon salt
Pepper to taste

Beat the eggs and flour until smooth. Mix spinach, Cheddar cheese, and cottage cheese together. Add salt and pepper. Bake uncovered in a 2-quart casserole in a preheated 350 degree oven for 1 hour. Let stand a few minutes before serving. Egg substitute and low-fat cheeses may be used to decrease total fat.

Yield: 6-8 servings

Catherine Blackwell, Faculty Wife

Green Bean Wraps

1 (15½-ounce) can whole green beans, drained
1 bottle Russian or Catalina salad dressing
8 slices bacon
Dash Worcestershire sauce
Pepper

Wrap a strip of bacon around bundles of 4-6 beans. Place the wraps into a 9x9 baking dish. Mix the dressing and Worcestershire sauce and pour over the wraps. Sprinkle with pepper. Bake in a preheated 350 degree oven for 30-45 minutes or until the bacon is done.

Yield: 4 servings

Amy Garner

Stir-Fried Green Beans

3 cloves garlic, sliced very thin
3 Tablespoons olive oil
2 pounds green beans, washed and snapped (must be fresh and tender)
Salt and pepper to taste
½ teaspoon Italian seasoning
5 leaves fresh basil (optional)
1 Tablespoon lemon juice

In a wok or large frying pan, sauté garlic in oil. Add green beans and seasonings. Cover and cook for about 30 minutes until tender, stirring often. Add lemon juice, toss, and serve.

Yield: 6 servings

Susan Newman, Staff

Sweet and Sour Green Beans

4 slices bacon
1 medium onion, chopped
½ cup slivered almonds
3 (16-ounce) cans green beans, French-style or cut
½ cup vinegar
½ cup sugar

In a large skillet cook bacon until crisp. Remove bacon from skillet and crumble. Sauté onion in bacon drippings. Mix together bacon, onion, slivered almonds, and green beans. Add vinegar and sugar. Simmer for 30-40 minutes. This can be made ahead and reheated when ready to serve or can be baked in a 9x13 casserole in a preheated 300 degree oven for 1½ hours.

Yield: 8 servings

Laura Sue Lofton (Widow of W. D. Lofton, Jr. '42)
Bobbie M. Gardner

W. D. Lofton, Jr., served on the Mississippi College Board of Trustees, 1965-71, 1972-78, 1979-85, 1986-92.

Green Beans and Artichokes

4 (16-ounce) cans cut green beans, drained
1 can artichokes, drained
1½ cups sugar
2 cups oil
1 cup apple cider vinegar
2 cloves garlic, sliced
1 Tablespoon salt

Drain beans and artichokes and place in a large container. Prepare marinade from sugar, oil, vinegar, garlic and salt. Pour over vegetables. Marinate in refrigerator for 24 hours. Heat in marinade, drain, and serve.

Yield: 12-15 servings

Mrs. Lloyd E. Roberts '80, Faculty Wife

A teaspoon of lemon juice or vinegar added to green vegetables will help them retain their color.

Green Beans Au Gratin

½ cup onions, chopped
1 Tablespoon parsley, chopped
2 Tablespoons butter or margarine
2 Tablespoons all-purpose flour
1 teaspoon salt
¼ teaspoon pepper
½ teaspoon grated lemon peel
1 cup sour cream
5 cups sliced green beans, cooked and drained

Topping:
½ cup grated Cheddar cheese
2 Tablespoons butter or margarine, melted
½ cup cracker crumbs

Cook onions and parsley in butter until tender but not brown. Stir in flour, salt, pepper, and lemon peel. Add sour cream, then mix in green beans. Pour mixture into a 2-quart casserole and set aside. Mix topping ingredients and spoon over bean mixture. Bake for 30 minutes in a preheated 350 degree oven.

Yield: 6-8 servings

Joann White

Swiss Green Beans

2 (16-ounce) cans French-style green beans, drained
½ pound Swiss cheese, grated
4 Tablespoons butter, melted, divided
2 Tablespoons all-purpose flour
1 teaspoon onion, grated
½ teaspoon salt
¼ teaspoon pepper
1 teaspoon sugar
1 cup sour cream
1 cup breadcrumbs

Place beans into a greased, 1½-quart casserole. Sprinkle with cheese. Melt 2 tablespoons butter in saucepan and blend in flour. Add onion, salt, pepper, sugar, and sour cream. Cook over low heat, stirring constantly. Pour mixture over beans and cheese. Sprinkle with breadcrumbs mixed with remaining 2 tablespoons melted butter. Bake for 25 minutes in a preheated 400 degree oven.

Yield: 6-8 servings

Jimmy Gartin, Jr. '58

Green Beans with Horseradish Dressing

5 (16-ounce) cans green beans
2 hard-cooked eggs, chopped fine
1 cup mayonnaise
Juice of 1 lemon
1 Tablespoon horseradish
1 teaspoon Worcestershire sauce
A dash of any of the following: celery salt, onion salt, garlic salt, parsley flakes

Drain the beans, rinse with cold water. Cover with fresh water and heat until very hot; do not boil. Drain beans and place in a serving dish. Mix the remaining ingredients and pour over hot beans. This is an easy, quick dish for a covered dish supper. The beans may also be served cold.

Yield: 12 servings

Marian Lyons

Green Bean and Corn Casserole

1 (16-ounce) can French-style green beans
1 (16-ounce) can shoepeg corn
½ cup sharp Cheddar cheese, grated
1 can cream of chicken soup
½ cup sour cream
½ cup margarine, melted
1 stack round buttery crackers, crushed

Drain beans and corn; mix the vegetables with cheese, soup, and sour cream and put into a 9x13 baking dish. Mix margarine with crushed crackers. Sprinkle crackers on top of casserole and bake for 40 minutes in a preheated 350 degree oven.

Yield: 6-8 servings

Melissa A. Thompson '82

Store vegetables such as corn, peas, and beans dry and unwashed in plastic bags in refrigerator. Potatoes and onions should be stored in a cool, dry, well-ventilated place out of direct sunlight.

Crusty Corn Casserole

1 can cream-style corn
1 can whole kernel corn, undrained
1 package Mexican cornbread mix
1 (8-ounce) carton sour cream
1 stick margarine, melted
1 cup cheese, grated
½ cup green pepper, chopped
Pimiento for color (optional)

Combine all ingredients. Bake uncovered for about 45 minutes in a preheated 325 degree oven.

Yield: 6 servings

Peggy F. Lovell '75

Sweet Corn Casserole

2 sticks butter, melted
1 Tablespoon butter flavoring
1 (16-ounce) carton sour cream
2 eggs, beaten
1 (15-ounce) can kernel corn, undrained
1 (15-ounce) can cream-style corn
1 (8½-ounce) box corn muffin mix

Mix all ingredients in a large bowl. Place ingredients in a 9x13 baking dish. Bake in a preheated 350 degree oven for 45 minutes or until edges turn golden brown and middle is firm.

Yield: 8-12 servings

Ruth Ann Gibson, Faculty

Corn Pudding

½ stick margarine
1 Tablespoon all-purpose flour
1 Tablespoon sugar
⅛ teaspoon salt
⅛ teaspoon black pepper
1 cup milk
2 eggs, beaten
1 (16-ounce) can cream-style yellow corn

Melt margarine and put into an 8x8 baking dish. Chill until margarine is hardened. Mix flour, sugar, salt, and pepper. Add milk gradually, mixing well. Stir in eggs and corn. Pour into the prepared baking dish and bake in a preheated 350 degree oven for about 1 hour or until lightly browned and set. Serve warm.

Yield: 6 servings

Genevieve S. Lassetter '37

Jade Green Broccoli

2 pounds fresh broccoli
1 Tablespoon cornstarch (or 2 Tablespoons flour)
2 Tablespoons soy sauce
½ cup water or chicken stock
1 teaspoon sugar (optional)
¼ cup oil
⅛ teaspoon salt
1 clove garlic, minced

Wash broccoli, blot dry, and cut into bite-sized pieces. Mix together sugar, cornstarch, soy sauce, and chicken stock; set aside. Heat wok or large skillet until hot. Add the oil, then the salt. Reduce heat to medium and add the garlic. When garlic is golden brown, add the broccoli. Increase heat and stir-fry 2 minutes. Cook covered for an additional 2 minutes. Remove cover and add the soy sauce mixture while stirring. Allow sauce to thicken. Serve broccoli and sauce over cooked rice.

Yield: 6 servings

Elaine Martin Barber '82

Broccoli with Cream Cheese and Chives

1 (40-ounce) bag frozen broccoli spears or cut broccoli
1 (12-ounce) carton cream cheese with chives, softened
2 cans cream of shrimp soup, undiluted
½ stick margarine or butter, melted
Juice of 1 lemon
4 ounces mild Cheddar cheese, grated
1 cup fine dry bread or cracker crumbs

Cook broccoli crisp-tender. Drain, place in bottom of a 13x9x2 baking pan which has been buttered or coated with cooking spray. Mix the cream cheese with the soup, margarine, and lemon juice. Pour over broccoli. Mix grated cheese with crumbs and spread over the soup mixture. Bake in a preheated 350 degree oven for 30 minutes.

Yield: 8-10 servings

Marian Lyons

Broccoli and Cauliflower Casserole

1 large package frozen mixed broccoli and cauliflower
1 can cream of mushroom soup
1 (8-ounce) jar process cheese spread (plain or mild Mexican)
3 cups cooked rice
Cracker crumbs

Cook vegetables; drain, reserving one-half cup liquid. Mix liquid with soup. Stir cheese spread into soup mixture and add rice. Combine vegetables with soup mixture. Top with cracker crumbs. Bake in a preheated 350 degree oven for 30 minutes.

Yield: 8 servings

Jean Lomax Irby '64

Lima Bean-Broccoli Casserole

1 (10-ounce) package frozen baby limas
1 (10-ounce) package frozen broccoli, chopped
1 can water chestnuts, sliced
1 cup sour cream
1 package dry onion soup mix
1 can cream of mushroom soup
1 stick butter or margarine, melted
3 cups crispy rice cereal

Coat a 2-quart casserole with vegetable cooking spray. Cook beans and broccoli until tender; drain. Add water chestnuts and spoon into casserole. Mix sour cream, onion soup mix, and mushroom soup and pour over vegetables. Mix melted margarine and crispy rice cereal and spread over top of vegetables. Bake for 30 minutes in a preheated 350 degree oven.

Yield: 6 servings

Shirley Voyles

To reduce the odor which results in cooking cabbage, broccoli, or other vegetables, add a little vinegar to the cooking water.

Spicy Lima Beans

6 slices bacon
⅓ cup celery, minced
¼ cup green pepper, minced
2 large cloves garlic, minced
2 Tablespoons all-purpose flour
Salt and pepper, to taste
2 Tablespoons sugar
1 cup canned tomatoes
2 (10-ounce) boxes frozen limas, cooked

Fry bacon; cook celery, green pepper and garlic in bacon fat. Add flour, salt, pepper, sugar, tomatoes, and cooked beans; blend well. Put mixture into a baking dish and crumble bacon over top. Cook covered in a preheated 350 degree oven for 30 minutes.

Yield: 10 servings

Ann Fisher Godwin '81

English Pea Casserole

1 cup milk
2 Tablespoons all-purpose flour
2 Tablespoons butter
1 (8-ounce) jar sharp cheese spread
½ pound pasteurized process cheese spread
¼ teaspoon black pepper
1 can English peas, drained
1 small can pearl onions, drained
½ cup buttery cracker crumbs

In a saucepan combine milk, flour, butter. Stir, cooking slowly until thickened. Add cheeses; heat until cheeses melt. Add black pepper, peas, and onions. Pour mixture into a baking dish. Top with crumbs. Bake in a preheated 350 degree oven for 20-25 minutes.

Yield: 6-8 servings

Lynn King

A teaspoon of honey in the water used for cooking frozen peas, corn, or lima beans adds zest and flavor to the vegetables.

Easy Cheesy Peas

1 (8-ounce) jar jalapeño pasteurized process cheese spread
1 can cream of mushroom soup
2 or 3 (16-ounce) cans tiny English peas

In a saucepan, over low heat, melt cheese spread and soup together. Drain English peas; add to the cheese sauce and heat thoroughly for 2-3 minutes or until the peas are hot. This recipe may be halved and made in the microwave. Plain process cheese spread may be substituted for jalapeño cheese if a milder taste is desired.

Yield: 6-8 servings

Irma M. Murray Glover '43

Mushroom Marinade

¾ cup oil
3 Tablespoons soy sauce
⅛ cup Worcestershire sauce
1 teaspoon salt
3 Tablespoons lemon juice
¼ teaspoon garlic salt
1 teaspoon pepper
1½ pounds fresh or canned whole mushrooms

Mix all ingredients for marinade together. Pour over mushrooms in a large skillet; simmer 20-25 minutes, stirring occasionally. Cool and refrigerate overnight. Reheat before serving. This may be used as an accompaniment to meat.

Yield: 6 servings

Mary Elizabeth Vickery

Mary Elizabeth Vickery is the daughter-in-law of Harry Vickery, a member of the Mississippi College Board of Trustees.

Vidalia Onion Casserole

5 large Vidalia onions, sliced
1 stack round buttery crackers, crushed
1 pound medium hot sausage, browned and drained
1 can cream of mushroom soup
½ teaspoon seasoned salt
½ cup sharp Cheddar cheese, grated

Put half of onion slices on bottom of a 12x17 casserole. Add a layer of crushed crackers, a layer of sausage, then another layer of onions. Spread soup on top and sprinkle with seasoned salt and then cheese. Bake for 45-55 minutes in a preheated 400 degree oven.

Yield: 8-12 servings

Cynthia B. Foster, Staff

Hot Curried Fruit

¾ cup sugar
2 teaspoons curry powder
⅓ cup margarine, melted
1 (14-ounce) can applesauce
1 (16½-ounce) can purple plums, pitted and drained
1 (29-ounce) can sliced peaches, drained
1 (20-ounce) can pineapple chunks, drained
1 (6-ounce) jar maraschino cherries, drained
½ cup brown sugar
½ cup pecans, chopped

Mix sugar, curry powder, margarine, and applesauce. Stir in fruit. Place in a 2-quart baking dish; top with a mixture of brown sugar and pecans. Bake at 350 degrees for 1½ hours, checking nuts to prevent over-browning.

Yield: 10-12 servings

Marva Nell King '62

Scalloped Apples

8-9 slices fresh bread, crumbed
1 (20-ounce) can apples
2 cups sugar, divided
3 eggs, beaten
1 cup butter, melted
Cinnamon

Toss breadcrumbs and apples in a buttered 2-quart baking dish. Combine 1¾ cups sugar, eggs, and butter. Pour over apples and breadcrumbs. Sprinkle with one-fourth cup sugar and desired amount of cinnamon. Bake for 30-40 minutes in a preheated 350 degree oven. This dish may be prepared ahead of time and refrigerated before baking.

Yield: 6-8 servings

Diane Legg Hutto '82

Scalloped Pineapple

4 cups fresh breadcrumbs
1 (20-ounce) can pineapple chunks, drained
3 eggs, beaten
1 cup sugar
½ stick butter or margarine, melted

Grease a 2-quart baking dish. Toss together the breadcrumbs and pineapple. Place in baking dish. Combine remaining ingredients and pour over pineapple mixture and breadcrumbs. Bake for 30 minutes in a preheated 350 degree oven. This dish may be made ahead and refrigerated overnight before baking.

Yield: 6-8 servings

Cindy Hampton, Staff

Papa's Pineapple Casserole

1 (20-ounce) can pineapple chunks
1 cup sugar
8 Tablespoons flour
8 Tablespoons pineapple juice
1½ cups Cheddar cheese, shredded
3 cups crushed round buttery cracker crumbs
1 stick butter or margarine, melted

Drain and reserve juice from pineapple chunks. Arrange chunks in greased casserole. Mix sugar, flour, pineapple juice, and cheese; spread over chunks. Top with crushed crackers and pour butter or margarine over entire casserole. Bake for 30 minutes in a preheated 350 degree oven.

Yield: 6-8 servings

Jeremy, Jeffrey, and Jamie Johnson

"Papa" is Michael Johnson, an associate professor of religion at Mississippi College.

Holiday Cranberry Casserole

2½ cups fresh cranberries
3 cups apples, unpeeled and diced
1¼ cups sugar
½ teaspoon cinnamon

Topping:
1 stick margarine, melted
1½ cups quick-cooking oats
½ cup brown sugar
¾ cup pecans, chopped

Preheat oven to 325 degrees. Greasea 2-quart casserole with margarine. Mix cranberries, apples, sugar, and cinnamon; put into dish. Mix topping ingredients and crumble over cranberry-apple mixture. Bake 45 minutes to 1 hour. This is a wonderful side dish with turkey and dressing.

Yield: 8 servings

Mary Lou Swogetinsky Nail '81

MISSISSIPPI
COLLEGE
SCHOOL OF LAW

THE SCHOOL OF LAW BUILDING

The School of Law Building, located in downtown Jackson, was presented to the College in 1979 as the largest single gift that the institution had received at that time. After extensive remodeling, it was occupied by the School of Law in January, 1981. It houses administrative and faculty offices, classrooms, and the Law Library. The building is ideally situated in the capital city at the center of county, state, and federal government. The resources of the Law Library are made available to members of the Mississippi Bar.

ENTREES

Natchitoches Meat Pies

1½ pounds lean pork, ground
1½ pounds lean beef, ground
1 Tablespoon all-purpose flour
2 medium onions
½ large bell pepper
2 medium cloves garlic
1 hot pepper
1 teaspoon parsley, chopped
2-3 green onions, ground (optional)
Salt to taste
Red and black pepper to taste

Crust:
4 cups all-purpose flour
½ teaspoon salt
2 teaspoons baking powder
2 eggs, beaten
¾ cup milk, at room temperature
½ cup shortening, melted

Have butcher grind both pork and beef to a very fine consistency. Brown meat in heavy Dutch oven; stir often and let cook for about 15 minutes. Add flour and brown. While meat is cooking, grind onions, bell pepper, garlic, and hot pepper. Add to meat mixture and cook slowly for about 30 minutes. Add parsley and green onions; cook for 10 more minutes. Add salt and peppers. To prepare crust, sift flour, salt, and baking powder. Mix eggs and milk and add to flour mixture. Stir in melted shortening. Knead until a stiff dough forms. Roll very thin. Place a saucer on pastry and cut around edges. Place a heaping tablespoon of filling on one side of the pastry round. Dampen edge of pie containing meat; fold top over meat and crimp with fork dipped in water. Prick with fork twice on top. Fry in deep fat fryer or skillet at 350 degrees or bake in a preheated 350 degree oven until golden brown. These meat pies freeze well and should not be thawed before baking.

Yield: 2 dozen pies

Ann McFarland, Faculty

Casseroles wrapped in foil, then again in newspaper, will stay hot for hours. To keep foods chilled, wrap in foil, then in wet newspaper, then again in foil to insulate.

Italian Scaloppine

1 large onion, chopped fine
1 pound tomatoes, fresh or canned, quartered
3 Tablespoons oil
1 teaspoon salt
1 teaspoon oregano
1 teaspoon basil
1 large eggplant
3 Tablespoons oil
8 very thin veal cutlets
Salt
Freshly ground pepper
5 Tablespoons all-purpose flour
2 Tablespoons butter or margarine
8 slices mozzarella cheese

Sauté onions in oil; add tomatoes, salt, oregano, and basil. Cook until thickened, stirring occasionally. Set aside. Wash and peel eggplant; cut into 8 slices. Salt both sides and let stand for 20 minutes, then dry with a paper towel. Lightly brush with oil and bake in a preheated 350 degree oven for 15 minutes or until soft. Set aside. Pound veal cutlets slightly. Sprinkle both sides with salt and pepper; dredge in flour, shaking off excess. Heat butter in a large skillet; add cutlets and cook for 5-6 minutes until golden brown. Into a baking dish large enough to hold 4 cutlets side by side, evenly spread half of tomato sauce. Add 4 cutlets and cover with remainder of tomato sauce. Add a second layer of cutlets, then add eggplant. Top with mozzarella cheese. Bake for 15 minutes or until mozzarella cheese is melted. This dish may be prepared in advance.

Variation: Cubed steak may be used instead of veal cutlets. Layer all ingredients as above except mozzarella cheese. Bake for 15 minutes, then add cheese and return to oven until cheese is melted.

Yield: 4 servings

Ina Stegen

Salt meat after cooking to prevent loss of natural juices.

Shish Kebab

Marinade Sauce:

1 cup oil
1 cup hot water
3 Tablespoons Worcestershire sauce
1 Tablespoon cider vinegar
1 cup catsup
1 teaspoon garlic salt
3 Tablespoons soy sauce
Salt

Shish Kebab:

3 pounds boneless chicken, sirloin, or orange roughy
2 large green peppers
1 large onion
1 (4-ounce) can whole mushrooms
Cherry tomatoes

Combine marinade sauce ingredients and boil for 10 minutes. Cool; cut meat into chunks and marinate for several hours or overnight in the refrigerator. Alternate pieces of meat and vegetables on skewers. Grill outdoors or broil in oven. This is good served over rice or with a baked potato.

Variation: Italian salad dressing may be used for a quick marinade. *Melanie Hodge '83* uses lamb for a different meat flavor.

Yield: 8 servings

Mrs. Bill Causey (Bill Causey '42)
Karen Killebrew Clark '83

Tofu Pesto

2 medium tomatoes, quartered
3 cloves garlic
4 cups fresh basil leaves
1½ cakes tofu
1 teaspoon salt
2 teaspoons soy sauce
1 Tablespoon lemon juice
1 cup walnuts, chopped
Cooked linguine
Parmesan cheese

Puree tomatoes and garlic in a food processor. Add basil and tofu. Blend until basil is finely chopped. Add salt, soy sauce, and lemon juice. Process until smooth. Stir in nuts. Keep pesto sauce at room temperature while cooking linguine. Sprinkle with Parmesan cheese to taste.

Yield: 6-8 servings

Cynthia Harmon '84

Hot French Bread Sandwiches

1½ pounds extra-lean ground beef, browned and drained
1 (4-ounce) can evaporated skimmed milk
½ cup onion, chopped
½ cup cracker crumbs
2 cups cheese, grated
¾ teaspoon garlic powder
1½ teaspoons parsley
1 teaspoon black pepper
1 egg, beaten
1 Tablespoon prepared mustard
1 loaf Italian or French bread
Green pepper, pimiento, or olives (optional)
Extra cheese

Mix all ingredients except bread in a large bowl. Slice bread in half lengthwise and scoop out some of the bread from the bottom half. Spread meat mixture into bread shell and replace top. Wrap in foil and bake in a preheated 350 degree oven for 30 minutes or longer. When sandwich filling is cooked, completely unwrap foil. Sprinkle some extra cheese on top of loaf and bake until cheese is melted.

Yield: 6 servings

Carol Barrett Kirk, Staff

Ladies' Luncheon Chicken Sandwich

1½ cups chicken, cooked and chopped fine
1 can cream of mushroom soup
1 (12-ounce) can chicken gravy
2 Tablespoons pimiento, chopped
2 Tablespoons onion, chopped
1 can sliced water chestnuts, drained (optional)
24 slices of bread, trimmed
4 eggs, beaten
2 Tablespoons milk
1 (6-ounce) bag plain potato chips, crushed

Mix chicken, mushroom soup, chicken gravy, pimiento, onion and chestnuts. Spread onto bread to make 12 sandwiches. Wrap sandwiches individually in plastic wrap and freeze. When ready to serve, grease a cookie sheet. Mix beaten eggs with milk and dip frozen sandwiches in mixture. Coat with crushed potato chips. Bake in a preheated 300 degree oven for 1 hour.

Yield: 12 servings

Carnette McMillan '50, Faculty Wife

Supper Sandwich

2 loaves French bread, unsliced
Margarine, softened
1 (14-ounce) can spaghetti sauce or pizza sauce
1 pound ground beef, cooked, crumbled, and drained
16 ounces mozzarella cheese, grated, divided
8 ounces Cheddar cheese, grated, divided
1 small onion, cut in strips
1 small bell pepper, cut in strips

Slice each loaf of bread lengthwise twice, creating three pieces from each loaf. Butter cut surface of each slice to prevent sauce from soaking the bread. Spread the bottom slice and top slices with sauce. On bottom slice place meat and half of the cheeses. Top with middle slice. On middle slice layer onion and bell pepper strips and the remaining cheeses. Add top slice. Brush the top of loaves with margarine and wrap in foil. Bake in a preheated 350 degree oven for about 20 minutes or until cheeses melt. Slice diagonally to serve. This sandwich may be frozen before baking.

Yield: 8 servings

Betty Love Lamb '63, Faculty Wife

Betty Lamb is the granddaughter of M.P.L. Love, who served on the Mississippi College Board of Trustees, 1911-14.

Hot Tuna Sandwiches

Margarine, softened
12 slices bread, trimmed
1 (6-ounce) can tuna, drained
2 eggs, hard-boiled and diced
½ cup mushrooms
2 Tablespoons onion, chopped
½ cup ripe olives, chopped
¼ cup mayonnaise
1 can cream of chicken soup
1 cup sour cream
1 cup Cheddar cheese, grated

Butter bread slices and place 6 slices in a 9x13 pan. Mix tuna, eggs, mushrooms, onion, olives, and mayonnaise. Spread onto bread slices. Place remaining bread slices on top. Mix soup and sour cream; pour over sandwiches. Sprinkle grated cheese on top. Bake in a preheated 350 degree oven for 20 minutes. This dish may be prepared up to 24 hours before baking.

Yield: 6 servings

Tina Griggs Clark '56

Go Chocs Pre-Game Sandwich

1 round loaf bread
2 cups garlic and herb soft cheese spread
⅓ pound prosciutto
⅓ pound mortadella
⅓ pound Genoese salami
⅓ pound dry salami
⅓ pound mozzarella cheese
⅓ pound Provolone cheese
⅓ pound Fontina cheese
1 bunch arugula
1 head lettuce
1 cup red peppers, roasted
3 Tablespoons balsamic vinegar
1 Tablespoon extra-virgin olive oil

Remove the top fourth of the bread and hollow the inside of the bread shell. Cover the bottom and sides of bread shell with cheese spread. Combine vinegar and oil. Layer all meats, cheeses, lettuces, and pepper, sprinkling the vinaigrette between layers. Replace top on bread and press down, packing the ingredients together. Secure sandwich with long toothpicks and wrap in foil. Cut sandwich into wedges to serve.

Yield: 5-6 servings

Douglass Foster Berg '90

Stuffed Cabbage Rolls

1 head cabbage
Salt and black pepper to taste
Sage to taste
¼ pound pork sausage
1 pound ground beef
1 egg, beaten
1 (8-ounce) can tomato sauce

Parboil entire cabbage. Separate 12 large leaves which will be used to wrap rolls. Mix salt, pepper, sage, and meats with egg. Form 12 meatballs. Wrap each ball in a cabbage leaf and place into a greased baking dish. Bake covered with heavy foil, for 30 minutes. Remove cover, pour tomato sauce over rolls, and recover with foil. Bake for an additional 30 minutes. Drain the rolls and serve.

Yield: 12 servings

Mary Pollan Lane

Pat's Catfish Fillets

Butter-flavored non-stick vegetable spray
¼ cup onion, chopped
1 cup fresh mushrooms, chopped or 1 can sliced mushrooms
4 catfish fillets (3-4 ounces each)
Juice of 1 orange, divided
Juice of 1 lemon, divided
Preferred seasonings (seasoned salt, garlic salt, lemon pepper, paprika, Creole seasoning, etc.)

Coat large non-stick skillet *liberally* with vegetable spray. Sauté onions and mushrooms until tender over *medium* heat. Remove vegetables from skillet and set aside. Coat catfish fillets on both sides with vegetable spray and place into skillet. Squeeze juice from half an orange and half a lemon over fillets and add seasonings. Cover and cook for approximately 5 minutes. Turn fillets; add remaining fruit juices and cook until done. Place catfish onto serving dish and cover with sautéed onions and mushrooms.

Yield: 4 servings

Pat Turner, Staff

Low-Fat Grilled Catfish

2 Tablespoons diet margarine
2 cloves garlic, chopped fine
Juice of 3 lemons
6 catfish fillets
Seasoned salt
1 or 2 bunches green onions, sliced

Preheat charcoal grill. Melt margarine with chopped garlic. Add lemon juice. Place fish onto heavy-duty aluminum foil and turn up edges to form pan. Put onto hot charcoal grill. Pour margarine mixture over fish. Sprinkle generously with seasoned salt. Sprinkle green onions over fish. Cover grill and cook 20-30 minutes or until fish is brown or liquid is absorbed. Fish may also be baked in a preheated 450 degree oven.

Yield: 6 servings

Nancy Lewis Franklin '69

Catfish Margurey

4 medium catfish fillets
4 Tablespoons olive oil
Salt and pepper to taste
1 lemon, sliced into rings

Sauce:
½ cup shrimp, chopped
½ cup mushrooms, chopped
3-4 Tablespoons olive oil
3 Tablespoons butter or margarine, melted
3 Tablespoons all-purpose flour
1 cup milk
2 egg yolks, beaten
2 Tablespoons lemon juice
Salt and pepper to taste
½ teaspoon parsley flakes

Coat fillets with olive oil; sprinkle with salt and pepper. Arrange in a shallow baking dish. Top with lemon rings and drizzle with any remaining oil. Bake in a preheated 350 degree oven for 25 minutes. Baste with drippings to maintain moistness. Prepare sauce: Sauté shrimp and mushrooms in olive oil until done. Drain and set aside. Stir flour into butter. Cook for 1 minute. Slowly add milk while stirring. Whisk until smooth and then remove from heat. Add egg yolks; cook for about 1 minute until sauce begins to thicken. Stir in lemon juice, shrimp, and mushrooms. Season to taste. Remove lemon rings from fillets and arrange fish on serving platter. Spoon sauce over fish. Garnish with parsley flakes.

Yield: 4 servings

Robert H. Pendleton '60

Crunchy Onion Catfish

2 pounds catfish fillets
1 cup sour cream
1 cup mayonnaise
1 package ranch-style salad dressing mix
2 cans French-fried onions, crushed

Pat fish dry. Mix sour cream, mayonnaise, and dressing mix. Dip fillets in sour cream mixture; roll in crushed onions. Place on a rack in a casserole and bake in preheated 350 degree oven for 20-25 minutes.

Yield: 8 servings

Ann Fisher Godwin '81

Lemon Catfish with Parmesan

4 catfish fillets
½ cup bottled lemon juice concentrate
⅓ cup all-purpose flour
⅓ cup Parmesan cheese, grated
⅓ cup seasoned breadcrumbs
Lemon wedges for garnish

Coat a 9x12x1 baking dish with non-stick cooking spray. Rinse fillets in cold water; pat dry with paper towels. Pour lemon juice into baking dish. Place fillets into baking dish with lemon juice and marinate in refrigerator for 30 minutes. Combine flour, Parmesan cheese, and breadcrumbs; thoroughly coat each marinated fillet in flour mixture. Place coated fillets in baking dish. Bake in a preheated 400 degree oven for 15 minutes on 1 side; turn fillets carefully with a pancake turner. Bake for 15-20 minutes on the other side or until fillets are golden brown and crispy. Serve on platter with lemon wedges. Fish may be marinated and coated ahead of time and left covered in the refrigerator until ready to bake.

Yield: 4 servings

Barbara Barber, Staff

Delta Baked Catfish

2 cups dry breadcrumbs
¾ cup Parmesan cheese, grated
¼ cup parsley, chopped
½ teaspoon oregano
1 teaspoon paprika
¼ teaspoon basil
2 teaspoons salt
½ teaspoon black pepper
6 whole catfish fillets
¾ cup margarine, melted
Lemon wedges

Grease a 13x9x2 baking dish well. Combine breadcrumbs, cheese, herbs, and seasonings. Dip catfish in melted margarine and roll in crumb mixture. Arrange fish into a baking dish. Bake in a preheated oven at 375 degrees for 25 minutes or until fish flakes easily. Garnish with lemon wedges.

Yield: 6 servings

Myrtilla Burris Kirk '59

Best Ever Catfish

Catfish fillets
Salt to taste
Plain yellow cornmeal
Peanut oil for frying
Potato slices
Onion slices

Score catfish fillets on flesh side every half inch. Salt to taste. Coat with cornmeal on each side. Heat peanut oil and drop in potato slice and onion slice. When they begin to brown, oil is ready to fry catfish. Cook until catfish is medium brown. Remove onion before it burns. Add an additional slice of potato and of onion with each batch of fish.

Yield: Allow 2-3 fillets per servings

Joe Rees, Staff

Herbed Fish Fillets

1 pound fish fillets (any kind, but catfish is best)
2 Tablespoons lemon juice
½ teaspoon salt
¼ teaspoon pepper
2 Tablespoons margarine, melted
1 cup onion, chopped
1 clove garlic, chopped
1 teaspoon parsley, chopped
¼ teaspoon crushed dry tarragon leaves
⅛ teaspoon thyme
½ cup breadcrumbs, lightly toasted
Paprika (optional)

Rinse fish in cold water. Pat dry and sprinkle with lemon juice, salt, and pepper. Place in an 11x8 casserole which has been sprayed or greased lightly. To margarine add onion, garlic, and parsley; sauté. Add herbs. Mix well. Spread half of this mixture over the fish. Add breadcrumbs to remaining herb mixture. Spoon over fish. Sprinkle with paprika if desired. Microwave for 6-8 minutes on High or bake for 16 minutes in oven preheated to 350 degrees. Fish will flake easily when done.

Yield: 4 servings

Bill Armstrong '78

Brazilian Coconut Fish

3 medium tomatoes, chopped or equivalent amount canned tomatoes, drained
1 small onion, chopped
1 small garlic clove, minced
½ medium green pepper, chopped
2 Tablespoons fresh coriander (optional)
1 Tablespoon oil
Salt and pepper to taste
2 Tablespoons tomato paste
1 pound salt water fish fillets (fresh or frozen)
1½ cups coconut milk
Hot cooked rice

Simmer chopped vegetables in a small amount of water with oil, salt, pepper, and tomato paste until tender. Add fish; cook until tender. Stir in coconut milk; heat but do not boil. Serve at once over cooked rice. Unsweetened coconut milk can be purchased in most large grocery stores. If unavailable, it can be made by grating pieces of fresh coconut in the blender. Scrape off the sides and add a cup of warm water to the grated coconut. Blend well. Pour into a sieve and squeeze all the liquid out of coconut. Peeled, deveined shrimp may be substituted for fish.

Yield: 4-5 servings

Freda Porter Trott '51
Ann Kolb, Faculty Wife (Raymond Kolb '39)

Thaw fish in milk to take out the frozen taste.

French (White) Shrimp Etouffeé

½ stick butter, melted
1 medium onion, chopped
¼ cup bell pepper, chopped
½ cup celery, chopped
3 cloves garlic, minced
2 pounds shrimp (or more)
2 cups water
Salt and pepper
All-purpose flour
Parsley
Hot cooked rice

Sauté onion, bell pepper, celery, and garlic in butter until tender. Peel, devein, and butterfly shrimp; season with salt and pepper. Add shrimp to sautéed vegetables. Cook, stirring gently until shrimp are pink. Pour in water. Make a paste of flour and water and add to shrimp mixture. Cook until thickened. For more sauce mix in additional water and flour paste. Stir in parsley. Serve over cooked rice. The amounts of the ingredients do not have to be exact in order for this dish to be successful.

Yield: 8 servings

Alice Ann McCann Smith '63, Staff

Mrs. Billy Smith shared this recipe with me when our daughters were roommates at Mississippi College.

Thibaut Crawfish Etouffeé

1 cup onion, chopped
1 cup bell pepper, chopped
1 cup celery, chopped
8 Tablespoons butter
2 pounds crawfish tails
1 teaspoon salt
1 teaspoon garlic powder
1 teaspoon seasoned salt
½ teaspoon Worcestershire sauce
½ teaspoon Tabasco sauce
¼ cup green onion, chopped
¼ cup parsley, chopped
Hot cooked rice

Sauté onion, bell pepper, and celery in butter until soft. Add crawfish, salt, garlic powder, seasoned salt, Worcestershire sauce, and Tabasco sauce. Cook for 15 minutes. Add green onion and parsley and continue cooking for 10 minutes at low heat. Serve over rice.

Yield: 8 servings

Jean Pittman Williams '55

Jean Williams is the wife of J. Kelley Williams, who served on the Mississippi College Board of Trustees.

Carolyn's Shrimp Etouffeé

½ stick margarine, melted
1 large onion, finely chopped
2 ribs celery, chopped
1 medium bell pepper, chopped
2 bunches green onions, chopped
8 ounces mushrooms, sliced
1 teaspoon garlic, minced
Juice of ½ lemon
1 (10-ounce) can diced tomatoes with green chilies
2 cans cream of mushroom soup
2 Tablespoons cornstarch
½ cup water
1 Tablespoon Worcestershire sauce
2 pounds cooked shrimp, peeled and deveined
Hot cooked rice

Sauté chopped vegetables and garlic with margarine in a heavy 4-quart saucepan. Add lemon juice, tomatoes, and soup; bring to a boil. Mix cornstarch with water and add to boiling mixture. Stir until thickened and remove from heat. Add Worcestershire sauce and shrimp. Serve over cooked rice. Flavor is enhanced if etouffeé is refrigerated for several hours and gently reheated.

Yield: 8 servings

Dorothy Ivey Carpenter '84, Faculty Wife

Easy Crawfish Etouffeé

1 stick margarine
1 cup onions, chopped fine
1 cup celery, chopped fine
2 cloves garlic, chopped fine
¼ cup green pepper, chopped fine
¾ cup green onions, chopped fine
3 Tablespoons flour
1 can chicken broth
1 Tablespoon Worcestershire sauce
2 teaspoons paprika
Salt and pepper (both red and black pepper)
1 pound crawfish or shrimp, shelled
Hot cooked rice

Sauté vegetables in margarine until tender; add flour. Stir until bubbly but not brown. Add chicken broth, Worcestershire sauce, and paprika; simmer covered for 20 minutes. Add crawfish or shrimp and simmer for 20 minutes more. Salt and pepper to taste. Serve over hot cooked rice. This freezes well.

Yield: 6 servings

Edith Pope Kitchens '39

Fish Soufflé

1 pound white boneless fish (snapper, catfish, etc., fresh or frozen)
Enough water to poach fish
2-3 teaspoons chicken bouillon granules
½ stick corn oil margarine, melted
2 cups milk
3 eggs
1 cup cracker crumbs
½ teaspoon salt
1½ Tablespoons lemon juice
1 Tablespoon onion, grated
1 Tablespoon parsley, chopped
Dash of Tabasco sauce
Additional buttered cracker crumbs (optional)
Dill Sauce

Lightly butter a flat casserole. Add chicken bouillon to water and poach fish for 4-7 minutes. Remove and cool fish; break into chunks. Combine margarine and milk; add beaten eggs, crumbs, salt, lemon juice, onion, parsley, and Tabasco sauce. Stir for about a minute. Add the fish chunks and pour into greased casserole. Bake in a preheated 350 degree oven for 25-35 minutes or until set. Buttered cracker crumbs may be sprinkled on top for the last 10 minutes of cooking. Serve with Dill Sauce.

Dill Sauce:
1 Tablespoon onion, chopped
Juice of 2 lemons
2 Tablespoons parsley
2 (6-inch) dill pickles
2 cups mayonnaise
1 teaspoon dill weed
Salt, pepper, and Tabasco sauce to taste

Puree onion and lemon juice in food processor and add in succession parsley and dill pickles, cut into chunks. Process until pieces are finely chopped. Add mayonnaise and dill weed. Season to taste with salt, pepper, and Tabasco sauce; let stand at room temperature for at least 2 hours.

Yield: 4 servings

Katty Ireland, Faculty Wife

To keep cleanup to a minimum when cleaning fish, use a scaler, vegetable peeler, or dull knife while holding the fish under water.

Shrimp or Crawfish Casserole

1 cup onion, chopped
1 cup celery, chopped
1 cup bell pepper, chopped
1 stick margarine
1 can cream of mushroom soup
1 can Cheddar cheese soup
1-2 teaspoons Tabasco sauce
1 cup green onion tops, chopped
1 (4-ounce) jar diced pimiento
2 cups cooked rice
2-3 cups boiled and shelled shrimp or crawfish tails
2 Tablespoons fresh parsley, chopped, or 2 teaspoons dried parsley
Italian style breadcrumbs

Sauté the onion, celery, and bell pepper in margarine. Mix soups and heat until warm. Add Tabasco sauce, sautéed vegetables, green onion tops, and pimiento to soups. Stir in the rice, crawfish or shrimp, and parsley; mix well. Pour into a 13x9x2 baking dish. Top with breadcrumbs. Bake uncovered in a preheated 350 degree oven for 30 minutes.

Yield: 6-8 servings

Elizabeth Adams Field '56

Oysters Mosca

1 large onion, chopped
3 cloves garlic, chopped
1 stick margarine
¼ teaspoon thyme
¾ teaspoon oregano
2 Tablespoons parsley
4 dozen oysters, drained (reserve liquid)
1 cup seasoned breadcrumbs
Salt and pepper to taste
Parmesan cheese

In a heavy skillet, sauté onion and garlic in margarine. Add thyme, oregano, parsley, and drained oysters. Cook until oysters begin to curl. Add oyster liquid. Fold in breadcrumbs. Mix and spoon into a buttered casserole. Salt and pepper as desired and sprinkle with cheese. Bake in a preheated 350 degree oven for 30 minutes.

Yield: 6 servings

Loretta Ford

Freeze fresh shrimp or fish in cold water to maintain freshness and decrease odor while cooking.

Shrimp and Pasta

1 stick margarine, melted
3-5 pounds raw shrimp, peeled
1 teaspoon salt
1 teaspoon celery salt
2 teaspoons basil
1 teaspoon thyme
½ teaspoon garlic powder
2 Tablespoons black pepper
2 Tablespoons parsley flakes
2 Tablespoons lemon juice
2 Tablespoons Worcestershire sauce
2 teaspoons liquid crab boil (optional)
1 (16-ounce) package linguine, cooked and drained
1 (16-ounce) box pasteurized processed cheese spread, cubed

Pour melted margarine into a 13x9x2 pan. Arrange shrimp evenly in pan. Combine salt, celery salt, basil, thyme, garlic powder, black pepper, and parsley flakes; sprinkle mixture over shrimp. Add lemon juice, Worcestershire sauce, and liquid crab boil. Bake uncovered in a preheated 350 degree oven for 25 minutes. Stir as needed. Combine cooked and drained linguine, cubed cheese, and shrimp. Return to oven until cheese is melted and bubbly. If using frozen shrimp, thaw and dry before using.

Yield: 10-12 servings

Mary Evelyn Dorsett Evans '57
Becky Jones Rogers

Easy Seafood Au Gratin

1 can Cheddar cheese soup
¼ cup milk
2 cups cooked shrimp
1 (6-ounce) can tuna, drained
½ cup celery, chopped
½ cup bell pepper, chopped
½ stick margarine
Salt and pepper
Cooked egg noodles

Combine soup and milk in the top of a 2-quart double boiler. Add shrimp and tuna and heat slowly. Sauté celery and green pepper in margarine until tender. Stir vegetables and seasonings into seafood mixture and heat thoroughly. Serve over cooked noodles.

Yield: 6-8 servings

Elizabeth Robertson

Low Country Boil

1 package crab boil
1 package smoked beef sausage, cut into 1-inch pieces
8 small onions, peeled
8-12 small red potatoes, well-scrubbed
8-12 (2-inch) pieces corn on the cob
3-4 pounds large shrimp (raw, unpeeled shrimp, allowing ½ pound per person)

Fill a stockpot with enough water to cover all ingredients and bring to a boil. Add crab boil, sausage, and onions. Cook for 2-3 minutes; then add the whole potatoes. When potatoes are almost done, add the corn on the cob; cook until all ingredients are tender. Add shrimp and cook for 3-4 minutes. Remove ingredients with a slotted spoon; drain before serving on a large, deep platter.

Yield: 6-8 servings

Hazle K. Anthony, Staff

Crabmeat Casserole

4 Tablespoons flour
4 Tablespoons margarine
2 cups milk
1 cup sharp Cheddar cheese, grated
2 egg yolks, beaten
2 cups crabmeat (fresh or canned)
2 Tablespoons margarine, melted
¼ cup breadcrumbs
Dashes of paprika (optional)

Prepare a white sauce by combining flour, margarine, and milk in a saucepan. Stir over low heat until thickened; remove from heat. Add grated cheese to white sauce and stir until melted; add beaten egg yolks gradually. Stir in crabmeat. Spoon into a greased 2-quart casserole. Mix margarine and breadcrumbs together; garnish top of casserole with crumb mixture. Add dashes of paprika. Bake in a preheated 350 degree oven for 30 minutes.

Yield: 6 servings

Joan Jolly

Hampton Plantation Shrimp Pilau

4 slices bacon
1 cup rice, uncooked
3 Tablespoons margarine
½ cup celery, chopped
2 Tablespoons bell pepper, chopped
1 pound shrimp, peeled
1 teaspoon Worcestershire sauce
1 Tablespoon all-purpose flour
Salt and pepper

Fry bacon until crisp; crumble and set aside. Cook rice according to package directions adding bacon drippings to water. In another pot, melt margarine; add celery and bell pepper. Cook until vegetables are tender. Add shrimp that have been sprinkled with Worcestershire sauce and dredged in flour. Stir and simmer until flour is cooked and the shrimp are pink. Season with salt and pepper. Add cooked rice and stir until rice is thoroughly mixed with shrimp sauce. More margarine may be added if mixture looks dry. Stir in crumbled bacon.

Yield: 4 servings

Mary Bevill, Staff

Shrimp-N-Squash Stir-Fry

Squash, chopped
Onions, chopped
Green onions, chopped
Salt
Pepper
Garlic salt
Seasoned salt
2-3 Tablespoons oil
Butter, melted
Soy sauce
Worcestershire sauce
Deveined shrimp

The amount of ingredients will vary according to preference and desired number of servings. Mix squash, onions, green onions, salt, pepper, garlic salt, and seasoned salt in a wok or deep skillet. In another skillet, combine butter, soy sauce, and Worcestershire sauce. Add shrimp; stir-fry until shrimp begin to turn pink. Drain shrimp and combine with the squash mixture. Cook for 3-4 more minutes at a setting equal to about 350 degrees. This may also be made using chicken breasts.

Yield: Variable

Melissa K. Janczewski Jones '92

Tuna Noodle Casserole

3 quarts water
3 teaspoons salt
1 Tablespoon olive oil
6 cups egg noodles
1½ cups celery, chopped
¾ cup onion, chopped
6 Tablespoons oil
3 cans cream of mushroom soup
2 cups English peas
2 cups milk
3 (6-ounce) cans tuna, drained
½ cup mayonnaise-type salad dressing
Bran flakes

Boil water in deep pot with salt and olive oil. Add egg noodles and cook uncovered for 4-5 minutes or until soft. Drain and rinse under hot water. In large skillet, sauté celery and onion in oil until tender. Blend in soup, peas, and milk; add tuna. Combine egg noodles and tuna mixture. Stir in salad dressing. Spoon into 2 (1½-quart) casseroles. Sprinkle bran flakes over the top of the casseroles. Bake in a preheated 350 degree oven for 20-25 minutes.

Yield: 12 servings

Brian W. Wells '88

Crusty Tuna Pie

1½ cups potatoes, cubed
2 cups carrots, sliced
½ cup onion, chopped
¼ cup parsley, chopped
¼ teaspoon salt
⅛ teaspoon pepper
¾ cup water
1 can cream of chicken soup
1 (6-ounce) can tuna, drained
½ cup milk
5 slices bread, buttered and cubed

Grease a casserole. Combine potatoes, carrots, onion, parsley, tuna, salt, pepper, and water in a covered saucepan. Bring to a boil; simmer until vegetables are tender. Add cream of chicken soup, tuna, and milk; pour into a prepared casserole. Top with the buttered bread cubes; bake in a preheated 350 degree oven for 30 minutes or until bubbly.

Yield: 4 servings

Debra Richmond King '77

Granna's Tuna Croquettes

1 (6-ounce) can tuna, water-pack, undrained
1 egg
¼ cup onion, chopped
½ cup self-rising cornmeal
Oil for frying

Mix all ingredients and shape into 6 patties. Fry in oil until golden brown.

Yield: 6 patties

Emily Kennedy, Staff

New Orleans Barbecued Shrimp

Butter or margarine
4-10 cloves garlic, chopped
1-5 Tablespoons whole peppercorns
Tabasco sauce to taste
Dash of salt
Shrimp, unpeeled, medium or large
French bread

In a large, flat baking pan or cookie sheet, melt enough butter or margarine to cover the bottom to about ⅛-inch thick. Combine garlic, peppercorns, red sauce, and salt in butter and heat for 3-5 minutes to meld flavors. Preheat broiler. Put single layer of shrimp into the butter in the baking pan. Cook about 6 inches from the broiler until pink. Turn shrimp and broil for 1-3 minutes. Do not overcook. Serve with the melted butter and French bread. Dip bread into seasoned butter.

Variation: Decrease garlic to 2 cloves; use ½ teaspoon each garlic salt, onion salt, and cayenne pepper and 1 1/2 teaspoons black pepper. Add juice of 1 lemon and 1 tablespoon Worcestershire sauce to butter sauce.

Yield: 4 servings

John H. Speights '64
Lisa Eichelberger, Faculty

Easy Shrimp Creole

1½ Tablespoons olive oil
1 large onion, chopped
1 (15-ounce) can tomato sauce
1 bay leaf
1 (16-ounce) can tomatoes, chopped and undrained
½ teaspoon thyme
1 teaspoon salt
½ teaspoon black pepper
1 teaspoon parsley
2 pounds raw shrimp, peeled
1½-2 green peppers, chopped
Hot cooked rice

In olive oil, sauté onion until golden. Add tomato sauce, bay leaf, tomatoes, thyme, salt, pepper, and parsley. Cook for 20 minutes. Add shrimp and bell pepper. Cook for 10 more minutes. Serve over cooked rice.

Yield: 6-8 servings

Abbi DuBose (Jonathan '83)

Shrimp in Angel Hair Pasta Casserole

1 Tablespoon butter
2 eggs
1 cup light cream
1 cup plain yogurt
½ cup Swiss cheese, shredded
⅓ cup feta cheese, crumbled
⅓ cup parsley, chopped
¼ cup fresh basil, chopped, or 1 teaspoon dried basil, crushed
1 teaspoon dried oregano, crushed
1 (9-ounce) package fresh, uncooked angel hair pasta
1 jar mild, thick and chunky salsa
1 pound medium shrimp, peeled and deveined
½ cup Monterey Jack cheese, shredded

Butteran 8x12 casserole. Combine eggs, cream, yogurt, Swiss cheese, feta cheese, parsley, basil, and oregano in medium bowl and mix well. Spread half of the pasta on bottom of prepared pan. Cover with salsa. Add half of the shrimp and cover with remaining pasta. Spread egg mixture over pasta and top with remaining shrimp. Sprinkle Monterey Jack cheese over top. Bake in a preheated 350 degree oven for 30 minutes or until bubbly. Let stand for 10 minutes before serving.

Yield: 4-6 servings

Gena Jackson, Faculty Wife

Shrimp Scampi

2 pounds cleaned shrimp, shelled and deveined
2 cloves garlic, crushed
1 Tablespoon olive oil
1 Tablespoon butter
1 Tablespoon oregano
1 (4-ounce) can sliced mushrooms (optional)
Chopped green onions (optional)
Angel hair pasta, cooked
1 cup Romano cheese, grated

Mix shrimp and crushed garlic in bowl. Chill for several hours or overnight. Preheat a large pot on rangetop at medium temperature. Add olive oil and butter. Stir in shrimp, then add oregano. Cook until mixture bubbles, then simmer for 3-5 minutes. Serve while warm over angel hair pasta. Sprinkle Romano cheese over all.

Variation: 1 can of sliced mushrooms and chopped green onions may be added as shrimp cooks.

Yield: 4-6 servings

Stacy McKay Goins '89
Gary Silverman '92

Mrs. Mayfield's Shrimp

6 Tablespoons butter or margarine
1 small onion, chopped
2 pounds shrimp, raw or boiled
8 ounces mushrooms
3 potatoes, peeled and boiled
1 (15-ounce) can small English peas, drained
Salt, pepper, garlic powder to taste

Sauté onion, shrimp and mushrooms in butter until shrimp turns pink. Cube potatoes; stir in a generous amount of pepper, a pinch of salt, and garlic powder. Combine potatoes and peas with shrimp mixture. Stir well until mixture is thoroughly heated.

Yield: 6-8 servings

Gayle Starnes Oakes '73

Spanish Shrimp

1 medium onion, chopped
1 green pepper, chopped
2 Tablespoons margarine
1 box Spanish rice vermicelli mix
1 (10-ounce) can tomatoes with chilies, diced
1 pound small shrimp, shelled

Sauté onion and pepper in margarine; set aside. Prepare rice mix according to directions on box, substituting tomatoes with chilies for tomatoes. Add onion, pepper, and shrimp. Simmer for 5 minutes and serve.

Yield: 6 servings

Stephanie M. Long

Shrimp Stroganoff

¼ cup minced onion
5 Tablespoons butter, divided
1½ pounds raw shrimp, peeled and deveined
½ pound fresh mushrooms, quartered
1 Tablespoon all-purpose flour
1½ cups sour cream, room temperature
1¼ teaspoons salt
Pepper to taste
Hot cooked rice
Artichoke hearts, quartered

In a large skillet sauté onion in 4 tablespoons melted butter until softened. Add shrimp and sauté for 3-5 minutes or until pink and just cooked. Transfer mixture to a heated dish and keep warm. (Don't heat too much or it will cause the juices to be too runny when added back to skillet). In same skillet sauté mushrooms in remaining butter over moderately high heat until browned. Sprinkle mushrooms with flour and cook mixture, stirring, for 2 minutes. Reduce heat to moderately low and stir in the shrimp mixture, sour cream, salt, and pepper. Cook mixture, stirring, for 2-3 minutes or until shrimp are thoroughly heated. Do not let mixture boil. Serve immediately over rice tossed with quartered artichoke hearts.

Yield: 4 servings

Jamie Walters Tice '90

Shrimp Creole

¼ cup oil
¼ teaspoon garlic powder
1 medium onion, chopped
1½ cups uncooked rice
1 green pepper, chopped
3 cups chicken broth
1 (16-ounce) can tomatoes, chopped
1 teaspoon salt
1 teaspoon sugar
1 pound shrimp, shelled
⅛ teaspoon red pepper

Heat oil in large heavy skillet. Add garlic powder, onion, and rice stirring constantly until rice is golden in color. Add green pepper, broth, tomatoes, salt, and sugar. Cover; boil gently for 20 minutes, stirring occasionally. Add shrimp and red pepper. Continue cooking covered for about 5 minutes. Shrimp will be pink. Serve immediately.

Yield: 6 servings

Irene Crocker Townsend '66

Asparagus Crab Soufflé

8 slices white bread, trimmed
3 cups crabmeat, fresh or frozen
¾ cup mayonnaise
2 small onions, chopped
2 small bell peppers, chopped
1½ cups celery, chopped
2¼ cups asparagus, tips and pieces (1½ cans)
6 eggs, beaten
4½ cups milk
1½ cans cream of mushroom soup
1 Tablespoon lemon juice
¾ cup cheese, grated
Parsley, chopped
Paprika

Place 4 slices bread into a large baking dish. Combine crabmeat, mayonnaise, onions, bell peppers, and celery; spread over bread. Top with asparagus. Cover with remaining bread. Mix eggs and milk; pour over mixture and refrigerate overnight. Bake in a preheated 325 degree oven for 15 minutes. Remove from oven; pour soup mixed with lemon juice over top and sprinkle with cheese, parsley, and paprika. Return to oven for 50 minutes.

Yield: 10-12 servings

Jean A. Jones '53

Cajun Fettuccine

3 medium onions, chopped fine
3 medium bell peppers, chopped
2 cloves garlic
2 Tablespoons jalapeño peppers (optional)
1½ cups butter
Cayenne pepper to taste
Salt to taste
¼ cup all-purpose flour
½ bunch parsley, chopped
2 Tablespoons lemon juice
1 pound pasteurized processed cheese, cut into cubes
3 pounds shrimp or crawfish tails
1 pound crabmeat
½ pint light cream (optional)
1 pound fettuccine noodles, cooked

In a large pot, sauté onions, peppers, garlic, and jalapeño peppers in butter for about 15 minutes or until onions are transparent. Add cayenne pepper and salt to taste. Add flour slowly, stirring steadily. Continue to cook for about 10 minutes. Add parsley and allow to soften in mixture while stirring. Add lemon juice and cheese, stirring until cheese is melted and has been blended well with mixture. Parboil crawfish or shrimp for 3 minutes. (If using crawfish, use fat also. If using shrimp, use small to medium size.) Strain crawfish or shrimp and add to mixture. Add crabmeat. Allow to cool for 15 minutes. If mixture is too stiff or thick, light cream may be added slowly until desired consistency is reached. Sauce may be served over noodles or noodles may be added to sauce. Serve hot in a 4-quart casserole. This dish freezes well.

Yield: 16 servings

Mrs. Glenn Jordan (Laura)

After peeling, deveining, and cooking, 2-2½ pounds raw shrimp will yield 1 pound of edible shrimp.

Stir-Fried Jambalaya

1-2 Tablespoons peanut oil
½ cup onion, chopped
½ cup green pepper, chopped
2 cloves garlic, minced
¼ cup parsley, chopped
½ pound ham, diced
½ pound Cajun sausage
2 boneless chicken breasts, cubed
3 Tablespoon tomato paste
2-3 cups chicken stock
¼ teaspoon thyme
1 teaspoon salt
½ teaspoon pepper
1 bay leaf
Tabasco sauce
1½ cups instant rice, uncooked

Heat oil in wok or large skillet with cover. Add onion and green pepper; stir-fry for 1-2 minutes. Add garlic and parsley; stir-fry briefly. Add ham, sausage, and chicken. Brown lightly. Combine tomato paste and chicken stock; pour into meat mixture and toss well. Add thyme, salt, pepper, bay leaf, and Tabasco sauce. Stir gently. Bring mixture to a boil. Add rice; cover and steam for 20-30 minutes until rice is tender. Remove bay leaf before serving.

Yield: 6-8 servings

Diane Nations Smith '76

Cheesy Enchilada Casserole

1 can cream of chicken soup
1 (8-ounce) jar sharp pasteurized processed cheese spread
½ teaspoon cumin
2 cups cooked chicken, chopped
1 (4-ounce) can diced green chilies
12 corn tortillas
1 (8-ounce) jar taco sauce or salsa

Combine soup, cheese spread, and cumin. Mix well. Add chicken and chilies. Spread one-half cup of this mixture over bottom of an 11x7 baking dish. Layer 4 tortillas dipped in taco sauce and one-third of the remaining mixture. Repeat layers twice. Cover and bake in a preheated 350 degree oven for 30 minutes. Remove cover and bake for 20 minutes more.

Yield: 6 servings

Janet Basford Newman '65

Natchez Chicken Casserole

5 chicken breast halves
2 cups water
¾ cup stock, reserved
2 teaspoons chicken bouillon granules
¾ cup frozen seasoning mix (onion, bell pepper, celery, red pepper)
2 Tablespoons margarine
1 (14½-ounce) can asparagus pieces
1 can cream of mushroom soup
¼ cup almonds, sliced and toasted
¼ cup margarine
1 (4-ounce) stack round buttery crackers, crushed

Boil chicken in 2 cups of water seasoned with bouillon until tender; set stock aside. Cut chicken into bite-size pieces. Grease an 11x7x2 baking dish. Sauté seasoning mix in margarine until softened. Add asparagus, soup, almonds, chicken and three-fourths cup stock. Stir well. Pour into prepared dish. Melt one-fourth cup margarine and stir in cracker crumbs. Spread crumbs over top of casserole and bake in a preheated 325 degree oven 45-50 minutes or until casserole is bubbly and crumbs are browned.

Yield: 6 servings

Rachel Smith '60, Faculty

Cheesy Chicken Skillet

2 whole chicken breasts, split
2 Tablespoons butter or margarine, melted
1 can Cheddar cheese soup
¼ cup water
2 medium potatoes, peeled and quartered
2 ribs celery, cut into 2-inch slices
½ cup carrots, sliced
1 bay leaf
¼ teaspoon poultry seasoning

Brown chicken in butter or margarine; add remaining ingredients to skillet. Bring to boil; cover and simmer for 30 minutes, stirring occasionally. Remove bay leaf and serve.

Yield: 4 servings

Ann Rogers McGraw '75

Chicken-Vegetable Pot Pie

1 (3-pound) broiler-fryer
3 teaspoons salt, divided
1 teaspoon pepper, divided
Water
4-5 medium-sized potatoes, pared
5 ribs celery
½ pound carrots
3 cups chicken broth
1 (17-ounce) can English peas
½ cup margarine
⅔ cup all-purpose flour
1 cup milk
1 chicken bouillon cube
2 teaspoons salt
½ teaspoon pepper
Pastry for double crust (9-inch pie)

Place chicken, one teaspoon salt, one-half teaspoon pepper, and enough water to cover chicken into a Dutch oven. Bring to a boil, cover, and simmer for 1 hour or until tender. Remove chicken from broth; cool and cut into bite-size pieces. Cut potatoes, celery, and carrots into 1-inch chunks. Place into broth; simmer until tender. Drain, reserving 3 cups broth. Combine chicken and vegetables; spoon into a 9x13 pan. Melt margarine in a heavy saucepan over low heat; add flour, stirring until smooth. Cook for 1 minute, stirring constantly. Gradually stir in milk, reserved chicken broth, and bouillon cube. Cook over medium heat, stirring constantly, until thick and bubbly. Stir in salt and pepper. Pour sauce evenly over chicken-vegetable mixture. Prepare pie crust; roll to fit 9x13 pan. Place crust over chicken mixture; cut 4-6 small slits in crust to allow steam to escape. Bake in a preheated 400 degree oven for 45-55 minutes, or until crust is golden brown.

Yield: 6-8 servings

Carolyn V. Hand '65, Staff

A sprig of tarragon pulled through an orange slice creates a lovely garnish for chicken dishes.

Country Captain

1 hen or large fryer
4 medium onions, chopped
1 bell pepper, chopped
1 full bunch of celery, chopped
2 (15-ounce) cans tomatoes
1 (8-ounce) can tomato sauce
1 (15-ounce) box white raisins
½ (¾-ounce) box curry powder
2 teaspoons salt
1 Tablespoon chili powder
Hot cooked rice
Chinese noodles

Boil hen, bone, and cut into small pieces. In a large Dutch oven, brown onions, pepper, and celery in fat from hen until tender. Add remainder of broth. Add the meat and all other ingredients except rice and Chinese noodles to this mixture. Simmer for 1 hour covered on rangetop. Stir occasionally. Serve over rice and top with crisp Chinese noodles. Sauce may be frozen or cooked several days in advance.

Yield: 12-14 servings

Ann Albritton '50

Chicken Tenders

1 (20-ounce) can evaporated milk
2 eggs, beaten
5 pounds boned, skinless chicken breast strips
Garlic salt to taste
Pepper
All-purpose flour

Add a little water to evaporated milk and combine with eggs. Marinate chicken overnight in milk/egg mixture. Sprinkle with garlic salt and pepper to taste. Dredge chicken in flour and fry until golden brown in hot oil.

Yield: 8-10 servings

Martha Rogers Elliott '63

Mrs. Elliott is the daughter of B. C. Rogers. Her family has been associated with the poultry industry for more than 30 years in Morton, Mississippi. B. C. Rogers served as a member of the Mississippi College Board of Trustees, 1951-60, 1962-68.

Special Creamy Chicken

1 (3-ounce) package cream cheese, softened
3 Tablespoons margarine, melted, divided
2 cups chicken, cooked, cubed
1 teaspoon salt
1/8 teaspoon pepper
2 Tablespoons milk
1 Tablespoon onion, chopped
1 Tablespoon pimiento, chopped
1 (8-ounce) can refrigerated crescent rolls
3/4 cup seasoned croutons, crushed

In a medium bowl blend cream cheese and 2 tablespoons margarine until smooth. Add chicken, salt, pepper, milk, onion, and pimiento. Mix well. Separate crescent rolls into 4 rectangles. Firmly press seams to seal. Spoon one-half cup mixture onto center of rectangles. Pull 4 corners of pastry dough to top center of chicken mixture. Twist slightly and seal edges. Brush top with reserved margarine. Dip in crouton crumbs. Bake on ungreased cookie sheet in a preheated 350 degree oven for 20-25 minutes until golden brown.

Variation: Place crescent dough into a 9x13 pan. Sprinkle 1 cup shredded Cheddar cheese over crust. Arrange 1 (10-ounce) package frozen chopped broccoli, cooked and drained, over cheese. Combine 4 eggs, slightly beaten, 1 can cream of chicken soup, 1/4 cup mayonnaise, and 1 teaspoon mustard. Stir in chicken and onions. Pour mixture over broccoli.

Yield: 6-8 servings

Nancy Worley Wilbanks '57
Susan Newman, Staff

For a brown crust on roasted chicken, rub chicken generously with mayonnaise before cooking.

Chicken And Rice Casserole

4 boneless, skinless chicken breasts
1 can cream of mushroom soup
1 can cream of chicken soup
Pepper and garlic powder, to taste
1 cup rice, uncooked
½ small onion, chopped
½ cup Cheddar or Monterey Jack cheese, grated

Grease or spray a 9x13 baking dish. In a mixing bowl combine soups. Set aside. Wash and pat dry chicken. Season with pepper and garlic powder. Arrange chicken pieces in greased dish. Add rice to soups and stir well. Pour rice/soup mixture over chicken breasts. Sprinkle with chopped onion and grated cheese. Bake in a preheated 350 degree oven for 1 hour or until chicken and rice are tender.

Variation: A package of wild and white rice and 1 can cream of celery soup may be used. To this add 1 (2-ounce) jar pimiento, 1 (16-ounce) can French-style green beans, drained, 1 cup mayonnaise, and 1 can water chestnuts. Cheese should be omitted.

Yield: 4 servings

Mary Johnson Dorsett '30
Becky Butler Wood '83
Joyce Byrd Ellis (Opie '49)

Chinese Chicken

Corn oil
3 whole chicken breasts, boned
3 eggs, beaten
Garlic salt
Pepper
All-purpose flour
Soy sauce

Place about 1 inch of corn oil into an electric skillet. Heat oil to 375 degrees. Cut chicken breast fillets into 2-inch pieces. Mix eggs, garlic salt, and pepper to taste. Dip pieces of chicken in egg mixture, then dredge in flour. Cook in oil until brown on each side and fork tender. Drain on paper towels. Sprinkle generously with soy sauce on top side only. Keep warm in oven until all chicken is ready to serve. If more chicken is being used, increase amount of egg mixture.

Yield: 6 servings

Donna J. Cooper '66

Chicken-To-Go Biscuits

2 Tablespoons butter or margarine
2 Tablespoons all-purpose flour
¼ teaspoon salt
Dash pepper
½ cup milk
2 cups chicken, cooked and cubed
1¼ cups Cheddar cheese, shredded
½ cup mushrooms, drained and sliced
1 (9½-ounce) can refrigerated buttermilk biscuits
1 egg, beaten
3 cups cornflakes, crushed

In a medium saucepan, melt margarine; stir in flour, salt, and pepper. Add milk. Cook for about 1 minute until mixture thickens, stirring occasionally. Add chicken, cheese, and mushrooms; set aside. Separate biscuit dough into 10 biscuits. Roll or pat out each biscuit into a 5-inch circle. Place about ¼ cup chicken mixture on each biscuit circle; shape mixture into rolls 4 inches long. Wrap dough around chicken mixture, pressing edges to seal. Dip rolls into egg; coat with crushed cornflakes. Place onto ungreased cookie sheet. Bake in a preheated 400 degree oven for 20-25 minutes until golden brown.

Variation: 3 (5-ounce) cans drained chicken or 2 cups any cooked or canned meat, cubed, may be substituted for the chicken. To reheat biscuits, wrap in foil and bake at 400 degrees for 15-20 minutes or until heated thoroughly. To prepare in advance, cover and refrigerate for up to 2 hours before baking. Bake as directed.

Yield: 10 servings

Norma Ruth Lee (Tom S. Lee '63)

Fruited Chicken

3/4 cup all-purpose flour
1/4 teaspoon each: salt, garlic salt, celery salt, and ground nutmeg
2 1/2-3 pound broiler-fryer chicken, cut-up
1/2 cup margarine or butter
1 (20-ounce) can pineapple tidbits
3 Tablespoons all-purpose flour
1 Tablespoon sugar
1/3 cup soy sauce

Place flour and seasonings into a brown paper bag. Add chicken pieces a few at a time. Shake to coat. Brown chicken in margarine. Place into a 13x9x2 casserole, reserving drippings. Drain pineapple, reserving 1 cup juice. Stir flour and sugar into drippings. Gradually add juice and soy sauce. Cook and stir until thickened and bubbly. Add pineapple. Spoon over chicken. Cover; bake in a preheated 350 degree oven for 1 hour.

Yield: 8 servings

Bessie Flowers Wallace '64

Chicken Okra Palau Over Rice

4 chicken breasts, cooked and chopped
1 cup onion, chopped
1 cup green pepper, chopped
2 Tablespoons margarine
2 cups fresh or frozen okra, sliced
1 can chicken broth or 2 cups fresh chicken broth
1 (14 3/4-ounce) can Italian-style stewed tomatoes
1 bay leaf (optional)
Dashes of garlic salt
Dashes of gumbo filé (optional)
Hot cooked rice

Sauté onion and pepper in a large skillet in margarine. Add okra, broth, Italian tomatoes, bay leaf, and garlic salt. Cook covered for about 30 minutes until okra is fork-tender. Stir chicken pieces into mixture. Serve mixture over hot rice; sprinkle with filé powder, if desired.

Yield: 8-10 servings

Mrs. Ray (Elizabeth) Poole

Marinated, Grilled Chicken

2 Tablespoons catsup
1 Tablespoon lemon juice
2 Tablespoons soy sauce
2½ Tablespoons oil
1 Tablespoon honey
1 teaspoon ginger
1 teaspoon dry mustard
Dash of garlic salt
4 boneless, skinless chicken breasts

Mix all marinade ingredients and pour over chicken. Cover and refrigerate overnight. To cook grill for 10-12 minutes, basting with marinade during the last 2 minutes of grilling.

Yield: 4 servings

Linda Cook '64

Sweet and Sour Chicken

2 pounds chicken breasts, boned
2 Tablespoons margarine
½ cup chicken bouillon
2 large carrots, sliced
1 (15-ounce) can pineapple chunks, undrained
½ cup brown sugar, firmly packed
2 Tablespoons cornstarch
½ cup white vinegar
4 Tablespoons soy sauce
½ green pepper, sliced
1 medium onion, sliced
1 can sliced water chestnuts
Hot cooked rice

Cut chicken breasts into slices and sauté in margarine in a skillet until no longer pink. Add bouillon and carrots. Cover and cook until carrots are tender. Drain pineapple, reserving juice, and set aside. Combine juice from pineapple, sugar, cornstarch, vinegar, and soy sauce. Add mixture to chicken and cook until sauce thickens. Just before serving add pineapple, pepper, onion, and water chestnuts. Heat thoroughly. Serve over hot rice.

Yield: 4 servings

Mrs. Walter G. Howell '79

Family Reunion Chicken

4 split chicken breasts, cooked and boned
1 stick margarine or butter
1 stack crackers
1 can cream of chicken soup
1 (8-ounce) carton sour cream
¼ cup chicken broth

Cut chicken into chunks. Melt butter and stir in crumbled crackers. Line a 9x13 glass baking dish with half of the cracker mixture. Add chicken. Mix sour cream, soup, and chicken broth. Spread on top of chicken. Top with remaining cracker crumbs. Bake uncovered in a preheated 350 degree oven for 35 minutes.

Yield: 6-8 servings

Ruthine Burkes '54

Chicken Spaghetti

4 large chicken breasts
1 rib celery
1 (16-ounce) package vermicelli
½ cup celery, chopped
¼ cup pimiento, chopped
½ cup green pepper, chopped
2 onions, chopped
1 stick margarine
2 (16-ounce) cans chopped tomatoes
1 (10-ounce) can tomatoes with chilies
Salt and pepper to taste
½ teaspoon oregano
½ teaspoon basil
1 teaspoon parsley flakes
1 cup cheese, grated

Boil skinned chicken breasts with a celery rib until tender. Bone and cube chicken. Boil vermicelli in chicken stock until tender; drain. Sauté celery, pimiento, green pepper, and onions in margarine. Add tomatoes and seasonings; simmer for 10 minutes. Add chopped chicken and vermicelli and mix well. Pour into a large casserole and cook in a preheated 350 degree oven for 30-40 minutes. In last 5 minutes of baking time, sprinkle cheese on top. This dish freezes well.

Yield: 10-12 servings

Elese Williams Sansing '64

Barrentine's Chicken

2 pounds boneless chicken, cubed
1-2 green peppers, thinly sliced
1 medium onion, chopped
1 teaspoon dried cilantro (optional)
1 teaspoon cumin
¼ teaspoon garlic salt, or to taste
¼ teaspoon red pepper
2 (8-ounce) cans tomato sauce
Hot cooked rice

Lightly grease or spray a large skillet. Brown chicken in skillet over medium heat. Add green pepper and onion and sauté until vegetables are tender and chicken is almost done. Add remaining ingredients and simmer for 5-10 minutes. Serve over rice. Refried beans and grated cheese make great accompaniments.

Yield: 10-12 servings

Mary Platt Barrentine '84

Easy Chicken Pie

1 fryer or chicken pieces, boiled and boned
1½ cups chicken broth
1 can cream of celery soup
Pepper
1 cup self-rising flour
1 stick margarine, melted
1 cup milk

Place chicken in a 9x13 casserole. Mix chicken broth and celery soup. Heat to boiling point. Pour mixture over the chicken and sprinkle with pepper. Mix flour, melted margarine, and milk. Spread the flour mixture over the chicken and soups to create a topping. Bake uncovered in a preheated 350 degree oven for about 1 hour or until golden brown.

Variation: Substitute cream of chicken soup for cream of celery and add 1 (10-ounce) box frozen mixed vegetables, cooked and drained. Slice 5 hard-boiled eggs over the chicken layer before adding the flour mixture.

Yield: 8-10 servings

Shirley Jackson Davis '61
Joyce D. Ivey, Staff

Mexican Chicken

1 chicken (cooked, boned, and cut into chunks)
2 cups chicken broth
1 can cream of chicken soup
1 can cream of mushroom soup
1 (8-ounce) jar pimiento strips, drained
1 (8-ounce) jar sharp pasteurized processed cheese spread
1 medium onion, chopped
2 teaspoons chili powder
1 cup instant rice, uncooked
1 medium bag corn chips

Combine broth, soups, pimiento strips, cheese spread, onion, and chili powder in a saucepan. Simmer for about 15 minutes, stirring occasionally. In a 9x13 Pyrex dish, layer the following: one-third of corn chips, half of chicken, half of sauce, one-third of corn chips, instant rice, half of chicken. Pour remaining sauce over this. Top with remaining corn chips. Bake uncovered in a preheated 350 degree oven for 25-30 minutes or until bubbly.

Yield: 6-8 servings

Jo Ellen Clark

Italian Chicken

4 chicken breasts
1 (15-ounce) jar spaghetti sauce
1½ cups Parmesan cheese
1 cup mozzarella cheese, grated

Place chicken meaty side down in a 9x13 baking dish. Pour half the spaghetti sauce and half of the Parmesan cheese over chicken. Bake in a preheated 400 degree oven for 20 minutes. Turn chicken. Pour remaining sauce and cheeses over chicken. Bake for an additional 20 minutes.

Yield: 4 servings

Ann P. Harris '69

Darlene's Glazed Chicken

4 chicken breast halves or 4 thighs, skinless
1 can Italian tomato soup
1 Tablespoon water
1 Tablespoon vinegar
1 Tablespoon Worcestershire sauce
Dash of pepper and salt
1 teaspoon oregano (optional)
1 Tablespoon brown sugar, packed

Arrange chicken in a 2-quart baking dish. Bake in a preheated 350 degree oven uncovered for 30 minutes. Combine remaining ingredients and spoon over chicken. Return to oven and bake for 30 minutes.

Yield: 4 servings

Darlene Hill Jezek '86

Chicken Cashew

4 chicken breast halves, skinned and boned
1 Tablespoon oil
2 cups fresh mushrooms, sliced
½ cup green onions, sliced
1 small green pepper, cut into 1-inch pieces
1 (8-ounce) can sliced water chestnuts, drained
2 teaspoons chicken-flavored bouillon granules
1¼ cups boiling water
2 Tablespoons soy sauce
1 Tablespoon cornstarch
2 teaspoons light brown sugar
½ teaspoon ground ginger
½ cup cashews, toasted
Hot cooked rice

Cut chicken into 1-inch pieces. Heat oil in a large skillet. Add chicken and cook until browned, stirring often. Remove chicken from skillet. Add mushrooms, onions, pepper, and chestnuts to skillet; sauté for 5 minutes or until tender. Dissolve bouillon in boiling water. Combine soy sauce, cornstarch, sugar, and ginger; stir into bouillon mixture. Add chicken to vegetables. Stir in bouillon mixture; cook over low heat, stirring constantly, for 1 minute or until thickened. Stir in cashews just before serving. Serve over hot cooked rice.

Yield: 4 servings

Bobbye Rankin '66

Poppy Seed Chicken

6-8 chicken breasts, cooked and boned
2 cans cream of mushroom soup
2 cans cream of chicken soup
2 (16-ounce) cartons sour cream
Round buttery crackers, crumbled
2 Tablespoons poppy seed
½ stick margarine, melted
Hot cooked rice

Cut chicken into bite-size pieces and place into the bottom of a 9x13 casserole. Mix soups and sour cream in a bowl and pour over chicken. Crumble enough crackers to cover the top. Sprinkle poppy seed over crackers and pour margarine over poppy seed. Bake in a preheated 350 degree oven uncovered for 30 minutes. Serve over rice. To freeze, omit crackers, poppy seed, and margarine until ready to bake.

Yield: 6 servings

Mary Atwood, Staff

Groundnut Stew

Stew:
1 (3-4 pound) chicken, cooked and boned
2 pints chicken stock
2 medium-size tomatoes, peeled and quartered
1 small onion, peeled and quartered
½ cup peanut butter
½ teaspoon salt
¼ teaspoon black pepper
Hot cooked rice

Measure 2 pints stock into a large boiler. Puree tomato and onion pieces in a blender for approximately 5 seconds on High. Add puree to the stock along with the peanut butter. Add salt and pepper. Bring mixture to a boil, reduce heat, and simmer for 1 hour. Add the chicken to the stew in the last few minutes before serving. Serve over hot rice. This stew may be served plain, but its flavors are enhanced when served with condiments such as mandarin oranges, sliced bananas, shelled whole peanuts, chopped green pepper, chopped onion, hard-boiled eggs or chopped tomatoes. "Groundnut" is another word for peanut, a staple in the diet of the people of Ghana.

Yield: 6-8 servings

Amy Jo Purl (John M. '91)

Chicken Las Vegas

6 boned chicken breasts
Salt and pepper
6 slices ham
6 slices Swiss cheese
1 egg, beaten
2 Tablespoons milk
All-purpose flour
½ stick margarine

Cheese Sauce (optional):
1 Tablespoon butter, melted
1 Tablespoon all-purpose flour
Salt and pepper to taste
½ cup milk
½ cup Swiss cheese, shredded

Flatten chicken breasts with a rolling pin until thin.

Salt and pepper to taste. Place one slice each of ham and cheese onto each chicken breast. Roll up and secure with toothpicks. Mix beaten eggs with milk. Dip breasts into egg-milk mixture and dredge in flour. Sauté lightly in margarine. Place into a baking dish and bake in a preheated 350 degree oven for 40 minutes. Cheese Sauce: Cover roll-ups with warm cheese sauce. Stir flour, salt, and pepper into butter. Add milk and shredded cheese; heat slowly using wire whisk to prevent lumps.

Yield: 6 servings

Tamra Potter Helms '81
Joanna Hall Mixon '83

Crispy "Tater" Chicken

¼ cup prepared mustard
2 eggs, beaten
1 Tablespoon water
2 teaspoons seasoned salt
1 (2½-pound) chicken, cut-up
1 cup instant mashed potato flakes
2 Tablespoons margarine, melted (optional)

Preheat oven to 375 degrees. Beat together mustard, eggs, water, and seasoned salt. Dip chicken pieces into mixture and coat evenly with potato flakes. Place chicken, skin-side up, into a foil-lined shallow baking pan. Bake in a preheated 375 degree oven for 50 minutes or until tender. For crispier chicken, drizzle with melted margarine the last 10 minutes of cooking time.

Yield: 6 servings

Nora Allard, Staff

Honey Curry Chicken

1 fryer chicken, cut-up
Salt and pepper to taste
4 Tablespoons butter
½ cup honey
¼ cup prepared mustard
1 teaspoon curry powder
1 teaspoon salt

Remove skin of chicken. Wash chicken and pat dry. Salt and pepper to taste. Melt butter in small saucepan. Blend in honey, mustard, curry powder, and salt. Dip chicken into butter sauce. Arrange in a 9x5x2 baking dish with meaty side up in a single layer. Bake covered in a preheated 375 degree oven for 45 minutes. Remove cover, turn or baste, and cook for 15 minutes more.

Variation: For a spicier taste, increase curry to 1 tablespoon and substitute one-half cup Dijon mustard for one-fourth cup prepared mustard.

Yield: 4-6 servings

Jimmy Gartin, Jr. '58
Sharlene Joh (Leopold Frederick '90)

Easy Chicken and Dumplings

4 chicken breasts, boiled or equivalent canned chicken
4 cups chicken broth
1 can cream of mushroom soup
1 can cream of chicken soup
12 flour tortillas, cut into 1-inch strips
All-purpose flour
Salt and pepper to taste
½ cup milk
¼ stick margarine

Save broth from chicken and add canned chicken broth as needed to make 4 cups. Cut chicken into bite-size pieces and return to broth. Add both soups and bring to a boil. Add strips of tortillas which have been dusted with flour. Add salt and pepper to taste. Cover and cook for 12-15 minutes, stirring occasionally. Add the milk and margarine just before removing from heat. Stir well and serve while hot.

Yield: 8 servings

Mary Etta Thompson, Faculty Wife

Russian Chicken

4-6 chicken breasts or 1 whole fryer, cut into pieces
1 (8-ounce) bottle Russian salad dressing
1 envelope onion soup mix
1 cup water
1 teaspoon garlic, chopped
Salt and pepper to taste
Hot cooked rice or pasta

Put chicken into a 9x13 baking dish. Mix dressing, soup mix, water, garlic, salt, and pepper in a separate bowl. Pour over the chicken and bake in a preheated 350 degree oven for approximately 45 minutes or until done. Serve with rice or pasta.

Variation: Omit the cup of water. Add apricot preserves to dressing, soup mix, and seasonings. This gives a sweeter taste.

Yield: 4-6 servings

Bae Brock Waller '87
Frances Skulley, Retired Faculty
Lisa R. Headley

Sadie's Baked Chicken Breasts

4-6 split chicken breast pieces, skinned
1 Tablespoon salt
Salt and pepper
1-2 Tablespoons lemon juice (optional)
All-purpose flour
1 stick margarine, melted
½ cup Italian-style breadcrumbs (optional)

Soak chicken overnight in salted ice water in refrigerator. Drain and pat chicken dry. Salt and pepper to taste. Sprinkle with lemon juice, if desired. Dredge in flour then dip in margarine. Place into a 9x13 baking dish. Bake uncovered in a preheated 350 degree oven for 1 hour. Do not turn chicken while baking. Sprinkle Italian-style bread crumbs over chicken after rolling it in butter.

Yield: 4-6 servings

Ralph L. Carroll, Faculty

Chicken Divan

6-8 chicken breasts, cooked and boned
2 (10-ounce) packages frozen broccoli spears
1 can cream of mushroom soup
1 can cream of chicken soup
¾ cup mayonnaise
1 teaspoon curry powder
1 teaspoon lemon juice
1 cup sharp Cheddar cheese, grated
Buttered breadcrumbs

Butter a 9x13 casserole. Cut chicken into bite-size pieces. Cook broccoli according to package directions. Place broccoli in bottom of dish. Mix soups, mayonnaise, curry powder, lemon juice, and cheese together in a large mixing bowl. Add chicken; spread chicken mixture over broccoli. Cover with buttered breadcrumbs. Bake in a preheated 350 degree oven for 30 minutes. Chicken may be prepared ahead and frozen.

Yield: 8-10 servings

Mrs. John G. McCall, Faculty Wife
Betty Robinson Oswald '50

Chicken Parmigiana

4 chicken breast halves, boneless and skinless
2 eggs, beaten
1 cup Italian-style breadcrumbs
¼ cup olive oil
1 (8-ounce) jar meat-flavored spaghetti sauce
½ cup Parmesan cheese, grated
1 cup mozzarella cheese, shredded

Dip chicken into egg and then into breadcrumbs, coating thoroughly. In a medium skillet, heat olive oil and cook chicken in oil until done and well browned on both sides. Pour spaghetti sauce into a 7x11 baking dish. Place chicken on sauce and top with Parmesan and mozzarella cheeses. Bake in a preheated 400 degree oven for 15 minutes or until cheese is melted and lightly brown.

Yield: 4 servings

Ann P. Harris '69
Maxine Crumpton

Bill's Chicken Breasts Florentine for Two

1 (10-ounce) package frozen chopped spinach, thawed
4 Tablespoons olive oil, divided
2 Tablespoons slivered almonds
2 Tablespoons shallots, minced
¼ cup raisins
2 chicken breast halves, boneless and skinless
2 Tablespoons all-purpose flour
Salt and pepper
½ cup chicken stock
½ cup light cream
Dash nutmeg

Heat 2 tablespoons of olive oil in a skillet; cook almonds and shallots until golden. Press thawed spinach between paper towels to remove as much water as possible. Add spinach and raisins and heat thoroughly; season and set aside to keep warm. Dredge the chicken breasts in flour, salt, and pepper. In a hot skillet cook the chicken breasts in the remaining oil until golden brown on both sides. Remove the chicken and heat the chicken stock in the skillet. Add the light cream and cook until sauce is thickened. Return the chicken to the skillet for reheating. Serve the chicken on a bed of the spinach mixture. Sprinkle with nutmeg.

Yield: 2 servings

Ruth Ashley McDonald '36

Chicken and Spinach Noodle Casserole

4 pound hen, cooked and boned
Reserved chicken stock
1 (12-ounce) package spinach noodles
1 stick margarine
1 cup celery, chopped
1 cup green pepper, chopped
1 cup onions, chopped
½ pound pasteurized process cheese spread
1 medium bottle stuffed olives, sliced
1 large can sliced mushrooms

Cut chicken into bite-size pieces. Cook noodles in reserved chicken stock; drain. Sauté celery, green pepper, and onion in margarine until tender. Add cheese, mushrooms, olives, chicken, and noodles to sautéed vegetables. Simmer until heated thoroughly. This dish freezes well.

Yield: 10-12 servings

Lynda Street '64, Staff

Baked Chicken Parmesan

1 teaspoon salt
¼ teaspoon pepper
¼ teaspoon paprika
1 Tablespoon fresh basil, chopped fine (1 teaspoon dried)
1 teaspoon fresh thyme, chopped fine (¼ teaspoon dried)
¼ cup Parmesan cheese (fresh if possible)
¼ cup fresh parsley, chopped (1 Tablespoon dried)
⅓ cup fine plain breadcrumbs
1 fryer (or 6 breasts), skin removed and cut into serving pieces
2-3 Tablespoons water
1 Tablespoon oil or liquid margarine

Coat a shallow 9x13 baking pan with cooking spray. Combine seasonings, cheese, parsley, and breadcrumbs; coat chicken. Place chicken into pan and add water. Drizzle oil or margarine on top of chicken. Bake uncovered in a preheated 350 degree oven for 30-45 minutes or until lightly brown.

Yield: 4-6 servings

Barbara E. Barnett '90

Chicken and Green Bean Casserole

3 (5-ounce) cans chunk chicken, drained
2 (16-ounce) cans French-style green beans, drained
½ stick margarine
1 onion, chopped
¾ cup mayonnaise
1 can cream of mushroom soup
1 can cream of chicken soup
8 ounces pasteurized processed cheese spread
1 can French fried onions

Place chunk chicken in bottom of a 9x13 glass baking dish. Spread green beans over chicken. In a saucepan, melt margarine; add onion and sauté. Add mayonnaise, soups, and cheese. Stir over medium heat until cheese is melted. Spread mixture over green beans. Bake in a preheated 325-350 degree oven for 25 minutes. Sprinkle French fried onions over casserole; return to oven until onions brown.

Yield: 6-8 servings

Christa Boykin Powell '92

Lemon Lover's Meat Loaf

¾ cup catsup
¼ teaspoon allspice
¼ cup brown sugar
¾ teaspoon dry mustard
1/16 teaspoon cloves
1½ pounds ground beef
3 slices day-old bread, cubed
1 egg, beaten
⅓ cup lemon juice
¼ cup onion, chopped
1 teaspoon seasoned salt
1 lemon, sliced (optional)

Mix catsup, allspice, brown sugar, dry mustard, and cloves; set aside. Mix the ground beef, bread, egg, lemon juice, onion, and salt; mold into a loaf shape. Place in a loaf pan (9x5x3). Spread the sauce over the meat loaf; top with lemon slices. Bake in a preheated 350 degree oven uncovered for 1 hour.

Yield: 6-8 servings

J. Kirk Gulledge '70

Apple Meat Loaf

1½ pounds ground beef
1 cup dry breadcrumbs
¼ cup milk
1 medium egg
½ cup apples, peeled and diced
1 teaspoon salt
1 teaspoon Worcestershire sauce
¼ cup catsup
¼ cup parsley
¼ cup onion, chopped
¼ cup celery, chopped

Topping:
6-8 apple slices
3 Tablespoons catsup
3 Tablespoons brown sugar

Mix all ingredients except topping. Press into an ungreased loaf pan (9x5). Arrange apple slices in a flower pattern on top. Mix catsup and brown sugar and pour over meat loaf and apple slices. Bake in a preheated 350 degree oven for 60 minutes or until done. Drain the fat while cooking, if desired. This meat loaf stays very moist; it may be prepared a day ahead.

Yield: 6-8 servings

Amy M. Hyde

Italian Meat Loaf

2 pounds lean ground beef
2 cups breadcrumbs
2 eggs, beaten
¼ cup onion, chopped
¼ cup Parmesan cheese
½ teaspoon salt
¼ teaspoon pepper
1 (8-ounce) can tomato sauce
½ teaspoon oregano leaves
1 (4-ounce) package mozzarella cheese, shredded

Combine first 7 ingredients; mix lightly and press into a 9x13 baking pan. Bake in a preheated 350 degree oven for 30 minutes. Pour off drippings. Combine tomato sauce and oregano; pour mixture over meat loaf. Top with mozzarella cheese and continue baking for another 30 minutes. Needs mushrooms or Killer flavor — try Morels.

Yield: 8-10 servings

Susan S. Slater '76

Meat Loaf Man

1 pound ground chuck
1 cup breadcrumbs
1 (8-ounce) can tomato sauce
1 egg
2 Tablespoons Tabasco sauce
1 Tablespoon salt
Black olives, bell pepper slice, pimiento for garnish

Mix all ingredients in bowl. Shape mixture into body parts: legs, arms, head, and main body. Place all parts together, forming man. Place onto a greased cookie sheet. Bake in a preheated 350 degree oven for 45 minutes. Remove from oven. Add black olives for eyes, slice of bell pepper for mouth, pimiento for tongue. Meat loaf may be topped with sour cream, brown gravy, or sweet and sour sauce. This is a kid-pleasing dish and a fun way to get children to eat their meat.

Yield: 4-8 servings

Paul W. Lewis '71

Fiesta Stack Ups

Meat Sauce:

4 pounds ground beef
3 large onions, chopped
2 (14½-ounce) cans whole tomatoes
2 (15-ounce) cans tomato sauce
2 (12-ounce) cans tomato puree
4 Tablespoons chili powder
2 teaspoons cumin
1 teaspoon garlic powder
2 Tablespoons salt
2 (23-ounce) cans ranch-style beans

Brown beef and onions; drain. Add all other ingredients except beans. Simmer for 1½ hours. Add beans and heat. Serve buffet-style over layers of corn chips and rice with the following items in separate dishes. Each person may arrange the ingredients to form a "stack."

Layers:

3 (12-ounce) packages corn chips, crushed
1 (14-ounce) box rice, cooked
1 pound or more Cheddar cheese, grated
2 large onions, chopped
1-2 large heads lettuce, chopped
5-6 medium tomatoes, chopped
1 (4½-ounce) can ripe black olives, chopped
1 cup pecans, chopped
1 (7-ounce) package shredded coconut
1 (16-ounce) jar picante sauce
Meat sauce, heated

Yield: 15-18 servings

Jan Simmons Cameron '78
JoAnn Leavell

JoAnn Leavell is the wife of Landrum P. Leavell, who served as a member of the Mississippi College Board of Trustees, 1957-63.

When browning ground beef, use a potato masher to separate the meat, then remove grease with a baster.

Best Eggplant Casserole

2 average size eggplants
2 Tablespoons oil
1 large onion, chopped
1 cup bell pepper, chopped
1 cup celery, chopped
1 pound fresh ground round beef
1 (8-ounce) can tomato sauce with mushrooms
Breadcrumbs, divided
½ teaspoon thyme
Salt and pepper to taste
2 Tablespoons butter, melted

Peel eggplant and cut in small pieces. Boil in water until tender. Drain and mash eggplant. In small amount of oil, sauté onion, bell pepper and celery; add ground beef and brown slightly. Combine eggplant, beef mixture, tomato sauce, and breadcrumbs. (Add only enough breadcrumbs to thicken mixture.) Season to taste with thyme, salt and pepper. Place in a greased casserole. Cover top with additional breadcrumbs. Top with melted butter. Bake in a preheated 375 degree oven until casserole is bubbly and top has browned slightly.

Yield: 6-8 servings

Mrs. Jack Parkman

Reuben Pie

1 (9-inch) deep-dish pastry shell
1 egg, beaten
⅓ cup evaporated milk
¾ cup soft rye breadcrumbs
¼ cup onion, chopped
¼ teaspoon salt
Dash pepper
1 (8-ounce) can sauerkraut, drained and snipped
½ pound ground chuck, browned
4 ounces Swiss cheese, grated
1 (15-ounce) can corned beef, flaked

Place pastry shell into pie plate. Combine all other ingredients and put into pastry shell. Place pie plate on a cookie sheet and bake in a preheated 400 degree oven for 25-30 minutes or until the crust is brown.

Yield: 6-8 servings

Libby Patterson '57, Staff

Beef-Vegetable Pie

1½ pounds beef stew meat
3 Tablespoons oil
1 medium onion, chopped
2 cloves garlic, minced
¼ teaspoon salt
¼ teaspoon pepper
⅓ cup soy sauce
1 cup water
2 small carrots, diced
1 small green pepper, cut into ¼-inch strips
4 medium potatoes, diced
3 Tablespoons cornstarch
3 Tablespoons cold water
2 medium tomatoes, sliced
1 (9-inch) pastry shell

In a Dutch oven, brown meat in oil. Stir in onion and garlic; add salt, pepper, soy sauce, and water. Cover and simmer for 1¼ hours or until tender. While meat is simmering, boil carrots, green pepper, and potatoes in salted water for 10-15 minutes until tender. Drain and set aside. When meat is cooked, drain liquid, reserving 1¼ cups. Spread meat evenly in a 9-inch pie plate. Arrange cooked vegetables over meat. In a Dutch oven, heat reserved meat liquid until boiling. Blend cornstarch and water until smooth; stir into liquid. Cook, stirring continuously, until clear and thickened. Pour gravy over meat and vegetables. Arrange tomato slices over meat, add pepper to taste, and cover with pastry shell. Bake in a preheated 450 degree oven for 25-30 minutes, or until crust is golden brown.

Yield: 6 servings

Peggy O'Neill Hewlett, Faculty

Potato Puff Casserole

2 pounds ground chuck
½ cup onion, chopped
Salt and pepper
1 can cream of mushroom soup
1 (8-ounce) carton sour cream
2 cups Cheddar cheese, grated
1 (2-pound) package frozen potato puffs

Brown ground chuck with onion, salt and pepper. Drain and place into a 3-quart casserole. Top with cream of mushroom soup, sour cream, and grated cheese. Arrange frozen potato puffs on top to cover. Bake in a preheated 400 degree oven for 45 minutes.

Yield: 8-10 servings

Rosemary Sudduth Rhodes '71

White Chili

1 pound dried white beans
6 cups chicken broth
2 cloves garlic, minced
2 medium onions, chopped, divided
1 Tablespoon oil
2 (4-ounce) cans mild diced green chilies
2 teaspoons ground cumin
1½ teaspoons oregano
¼ teaspoon ground cloves
¼ teaspoon cayenne pepper
4 cups chicken breasts, cooked, diced
3 cups Monterey Jack cheese, grated
Salsa
Sour cream

Combine beans, broth, garlic, and half the onions in a large stockpot. Bring to a boil. Reduce heat. Simmer for 2 hours or until beans are soft, adding broth or water as necessary. Sauté remaining onions in oil until tender. Add chilies, seasonings, and chicken to bean mixture. Simmer for 1 hour. Serve topped with grated cheese, salsa, and sour cream. This may be frozen.

Yield: 8-10 servings

Libby Allen, Faculty Wife

Burrito Bake

1 pound ground beef, browned, drained
½-1 cup picante sauce
1 cup biscuit mix
¼ cup water
1 (16-ounce) can refried beans
Cheddar cheese, shredded
Sour cream

Grease bottom and sides of a 10-inch pie plate. Stir picante sauce into ground beef. Set aside. Combine biscuit mix, water, and refried beans. Spoon bean mixture into pie plate. Top with ground beef mixture. Bake in a preheated 400 degree oven for 30-35 minutes. Remove from oven and top with shredded cheese; return to oven to melt cheese. Serve with additional picante sauce and sour cream.

Yield: 6-8 servings

Robin Lackey '91

Sweet and Sour Beef Balls

Meatballs:
1 pound ground beef
1 Tablespoon cornstarch
2 Tablespoons onion, chopped
1 egg
1 teaspoon salt
Pepper
2 Tablespoons oil

Sauce:
1 Tablespoon oil
1 cup pineapple juice
1 Tablespoon soy sauce
6 Tablespoons water
3 Tablespoons cornstarch
3 Tablespoons vinegar
½ cup sugar

Stir Fry:
4 slices pineapple, chopped
3 green bell peppers, sliced into strips
Hot cooked rice

Mix beef, cornstarch, onion, egg, salt and pepper to form about 18 balls. Brown the meatballs in oil and drain fat. Sauce: Mix oil and pineapple juice together and cook over low heat for 2-3 minutes. Add soy sauce, water, cornstarch, vinegar, and sugar. Cook until juice thickens, stirring constantly. Add meat balls, pineapple, and green pepper. Heat thoroughly. Serve over cooked rice.

Yield: 6-8 servings

Marjorie Dean, Former Faculty Wife

Sprinkle salt in the bottom of the skillet when pan broiling chops, hamburgers, or steaks to prevent sticking and to help absorb the grease.

Classic Meat Sauce

1-1½ pounds ground beef
½ large onion, chopped fine
½ medium bell pepper, chopped (optional)
1-2 Tablespoons all-purpose flour
1 (6-ounce) can tomato sauce
3 (6-ounce) cans water
1 Tablespoon Worcestershire sauce
1 teaspoon celery salt
½ teaspoon garlic powder
1 teaspoon oregano
1 bay leaf
3 Tablespoons Parmesan cheese, grated
Salt and pepper to taste

In a large skillet, brown ground beef; drain fat. Add onion, bell pepper, and flour, stirring well. Mix in tomato sauce and water. Stir in remaining ingredients. Bring mixture to a boil, lower heat, and simmer for 1-1½ hours, stirring frequently. Add additional water as needed. Remove bay leaf before serving. This sauce may be used with cooked pasta or as a casserole ingredient.

Yield: 6 servings

Anne Fortenberry '84, Faculty

Stuffed Zucchini

¾ pound ground beef
¾ cup onion, minced
Salt and pepper
1 (6-ounce) can tomato paste
1 Tablespoon sugar
¼ cup water
¼ pound cheese, grated
4 medium zucchini
Seasoned salt

Brown ground beef with onion, salt, and pepper; drain. Stir in tomato paste, sugar, and water. Remove from heat and stir in cheese. Cut zucchini in half lengthwise. Scoop out and discard seeds. Blanch zucchini in boiling water. Remove from water, put into casserole, and sprinkle with seasoned salt. Fill each zucchini shell with meat mixture. Bake covered in a preheated 275 degree oven for 30 minutes. This dish freezes well.

Yield: 4 servings

Clyde P. Mahaffey '47

Casa Myers Lasagna

1 (18¾-ounce) can Italian tomatoes
1 (8-ounce) can tomato sauce
1 (6-ounce) can tomato paste
2 teaspoons oregano
¼ teaspoon black pepper
Dash of rosemary, thyme, marjoram, and basil
Salt
2 Tablespoons olive oil
½ cup onions, minced
2 small cloves garlic, minced fine
2 pounds ground chuck or round steak
½ pound lean ground pork
9-12 lasagna noodles
1 pound mozzarella cheese, shredded
2 ounces provolone cheese, shredded
¾ cup Parmesan cheese, grated, divided
2 cups Rich White Sauce

In a saucepan combine tomatoes, tomato sauce, tomato paste, and seasonings; heat and set aside. In a heavy Dutch oven heat olive oil and sauté onions, garlic, and ground meats until red color disappears from meats. Add tomato mixture to meat mixture; cover and simmer 2-3 hours, stirring occasionally. Add additional seasonings as desired. When meat sauce is cooked, prepare lasagna noodles according to package directions. While noodles are cooking, prepare white sauce. Coat a 9x13 baking dish with cooking spray and spread with one-third meat sauce. Place half the cooked noodles side by side without overlapping and spread with half of the shredded cheeses. Sprinkle with one-fourth cup Parmesan cheese, and spread with half of the white sauce. Repeat layers; cover with remaining meat sauce and sprinkle with remaining Parmesan. Bake in a preheated 350 degree oven for 30-40 minutes or until bubbly in center. Remove from oven and let stand 10-15 minutes before cutting into squares.

Yield: 10-12 servings

Rich White Sauce:
5 Tablespoons butter
3 Tablespoons flour
1 teaspoon salt
2 cups light cream or milk
¼ teaspoon nutmeg

Melt butter in saucepan; add flour and blend well. Add salt and nutmeg; slowly add milk, stirring constantly over medium heat until mixture thickens.

Yield: 2 cups

Lynn Myers, Former Staff

Chinese Ground Beef Casserole

½ pound fine noodles
2 pounds ground beef
2 cups onions, chopped
1 can cream of chicken soup
1½ cups milk
1 (4-ounce) can mushrooms
Salt, pepper and Worcestershire sauce to taste
¼ cup soy sauce
1 (8-ounce) can sliced water chestnuts, drained
½ pound cheese, grated
1 can Chinese noodles
½ pound cashews

Butter a 3-quart casserole. Cook and drain noodles. Brown meat and onions; drain. Combine soup, milk, mushrooms, salt, pepper, and sauces; add to meat mixture. Add chestnuts and mix lightly. Place noodles into casserole and cover with mixture. Top with cheese. Bake in a preheated 350 degree oven for 25 minutes or until cheese bubbles. When ready to serve, top with Chinese noodles and nuts; return to oven for about 10 minutes.

Yield: 8-10 servings

Ann McFarland, Faculty

Zucchini and Cheese Casserole

1½ pounds zucchini
1 pound lean ground beef
1 onion, chopped
2 Tablespoons olive oil
½ pound Monterey Jack cheese
1½ cups diced French bread
1 teaspoon garlic salt
1 teaspoon oregano
1 teaspoon basil
Salt and pepper
Parmesan cheese, grated

Cook zucchini in lightly salted water until tender. Drain for at least 1 hour to remove excess moisture. Combine oil, chopped onion, and ground beef in a large skillet. Sauté until meat is well cooked, stirring frequently. Add zucchini, Monterey Jack cheese, bread, and spices. Mix and cook on low heat for about 5 minutes or until all ingredients are blended. Add pepper and salt to taste. Pour into a greased casserole and sprinkle with Parmesan cheese; bake in a preheated 350 degree oven for 15 minutes or until thoroughly heated.

Yield: 6 servings

Grace Sinclitico, Former Faculty Wife

Easy Spaghetti

1 pound ground beef, browned
3 teaspoons minced onions
1 (15-ounce) can tomato sauce
1 (12-ounce) can tomato paste
2 cups water
½ teaspoon salt
½ teaspoon garlic powder
½ teaspoon oregano, crushed
½ teaspoon basil
Cooked spaghetti

Stir all ingredients together. Heat to boiling. Reduce heat; cover and simmer for 1 hour. Serve over cooked spaghetti.

Variation: Mix three-fourths pound pasteurized process cheese with cooked spaghetti and sauce. Pour into a casserole and top with quarter pound cubed pasteurized process cheese. Bake at 350 degrees for 20 minutes until cheese is bubbly.

Yield: 6-8 servings

Carol Hixon Dunn '57
Karon Quick McMillan '81

Sauerbraten

2 pounds beef (pot roast or brisket)
8 ounces wine vinegar
8 ounces water
1 Tablespoon sugar
3 dry bay leaves
6 peppercorns
1 pound onions, divided
Oil
8 ounces beef broth
3 Tablespoons sour cream
Salt and pepper

Prepare marinade mixture of vinegar, water, sugar, bay leaves, peppercorns, and 1 peeled and sliced onion. Add beef and marinate in refrigerator for 1-2 days in a Dutch oven. Drain meat, reserving the marinade. Brown beef and remaining sliced onions in oil. Add beef broth and marinade liquid gradually. Simmer all ingredients partially covered for about 90 minutes. Turn beef every 30 minutes. When meat is tender, stir in sour cream to form sauce. Add salt and pepper to taste.

Yield: 4 servings

Volker Held '66

Eye of Round Roast

Eye of round roast
1 teaspoon unseasoned meat tenderizer
1 teaspoon seasoned salt flavor enhancer
1½ teaspoons seasoned salt
½ teaspoon pepper
Garlic salt

Place the roast in a roasting pan and add the other ingredients. Let stand at room temperature for 1 hour. Preheat oven to 500 degrees. Cook only 5 minutes per pound. Turn oven off and leave for 2 hours. Do not open oven door.

Yield: 8-10 servings

Jerry Lyons '66

Easy Autumn Pot Roast

1 (3½-4½-pound) beef pot roast
2 Tablespoons all-purpose flour
3 Tablespoons oil
1 envelope onion soup mix
½ cup apple cider
½ teaspoon celery seed
6 potatoes, quartered
6 carrots, quartered
All-purpose flour
Water
2 Tablespoons snipped parsley or parsley flakes

Dredge beef in flour and brown the roast in oil in large skillet or Dutch oven; pour off drippings. Combine onion soup mix, cider, and celery seed. Stir well and add to meat. Cover tightly and cook slowly for 2 hours on rangetop. Add potatoes and carrots; cover and cook slowly for 50 minutes longer or until meat and vegetables are tender. Remove pot roast and vegetables to hot platter. Thicken cooking liquid with blend of flour and water, if desired. Sprinkle vegetables with parsley and add remaining parsley to gravy.

Yield: 8 servings

Sharon Meagher '78

Spicy Italian Roast

3-4 pounds beef rump roast
1½ teaspoons garlic salt
1 (4-ounce) can sliced mushrooms, drained
1 onion, diced
1 (1½-ounce) package spaghetti sauce seasoning mix
1 (8-ounce) can tomato sauce
2 Tablespoons butter, melted
2 Tablespoons all-purpose flour
2 Tablespoons tomato paste
Hot cooked pasta

Season roast with garlic salt and place into a slow cooker. Add mushrooms and onion. Combine seasoning mix and tomato sauce; pour over meat. Cover and cook on High 4-5 hours or on Low heat 8-10 hours. Mix butter and flour. Add tomato paste and stir into meat drippings in slow cooker. Cover and cook on High for about 30 minutes or until thickened. Serve over hot pasta.

Yield: 6 servings

Jan Simmons Cameron '78

Grilled Sirloin Tip Roast

1 (3-inch thick) sirloin tip roast
2 Tablespoons oil
1 (5-ounce) bottle soy sauce
2 Tablespoons vinegar
Garlic salt or minced garlic
Seasoned salt

Place roast into a plastic bag. Mix oil, soy sauce, vinegar, garlic, and salt. Pour oil mixture into bag and cover all surfaces of roast with marinade. Seal bag and let stand in refrigerator for at least 3 hours or overnight. Cook on the grill for 30-40 minutes, turning twice, or until roast reaches desired degree of doneness. Remove to a 9x13 dish and slice very thin across the grain. Heat marinade and pour over meat.

Yield: 8 servings

Mrs. M. C. Harris

Bar-B-Q Brisket

5-6 pounds fresh beef brisket
1 teaspoon celery salt
1 teaspoon garlic salt
2 teaspoons salt
½ teaspoon pepper
2 Tablespoons Worcestershire sauce
1½ ounces liquid smoke
6 ounces barbecue sauce

Put brisket into a 9x11 baking pan. Add salts, pepper, Worcestershire sauce, and liquid smoke. Cover with aluminum foil and seal. Refrigerate overnight. Place sealed pan into a preheated 225 degree oven and bake 4-5 hours or until tender. Drain liquid and cover brisket with barbecue sauce. Bake for 1 hour longer; cool, slice, and serve.

Yield: 20 servings

Mrs. Russell McIntire (Maellen) '59, Faculty Wife

English Beef Short Ribs

3-4 pounds beef short ribs
2 teaspoons salt
1 teaspoon thyme
½ teaspoon savory
⅛ teaspoon pepper
1¼ cups water, divided
4 small onions, sliced
1 Tablespoon brown sugar
1 Tablespoon vinegar
1 Tablespoon prepared mustard
2 Tablespoons all-purpose flour
½ cup buttermilk

Put short ribs into a large heavy skillet or Dutch oven; cover tightly and cook slowly for 1½ hours, turning occasionally to brown all sides. Pour off drippings. Sprinkle salt, thyme, savory, and pepper over meat. Add 1 cup water, cover and cook for 30 minutes. Place onions on top of meat; continue cooking covered for another 30 minutes or until meat is tender. Remove ribs to warm platter. If needed add water to cooking liquid to make 1 cup. Stir in brown sugar, vinegar, and mustard. Blend flour with ¼ cup water; gradually add to liquid and cook, stirring until thickened. Add buttermilk and cook slowly for 2 minutes. Pour sauce over ribs and serve.

Yield: 6-8 servings

Lois C. Mitcheltree '51

Spiced Orange Pot Roast

5 pound lean boneless beef chuck roast
1 Tablespoon oil
½ onion, chopped fine
1 clove garlic, minced, or ¼ teaspoon garlic salt
1 (8-ounce) can tomato sauce
1-2 cups mandarin orange sections with juice
1 Tablespoon sugar
1 Tablespoon orange rind, grated (optional)
1½ teaspoons salt
½ teaspoon nutmeg
½ teaspoon cinnamon
¼ teaspoon cloves
Dash of pepper
Oranges slices and/or parsley for garnish

Preheat oven to 325 degrees. Brown meat slowly on both sides in hot oil using a deep iron skillet. Add onion and garlic; cover and cook over medium heat for 20 minutes. Pour tomato sauce, orange sections with juice, sugar, and grated orange rind over meat. Sprinkle with salt, spices, and pepper. Cover and brown for approximately 4 hours, or until meat is tender. Garnish with orange slices and parsley and serve broth-type gravy as optional sauce.

Yield: 12-16 servings

Anne Greene Eaves, Faculty Wife

Mexican Steaks

¾ cup all-purpose flour
¼ teaspoon salt
¼ teaspoon pepper
4 beef steaks, cubed
3 Tablespoons oil
½ cup onion, chopped
½ cup green pepper, chopped
1 Tablespoon margarine
1 (10-ounce) can tomatoes and green chili peppers, undrained
1 cup cheese, grated

Blend flour, salt, and pepper. Dip meat in flour mixture. Heat oil in large skillet. Cook meat over medium heat for 8-10 minutes on each side. Remove to platter. Cook onion and green pepper in margarine until tender. Add undrained tomatoes; heat thoroughly. Add cheese and stir until melted. Pour sauce over steaks.

Yield: 4 servings

Carolyn M. Kilgore '84

Lady Astor's Plush Steak

3 Tablespoons prepared mustard
3 teaspoons fresh lemon juice
3 pounds sirloin steak, room temperature

Sauce:
½ cup catsup
¼ cup water
½ cup oil
4 Tablespoons red wine vinegar
4 Tablespoons soy sauce
5 Tablespoons cherry jam
5 Tablespoons brown sugar
⅛ teaspoon fresh ground pepper
5 drops Tabasco sauce

Mix mustard and lemon juice; spread on both sides of steak.

Combine all sauce ingredients in a small saucepan. Boil and stir for 2 minutes. Place steak into a large shallow glass dish or large plastic bag. Pour sauce over steak; allow to stand for at least 2 hours. Turn steak twice. Grill over very hot coals or broil in oven. Allow 5-6 minutes on each side for rare, 7-8 minutes for medium. Baste with sauce. Use tongs to turn the meat. Cut meat diagonally; serve on a hot platter or a wooden carving board.

Yield: 4-6 servings

June Campbell (Richard Campbell '50)

Pop Earley's Marinated Steaks

⅓ cup steak sauce
2 Tablespoons teriyaki sauce
2 (8-ounce) ribeye steaks
Garlic salt with herbs

Mix steak sauce and teriyaki sauce; pierce steaks with fork on both sides. Sprinkle garlic salt on steaks and rub into steak with fingers. Marinate steaks in sauce mix for at least 2 hours, turning every half hour. Cook steaks as desired on a barbecue grill or on indoor grill.

Yield: 2 servings

Paul E. Earley '75

Venison Crockpot Steak

3 or 4 half-inch venison steaks
Seasoned salt
Unseasoned meat tenderizer
½-1 cup all-purpose flour
¼ cup shortening
½-1 cup water
1 large onion, sliced
2 beef bouillon cubes
Hot cooked rice or creamed potatoes

Remove all fat and white membrane from partially frozen steaks. Sprinkle generously with seasoned salt and meat tenderizer. Pound steaks with meat mallet on both sides to tenderize steak. Dredge in flour. Heat shortening in black skillet. Add steaks and brown on both sides. Remove steaks to crockpot. Sprinkle flour over bottom of skillet and brown. Add water, onion, and bouillon cubes. Bring to a boil, dissolving bouillon cubes. Let gravy thicken and pour over steaks in crockpot. Cook 8 hours on Low or 4 hours on High. Add more water if needed. Serve over rice or creamed potatoes.

Variation: Venison may be cooked in skillet on rangetop for 40 minutes.

Yield: 4 servings

Sue Lewis Addy '66

Mexican Casserole

1½ pounds ground beef
½ onion, chopped
1 (12-ounce) can evaporated milk
1 (4-ounce) can green chilies, chopped
1 (10-ounce) can enchilada sauce
1 can cream of mushroom soup
1 can cream of chicken soup
1 (16-ounce) bag corn chips, crushed
2 cups cheese, shredded

Brown ground beef and onions. Mix milk, chilies, enchilada sauce, and soups. In a 9x13 pan, layer half of corn chips, half of liquid mixture, and half of ground beef mixture; top with half of cheese. Repeat layers. Bake in a preheated 350 degree oven for 45 minutes.

Yield: 8-10 servings

Norman H. Gough, Jr. '84

Carne Mechada

2 pounds chuck steak
1 green pepper, diced
1 onion, diced
1 tomato, diced
1 cup water
½ teaspoon salt
½ teaspoon garlic
½ teaspoon cumin

Place all ingredients in a deep skillet and cook covered on low heat for 1-1½ hours on the rangetop. When meat has cooled, remove from skillet and shred. Return meat to skillet and simmer in liquid. Serve hot.

Yield: 4-6 servings

Martha Beal '69

Taco Casserole

1½ pounds ground chuck
1 (5-ounce) package yellow rice
2 cans chili with beans
8 ounces sharp Cheddar cheese, grated
1 (16-ounce) jar taco sauce
1 (16-ounce) carton sour cream

Brown meat and drain. Cook rice according to package directions. Combine the cooked rice with meat; mix well. Add chili and stir. Pour into a large casserole and sprinkle with the grated cheese. Bake in a preheated 350 degree oven for 25 minutes. Top with sour cream mixed with taco sauce. Serve with tortilla chips.

Yield: 16 servings

Lynn King

Tamale Casserole

1 (15-ounce) can tamales, sliced lengthwise
2 cups cooked rice
1 onion, diced
½ (12-ounce) bottle taco sauce
1 (6-ounce) can sliced ripe olives
1 (15-ounce) can chili without beans
½ pound cheese, grated

Grease a medium casserole. Layer ingredients in order listed. Bake in a preheated 350 degree oven for about 30 minutes.

Yield: 8-12 servings

Grace M. Elsey '53, Former Staff

Favorite Fiesta Casserole

2 pounds ground beef
½ cup celery, chopped
½ cup onion, chopped
1 (16½-ounce) can kernel corn, drained
1 package taco seasoning
2 (8-ounce) cans tomato sauce
8 flour tortillas
4 ounces Cheddar cheese, grated

Brown meat with celery and onions; drain. Stir in corn. Add taco seasoning to tomato sauce. Reserve one-third cup of sauce mixture and add remainder to meat mixture. Reserve two-thirds cup of meat mixture; pour remainder into casserole. Put 2 tablespoons of meat mixture on each tortilla. Roll up and place filled tortilla, seam side down, into casserole. Pour reserved sauce over top. Bake in a preheated 375 degree oven for 20 minutes. Sprinkle with cheese.

Yield: 8 servings

Faye Robertson

Beef Patties

Patties:
1 pound ground beef
½ cup breadcrumbs
Salt and pepper to taste
⅓ cup evaporated milk
¼ cup onion, chopped
All-purpose flour
2 Tablespoons oil

Sauce:
¾ cup water
1 Tablespoon catsup
1 Tablespoon Worcestershire sauce
¼ cup celery, chopped
¼ cup onion, chopped

Combine beef, breadcrumbs, salt, pepper, milk, and onion; shape into 4 patties. Coat with flour and brown in hot oil; drain. Mix the sauce ingredients and spoon over patties in pan. Cover and simmer (or bake in a preheated 350 degree oven) for 1 hour.

Yield: 4 servings

Ruby Nell Johnson Stancill '50

One-Dish Meal

1½ pounds ground chuck, browned and drained
1 large potato, cubed
2-3 carrots, chopped
3 small celery ribs, chopped
1 medium onion, chopped
Salt and pepper to taste
1 (8½-ounce) can English peas

Mix all ingredients except peas in an iron skillet; pour in liquid from peas. Cover and bake in a preheated 350 degree oven for 1¼ hours. Remove from oven and stir in peas; cover and bake for 15 minutes longer.

Yield: 4-6 servings

Angela Gilstrap Robison '91

Bobotee

2 onions, sliced thin
1 apple, diced
2 teaspoons margarine
2 slices bread
1 cup milk
2 pounds ground meat, cooked and drained
2 teaspoons curry powder
1 teaspoon turmeric
2 teaspoons sugar
2 eggs
2 teaspoons vinegar
2 teaspoons salt
¼ teaspoon pepper
¼ cup raisins
12 whole almonds (optional)
6 lemon or bay leaves
Hot cooked rice
Chutney

Grease an 8x8x2 baking pan. Sauté onion and apple in the margarine; set aside. Soak bread in milk, then squeeze dry; reserve milk. Mix bread with onion, apple, meat, curry powder, turmeric, sugar, 1 egg, vinegar, salt, pepper, and raisins. If almonds are used, blanch almonds and remove skins; cut into quarters and add to mixture, stirring well. Place into prepared baking pan. Roll the lemon leaves and insert them well into the mixture in an upright position. Bay leaves are not rolled. Bake in a preheated 350 degree oven for 30 minutes. Beat the second egg with the reserved milk and pour it over the bobotee; bake for another 10-15 minutes. Serve with rice and chutney. Bobotee is a dish from South Africa.

Yield: 6-8 servings

Hugh A. Brown '39

Pizza Squares

1 pound ground turkey or beef, browned and drained
1 (32-ounce) jar spaghetti sauce
½ cup Cheddar cheese, shredded
½ cup mozzarella cheese, shredded
1⅛ cups biscuit mix
3 eggs or equivalent egg substitute
2¼ cups skim milk

Coat a 9x13 baking pan with a non-fat spray. Spread meat evenly in pan. Pour spaghetti sauce over meat, spreading evenly. Sprinkle both cheeses over sauce. Combine biscuit mix, eggs, and milk; pour over cheese. Bake in a preheated 350 degree oven for approximately 45 minutes or until crust is brown and done through the middle.

Yield: 8 servings

Bettye R. Coward, Faculty

Beef and Noodle Skillet

1 pound ground beef
1 onion, chopped fine
½ green pepper, chopped fine
1 (8-ounce) package egg noodles
1 (4-ounce) jar mushrooms, chopped
1 (20-ounce) can tomatoes
Salt and pepper
8 ounces mozzarella cheese, sliced

Brown ground beef, onions, and pepper in a deep skillet; drain. Return meat mixture to skillet. Place noodles on top of meat mixture; cover with mushrooms and tomatoes. Arrange cheese slices on top. Cook covered on low heat on rangetop for about 15-20 minutes until noodles are tender.

Yield: 6-8 servings

Eleanor Testerman '78

Hamburger Pie

½ medium onion, chopped
½ medium bell pepper, chopped
1 pound ground chuck, browned and drained
1 can tomato soup
2 (9-inch) refrigerated crusts

Add onion and pepper to ground chuck. Mix in tomato soup. Pour mixture into a pie pan lined with one crust and top with second crust. Cut several slits in top crust. Bake in a preheated 400 degree oven for 40 minutes or until crust is golden brown. Let stand for 5 minutes before serving.

Yield: 6-8 servings

Karen Nelson Sanders '81

Eggplant Parmesan

1 large eggplant
2 eggs
1½ cups milk
All-purpose flour
Oil for frying
2 cups Cheddar cheese, grated

Sauce:
1 (32-ounce) jar thick and zesty spaghetti sauce
1 onion, chopped
1 pound ground beef, cooked and drained
¼ cup Parmesan cheese
1 teaspoon oregano

Peel and slice eggplant ¼-inch thick. Mix eggs and milk. Dip eggplant slices in egg mixture, then dredge in flour; fry in small amount of oil until brown. Mix together sauce ingredients and heat thoroughly. Layer eggplant, sauce, grated cheese, and a little Parmesan cheese. End with sauce and cheese on top. Bake for 30 minutes. This dish may be made ahead and frozen.

Yield: 4-6 servings

Rachel A. Wooten '93

Breakfast Pizza

2 (8-ounce) cans refrigerated crescent rolls
2 pounds hot sausage, cooked and drained
2 cups Monterey Jack cheese, grated
12 eggs, scrambled and seasoned to taste
2 cups Cheddar cheese, grated

Flatten rolls and pat into an 11x15 pan to form a crust. Sprinkle cooked sausage evenly over crust. Sprinkle grated Monterey Jack cheese over sausage. Spoon cooked eggs over Monterey Jack cheese and top with Cheddar cheese. Bake in a preheated 350 degree oven for 30 minutes until crust is done. This may be assembled and refrigerated the night before it is cooked and served.

Yield: 8-10 servings

Carolyn V. Hand '65, Staff

Creole Black-Eyed Peas

1 (16-ounce) package dried black-eyed peas
½ pound salt pork or bacon, cubed
6 cups warm water
3 cups onion, chopped
1 bunch green onions, chopped (use some of the green tops)
1 cup fresh parsley, chopped
1 cup bell pepper, chopped
2 cloves garlic, pressed
1½ teaspoons salt
1 teaspoon black pepper
3 dashes Tabasco sauce
1 Tablespoon Worcestershire sauce
1 (8-ounce) can tomato sauce
¼ teaspoon oregano
¼ teaspoon thyme
1 pound smoked sausage, sliced into rounds
Hot cooked rice

Simmer dry peas (do not soak) and pork in water for 45 minutes. Add the remaining ingredients except sausage. Cover and simmer for 1 hour. Add sausage to mixture. Uncover and cook for 45 minutes longer. It may be necessary to add additional water during cooking. Serve over rice.

Yield: 16 servings

Robert Glenn Luke '92

Sausage Jambalaya

1½ pounds link sausage
2 cans French onion soup
1 (10-ounce) can tomatoes with chilies
5 beef bouillon cubes
2 large onions, chopped
1 cup green pepper, chopped
1½ cups water
2½ cups long grain rice, uncooked
1 teaspoon sugar

Cook sausage in boiling water. Drain and cut into small pieces. In a 6-quart saucepan combine sausage, soup, tomatoes, bouillon cubes, onions, peppers, and water. Bring to a boil, then add rice and sugar. Stir ingredients well, cover, and cook for about 20 minutes. Do not stir.

Yield: 8-10 servings

Anna Dell Creel

Sausage and Rice Casserole

1 large onion, chopped
1 medium green pepper, chopped
1 cup celery, chopped
2 Tablespoons oil
2 envelopes chicken noodle soup mix
½ cup uncooked rice
4½ cups water
1 pound hot sausage, cooked and drained
Slivered almonds
Parsley, chopped (optional)

Sauté onion, pepper, and celery in oil and set aside. Add soup mix and rice to boiling water. Cook for 7 minutes, covered. Do not drain. Stir in sausage and vegetables. Pour into a prepared casserole. Sprinkle top with almonds and parsley. Bake in a preheated 350 degree oven for 30 minutes.

Yield: 6 servings

Dorothy Boyd Carpenter (Ray W. Carpenter '49)

Ratatouille

(Pronounced "rat-a-too-ya")

2 pounds sweet Italian sausage links
⅓ cup olive oil
2 large onions, sliced
2 bell peppers, seeded and cut in chunks (1 red and 1 green)
3 ribs celery, cut in ¾-inch chunks
3 cloves garlic, minced
1 small eggplant, peeled and cut in chunks
4-5 zucchini, sliced
1 (10-ounce) package frozen French-style green beans
1 (20-ounce) can tomatoes
1 (4-ounce) can mushrooms, sliced
3 teaspoons beef bouillon granules
Sugar, salt, pepper, and basil to taste
Parmesan cheese, grated
Parsley, chopped

Remove casings from sausage, break into chunks, and sauté in olive oil over medium heat in a non-stick or well-greased 8-quart Dutch oven. Remove and drain, reserving the oil. Sauté onions, peppers, and celery in the oil until onion is translucent. Add garlic, eggplant, zucchini, beans, tomatoes, mushrooms, and bouillon; cook until done but crisp. Add sausage and seasonings; simmer for a few minutes. Serve in individual bowls with Parmesan cheese and parsley on top. This dish freezes well. It may be prepared ahead and reheated.

Yield: 8-10 servings

Norman S. Deaton '54

Sausage Casserole

1 pound link sausage
8 ounces fresh mushrooms
¾ cup celery, diced
¾ cup bell pepper, diced
½ cup onion, chopped
4 or 5 medium potatoes, cubed
Salt and pepper

Cut sausage into ¼-inch rounds and place into the bottom of a Dutch oven. Wash and slice mushrooms; place on top of sausage. Add celery, pepper, and onions and sauté lightly. Arrange potatoes on top of other ingredients, then salt and pepper to taste. Cover and simmer until potatoes are tender, stirring occasionally. Add one-half cup water if needed.

Yield: 6 servings

Neal Brashier, Staff

Stuffed Pork Loin

1 (2½-pound) pork loin, boneless
1 link smoked sausage
Seasoned salt
Ground thyme
Dried parsley
Garlic butter (optional)
Dark molasses or cane syrup

With an electric knife or a long, sharp fillet knife, cut a hole lengthwise through pork loin. Insert smoked sausage into pork loin. Place loin onto double thickness of heavy aluminum foil. Sprinkle heavily with seasoned salt and rub it into the meat. Sprinkle thyme and parsley onto meat and spread with garlic butter. Pour molasses over pork loin and fold up foil to securely wrap. Cook over grill for approximately 30 minutes per pound. Slice crosswise when done.

Yield: 10-12 servings

Dane A. Evers '90

Pork Chop Casserole

6 pork chops, boneless, trimmed
Seasoned salt
1 can cream of celery soup
½ cup milk
½ cup sour cream
¼ teaspoon black pepper
1 (24-ounce) package hash brown potatoes, thawed
1 cup Cheddar cheese, shredded, divided
1 can French-fried onions, divided

Brown pork chops in lightly greased skillet. Sprinkle with seasoned salt and set aside. Combine soup, milk, sour cream, pepper, and one-half teaspoon seasoned salt. Stir in potatoes, one-half cup cheese, and one-half can of onions. Spoon mixture into a 9x13 glass baking dish. Arrange pork chops over potatoes. Bake covered in a preheated 350 degree oven for 40 minutes. Top with remaining cheese and onions. Bake uncovered for 5 minutes longer.

Yield: 8-10 servings

Mrs. John G. McCall, Faculty Wife

Easy and Delicious Pork Chops

4-6 pork chops
1½ cups cola-flavored carbonated drink
¾ cup soy sauce

Marinate pork chops overnight in cola and soy sauce mixture. Grill to desired doneness on gas or charcoal grill. To cut the grilling time, cook pork chops in microwave for 5 minutes before grilling.

Yield: 4-6 servings

Amy Turner Rowan '85

Khao Phat Mu Kung Sai Khai

(Thai Fried Rice with Pork, Shrimp and Egg)

6 ounces lean pork, sliced into small strips
3 Tablespoons soy sauce, divided
¼ cup oil
1 onion, thinly sliced
6 ounces shrimp, peeled and deveined
2 Tablespoons catsup
1 Tablespoon sugar
4 cups cooked rice
1 Tablespoon oil
2 eggs

Marinate pork strips in 1 tablespoon soy sauce for a few minutes. Heat one-fourth cup oil in a wok or skillet over medium heat. Sauté onion until yellow; add pork, shrimp, catsup, sugar, and remaining soy sauce. Stir-fry until pork is fully cooked. Add rice and stir constantly until desired degree of dryness is reached. Remove rice mixture from wok. Return wok to heat and add 1 tablespoon oil. When hot, break eggs into wok. With spatula, break, spread, and turn eggs; when done, cut into strips. Add rice mixture and mix well. Serve with sliced cucumbers, spring onions, cabbage, lettuce, and wedges of lime.

Yield: 4 servings

Direk Arayakosol '56

Sweet and Sour Pork Chops

4 lean pork chops
Salt
All-purpose flour
2 Tablespoons oil
1 (13¼-ounce) can pineapple chunks, drained
1 small green pepper, cut into rings
1 cup chicken broth
1 cup sugar
1 cup vinegar
⅓ cup catsup
2 Tablespoons cornstarch
¼ cup water
Hot cooked rice

Sprinkle chops with salt and dredge in flour. Brown on both sides in oil. Place chops into a shallow 10-inch square casserole. Top with pineapple and pepper. Combine chicken broth, sugar, vinegar, and catsup in a small saucepan; bring to a boil. Reduce heat to medium. Combine cornstarch and water; stir well and add to chicken broth mixture. Stir constantly until thickened and bubbly. Pour chicken broth mixture over chops. Cover and bake in a preheated 325 degree oven for 1 hour or until done. Serve over rice.

Yield: 4 servings

Bettye Stewart, Staff (Franklin D. '71)

Bacon-Wrapped Pork Tenderloin

1 whole fresh tenderloin, cut in half lengthwise
8 slices bacon
1 (8-ounce) bottle Russian salad dressing

Wrap slices of bacon around each half of tenderloin and secure with a toothpick. Place meat into casserole and add salad dressing. Marinate in dressing for 24 hours. Bake in a preheated 350 degree oven for 1 hour.

Yield: 6-8 servings

Libby Patterson '57, Staff

Try hot pepper jelly with ham or pork.

Baked Ham

½ ham
2-3 teaspoons tart jelly
1 onion, quartered
1 tart apple, quartered
Black pepper
Sugar
Whole cloves

Rinse ham thoroughly. Place into a roasting pan and rub with jelly. Place apple and onion around ham and add water to pan to a 1-inch depth. Cover tightly with foil or the roaster top. Cook for about 20 minutes per pound in a preheated 325 degree oven. This may take longer depending on the water content of the ham. Check after 2 hours. Ham is done when skin is loose, fork pierces meat easily, and fat is soft. Let ham cool enough to handle; then remove from roasting pan to a flat broiler-type pan. Do not use a cookie sheet. Remove the skin and trim the fat carefully so that only a ¼-inch layer remains. Patch any meat that is bare with little pieces of the discarded fat. Coat the fat with thick layer of sugar and black pepper. Score fat in a diamond pattern with a sharp knife; place a clove in the middle of each diamond. Reduce heat and bake at 275 degrees. Cook for about 1 hour or until coating is brown and crusty.

Yield: Variable

Katty Ireland, Faculty Wife

Sweet and Sour Ham Loaf

1 pound cooked ham, ground
½ pound fresh lean pork, ground
1 cup cracker crumbs
½ teaspoon dry mustard
2 eggs, beaten
1 cup milk

Sweet and Sour Sauce:
¾ cup brown sugar
½ teaspoon dry mustard
2 Tablespoons water
2 Tablespoons vinegar

Mix ham, pork, cracker crumbs, mustard, beaten eggs, and milk. Combine lightly with a fork. Shape and place into a loaf pan. Combine ingredients for sauce in small bowl. Stir to mix. Spoon over ham loaf. Bake in a preheated 350 degree oven for 50 minutes. Baste with sauce often during cooking.

Yield: 6 servings

Mary H. Thurman

Ham Loaf

Loaf:
2 pounds smoked ham, ground
2 pounds lean pork, ground
1½ cups soda crackers, crumbled
⅓ cup onion, chopped
4 eggs, beaten well
1½ teaspoons salt
2 Tablespoons parsley, chopped

Basting Sauce:
½ pound brown sugar
½ cup apple cider vinegar
1½ Tablespoons dry mustard

Zippy Sauce:
½ cup mayonnaise
½ cup sour cream
¼ cup prepared mustard
1 Tablespoon chives
2 Tablespoons horseradish
Salt and lemon juice to taste

Grease 2 loaf pans (9x5x3). Have the butcher mix the ham and pork together. Mix all loaf ingredients together and place into pans. Bake in a preheated 350 degree oven for 30 minutes. Mix ingredients for basting sauce and boil for 1 minute. Baste meat with half the basting sauce. Cook ham loaves for another 30 minutes. Baste with remaining sauce. Bake for 30 minutes more. Cool before slicing. Mix ingredients for Zippy Sauce and serve as a condiment.

Yield: 12 servings

Dell Dickins Scoper '56

Mrs. Scoper's father, John W. Dickens, served on the Mississippi College Board of Trustees.

Blend honey with peanut butter to create a wonderful glaze for ham.

Ham Rolls

Cheese slices
Ham, sliced thin
Bacon
1 cup catsup
3 Tablespoons catsup-type steak sauce
¼ cup water
1 Tablespoon Worcestershire sauce
1 Tablespoon prepared mustard

Place a piece of cheese onto each ham slice and roll. Wrap each roll with a half slice of bacon and secure with toothpick. Place into a shallow baking dish. Make a sauce with the remaining ingredients and pour over rolls. Bake in a preheated 350 degree oven about 30 minutes or until bacon is cooked.

Yield: 2-3 ham rolls per serving

Mrs. L. Bracey Campbell III (Bracey Campbell '69)

From the recipes of Electra Warren Campbell '40

Broccoli, Ham, and Macaroni Bake

1 (8-ounce) package macaroni
3 quarts boiling water
1 Tablespoon salt
½ cup butter
¼ cup all-purpose flour
2½ cups milk
¾ cup cheese, grated
1 teaspoon onion, grated
½ teaspoon dry mustard
1 cup mayonnaise
1 (10-ounce) package frozen chopped broccoli, cooked
2 cups ham, cubed
2 teaspoons salt
⅛ teaspoon pepper
Buttered breadcrumbs

Slowly add macaroni to boiling, salted water. Allow water to return to boil and cook for 7-9 minutes, stirring occasionally. Melt butter in saucepan, blend in flour. Add milk and stir until sauce thickens. Add grated cheese, onion, and mustard to sauce mixture and fold in mayonnaise. Combine macaroni, cooked broccoli, ham, and sauce; season with salt and pepper. Pour into a 2-quart casserole, top with buttered breadcrumbs and bake in a preheated 375 degree oven for 25-30 minutes.

Yield: 8 servings

Joan Bailey (Mrs. Perry)

Red Beans and Rice

1 pound dried red kidney beans
1½ quarts water
1 cup onion, chopped
½ cup green pepper, chopped
3-4 cloves garlic, minced
1 Tablespoon parsley
¼ teaspoon cayenne pepper
2 bay leaves
¼ teaspoon thyme
⅛ teaspoon basil
6-7 ham hocks
¾ teaspoon salt
½ teaspoon black pepper
1 pound smoked sausage, diced
Cured ham cubes (optional)
Hot cooked rice

Cover beans with water and soak overnight; drain. Add fresh water and remaining ingredients. Bring to a boil over high heat, then reduce the heat and simmer for 2 hours or until the beans are tender and a thick, natural sauce has formed. Stir the mixture once every half hour. Serve over rice.

Yield: 6-8 servings

Terry Blais Compton '79

Eggs McMurff

6 Tablespoons butter
6 Tablespoons all-purpose flour
2 cups milk
1 (8-ounce) jar sharp pasteurized processed cheese spread
1 (8-ounce) carton sour cream
1 teaspoon salt
1 teaspoon pepper
Paprika
18-20 hard-boiled eggs, sliced
1 pound bacon, cooked and crumbled
10-12 English muffins

To make white sauce, melt butter in a small saucepan over medium heat. Blend in flour until smooth. Gradually add milk, stirring constantly. Continue cooking over medium heat until mixture thickens. Remove from heat and cover with wax paper until cool. Add cheese spread, sour cream, salt, pepper, and paprika. In a deep casserole, layer eggs, sauce, and bacon; repeat, ending with sauce. Bake in a preheated 350 degree oven until bubbly. Serve over English muffins.

Yield: 10-12 servings

Becky DeLashmet Fisk '81

Egg and Sausage Bake

2 cups herbed croutons
1 pound sausage, cooked and drained
4 eggs, beaten
3 cups milk, divided
1 teaspoon dry mustard
8 ounces Cheddar cheese, grated
1 can cream of mushroom soup

Place croutons in bottom of a 9x13 baking dish. Cover croutons with cooked sausage. Combine eggs, 2½ cups milk, and dry mustard; pour over sausage. Sprinkle with cheese. Combine soup and one-half cup milk; pour over cheese. Bake uncovered in a preheated 325 degree oven for 45-55 minutes. Casserole should be firm in center and browned on top.

Yield: 6-8 servings

Stephen W. Blackburn '70

Breakfast Casserole

6 slices bread, cubed
1 pound pork sausage, sausage links, or chopped ham
1 cup Cheddar cheese, grated
6 eggs, beaten slightly
2 cups milk
¼ teaspoon dry mustard
1 teaspoon salt
Pepper to taste

Coat a 9x9 casserole with non-stick vegetable spray. Cook meat and drain. In casserole layer bread, meat, and cheese. Mix eggs, milk, mustard, salt and pepper. Pour over layers. Bake in a preheated 325 degree oven for 45 minutes. This may be made the night before and baked just prior to serving.

Variation: Decrease eggs to 4. In place of seasonings listed above, use 1 teaspoon brown sugar, ¼ teaspoon paprika, ½ teaspoon dry mustard, ½ teaspoon salt, ½ teaspoon pepper, ⅛ teaspoon Tabasco sauce, and ½ teaspoon Worcestershire sauce.

Yield: 6-8 servings

Fannie Peeples (widow of Sam A. Peeples '35)
Ann Patterson Cameron '70
Sarah N. Spencer, Staff

Stuffed French Toast Casserole

8-10 slices bread, cubed
2 (8-ounce) packages cream cheese, cubed
1 dozen eggs
⅓ cup maple syrup
2 cups milk
Confectioners' sugar
Fresh fruit
Butter
Maple Syrup

Butter a 9x13 baking dish. Put half of the cubed bread into prepared dish and add cream cheese. Top with remainder of bread and set aside. Mix eggs, syrup, and milk. Pour over bread and cream cheese. Cover with plastic wrap and refrigerate overnight. Bake in a preheated 375 degree oven for 45-50 minutes until golden brown. Cut into squares and dust with confectioners' sugar. Serve with fresh fruit, butter, and syrup.

Yield: 10-12 servings

Joseph Batton '87

Shrimp Quiche

3 eggs
1 cup light cream
½ cup Swiss or Gruyère cheese, shredded
½ teaspoon salt
1 onion, thinly sliced
4 Tablespoons margarine
½ teaspoon chives, chopped
½ teaspoon parsley, chopped
1 pound shrimp, peeled
1 (9-inch) unbaked pastry shell

Mix eggs, cream, cheese, and salt. Cook onion in margarine until soft but not brown. Add onion, seasonings, and shrimp to egg mixture. Spoon into the pie shell. Bake in a preheated 350 degree oven for 30-35 minutes.

Yield: 6 servings

Suzanne Murray Damron '73

Quick Quiche

Any or all of the following as desired: onion, celery, bell pepper, ham, sausage, broccoli, spinach
¼ cup margarine
3 eggs
1 cup cheese, shredded
1½ cups milk
½ cup biscuit mix

Grease a quiche pan or 2 smaller pie plates. Chop vegetables and sauté in margarine; if using meat, precook. Sprinkle vegetables and meat into bottom of prepared pan. Combine eggs, cheese, milk, and biscuit mix. Pour egg mixture over vegetables and meat. Bake in a preheated 350 degree oven for 30-45 minutes or until brown and firm. This dish freezes well. This recipe makes 1 regular quiche, 2 smaller ones, 3 dozen miniature quiches or 18 regular muffin-sized quiches.

Yield: 4-6 entree servings or 36 appetizer servings

Sonia Gilliam Truitt '59

Crustless Sausage-Apple Quiche

1½ cups apple, peeled and chopped fine
½ teaspoon ground cinnamon
½ teaspoon ground nutmeg
4 ounces sharp Cheddar cheese, shredded
½ pound pork sausage, browned and drained
4 eggs, beaten
1 cup light cream
½ cup biscuit mix

Lightly grease a 9-inch quiche dish or deep pie plate. Combine apple, cinnamon, nutmeg, cheese, and sausage. Spoon into dish. Combine eggs, cream, and biscuit mix. Pour over apple mixture. Bake in a preheated 375 degree oven for 35-40 minutes.

Yield: 6 servings

Beverly Craig McBride '61

Breakfast Quiche

1 deep-dish pie shell, unbaked
½ cup sharp Cheddar cheese, divided
4 eggs, beaten
1 cup milk
½ pound sausage, browned and drained

Prick the pie shell well with a fork. Spread one-fourth cup cheese on pie shell. Add milk to beaten eggs and pour mixture over cheese. Sprinkle sausage into pie shell. Bake in a preheated 375 degree oven for 35 minutes. Remove from oven and sprinkle top with remaining one-fourth cup cheese. Bake for an additional 5 minutes or until cheese is melted.

Yield: 6-8 servings

Scott Hodges '92

Spinach and Bacon Soufflé

1 (15-ounce) can spinach
4 eggs, beaten
1 cup milk
1 cup Swiss cheese, shredded
1 cup firm white bread, cubed
½ cup green onions, chopped
¼ cup Parmesan cheese, grated
¾ cup crumbled bacon

Coat a 1-quart baking dish with non-stick spray. Drain spinach thoroughly and set aside. Combine eggs, milk, Swiss cheese, bread, onions, Parmesan cheese, and bacon. Add spinach. Pour into the baking dish and bake covered in a preheated 375 degree oven for 20 minutes. Remove cover and bake for another 10 minutes or until browned on top.

Yield: 6 servings

Andrea Lott Roberts '89

Easy Mexican Omelette

½ pound sharp Cheddar cheese, grated
½ cup all-purpose flour
2 eggs, beaten
1 (4-ounce) can green chilies, chopped and drained
1 teaspoon salt
2 cups milk

Grease a 2-quart baking dish. Mix ingredients in order listed and pour into prepared baking dish. Bake in a preheated 350 degree oven for 45-50 minutes.

Yield: 8 servings

Grace M. Elsey '53, Former Staff

Spaghetti Pie

6 ounces spaghetti, cooked and drained
2 Tablespoons olive oil or butter
2 large eggs, beaten well
¾ cup Parmesan cheese, divided
1 cup ricotta cheese
1 cup spaghetti sauce
½ cup mozzarella cheese, shredded

Lightly grease a 10-inch pie plate; set aside. Toss hot spaghetti with olive oil or butter. Combine eggs and one-half cup Parmesan cheese; stir into spaghetti. Pour spaghetti mixture into prepared pie plate. Form into a crust. Spread ricotta over spaghetti crust. Top with spaghetti sauce. Bake uncovered in a preheated 350 degree oven for 25 minutes. Top with shredded mozzarella. Bake for 5 minutes more or until cheese melts. Remove from oven. Sprinkle with reserved one-fourth cup Parmesan. Cool for 10 minutes before cutting into wedges. Serve immediately.

Yield: 6 servings

Amy McCarty (Britt McCarty '81)

Macaroni and Cheese

2 cups water
1½ teaspoons salt, divided
1 cup dry macaroni
1 cup milk
1 Tablespoon butter, melted
1 egg, beaten
1 teaspoon dry mustard
3 cups sharp cheese, grated, divided

In a 1-quart saucepan, combine water and one-half teaspoon salt. Cover and bring to a boil. Add macaroni; reduce heat and simmer for 8-9 minutes. Drain macaroni and place into a 1-quart casserole. Stir in milk, butter, egg, salt, dry mustard, and 2½ cups cheese. Cover with foil. Bake in a preheated 350 degree oven for 20 minutes. Uncover casserole; top with remainder of cheese and bake for another 10-12 minutes. This is a good, old-fashioned "comfort food" that doesn't take a lot of preparation time.

Yield: 6 servings

Carolyn M. Kilgore '84

Broccoli-Cheese Strata

12 slices white bread, frozen
12 ounces sharp Cheddar cheese, sliced
1 (10-ounce) package frozen chopped broccoli, cooked and drained
2 cups cooked or canned ham, diced fine
6 eggs, slightly beaten
3½ cups milk
2 Tablespoons instant minced onion
½ teaspoon salt
¼ teaspoon dry mustard
Shredded cheese (optional)

Cut 12 "doughnuts and holes" from bread. Fit the scraps of bread (top crusts removed) into the bottom of a 9x13 baking dish. Layer cheese over bread; add a layer of broccoli, then ham. Arrange bread "doughnuts and holes" on top. Combine remaining ingredients; pour over bread. Cover and refrigerate for at least 6 hours or overnight. Bake uncovered in preheated 325 degree oven for 55 minutes. For a pretty finish, sprinkle with shredded cheese 5 minutes before end of baking time. Let stand for 10 minutes to firm.

Yield: 12 servings

Nancy Farr Hughes '56

Black Bean and Zucchini Chilaquiles

12 corn tortillas
2 Tablespoons olive oil
1 cup onions, chopped
1 medium green bell pepper, chopped fine
1 (28-ounce) can crushed or pureed tomatoes
2 teaspoons chili powder
1 teaspoon dried oregano
½ teaspoon ground cumin
2½ cups black beans, cooked
1 medium zucchini, grated
½ pound Cheddar cheese, grated

Place tortillas onto a large baking sheet and bake for 10-15 minutes until the tortillas are dry and crisp. When cool enough to handle, crumble into small pieces and set aside. Heat oil in a heavy saucepan. Sauté onions until translucent. Add green pepper and continue to sauté until onions and pepper are soft. Stir in tomatoes, chili powder, oregano, and cumin; simmer over low heat for 10 minutes. Layer in a greased 9x13 casserole as follows: half the tortilla pieces, half the tomato sauce, half the black beans, half the zucchini, and half the cheese. Repeat layers. Bake in a preheated 350 degree oven for 25-30 minutes or until the cheese is bubbly. Let stand for 5-10 minutes; cut into squares and serve at once.

Yield: 6-8 servings

Betty Stovall Thompson '62

Garlic Cheese Grits

1 cup grits
1 Tablespoon salt
4 cups water
1 stick margarine
1 (6-ounce) roll garlic cheese, cubed
½ pound sharp cheese, grated
2 Tablespoons Worcestershire sauce
Paprika

Lightly grease a casserole. Cook grits in salted water until smooth and creamy. Stir in margarine, cheeses, and Worcestershire sauce. Place into prepared casserole and sprinkle top with paprika. Bake in a preheated 350 degree oven for 30-35 minutes or until top is slightly brown. Do not overcook.

Yield: 8 servings

Ruby Rae Stampley '67

Spinach Lasagna

1 (1½-ounce) package spaghetti sauce mix
1 (6-ounce) can tomato paste
1 (8-ounce) can tomato sauce
1¾ cups water
2 eggs, beaten
1 (16-ounce) carton ricotta or cottage cheese
1 (10-ounce) package frozen chopped spinach, thawed and drained
½ cup Parmesan cheese, grated, divided
1 (8-ounce) package lasagna noodles, uncooked
1 (8-ounce) package mozzarella cheese, sliced

Combine spaghetti sauce mix, tomato paste, tomato sauce, and water in a medium saucepan; bring to a boil over low heat. Remove from heat. Combine eggs, ricotta cheese, spinach, and one-fourth cup Parmesan cheese, mixing well. Set aside. Spread one-half cup tomato sauce mixture into a greased 13x9x2 baking dish. Place half the noodles over sauce; spread with half the spinach mixture, half the mozzarella cheese, and half the tomato sauce. Repeat layers, using remaining ingredients. Sprinkle with remaining Parmesan cheese. Cover dish securely with aluminum foil, and bake in a preheated 350 degree oven for 1 hour. Let stand for 10 minutes before serving. This dish freezes well, but should thaw at room temperature before cooking. A (32-ounce) jar or can of commercial spaghetti sauce may be substituted for the first 4 ingredients.

Yield: 6-8 servings

Joann Branson Cunningham '84

LATIMER HOUSE

Latimer House, later called Twin Oaks, was built circa 1895 by Warren S. Webb, President of Mississippi College, 1873-91. President Webb's daughter, Leura Myrtle, married Murray E. Latimer, professor of Greek at Mississippi College from 1898 until the late 1940's; he also served as college registrar and as mayor of Clinton, 1906-1919. Mississippi College purchased the home in 1969 and used it for a time as faculty housing. In 1991, after extensive renovation and restoration, the late-Victorian era building took on new life as the College guest house and as a unique setting for art exhibits.

DESSERTS

Quick Chocolate Mousse

1 (3½-ounce) box instant chocolate pudding
1 can sweetened condensed milk
1 cup cold water
½ pint heavy cream, whipped
1 (8-ounce) carton whipped topping
Toasted nuts or fresh strawberries

In a large mixer bowl, combine pudding mix, condensed milk, and water. Beat well. Chill for 10 minutes. Fold in whipped cream. Spoon mixture lightly into serving dishes; chill for 2-4 hours. At serving time, garnish with whipped topping and fresh strawberries or toasted nuts.

Yield: 6-8 servings

Rebecca L. Thames

Death By Chocolate

1 box chocolate cake mix
1 (16-ounce) can chocolate syrup
3 (3½-ounce) boxes instant chocolate pudding
6 cups milk
6 chocolate-covered toffee candy bars
1 (16-ounce) carton whipped topping

Bake chocolate cake in a 9x13 pan according to package directions. Punch holes and pour chocolate syrup over cake. Cool. Prepare instant pudding with milk as directed and chill. Crush candy bars. Crumble cake and layer half of it in the bottom of a large trifle or glass salad bowl. Add half the pudding, half the topping, and half the candy bars. Repeat the layers. Refrigerate.

Yield: 15 servings

Vicki Fioranelli

Birchermuesli

4 Tablespoons sweetened condensed milk
4 Tablespoons lemon juice
4 Tablespoons raw (old-fashioned) oatmeal
½ teaspoon lemon rind, grated
1 cup fresh or frozen strawberries, drained
Pecans, chopped (optional)
1 (6-ounce) can crushed pineapple, drained
2 red apples, grated (include peeling for color)
2 bananas, grated or mashed
¾ carton whipped topping

Mix condensed milk, lemon juice, oatmeal, lemon rind, strawberries, pecans, and pineapple. At serving time, add apples, bananas, and whipped topping. Mix well; serve in chilled sherbet glasses. Garnish with a teaspoon of whipped topping and a strawberry or cherry.

Yield: 8 servings

Billie Hilburn Sartin '52

This dish was created in the early 1900's by a Dr. Bircher, renowned for his knowledge of nutrition. In the 1950's it became a popular dessert in Switzerland. The concoction made its way to MC through Marilyn Hubbell, who obtained the recipe while she and her husband were at Ruschlikon Baptist Seminary in Zurich, Switzerland.

Norwegian Apple Dessert

¾ cup sugar
1 teaspoon baking powder
½ cup all-purpose flour
½ cup pecans, chopped
¼ teaspoon salt
1 egg
1 teaspoon vanilla
2 cups tart apples, sliced
Ice cream (optional)

Preheat oven to 350 degrees. Grease a 9-inch square baking dish. Mix sugar, baking powder, flour, pecans, salt, egg, vanilla, and apples. Pour into greased pan and bake for 30 minutes. Serve with a scoop of ice cream, if desired.

Yield: 6 servings

Alicia F. Castillo '87

Caramel Nougat Dessert

Puff pastry shells
Bite-size chocolate covered caramel nougat candy bars
Confectioners' sugar

Preheat oven to 400 degrees. Place pastry shells on an ungreased cookie sheet and bake for 10-15 minutes, or until pastries puff up 1½-2 inches. Remove from oven and slice top from each shell, dropping 1 or 2 candy bars into each shell; replace top of shell. Bake for 5-10 minutes more, until pastry is light golden brown. Remove from oven and sprinkle lightly with confectioners' sugar. Serve warm.

Yield: Variable

Donna Powell Diaz '80

Four-Layer Chocolate Delight

Bottom Layer:
1 cup biscuit mix
1 stick butter or margarine
½ cup nuts, chopped very fine

Preheat oven to 350 degrees. Spread this mixture over bottom of a 9x13 baking pan. Press firmly to make crust. Bake for about 15 minutes. Do not overbake. Cool completely.

Top Layers:
1 (8-ounce) package cream cheese
2 cups confectioners' sugar
1 (6-ounce) box instant chocolate pudding
1 (12-ounce) carton whipped topping

Mix cream cheese and confectioners' sugar. Spread cream cheese mixture over cooled crust. Prepare pudding according to directions. Spread pudding mix over cream cheese layer. Spread whipped topping on top of chocolate pudding. Sprinkle with shaved chocolate and nuts, if desired.

Yield: 14-16 servings

Dorothy Prestridge

Quick Blueberry Dessert

2 cups blueberries, washed and drained
1¼ cups sugar, divided
3 Tablespoons margarine
1 teaspoon baking powder
1 cup plus 1 Tablespoon all-purpose flour, divided
½ cup milk
1 cup boiling water
Ice cream (optional)

Preheat oven to 400 degrees. Place blueberries in a greased 8-inch square pan. Mix ¾ cup sugar, margarine, baking powder, 1 cup flour, and milk. Spoon batter over berries. Combine remaining one-half cup sugar and 1 tablespoon flour. Sprinkle over batter. Pour boiling water over batter and bake for 40-45 minutes. Serve warm with ice cream.

Yield: 6-8 servings

Rita Ladner

Raspberry Delight

1 package frozen raspberries
½ cup lemon juice
1 can sweetened condensed milk
1 (9-inch) graham cracker crust
¼ teaspoon cream of tartar
3 egg whites
6 Tablespoons sugar

Preheat oven to 350 degrees. Thaw berries and drain well. Mix lemon juice and milk until thick. Add drained berries. Place into crust. For meringue: mix cream of tartar into egg whites and beat until stiff, adding sugar gradually. Pile lightly onto pie, sealing edges to crust, and bake until lightly browned. Refrigerate before serving.

Yield: 1 (9-inch) pie

Mrs. Van H. Hardin '37
Holly Monette Hardin '93

This recipe must be a favorite of the Hardin family, as it was submitted by Holly and her grandmother, each without the knowledge of the other.

Nut Torte

1½ cups brown sugar
1½ cups granulated sugar
1½ cups egg whites (6-8 large eggs), room temperature
½ teaspoon cream of tartar
2 Tablespoons vanilla
1¼ cups graham cracker crumbs
1 cup nuts, chopped
1 (16-ounce) carton whipped topping

Preheat oven to 350 degrees. Heavily grease 3 (9-inch) pie tins. Combine both sugars. Beat egg whites, gradually adding cream of tartar until frothy. Gradually add sugar mixture while beating on medium speed. Beat for 25 minutes. Add vanilla during the last few minutes. Fold in graham cracker crumbs and nuts. Spread into prepared pie tins, leaving a slight depression in the center. Bake for about 20 minutes or until brown. Cool. Spread with whipped topping. Pies may be frozen before topping is added. They keep beautifully.

Yield: 3 (9-inch) pies

Morrison's Hospitality Group

Raspberry Chocolate Delight

1 box lite or regular brownie mix
½ gallon raspberry frozen yogurt, softened
45-50 chocolate snack cookies
2 cups fresh or frozen raspberries

Bake brownies in an 8x8 pan according to package directions. Don't overbake. Cool. Spread with frozen yogurt. Crush cookies and sprinkle on top. Freeze. Before serving, thaw slightly and cut into squares. Top with raspberries before serving.

Variation: Substitute strawberry or blueberry for raspberry yogurt and raspberries.

Yield: 12 servings

Brenda Crumpton Sumrall '72

Party Trifle

1 box yellow cake mix or prepared 2-layer yellow cake
1 (3-ounce) box strawberry gelatin
1 (6-ounce) box instant vanilla pudding
1 (16-ounce) carton whipped topping
1 container fresh strawberries or 1 box frozen berries, drained

Prepare cake, gelatin, and pudding as directed on packages. Crumble cake (1 layer at a time), in the bottom of a trifle bowl or any large glass bowl. On top of the first layer of cake, spread 1 layer of vanilla pudding, 1 layer of whipped topping, and 1 layer of strawberries. Continue layering until the container is filled. Garnish with additional berries. Refrigerate overnight to serve the next day.

Yield: 20 servings

Eva Aultman Hart '68, Faculty

Eva Hart is the daughter of Howard H. Aultman, a member of the Mississippi College Board of Trustees, 1956-62, 1963-69, 1971-77.

Chess Squares

2 sticks margarine
1 (1-pound) box light brown sugar
½ cup granulated sugar
4 eggs
1 teaspoon vanilla
2½ cups all-purpose flour
1 teaspoon baking powder
⅛ teaspoon salt
1 cup nuts, chopped
Confectioners' sugar

Preheat oven to 325 degrees. Heat margarine and brown sugar until margarine is melted. Remove from heat and stir in granulated sugar, eggs, and vanilla. Sift flour, baking powder, and salt and add to sugar mixture. Blend well; stir in nuts and pour into a 9x13 pan. Bake for 35 minutes; check for doneness. Cool for 20 minutes. Sprinkle with confectioners' sugar and cut into squares.

Yield: 36 servings

Faye M. Rogers '49

Strawberry Pizza

Crust:
1 cup all-purpose flour
¼ cup confectioners' sugar
½ cup margarine
½ cup pecans, chopped (optional)

Preheat oven to 325 degrees. Cut margarine into flour and sugar. Mix in pecans and press into a 13-inch pizza pan. Bake for 15 minutes. Cool.

Filling:
1 (8-ounce) package cream cheese
½ cup sugar
½ teaspoon vanilla
¼ teaspoon almond flavoring

Beat all together until fluffy and spread over cooled crust.

Topping:
1 jar strawberry glaze

Top crust and filling with strawberry glaze. Spread to cover filling.

Yield: 10-12 servings

Mary Bevill, Staff

Butter or oil the cup before melting chocolate or measuring honey, molasses, or syrup. They will pour faster and leave no residue.

Elegant Chocolate Party Roll

Roll:
6 eggs, separated
6 Tablespoons cocoa
6 Tablespoons sugar
2 teaspoons vanilla

Frosting:
¾ stick margarine
1 (1-pound) box confectioners' sugar
5 Tablespoons cocoa
5 Tablespoons milk
¾ Tablespoon vanilla

Filling:
8 ounces whipped cream or frozen non-dairy topping

Preheat oven to 325 degrees. Grease a 12x16 cookie sheet or jelly roll pan heavily and line with greased wax paper. Beat egg whites until stiff. Beat yolks until lemon-colored; then add cocoa, sugar, and vanilla, beating yolk mixture after each ingredient is added. Fold the 2 mixtures together. Spread out on prepared cookie sheet. Bake for 20-25 minutes. Do not overbake. Check after 15 minutes. Turn out onto a very soft tea towel. Peel off paper and roll up jelly roll style. Allow roll to cool. For frosting, melt margarine in a double boiler and add other ingredients. Stir until smooth. Unroll chocolate roll and spread with whipped cream or frozen topping. Re-roll and frost. Refrigerate until serving time. Slice into ½-inch pieces to serve.

Yield: 24 slices

Jean Harvey '79, Former Faculty Wife

Preheat the oven for at least twenty minutes before baking cakes unless directions specify otherwise.

Miss Nelly Magee's Honeyballs

1 cup shortening
¼ cup honey
2 cups sifted all-purpose flour
½ teaspoon salt
2 teaspoons vanilla
2 cups pecans, finely chopped
Confectioners' sugar

Cream shortening and honey. Sift together flour and salt. Add flour mixture gradually to shortening mixture. Add vanilla and pecans. Blend thoroughly and chill. Preheat oven to 300 degrees.

Form dough into small balls (half a teaspoon size) and place on lightly greased baking sheet. Bake for 25-30 minutes or until lightly browned. Roll in confectioners' sugar while hot. Cool and store in airtight containers. These will keep for a week or more. For longer storage freeze in freezer bags. Thaw at room temperature and re-roll in confectioners' sugar if desired.

Yield: 10 dozen

John P. Rushing '50

Lollypop Cookies

½ cup granulated sugar
½ cup brown sugar, firmly packed
½ cup butter or margarine, softened
½ cup chunky peanut butter
1 teaspoon vanilla
1 egg
1½ cups all-purpose flour
½ teaspoon baking powder
½ teaspoon soda
¼ teaspoon salt
10 wooden sticks (craft sticks or tongue depressors)
10 caramel-peanut fun-size candy bars

Preheat oven to 375 degrees. In large bowl combine sugars, margarine, peanut butter, vanilla, and egg. Beat well. Add flour, baking powder, soda, and salt. Mix well. Securely insert a wooden stick into small end of each candy bar, forming a lollypop. Shape about one-third cup cookie dough smoothly around each candy bar, making sure bar is completely covered. Place 4 inches apart on ungreased cookie sheets. Bake for 13-16 minutes or until golden brown. Cool for 10 minutes (after 1 minute, gently slide stick deeper into cookie to secure it). Remove from sheet and cool completely. These cookies make a wonderful "treat" for children and grandchildren!

Yield: 10 cookies

Nan Laurence Grantham '57

Old-Fashioned Tea Cakes

¾ cup shortening
2 cups sugar
¼ cup milk
2 eggs
2 teaspoons vanilla
4 cups all-purpose flour
3 teaspoons baking powder

Cream shortening and sugar; add eggs to milk and beat well. Stir in vanilla; add milk mixture to shortening and sugar mixture. Sift baking powder with flour and add to mixture. Dough will be stiff and hard to stir. Add more flour if necessary. Chill the dough. Preheat oven to 375 degrees. Roll out half the dough at a time on a well-floured board, about ⅛-inch thick. Cut with floured cookie cutter and place on greased cookie sheet. Bake for 10 minutes. Cookies are done when edges are light brown. Do not overcook. Remove to wire racks to cool.

Yield: 4 dozen

Hazle Dean Jackson Morton '29, Hillman

Sara's Teacakes

2 sticks margarine
1½ cups sugar
2 eggs
1 teaspoon vanilla
3 cups all-purpose flour
Food coloring (optional)

With mixer, cream margarine and sugar, add eggs, vanilla, and food coloring; mix well. Add 2 cups flour, 1 cup at a time, mixing with mixer. Add 3rd cup of flour, stirring by hand. Add additional flour if needed until mixture has soft dough consistency. Do not add too much flour! Roll into ball, wrap in wax paper, and chill for 3-4 hours or overnight. Preheat oven to 400 degrees. Roll out on floured board and cut with well-floured cookie cutters. Bake on lightly greased cookie sheet for 8-10 minutes. These cookies may be made in appropriate colors and shapes for each season or special occasion.

Yield: 4 dozen

Mary Carol Criss Miller '75

Easy Dropped Tea Cakes

2 cups self-rising flour
1 cup sugar
½ cup butter or margarine
2 eggs, lightly beaten
1 teaspoon vanilla
Sugar

Preheat oven to 350 degrees. Mix all ingredients thoroughly with mixer. Drop by teaspoonsful onto greased cookie sheet and sprinkle with sugar. Bake for approximately 8-10 minutes.

Yield: 5 dozen

Jimmy Shows '92

7-Layer Bars

1 stick margarine, melted
2 cups graham cracker crumbs
1 cup coconut
1 (6-ounce) package butterscotch chips
1 (6-ounce) package semi-sweet chocolate chips
1 can sweetened condensed milk
1 cup unsalted nuts, chopped

Preheat oven to 350 degrees. Pour margarine into a 9x13 pan; sprinkle graham cracker crumbs evenly in the pan. Next sprinkle coconut over crumbs; add butterscotch chips, then a layer of chocolate chips. Cover with condensed milk and top with nuts. Bake for 25-30 minutes.

Yield: 18-20 servings

Maida Wright

Chewy Walnut Squares

1 egg, unbeaten
1 cup light brown sugar, packed
1 teaspoon vanilla
½ cup all-purpose flour
¼ teaspoon baking powder
¼ teaspoon soda
1 cup walnuts, chopped

Preheat oven to 350 degrees. Grease or spray an 8-inch square pan. Stir together egg, sugar, and vanilla. Quickly stir in flour, baking powder, and soda. Add nuts. Bake for 18-20 minutes. Cool in pan. Cut into 2-inch squares.

Yield: 16 servings

Ernestine M. Daniel, Staff

Chocolate-Caramel Squares

1¾ cups all-purpose flour, divided
1½ cups rolled oats
¾ cup brown sugar
½ teaspoon salt
¾ cup margarine, melted
1 (6-ounce) package semi-sweet chocolate chips
1 (12-ounce) jar caramel topping

Preheat oven to 375 degrees. Combine 1½ cups flour, oats, brown sugar and salt. Add margarine and mix until crumbly. Reserve three-fourths cup of crumb mixture for topping. Press remaining mixture into a greased 9x13 pan. Bake for 10 minutes. Sprinkle reserved crumb mixture over caramel mixture and continue baking for 20 minutes. Cool thoroughly. Chill for a few minutes to set chocolate. Cut into bars.

Yield: 24 bars

Ann Harding Drane '76

Lemon Squares

½ cup butter
¼ cup confectioners' sugar
1 cup plus 2 Tablespoons all-purpose flour, divided
¼ teaspoon salt, divided
2 eggs, slightly beaten
2 Tablespoons lemon juice
½ teaspoon baking powder
1 cup granulated sugar
⅛ teaspoon lemon rind, grated

Lemon Glaze:
2 Tablespoons lemon juice
¾ cup confectioners' sugar
1 Tablespoon butter or margarine, melted

Preheat oven to 350 degrees. Combine butter, confectioners' sugar, 1 cup flour, and ⅛ teaspoon salt; blend until smooth. Pat dough into a lightly greased 8-inch square pan. Bake for 15 minutes. Set aside. Combine eggs, lemon juice, baking powder, granulated sugar, and ⅛ teaspoon salt and mix until blended. Pour over crust; bake for 25 minutes. Lemon Glaze: Combine lemon juice, confectioners' sugar, and butter; mix until smooth. Brush the glaze over lemon layer while warm. Cut into squares.

Yield: 16 (2-inch) squares

Lee E. Harding '73, Faculty

Date Squares

3 eggs, beaten
1 cup sugar
1 teaspoon vanilla
1½ cups all-purpose flour, sifted
1 teaspoon baking powder
½ teaspoon salt
1 cup pecans, chopped
1½ cups dates, chopped
Flour for dredging
Confectioners' sugar, sifted

Preheat oven to 325 degrees. Beat eggs and sugar together. Add vanilla. Sift flour, baking powder, and salt together and add to egg mixture. Mix the nuts and dates with some flour and add last. Spread in a greased 8-inch square pan and bake for about 20-25 minutes. When done, cut into squares while hot and roll in confectioners' sugar. These will keep for 4-5 weeks if stored in a cool, dry place.

Yield: 24 servings

Kathleen Martin, Staff

Apricot Squares

¾ cup margarine
1 cup sugar
1 egg
2 cups all-purpose flour
½ teaspoon baking powder
¼ teaspoon salt
1 (12-ounce) jar apricot preserves
1 cup flaked coconut

Preheat oven to 350 degrees. Mix margarine and sugar with fork; add egg and continue to mix with fork. Sift together flour, baking powder, and salt and add to margarine mixture. Press two-thirds of the mixture into a 9x13 pan. Spread over this mixture apricot preserves. Add flaked coconut to remaining one-third of the crumb mixture; sprinkle over apricot layer. Bake for 35 minutes. Cool for 2 hours before cutting into squares.

Yield: 24 small servings

Nan M. Sibley '56, Staff

Orange Slice Bars

4 eggs, beaten
1 (1-pound) box brown sugar
1 teaspoon vanilla
1 cup pecans, chopped
1 pound orange slice candy, cut up
2 cups all-purpose flour
½ teaspoon salt

Preheat oven to 350 degrees. To beaten eggs add sugar and mix well. Stir in vanilla, nuts, and cut-up orange slices, mixing well. Add flour and salt. Mix very well. Spread in a 9x13 pan. Bake for 30 minutes.

Yield: 2 dozen

Elizabeth Lee '91

Almond-Brown Sugar Bars

½ cup plus 3 Tablespoons butter, divided, softened
½ cup confectioners' sugar
1 cup all-purpose flour, sifted
1½ cups light brown sugar, packed
1 Tablespoon water
¾ teaspoon lemon juice
¾ cup almonds, sliced
¾ teaspoon vanilla

Preheat oven to 350 degrees. Cream one-half cup butter and confectioners' sugar. Add flour and mix well. Pat into ungreased 9x9x2 baking pan. Bake for 12-15 minutes. Melt remaining 3 tablespoons butter in saucepan. Add brown sugar, water, and lemon juice and heat to boiling, stirring constantly. Remove from heat; add almonds and vanilla. Spread over baked crust. Bake for an additional 15-20 minutes. Cut into bars while warm.

Yield: 12 servings

Jill Baker, Faculty Wife

Brown quick-cooking oats in a little margarine or butter and use as a substitute for chopped nuts in cookie recipes.

Easy Brownies

1½ cups self-rising flour
2 cups granulated sugar
8-10 Tablespoons cocoa (maximum amount for "chocaholics")
1 cup oil
4 eggs
1 teaspoon vanilla
Confectioners' sugar

Preheat oven to 350 degrees. Thoroughly blend flour, sugar, and cocoa. Add remaining ingredients, and stir until blended. Bake in a 9x13 pan for 25-28 minutes. Do Not Overbake. Sift confectioners' sugar on top of warm brownies. Cut into squares.

Variations: Add 1 cup chopped pecans or 1 cup chocolate chips.

Yield: 24 small servings

Patricia Hasselman '68

Turtle Brownies

1 (14-ounce) bag caramels
⅔ cup evaporated milk, divided
1 box regular German chocolate cake mix
¾ cup butter or margarine, softened
1 cup pecans, chopped
1 (6-ounce) package milk chocolate chips

Preheat oven to 350 degrees. Combine caramels and one-third cup evaporated milk in top of double boiler; cook, stirring constantly, until the caramels are completely melted. Remove from heat. Combine cake mix, remaining one-third cup milk, and butter, mixing with electric mixer until dough holds together. Stir in pecans. Press half of cake mixture into a greased 9x13 baking pan. Bake for 6 minutes. Sprinkle chocolate chips over crust. Pour caramel mixture over chips, spreading evenly. Crumble remaining cake mixture over the caramel mixture. Return pan to oven and bake for 15-18 minutes. Cool for 30 minutes. Cut into small bars.

Yield: Approximately 4 dozen

Patti Guyton Nuermberger '58
Mary Alta Jackson Clark '71

The Ultimate Chocolate Bar

Base:
½ cup margarine or butter
1 (1-ounce) square unsweetened chocolate
1 cup sugar
1 cup all-purpose flour
1 teaspoon baking powder
1 teaspoon vanilla
2 eggs
½ cup nuts, chopped

Filling:
1 (8-ounce) package cream cheese, softened (reserve 2 ounces for frosting)
¼ cup margarine or butter, softened
½ cup sugar
2 Tablespoons all-purpose flour
1 egg
½ teaspoon vanilla

Frosting:
2 cups miniature marshmallows
⅓ cup margarine or butter
⅓ cup milk, warmed
2 (1-ounce) squares unsweetened chocolate
Reserved 2 ounces cream cheese
4 cups confectioners' sugar
1 teaspoon vanilla

Preheat oven to 350 degrees. Grease and lightly flour a 9x13 pan. In large saucepan, melt margarine and chocolate over low heat. Remove from heat and stir in remaining base ingredients, mixing well after each. Spread in prepared pan. In small bowl, combine all filling ingredients. Beat for 1 minute at medium speed until smooth and fluffy. Spread over chocolate mixture. Bake for 25-30 minutes. Sprinkle with marshmallows during the last 2 minutes of baking time. While brownie is baking, melt margarine, chocolate squares, and reserved cream cheese over low heat. Add warm milk and remove from heat. Add vanilla and confectioners' sugar; blend well. Immediately pour over marshmallows and swirl together. Chill until firm; cut into bars. Store in refrigerator.

Yield: 36 bars

Johnnie Harper, Faculty Wife

Incredible Disappearing Brownies

Brownie:

4 (1-ounce) squares unsweetened chocolate
1¼ cups sugar
3 large eggs
6 Tablespoons unsalted butter, softened
2 teaspoons vanilla
½ cup all-purpose flour

Walnut Layer:

4 Tablespoons unsalted butter
½ cup light brown sugar, firmly packed
¼ cup sugar
2½ cups walnuts, chopped
2 large eggs
3 Tablespoons all-purpose flour
1 Tablespoon vanilla

Glaze:

½ cup unsalted butter
4 (1-ounce) squares semi-sweet chocolate

Melt chocolate in the top of a double boiler over simmering water and cool. Mix sugar, eggs, and butter until light and fluffy. Stir in cooled chocolate, vanilla, and flour. Pour batter into a buttered 9-inch square pan and spread evenly. Place brownie layer in freezer for at least 1 hour. This will keep the brownie and walnut layers separate. For walnut layer: preheat oven to 325 degrees. Melt butter in a small pan. Add both sugars and cook over high heat, stirring often until sugar is completely dissolved, about 2 minutes. Add walnuts, eggs, flour, and vanilla. Mix just until blended. Remove brownie layer from freezer and spread walnut mixture evenly on top. Bake for about 45 minutes or until a toothpick inserted in the center comes out with moist but not wet crumbs. Cool on wire rack. For glaze: melt butter and chocolate in the top of a double boiler. Cook until thickened slightly, then pour over cooled brownies. Refrigerate for at least 4 hours or up to 5 days before serving. Cut into squares and serve chilled. This may be frozen, if wrapped well, for several months.

Yield: 16 servings

June Campbell (Richard E. Campbell '50)

Outstanding Oatmeal Cookies

2 sticks butter or margarine
¾ cup brown sugar
¾ cup granulated sugar
2 large eggs
1 teaspoon vanilla
1½ cups all-purpose flour
1 teaspoon soda
1 teaspoon salt
2 cups uncooked oatmeal
1 cup nuts, chopped

Preheat oven to 350 degrees. Cream margarine and the sugars; add eggs and vanilla and beat well. Sift flour, soda, and salt and add to creamed mixture. Mix well. Stir in oatmeal and nuts by hand. Drop by teaspoonsful onto ungreased cookie sheet. Bake for 10-15 minutes. Gently lift each cookie and leave on the cookie sheet until cool.

Variation: Substitute one-half cup shortening for 1 stick butter. Increase brown sugar and granulated sugar to 1 cup each. Increase flour to 2 cups. Add one-half teaspoon baking powder and decrease salt to one-half teaspoon. Add 1 (12-ounce) package chocolate chips. Mix and bake as directed above.

Yield: 3 dozen large cookies or 6 dozen small cookies

Mella Joan Gentry Tarbet '74
Cynthia Lee Elgin Perry '85

Chocolate-Oatmeal Cookies

2 cups butter
2 cups granulated sugar
2 cups brown sugar
4 eggs
2 teaspoons vanilla
4 cups all-purpose flour
5 cups oatmeal, ground to fine powder
1 teaspoon salt
2 teaspoons baking powder
2 teaspoons soda
1 (24-ounce) package chocolate chips
1 (8-ounce) chocolate bar, crushed or chopped
3 cups nuts, chopped

Preheat oven to 375 degrees. Cream butter and sugars. Add eggs and vanilla. Mix together with flour, oatmeal, salt, baking powder, and soda. Add chocolate chips, chocolate bar, and nuts. Roll into balls and place 2 inches apart on a cookie sheet. Bake for 10 minutes.

Yield: 112 cookies (recipe may be halved)

Emma Ruth Smith Everett (Wilbourne Everett '42)
Connie B. Evans, Staff

Almond Bark and Cherry Drop Cookies

1 cup all-purpose flour
1 teaspoon baking powder
¼ teaspoon salt
½ cup butter or margarine, softened
½ cup granulated sugar
⅓ cup brown sugar, firmly packed
1 egg
1½ cups pecans, chopped
6 ounces almond bark, coarsely chopped
½ cup maraschino cherries, quartered
1 teaspoon vanilla

Preheat oven to 350 degrees. Lightly grease 2 cookie sheets. In medium bowl, combine flour, baking powder, and salt. In mixing bowl, cream butter, sugars, and egg until light and fluffy. Beat in flour mixture. Stir in pecans, almond bark, cherries, and vanilla. Drop by teaspoonsful, 2 inches apart, onto prepared cookie sheets. Bake for 12-15 minutes, until golden. Cool on cookie sheets for 5 minutes then transfer to wire racks to cool.

Yield: 3-4 dozen

Penny E. Pollard '87

Holiday Hunks

1 cup butter, softened
1½ cups sugar
3 eggs
1 teaspoon soda
2 Tablespoons hot water
3 cups all-purpose flour
1 teaspoon cinnamon
1 teaspoon ground cloves
1 pound pecans, chopped
1 pound raisins
1 pound dates, chopped
½ cup maraschino cherries, chopped

Preheat oven to 350 degrees. Mix butter and sugar until creamy. Add eggs. Dissolve soda in hot water and add to mixture. Mix in flour and spices. Stir in nuts and fruits. Drop teaspoon-size hunks onto greased cookie sheet. Bake for 7-10 minutes for chewy cookies, 10-12 minutes for crispy cookies.

Yields: 8-10 dozen cookies

Lucy A. Felder '64, Faculty Wife

Chewy Coconut Bars

1 cup all-purpose flour, sifted
½ teaspoon salt
1½ cups dark brown sugar, divided
½ cup shortening
2 eggs, beaten
2 Tablespoons all-purpose flour
½ teaspoon baking powder
1½ cups flaked coconut
1 cup nuts, coarsely chopped

Preheat oven to 375 degrees. Sift flour and salt together into bowl. Add one-half cup brown sugar and blend thoroughly. Cut in shortening with pastry blender. Spread mixture into a 9x13 baking pan. Bake for 10 minutes until lightly browned. Combine eggs, 1 cup brown sugar, and vanilla. Add 2 tablespoons flour, baking powder, coconut, and nuts. Blend well. Spread over baked mixture. Return to oven and bake for 15-20 minutes longer. Cool. Cut into bars.

Yield: 3 dozen bars

Marion Toler Hewitt, Faculty Wife (F. D. Hewitt, Jr. '31)

Crescent Cream Cheese Bars

2 large packages crescent rolls
2 (8-ounce) packages cream cheese
1 cup sugar
1 teaspoon vanilla
1 egg

Topping:
½ cup sugar
1 teaspoon cinnamon
½ cup nuts, chopped

Preheat oven to 350 degrees. In a 9x13 pan, place 1 package crescent rolls. Flatten in bottom of pan. Mix and beat cream cheese, sugar, egg yolk, and vanilla. Spread over top. Place second layer of crescent rolls over mixture. Spread slightly beaten egg white over dough. Mix topping ingredients and sprinkle over dough. Bake for 30 minutes.

Yield: 10-12 servings

Missy Hutto '91

Meringues

2 egg whites
⅛ teaspoon salt
¼ teaspoon cream of tartar
¼ cup sugar
1 (6-ounce) package chocolate chips
1 teaspoon vanilla

Preheat oven to 350 degrees for 15 minutes. Beat egg whites, until frothy; add salt and cream of tartar. Gradually add sugar and continue to beat for 15 minutes. Fold in chocolate chips and vanilla. Drop by teaspoonsful onto ungreased cookie sheet (turn off oven). Place cookies in oven for 1½ hours. Do not open oven door during cooking time.

Yield: 4 dozen

Carroll Waller '48

Molasses Cookies

¼ cup sorghum molasses
¾ cup oil
1 egg
1 cup sugar
2 cups all-purpose flour
2 teaspoons soda
½ teaspoon salt
½ teaspoon ginger
1 teaspoon cinnamon
Sugar

Preheat oven to 350 degrees. Lightly grease a cookie sheet. Add molasses to oil. Mix egg and sugar and add to oil and molasses. Sift flour, soda, salt, ginger, and cinnamon. Add to mixture, stir and chill. Form dough into small balls and dip in sugar. Place on cookie sheet and bake for about 8 minutes.

Yield: 2½-3 dozen

Mrs. Gowan Ellis (Gowan '57)

Mix several batches of different varieties of cookie dough; shape into cookies and freeze on cookie sheets. When they are frozen hard, store in plastic zipper freezer bags up to three months. When hot, fresh-baked cookies are needed, place a desired number and varieties on a cookie sheet and bake, adding three minutes to the normal cooking time.

Chocolate Raisin Cookies

½ cup shortening
½ cup brown sugar
¼ cup granulated sugar
1 egg
½ teaspoon vanilla
1 cup plus 2 Tablespoons all-purpose flour
½ teaspoon salt
½ teaspoon soda
1 cup chocolate covered raisins
½ cup pecans, chopped

Preheat oven to 350 degrees. Combine shortening and sugars. Beat until smooth. Add egg and vanilla and beat until blended. Gradually add flour, salt and soda. Stir in chocolate covered raisins and nuts. Drop by tablespoonful onto greased cookie sheet. Bake for 10-12 minutes.

Yield: 2 dozen

Sherry Rhodes '68

Best Ever Sugar Cookies

1 cup granulated sugar
1 cup confectioners' sugar
1 cup butter or margarine (or ½ cup each)
1 cup oil
2 eggs, beaten
2 teaspoons vanilla
5 cups all-purpose flour, sifted
1 teaspoon soda
1 teaspoon cream of tartar
¼ teaspoon salt

Preheat oven to 350 degrees. Cream together the sugars and butter. Blend in oil, eggs, and vanilla. Sift dry ingredients together, add to mixture and mix well. Roll into balls about the size of a small walnut. Place an inch apart on a greased cookies sheet. Press with the bottom of a glass dipped in sugar. Bake for about 10 minutes. Watch carefully. For best flavor use ½ cup butter and ½ cup margarine.

Yield: 100 cookies

Lola Weaver Waldrip '53
Annie Ruth McPhail, Faculty Wife (Hartwell McPhail '41)

Cookies will remain soft and fresh if a slice of bread is stored with them in a cookie jar.

Honey Ozark Oatmeal Cookies

½ cup shortening, regular or butter flavor
1¼ cups sugar
2 eggs
⅓ cup honey
1 teaspoon vanilla
1 teaspoon soda
1 teaspoon salt
1¾ cups unsifted all-purpose flour
2 cups quick oatmeal
1 cup flaked coconut
½ cup raisins (optional)

Preheat oven to 375 degrees. Cream shortening, sugar, eggs, honey, vanilla, soda, and salt thoroughly on medium speed of an electric mixer. Stir in remaining ingredients. Drop by teaspoonsful onto an ungreased cookie sheet. Bake for 5-8 minutes.

Yield: 4 dozen

Beth Henry '87

Cream Cheese Cookies

Cookie:
¼ cup margarine
1 (8-ounce) package cream cheese
1 egg yolk
1 teaspoon vanilla
1 box white cake mix

Icing:
¼ cup margarine
1 (3-ounce) package cream cheese
½ (1-pound) box confectioners' sugar
½ teaspoon vanilla

Cookie: Blend margarine and cream cheese until creamy. Add egg yolk and vanilla and mix well. Add one-third of cake mix and beat with mixer; add another third and beat. Add final third of cake mix and blend with spoon instead of mixer. Chill for 30-60 minutes. Preheat oven to 375 degrees. Form dough into balls and place onto ungreased cookie sheet. Bake for 12-15 minutes until the bottoms of the cookies just begin to brown. Let cool and remove from cookie sheet. Icing: Blend margarine and cream cheese. Add enough confectioners' sugar to make icing the right consistency. Add vanilla and blend well. Spread on tops of cookies.

Yield: 3 dozen

Nancy Tillotson Evans '72

Secret Kiss Cookies

1 cup butter or margarine, softened
½ cup sugar
1 teaspoon vanilla
2 cups sifted all-purpose flour
1 cup nuts, chopped fine
48 chocolate kisses
Confectioners' sugar

At medium speed beat sugar and vanilla until light and fluffy. Add flour and nuts; beat on low speed until well blended. Chill dough. Using approximately 1 tablespoon of dough, shape around an individual chocolate kiss and roll to make a ball. Be sure to cover kiss completely. Place on ungreased cookie sheet. Bake for 12 minutes or until cookies are set but not brown. Cool slightly. Roll in confectioners' sugar. Store in tightly covered container. Roll in sugar again before serving, if desired.

Yield: 4 dozen

Rosalee Hayden Meredith '45

Peanut Butter-Chocolate Kiss Cookies

½ cup shortening
½ cup peanut butter
¾ cup sugar, divided
½ cup brown sugar, firmly packed
1 egg
2 Tablespoons milk
1 teaspoon vanilla
1¾ cups all-purpose flour
1 teaspoon soda
½ teaspoon salt
48 chocolate kisses

Preheat oven to 350 degrees. Cream shortening and peanut butter. Gradually add one-half cup granulated sugar and brown sugar, beating until light and fluffy. Add egg, milk, and vanilla. Beat well. Combine flour, soda, and salt. Add to creamed mixture. Roll dough into 1-inch balls, then roll in ¼ cup granulated sugar. Place balls 2 inches apart on a lightly greased cookie sheet. Bake for 8 minutes. Remove from oven, press a chocolate kiss into the center of each cookie. Return to oven for an additional 2 minutes or until lightly browned. Cool slightly and remove from cookie sheet.

Yield: 4 dozen

Natasha Shirley Griffis '85

Nutty Fingers

½ cup shortening
½ cup butter
½ cup confectioners' sugar
2 teaspoons vanilla
2 Tablespoons water
2 cups all-purpose flour
1 cup pecans, chopped
Confectioners' sugar

Cream shortening, butter, and one-half cup confectioners' sugar in a large bowl. Add vanilla and water. Mix well. Blend in flour; add chopped pecans and mix well. Chill dough until hard. When ready to bake, preheat oven to 350 degrees. Shape dough into fingers and place onto ungreased cookie sheet 2 inches apart. Bake for 20 minutes or until golden brown. Coat with the confectioners' sugar. Cool and store in a plastic box or tin, separating each layer with foil, wax paper, or plastic wrap. Freeze, if desired. Do not store with other cookies.

Yield: 3 dozen

Leigh H. Rudacille '61
Gayle McGee Knight '68
Annette Daniels '93

No-Bake Cookies

2 cups sugar
1 stick butter
½ cup milk
¼ cup cocoa
½ cup peanut butter, regular or crunchy
3 cups uncooked oatmeal
1 teaspoon vanilla

Combine sugar, butter, milk, and cocoa in a saucepan. Bring mixture to boil over medium heat. Remove from heat and let stand for 1 minute. Add peanut butter, oatmeal, and vanilla to this mixture. Mix well and drop by teaspoonsful onto wax paper.

Yield: 3 dozen

Beth Hendrix Green '82
Christopher Allard '89

Deluxe Pound Cake

Cake:

1½ cups shortening
2¾ cups sugar
5 large eggs
1 cup milk
1 teaspoon rum flavoring
1 teaspoon coconut flavoring
½ teaspoon almond flavoring
3 cups cake flour
1 teaspoon salt
½ teaspoon baking powder

Preheat oven to 325 degrees. Cream sugar and shortening until smooth. Add eggs 1 at a time. Add flavorings to milk. Sift baking powder and salt with flour. Add flour and milk mixtures alternately to the creamed mixture. Pour batter into a greased and floured large tube cake pan and cook for 1½ hours.

Glaze:

½ cup sugar
¼ cup water
½ teaspoon almond flavoring

Bring sugar and water to a boil; boil for approximately 2 minutes, then add flavoring. With wooden pick, punch holes in hot cake and spread glaze on top of cake. Cool in pan for 20 minutes.

Yield: 16-20 servings

Annie Ruth McPhail, Faculty Wife (Hartwell McPhail '41)

Quick Sour Cream Pound Cake

1 box yellow butter cake mix
½ cup sugar
4 eggs
1 (8-ounce) carton sour cream
1 cup oil

Preheat oven to 350 degrees. Grease Bundt pan or tube pan. Mix all ingredients, pour into pan and bake for 55-60 minutes. This freezes well and keeps well in refrigerator.

Yield: 16-20 servings

Peggy Rae Dorris '56

Cream Cheese Pound Cake

1 cup butter, softened
1 (8-ounce) package cream cheese, softened
3 cups sugar
6 eggs
3 cups all-purpose flour
¼ teaspoon soda
¾ teaspoon lemon flavoring
1½ teaspoons vanilla

Preheat oven to 325 degrees. Grease and flour a 10-inch Bundt pan. Cream butter and cream cheese until well blended. Gradually add sugar. Beat at medium speed for 5-7 minutes. Add eggs 1 at a time, beating just until yellow disappears. Sift together flour and soda. Beating at low speed, gradually add flour mixture to creamed mixture, mixing well after each addition. Stir in lemon and vanilla flavorings. Spoon thick batter into prepared Bundt pan. Bake for 1 hour 20 minutes or until wooden pick inserted in middle pulls out clean. Cool in pan for 10 minutes.

Yield: 16-20 servings

Robin Lackey '91

Peach Pound Cake

1 cup butter or margarine, softened
3 cups sugar
6 eggs, room temperature
3 cups all-purpose flour
¼ teaspoon soda
¾ teaspoon salt
½ cup sour cream, room temperature
2 cups peaches, peeled and finely chopped
1 teaspoon vanilla
½-1 teaspoon almond flavoring

Preheat oven to 350 degrees. Grease and flour a 10-inch tube or Bundt pan or 2 loaf pans (9x5). Cream butter and sugar together until light and fluffy. Add eggs 1 at a time mixing after each. Combine flour, soda, and salt in a separate bowl; set aside. Mix sour cream and peaches together. Add dry ingredients alternately with sour cream/peach mixture to creamed ingredients. Stir in flavoring. Bake in prepared tube or Bundt pan for 70-80 minutes or in loaf pans for 1 hour. Remove from pans to cooling rack. Dust with confectioners' sugar, if desired.

Yield: 16-20 servings

LaVerne Walton Fountain '38

Lemon Poppy Seed Cake

1 box lemon cake mix
1 (3½-ounce) box instant lemon pudding and pie filling
½ cup sifted all-purpose flour
1½ cups water
½ (pint) carton egg substitute (or 4 egg whites)
2 Tablespoons poppy seed
Confectioners' sugar (optional)

Preheat oven to 350 degrees. Spray Bundt pan with non-stick vegetable spray. Mix cake mix, pudding mix, and flour. Add water and egg substitute. Beat at high speed for 2 minutes. Fold in poppy seed. Pour into pan and bake for 30-35 minutes or until cake tests done. Let cool in pan for 10 minutes before turning onto cake plate. Sprinkle with confectioners' sugar, if desired.

Yield: 16-20 servings

Rowena Gunter Falwell '34, Hillman

Strawberry Cake Supreme

2 (10-ounce) boxes sliced frozen strawberries ***or*** **3 pints fresh strawberries plus ½ cup sugar**
1 box white cake mix
3 cups heavy cream
⅓ cup sugar
1 teaspoon vanilla

If using fresh strawberries, prepare by slicing the berries lengthwise and adding one-half cup sugar. Fresh berries should be prepared 2 hours before baking cake. Bake cake according to package directions for layer cake. Let cake cool. Whip cream very stiff with sugar and vanilla. Put berries on first layer, letting juice seep into cake. Cover with whipped cream. Repeat process with the second layer. Frost rest of cake with remaining whipped cream.

Yield: 16 servings

Ethelyn Mayfield (Clifton Mayfield '49)

Blueberry Cake

3 eggs
½ cup oil
1 (8-ounce) package cream cheese
1 box butter cake mix
1 (15-ounce) can blueberries, drained
1 cup pecans, chopped fine

Do not preheat oven. Grease and flour tube pan. Beat eggs, oil, and cream cheese. Add cake mix; mix well. Stir in blueberries and pecans. Bake at 350 degrees for 40-45 minutes.

Yield: 16-20 servings

Pauline Greer Corban '52

Date Cake

1 cup flour
1 teaspoon salt
2 teaspoons baking powder
3 (8-ounce) packages dates, chopped
4 cups pecans, chopped
4 whole eggs (beaten lightly)
1 cup sugar
1 teaspoon vanilla

Preheat oven to 300 degrees. Mix flour, salt, and baking powder. Mix with dates and pecans, coating dates thoroughly. Mix eggs, sugar, and vanilla. Add to date mixture. Pour mixture into tube pan. Cook, covered loosely, in shallow water bath (an iron skillet works well) for about 2 hours and 15 minutes, until firm.

Yield: 16-20 servings

Pauline May (A. E. May '35)

Lemon Cream Cake

1 box lemon cake mix
1 can sweetened condensed milk
½ cup lemon juice
1 (12-ounce) carton extra creamy whipped topping

Coat 2 (9-inch) cake pans with non-stick vegetable spray. Prepare cake according to package directions. Let cool and slice each layer to make 4 layers. Mix milk and lemon juice well. Add whipped topping to the mixture and mix well. Spread mixture between layers and on top. Cover cake and refrigerate for 8 hours before serving. This cake may be frozen.

Yield: 16-20 servings

Jeanette B. Dunaway (Bob Dunaway '61), Staff

Holiday Cake

1 box white cake mix
2 (3-ounce) boxes gelatin, different flavors
1 cup hot water for each gelatin
1 (16-ounce) container whipped topping
Colored sprinkles or small holiday candies (optional)

Make cake in 2 layers according to package directions. When cake is done, cool slightly, and refrigerate for an hour. Turn layers out onto separate plates; dissolve each gelatin package in 1 cup hot water. Allow gelatin mixtures to cool completely. Using an ice pick, poke holes in each layer of cake. Pour one color cooled gelatin onto each layer. Refrigerate until set enough to be handled. Stack layers and cover with whipped topping. Cake may be decorated with sprinkles or candies, if desired. At Christmas, use red and green; Easter, use yellow and green; Halloween, use yellow and orange; Valentine's Day, use red and white (using gelatin just for the red layer).

Yield: 16-20 servings

Richard DeLoss Copeland '68

Coconut Cake

1 box yellow cake mix
1 can sweetened condensed milk
1 (8-ounce) can cream of coconut
1 (16-ounce) container whipped topping
1 (7-ounce) can flaked coconut

Make cake according to package directions, using a 9x13 pan. While cake is hot punch holes in top with ice pick. Mix condensed milk with cream of coconut and pour over hot cake. Let cake cool. Spread whipped topping on top and sprinkle coconut on surface. Cover and store in refrigerator.

Yield: 12 servings

Mrs. Henry A. Carlock (Mary) '59, Faculty Wife

Chocolate Sheet Cake

2 cups all-purpose flour
½ teaspoon salt
2 cups sugar
1 stick margarine
½ cup shortening
3 Tablespoons cocoa
1 cup water
2 eggs, beaten
½ cup buttermilk
1 teaspoon soda
1 teaspoon vanilla

Chocolate Sheet Cake Icing
1½ sticks margarine
1½ (1-ounce) squares unsweetened chocolate
⅓ cup warm milk
1½ teaspoons vanilla
1½ (1-pound) boxes confectioners' sugar, sifted
Miniature marshmallows
¾ cup pecans, chopped and toasted

Preheat oven to 375 degrees. Line bottom and sides of a 15x10x1 pan with brown paper and grease. Sift together flour, salt, and sugar. Combine in a saucepan margarine, shortening, cocoa, and water and bring to boil. Pour the hot mixture over the flour mixture and mix well. Add eggs, buttermilk, soda, and vanilla. Mix to blend. Pour batter into prepared pan and bake for 15-20 minutes. While cake is baking prepare icing. For icing: melt together margarine and chocolate; add milk and vanilla. Beat in sifted sugar and keep warm over hot water in double boiler until cake is done. Turn sheet cake out onto tray; while warm sprinkle top with marshmallows and pecans. Pour icing slowly over cake, marshmallows and nuts.

Yield: 12-16 servings

Henry Hederman '42, served as a member of the Mississippi College Board of Trustees, 1985-88, 1988-91.

To reduce fat in many cakes and muffins, substitute an equal amount of applesauce for the oil or shortening. Experiment with amounts to achieve the texture desired.

Chocolate Chip Cake

1 box yellow deluxe cake mix
1 (8-ounce) carton sour cream
4 eggs
½ cup oil
½ cup water
1 (3½-ounce) box instant chocolate pudding
1 (6-ounce) package milk chocolate chips

Preheat oven to 350 degrees. Grease and flour a Bundt pan. Mix cake mix, sour cream, eggs, oil, water, and pudding together and beat for 6 minutes. Fold in chocolate chips. Pour into a prepared Bundt pan and bake for 50 minutes.

Yield: 16-20 servings

Sue Epting Lee '39

Sue Lee is the wife of Roy Noble Lee '38, who has served as a member of the Mississippi College Board of Trustees, 1967-73, 1974-80, 1984-90, 1991- .

Amalgamation Cake

1 box white cake mix
8 egg yolks, beaten lightly
1 cup butter or margarine
2 cups sugar
1 cup pecans, chopped
1 cup English walnuts, chopped
1 cup coconut
1 (15-ounce) box raisins, chopped

Prepare cake mix according to package directions, making 3 (9-inch) layers. Cool thoroughly. Filling: In double boiler, combine egg yolks, butter or margarine, and sugar. Cook, stirring until thick. Pour over pecans, walnuts, coconut, and raisins. Stir thoroughly. Spread between layers and on sides of cake. Cake is best when made ahead.

Yield: 16-20 servings

Martha Rackley Rodgers '49

Rich Layer Fruitcake

2 cups sugar
1 cup butter or margarine
3 eggs, beaten well
1 cup buttermilk
1 teaspoon soda
1 cup blackberry jam
1 Tablespoon allspice
3 cups flour
1 cup pecans, chopped
1 cup raisins, chopped
1½ cups grated coconut

Preheat oven to 350 degrees. Grease and flour 3 (9-inch) cake pans. Cream sugar and butter well. Add eggs, buttermilk (with soda dissolved in it), jam, spice, flour, pecans, raisins, and coconut. Mix well after each addition. Bake layers for 30-35 minutes or until done; cool. The cake may be baked up to 30 days before using. Fill with Fruitcake Filling, page 289.

Yield: 24 servings

Nell Porter Ratliff

This recipe appeared in Holland Magazine December, 1939.

Japanese Fruitcake

1 cup butter or margarine
2 cups sugar
4 eggs
3 cups all-purpose flour
½ teaspoon salt
1 teaspoon each: cinnamon, allspice, cloves, nutmeg and soda
1 cup raisins, chopped
1 cup pecans, chopped
1 cup buttermilk
Nuts for garnish (optional)

Preheat oven to 300 degrees. Grease 3 (9-inch) pans, dust with flour. Cream butter and sugar together; add eggs, 1 at a time, beating well after each addition. Sift dry ingredients together. Alternately add flour mixture and buttermilk to butter mixture. Dredge raisins and pecans in flour. Stir into batter. Pour into prepared pans and bake for 1 hour or until cake leaves sides of pan. Fill with Fruitcake Coconut Filling, page 290. The cake may be garnished with chopped nuts. It freezes well.

Yield: 16-20 servings

Mrs. (M.D.) Katherine Crouch

Mama Griffis' No-Bake Fruitcake

1 pound graham crackers, crushed
½ pound candied cherries (red and green)
½ pound candied pineapple
1 cup white raisins
1 pound pecans, chopped
1 (7-ounce) can flaked coconut
1 pound marshmallows (cut into pieces)
¾ pound butter (no substitutes)
1 cup mixed candied fruit

Mix graham cracker crumbs with candied cherries and pineapple, raisins, pecans, and coconut. Melt butter and marshmallows together. Add to crumb mixture. Pack into 2 loaf pans lined with wax paper. Decorate with mixed candied fruit. Refrigerate until ready to cut and serve.

Yield: 16-20 servings

Tim '86 and Natasha Griffis '85
Keith '83 and Myrtle G. Hill '83

The Byrds' Fruitcake

1 can sweetened condensed milk
1 pound dates, chopped
1 (7-ounce) package coconut
¼ teaspoon salt
2 cups pecans, chopped
1 pound candied fruit (chop 1 cup into cake; then decorate the top with rest)
1 Tablespoon vanilla

Preheat oven to 325 degrees. Coat a loaf pan (9x5x3) with non-stick spray. Mix ingredients together well. Pack into prepared pan. Cook for 45-50 minutes.

Yield: 16-20 servings

Mrs. David Q. Byrd, Jr. (David Q. Byrd, Jr. '43)

Maude Byrd made this every Christmas for 62 years as it was David, Sr.'s favorite.

Fudge Pudding Cake

½ cup all-purpose flour
1 teaspoon baking powder
¼ teaspoon salt
⅓ cup granulated sugar
2 Tablespoons cocoa, divided
1 Tablespoon butter, melted
¼ cup milk
½ cup nuts, chopped (optional)
½ cup brown sugar, sifted
⅞ cup boiling water

Preheat oven to 350 degrees. Butter a 1-quart baking dish. Combine flour, baking powder, salt, sugar, and 1 tablespoon cocoa. Sift 3 times. Combine butter and milk. Add flour mixture and blend lightly. Add nuts, if desired. Pour into prepared baking dish. Combine brown sugar and 1 tablespoon cocoa. Sprinkle, dry, over batter. Gently pour boiling water over the top. Bake for 30 minutes. Serve hot. As mixture bakes, it makes 2 layers: a chocolate cake layer on top and a chocolate fudge pudding layer below. To serve, place a serving of cake on dish and spoon pudding over it.

Yield: 6 servings

Barbara Parks, Faculty Wife

Turtle Cake

1 (16-ounce) package caramels
1 can sweetened condensed milk
1 cup pecans, chopped
1 box German chocolate cake mix
1 cup water
3 eggs
1 stick margarine

Preheat oven to 325 degrees. Grease and flour a 9x13 baking dish. Melt the caramels in half of the condensed milk. Add pecans, keep mixture warm over hot water while mixing the cake. Mix cake mix, water, eggs, margarine, and the other half of the condensed milk. Pour half of the cake batter into the prepared dish. Bake for 15-20 minutes. Remove from oven, swirl the caramel mixture over the cake. Pour the remaining batter over the caramel mixture, return to oven and bake for 20-25 minutes longer. Test for doneness with a wooden pick. Frost with a chocolate butter cream frosting of your choice or use light chocolate prepared frosting.

Yield: 12 servings

Dorothy Davis Miley '64

Chocolate Icebox Cake

2½ dozen ladyfingers
2 (1-ounce) squares chocolate
½ cup sugar
¼ cup water
4 eggs, separated
1 cup unsalted butter
1 cup confectioners' sugar
½ pint heavy cream, whipped
Cherries for garnish (optional)

Line bottom and sides of a springform pan with ladyfingers, separated with rounded sides toward pan and close together. Prepare chocolate filling: place chocolate, sugar, and water in double boiler. When melted gradually add egg yolks, well beaten. Cook until thick and smooth, stirring constantly. Remove from heat and cool. Cream butter and confectioners' sugar together. Add egg mixture, stirring well. Fold in the stiffly beaten egg whites. Place part of filling in pan for first layer. Arrange on top of filling a layer of ladyfingers (arranged like spokes of wheel), then more filling and ladyfingers until used up. Refrigerate for 20-24 hours. Remove springform rim. Top cake with whipped cream. Add a cherry per serving, if desired.

Variation: Chopped nuts may be added to the chocolate filling.

Yield: 10 servings

Klare Sullivan

Devil's Food Cake

1 cup butter
2 cups sugar
4 (1-ounce) squares unsweetened chocolate
4 eggs, separated
1 cup milk
3 cups all-purpose flour
½ teaspoon salt
4 teaspoons baking powder
1 teaspoon vanilla

Preheat oven to 300 degrees. Grease and flour a 9x13 cake pan. Cream butter and sugar. Melt chocolate in double boiler; add to creamed mixture and beat well. Stir in egg yolks, milk, and 2 cups of flour. Add salt and baking powder to 1 cup of flour and combine. Fold in beaten egg whites and vanilla. Pour into prepared pan and bake for about 1 hour. Frost with a chocolate or a brown sugar icing.

Yield: 15-20 servings

Mary Gray Turley

Mary Gray Turley was a housemother at Jennings Hall in the late 1920's and 30's.

Flower Pot Surprise

1 package chocolate sandwich cookies
½ stick butter
1 (8-ounce) package cream cheese, softened
1 cup confectioners' sugar
3½ cups milk
1 (6-ounce) box instant vanilla pudding
1 (12-ounce) carton whipped topping
1 (8-inch) plastic flower pot
Artificial or fresh flower
Small trowel

Crush chocolate sandwich cookies in food processor or blender. Set aside. Cream together butter, cream cheese, and confectioners' sugar. In a separate bowl mix milk, instant vanilla pudding, and whipped topping. Blend cream cheese and pudding mixtures together. Line bottom of plastic flower pot with wax paper. Alternate layers of crushed cookies and cream mixture in pot, ending with crushed cookies. Cover and chill overnight. Place artificial or fresh flower (wrap stem in wax paper) in center of pot. Use as a centerpiece and serve with small trowel.

Variations: Substitute light cream cheese and whipped topping, skim milk, and sugar-free pudding for lower fat version. Chocolate pudding could be used instead of vanilla.

Yield: 12-15 servings

Gloria Camp Lawrence (Frank C. Lawrence, Jr. '60)

Christmas Date Loaf

2 cups sugar
1½ cups milk
1 (8-ounce) package dates, chopped
1 cup pecans, chopped
1 Tablespoon butter
1 teaspoon vanilla

Combine sugar and milk in a heavy 1½-quart saucepan. Boil to soft ball stage (240 degrees). Add dates and cook for an additional 10 minutes, stirring frequently. Remove from heat. Add pecans, butter, and vanilla. Mix well. Place onto a damp cloth and form into an 18-inch roll. Store, wrapped in the cloth, in a cool place overnight. Slice and serve.

Yield: 5 dozen slices

Betty Joyce Upton Magee '55

Chocolate Chip Oatmeal Cake

1¾ cups boiling water
1 cup uncooked oatmeal
1 cup brown sugar, lightly packed
1 cup granulated sugar
1 stick margarine
2 large eggs
1 teaspoon soda
1¾ cups all-purpose flour
½ teaspoon salt
1 Tablespoon cocoa
1 (12-ounce) package semi-sweet chocolate chips
¾ cup nuts, chopped

Preheat oven to 350 degrees. Grease and flour a 9x13 pan. Pour water over oatmeal and let stand for 10 minutes. Add sugars and margarine. Stir until margarine melts. Add eggs, mixing well. Add soda, flour, salt, and cocoa. Add half a package chocolate chips. Mix well and pour batter into prepared pan. Sprinkle nuts and remaining chocolate chips on top. Bake for 35 minutes.

Yield: 24 servings

Barbara (Milne) Deutsch '56

Red Velvet Cake

½ cup shortening
1½ cups sugar
2 eggs
1 Tablespoon vinegar
2 ounces red food coloring
2¼ cups all-purpose flour, sifted
2 Tablespoons cocoa
1 teaspoon soda
Pinch of salt
1 cup buttermilk

Preheat oven to 350 degrees. Grease and flour 3 (9-inch) cake pans. Cream shortening and sugar. Add eggs and beat well. Add vinegar and food coloring and mix well. Sift together flour, cocoa, soda, and salt. Add flour mixture alternately with buttermilk. Pour batter into prepared pans. Bake for 20-25 minutes or until a wooden pick comes out clean. Cool and frost with Cream Cheese Frosting, page 290.

Yield: 16 servings

Lula McCaa

Vanilla Wafer Cake

1 cup margarine
2 cups sugar
6 eggs
½ cup milk
12 ounces vanilla wafers, coarsely chopped
1 (7-ounce) package flaked coconut
1 cup pecans, chopped

Preheat oven to 275 degrees. Grease a tube pan. Cream margarine, add sugar, beat until smooth. Add eggs 1 at a time, beating well. Alternately add milk and crushed wafers. Add coconut and pecans. Bake for 1¾-2 hours in prepared tube pan.

Variation: This may be baked in a 9x13 pan and cut into squares. Reduce baking time.

Yield: 16-20 servings

Carnette R. McMillan '50, Faculty Wife

Delicious Plum Cake

2 cups sugar
1 cup oil
3 eggs
2 cups self-rising flour
1 teaspoon cinnamon
1-2 teaspoons ground cloves
2 (4¾-ounce) jars strained plums

Preheat oven to 350 degrees. Grease and flour a tube pan. In a large mixing bowl, place all the ingredients and mix thoroughly. Bake in prepared tube pan for 55 minutes. Let the cake stand for 20 minutes before cutting.

Variation: Strained apricots, prunes, or apples may be substituted for plums.

Yield: 16-20 servings

Audra T. O'Neal '55, Faculty Wife

Miss Esther's Squaw Valley Cake

1 cup quick oatmeal
1½ cups boiling water
½ cup shortening
1 cup brown sugar, sifted and packed
1 cup granulated sugar
1 teaspoon salt
2 eggs
1½ cups flour, sifted
1 teaspoon soda
1 teaspoon cinnamon

Topping:
6 Tablespoons margarine, softened
¾ cup brown sugar
¼ cup evaporated milk
1 teaspoon vanilla
1 cup nuts, chopped
1 cup coconut

Preheat oven to 350 degrees. Lightly grease a 9x13 pan. Pour boiling water over oatmeal and let stand until cool. Stir and set aside. Cream together shortening, sugars, and salt. Add in and beat together eggs, flour, soda, and cinnamon. Add the oatmeal mixture and spread into prepared pan. Bake for 35-40 minutes and cool in pan. Mix topping ingredients well. Spread topping over cool cake and broil until bubbly.

Yield: 12 servings

Kathryn Scott, Faculty Wife

Pumpkin Cake

½ cup shortening
1 cup sugar
1 egg
1½ cups pumpkin
2 cups all-purpose flour, sifted
1 teaspoon soda
1 teaspoon baking powder
¼ teaspoon salt
1 teaspoon cloves
1 teaspoon cinnamon
½ teaspoon nutmeg
1 cup raisins
1 cup nuts (optional)

Preheat oven to 350 degrees. Grease and flour a Bundt pan. Cream shortening and sugar. Add unbeaten egg, pumpkin and all dry ingredients. Add raisins; stir in nuts if desired. Bake in a prepared Bundt pan. When wooden pick comes out clean, it's done.

Yield: 16-20 servings

From the recipes of Laverne Deevers '63, Faculty Wife

Irene's Sour Cream Cake

2 sticks margarine, softened
2 cups sugar
2 eggs
2 cups all-purpose flour
¼ teaspoon salt
1 cup sour cream
½ teaspoon vanilla

Topping:
½ cup pecans, chopped
2 Tablespoons sugar
½ teaspoon cinnamon

Preheat oven to 325 degrees. Grease tube pan with shortening and flour heavily. Bump pan to remove excess flour. In a mixing bowl, cream margarine and sugar; add eggs and beat. Mix flour and salt. Stir in half of the flour mixture, add sour cream. Add remaining flour and vanilla. Pour half of the batter into pan and sprinkle with half of the topping mixture. Add remaining batter and sprinkle with remaining topping mixture. Bake for 1 hour and 15 minutes. Turn upside down and sprinkle with confectioners' sugar.

Yield: 16-20 servings

Sharon Johnston Scholle '70

Nut Cake

3 eggs
2 cups sugar
2½ cups margarine
1 (16-ounce) box raisins
2 pounds pecans, chopped
¾ cup all-purpose flour for dredging
1 cup molasses
1 teaspoon soda
1½ teaspoons nutmeg
1½ teaspoons cinnamon
1½ teaspoons cloves
2¼ cups all-purpose flour
1 cup grape juice

Preheat oven to 250 degrees. Grease and flour 2 tube pans. Combine eggs, sugar, and margarine. Dredge raisins and nuts in flour. Combine all ingredients except grape juice and flour. Mix these ingredients well. Add flour and grape juice alternately. Pour into 2 prepared tube pans and bake for approximately 3-4 hours. It takes this cake a long time to bake.

Yield: 30-40 servings

Andy Graves '76

Old Tyme Pineapple Upside Down Cake

½ cup butter
1½ cups brown sugar
1 (15-ounce) can sliced pineapple (reserve juice)
Nut halves
Maraschino cherries
1 cup cake flour, sifted
1 teaspoon baking powder
Dash of salt
3 eggs, separated
1 cup granulated sugar
5 Tablespoons pineapple juice (reserved from canned pineapple)
Whipped cream (optional)

Preheat oven to 375 degrees. Melt butter in heavy baking pan or iron skillet. Spread brown sugar evenly in pan; arrange pineapple slices on sugar-butter, filling in spaces with nuts and red cherries. In mixing bowl, sift flour, baking powder, and salt together. Beat egg yolks until lemon-colored; add sugar to egg mixture gradually. Add pineapple juice and flour mixture. Fold in stiffly beaten egg whites. Spoon batter over pineapple-nuts-cherries in bottom of skillet or baking pan. Bake for 30-35 minutes. Turn out upside down on large cake plate. Serve with whipped cream, if desired.

Yield: 8-10 servings

Effie Speights

Heavenly Hash Cake

4 eggs
1½ cups sugar
1¼ cups all-purpose flour
⅛ teaspoon salt
1 teaspoon vanilla
2 sticks margarine, melted
⅓ cup cocoa
1½ cups pecans, chopped
1 box miniature marshmallows

Preheat oven to 350 degrees. Grease and lightly flour a 9x13 pan. Mix eggs, sugar, flour, salt, and vanilla together well. Separately, mix margarine, cocoa, and pecans. Add second mixture to first mixture and blend. Pour into prepared pan and bake for 25 minutes. When cake is taken from oven, spread 1 package miniature marshmallows over the top of the hot cake. Leave cake in pan. Top with Chocolate-Pecan Frosting, page 290, omitting pecans if desired.

Yield: 24 servings

Mrs. Walter G. Howell '79

My Favorite Cake

3 cups all-purpose flour
1 teaspoon soda
½ teaspoon salt
2 cups sugar
½ teaspoon cinnamon (if desired)
4 egg whites and 3 egg yolks, beaten
¾ cup oil
1 teaspoon vanilla
2 teaspoons coconut flavoring
1 (15-ounce) can crushed pineapple, drained (reserve juice for glaze)
1½ cups bananas, mashed
½ cup raisins (optional)
Flour for dredging
1 cup pecans, chopped

Glaze:
½ cup pineapple juice (reserved)
1 cup sugar
Juice of 1 lemon or 1 orange (optional)

Preheat oven to 325 degrees. Combine flour, soda, salt, sugar, and cinnamon in a large bowl. Add eggs and oil, stirring until dry ingredients are moistened. Do not beat. Stir in vanilla and coconut flavoring, pineapple, and bananas. Add flour-coated raisins and pecans. Pour batter into a buttered 9x13 glass Pyrex baking dish. Bake for 25-30 minutes or until done. Leave cake in the baking dish. Glaze: Boil pineapple juice and sugar on top of stove until syrup forms. Add lemon or orange juice. Make holes in the cake with a sharp wooden pick. Pour glaze over cake while hot. Refrigerate to store.

Variation: Cake may be baked in a tube pan for 1 hour and 20 minutes at 300 degrees; serve without a glaze.

Yield: 16 servings

Lorene Burris
Lavonne Rouse

Before turning cake out onto a serving plate, sprinkle the plate with a teaspoon of granulated sugar. This allows the cake to be easily moved on the plate.

Gold and Silver Coconut Cake

Gold Layers:
¾ cup butter
1 cup sugar
8 egg yolks, beaten
2 cups all-purpose flour, sifted
2 teaspoons baking powder
½ cup milk
1 teaspoon vanilla

Silver Layers:
2 cups sugar
½ cup shortening
3 cups all-purpose flour, sifted
2 teaspoons baking powder
8 egg whites
¾ cup milk
1 teaspoon vanilla

Coconut Filling:
2 cups sugar
¾ cup butter (do not substitute)
1 cup milk
2 cups grated coconut

Preheat oven to 375 degrees. Gold layers: Cream butter and sugar. Add beaten egg yolks. Sift flour and baking powder together, and add alternately with milk and vanilla. Bake in 3 (8-inch) square pans or 3 (9-inch) round cake pans for about 25 minutes. (Line aluminum pans with oiled paper). Silver layers: Cream sugar and shortening. Sift flour and baking powder together. Beat egg whites until peaks form. Add flour mixture alternately with the milk and vanilla to the creamed sugar and shortening. As the mixture gets too stiff to handle easily, add about half of the beaten egg whites. Add the rest of the flour mixture and then fold in the remaining egg whites last. Bake in 4 (8-inch) square pans or 4 (9-inch) round cake pan for about 20 minutes. Filling: Cook sugar, butter, and milk until the mixture begins to thicken like soft jelly (about 20-25 minutes). Stir to keep mixture from sticking to the pan. Add freshly grated coconut (or frozen grated coconut, unsweetened) to cooled filling. Spread between layers, alternating white and gold layers, and on top layer. Sprinkle extra coconut on top of the cake.

Yield: 16-20 servings

Hortense Inmon Burns '68

This recipe dates back to 1895.

Carrot Cake

2 cups sugar
1 cup oil
4 eggs
2 (4-ounce) jars strained carrots
1 teaspoon vanilla
2 cups all-purpose flour
1½ teaspoons soda
2 teaspoons ground cinnamon
¼ teaspoon ground nutmeg
¼ teaspoon ground cloves
Pecan halves (optional)

Preheat oven to 350 degrees. Grease and flour 3 (9-inch) cake pans. Combine sugar and oil; beat well. Add eggs, carrots, and vanilla; beat mixture until smooth. Combine flour, soda, cinnamon, nutmeg, and cloves; add to creamed mixture, beating well. Pour batter into prepared pans. Bake for 30 minutes or until a wooden pick inserted in center comes out clean. Cool in pans 10 minutes; remove layers from pans. Cool on wire racks. Spread Cream Cheese Frosting, page 290, between layers and on top and sides of cake. Garnish with pecans, if desired.

Yield: 1 (3-layer) cake

Mrs. Mary Sims

Fresh Apple Cake

2 cups sugar
1¼ cups oil
3 eggs
3 cups self-rising flour, sifted
1 teaspoon almond flavoring
1 cup nuts, chopped
4 medium apples, peeled and diced

Preheat oven to 350 degrees. Lightly grease and flour a tube pan. Mix sugar, oil, and eggs. Add flour. Add flavoring, nuts, and apples. Stir well. Place into the prepared tube pan. Bake for 1 hour.

Yield: 16-20 servings

Emily Esteen Quinn '87

Nuts will not settle to the bottom of cake batter if they are first heated in the oven and then dusted with flour before being added to the batter. Raisins can be dusted with flour without being heated.

St. Louie Gooie Butter Cake

Crust:
1 box butter recipe cake mix
1 egg, well beaten
1 stick butter, softened

Topping:
1 (8-ounce) package cream cheese, softened
2 eggs, well beaten
1 (1-pound) box confectioners' sugar
2 teaspoons vanilla, almond, or lemon flavoring
Coconut, chopped nuts, confectioners' sugar (optional)

Crust: Mix together ingredients until crumbly and press into bottom of a lightly greased 9x13x2 pan. Refrigerate. Topping: Beat cream cheese, eggs, and desired flavoring; add sugar gradually. Pour over crust. Bake at 325 degrees for 35-40 minutes. Garnish with coconut, chopped nuts, or confectioners' sugar. Allow to cool thoroughly before slicing.

Yield: 10-12 servings

Audrey Adair

Jello Cake

1 box white cake mix
⅔ cup oil
⅔ cup water
4 eggs
1 teaspoon vanilla
1 (3-ounce) box gelatin (any flavor)

Preheat oven to 350 degrees. Grease a tube pan. Mix all ingredients. Beat at medium speed for 2 minutes. Bake for 45 minutes or until sides loosen from cake pan. Cool for 25 minutes before removing from pan.

Yield: 16-20 servings

Billye Ainsworth '58

This recipe appeared in Cooking is Fun, a cookbook compiled in 1974 by Mrs. Homer Ainsworth, sponsor of the M.C. Ministerial Wives' Association.

Gingerbread

1½ cups all-purpose flour, sifted
1½ teaspoons soda
½ teaspoon salt
1 teaspoon ground ginger
1 teaspoon ground cinnamon
½ teaspoon ground cloves
½ cup shortening
½ cup brown sugar
2 eggs, beaten
1 cup molasses
1 cup boiling water

Preheat oven to 350 degrees. Grease a 9x13 baking pan. Sift flour, soda, salt, and spices; set aside. Cream together shortening and sugar, beating at medium speed of electric mixer until light and fluffy. Add eggs, beating well; mix in molasses. Beginning and ending with flour mixture, add flour mixture and boiling water alternately. Pour batter into baking pan and bake for 30-35 minutes or until done.

Lemon Sauce:
1 stick butter, melted and cooled
1¼ cups sugar
2 eggs, beaten
¼ cup lemon juice
Grated rind of 1 lemon
½ cup water
⅛ teaspoon nutmeg

Combine all ingredients in a small heavy saucepan and whisking constantly, bring to a boil over medium heat. Continue beating; boil for 2-3 minutes. Serve hot or cold over gingerbread, pound cake, or angel food cake. This sauce is thin when hot but thickens when cold.

Yield: 12-15 servings

Dorothy Ivey Carpenter '84, Faculty Wife

To determine a cake pan size, measure across the inside top edges.

Apricot Nectar Cake

Cake:
1 box lemon cake mix
1 Tablespoon lemon juice
¾ cup apricot nectar
½ cup oil
4 eggs

Glaze:
1 cup confectioners' sugar
Juice and grated zest of 2-3 lemons

Preheat oven to 350 degrees. Grease and flour tube pan. Mix juice, nectar, and oil with cake mix. Blend well. Add eggs, 1 at a time, blending well after each addition. Bake for 40 minutes or until done. Mix glaze ingredients and pour over cake while warm.

Yield: 16-20 servings

Rachel Williams Jacobson '82

Blackberry Jam Cake

1 cup butter or margarine
2 cups sugar
4 eggs, beaten
1 cup blackberry jam
3 cups all-purpose flour
1 teaspoon soda
½ teaspoon each: allspice, cloves, nutmeg, and cinnamon
1 cup buttermilk
Pinch of salt

Preheat oven to 350 degrees. Cream butter and sugar together until fluffy; add eggs and jam. Sift dry ingredients together twice. Add to first mixture alternately with the milk. Depending on whether layers are to be thick or thin, prepare 3 or 4 (9-inch) pans. Bake for 25-30 minutes until done. Stack with Caramel Icing, page 291, spreading between layers, on top, and on sides of cake.

Yield: 16-20 servings

Anise P. McDaniel (Major C. McDaniel '21)

I baked this cake in my mother's kitchen on an old wood stove just after the turn of the century. It has been a favorite for birthdays and holidays for 4 generations including my 6 children who are Mississippi College graduates.

Fresh Apple Spice Cake

1½ cups oil
2 cups sugar
2 eggs, beaten
1 teaspoon vanilla
3 cups flour, sifted
¼ teaspoon salt
1½ teaspoons soda
1 cup nuts, chopped
1 teaspoon cinnamon
1 teaspoon nutmeg
3 cups apples, sliced thin

Preheat oven to 350 degrees. Grease and flour a 9x13 pan. Preheat oven to 350 degrees. Beat oil and sugar at low speed of mixer until creamy. Add eggs and vanilla. Sift flour, salt, soda, and add to mixture; add nuts, cinnamon, nutmeg, and apples. Pour into prepared pan and bake until done. Frost with Creamy Caramel Icing, page 291, or Old-Fashioned Caramel Icing, page 291.

Yield: 16-20 servings

Ann Wilkinson

Yuma Dump Cake

1 (21-ounce) can apple pie filling
2 eggs
2 cups sugar
2 cups all-purpose flour
2 teaspoons soda
2 teaspoons cinnamon
½ teaspoon salt
½ cup oil
1 cup nuts, chopped, or raisins (optional)
Ice cream or whipped topping (optional)

Preheat oven to 325 degrees. Dump ingredients together and mix well. Pour into a buttered 9x13 pan and bake for 1 hour. This may be served with ice cream or whipped topping.

Yield: 12-16 servings

Diane Chaffins, Staff

Italian Cream Cake

1 stick margarine
½ cup shortening
2 cups sugar
5 eggs, separated
1 teaspoon soda
1 cup buttermilk
2 cups all-purpose flour, sifted
1 teaspoon salt
1 can flaked coconut
1 cup pecans, chopped
1 teaspoon vanilla

Preheat oven to 325 degrees. Grease and flour 3 cake pans (9-inch). Cream margarine, shortening, and sugar. Beat well and add egg yolks 1 at a time, beating for 1 minute, after each addition. Mix soda and buttermilk, add alternately with flour and salt. Add coconut, pecans and vanilla. Fold in beaten egg whites. Bake for 30 minutes. Frost with Cream Cheese Frosting, page 290.

Yield: 20 servings

Bonnie Peoples Elliott '59

Cranberry Cake

Cake:
2 cups all-purpose flour
1 cup sugar
2 teaspoons baking powder
½ teaspoon salt
1 cup milk
4 Tablespoons melted butter (no substitutes)
2 cups fresh or frozen cranberries

Sauce:
½ cup butter (no substitutes)
1¼ cups sugar
½ pint whipping cream

Preheat oven to 325 degrees. Grease an 8x12 and an 8x8 pan. Sift together dry ingredients; add milk and melted butter, mixing well. Dust cranberries with flour and add, mixing well. Bake for 30 minutes. Combine sauce ingredients and bring to a boil. Serve hot over cake. This must be served while warm. The recipe is more than 100 years old.

Yield: 8-10 servings

Marion Sessums '50

Apple-Date Cake

1 cup oil
2 cups sugar
3 eggs
1 package dates, chopped
1½ cups apples, chopped
1 cup flaked coconut
2 teaspoons vanilla
1 cup pecans, chopped
3 cups all-purpose flour
1 teaspoon cinnamon
2 teaspoons baking powder
1 teaspoon salt

Preheat oven to 325 degrees. Grease and flour a Bundt pan. Cream oil with sugar, add eggs, 1 at a time. Add dates, apples, coconut, vanilla, and pecans. Sift dry ingredients together and add. Mix well. Bake for 1½ hours.

Yield: 16 servings

Marie Peden

Apfel Kuchen

(Apple Cake)

½ cup butter or margarine, softened
1 box yellow cake mix
½ cup flaked coconut
2½ cups canned or fresh sliced apples
½ cup sugar
1 teaspoon cinnamon
1 cup sour cream
2 egg yolks or 1 egg
Whipped topping (optional)

Preheat oven to 350 degrees. Cut butter into cake mix until crumbly. Mix in coconut. Press mixture into an ungreased 9x13 pan. Build up the edges slightly. Bake for 10 minutes. Arrange drained apple slices on warm crust. Mix sugar and cinnamon. Sprinkle on apples. Blend sour cream and egg yolks. Drizzle over apples. Bake for 25 minutes or until edges are light brown. Do not overbake! Serve warm with whipped topping, if desired.

Variation: Pears or peaches may be substituted for apples.

Yield: 12-15 servings

Elizabeth Rogers Bilbo '53

Chocolate Surprise Cupcakes

1 box chocolate cake mix
1 (8-ounce) package cream cheese, softened
⅓ cup sugar
1 egg
1 teaspoon vanilla
1 (6-ounce) package semi-sweet chocolate chips
1 cup nuts, chopped

Mix cake according to package directions. Using paper liners, fill muffin cups half full. Mix cream cheese, sugar, egg, and vanilla. Beat until creamy. Fold in chocolate chips and nuts. Add 1 tablespoon of cream cheese mixture to each cupcake. Bake according to package directions for cupcakes. These are delicious without icing.

Yield: 24-30 cupcakes

Ann Patterson Cameron '70

Chocolate Cupcakes

4 (1-ounce) squares semi-sweet chocolate
2 sticks margarine or butter
1¾ cups sugar
¼ teaspoon salt
1 cup all-purpose flour
4 eggs
1 teaspoon vanilla
2 cups pecans, toasted and chopped

Preheat oven to 325 degrees. Melt chocolate and margarine together; add sugar, salt, and flour mixing by hand (do not use mixer). Add eggs 1 at a time. Stir, don't beat. Add vanilla and pecans. Fill paper muffin cups half full. Bake for 25 minutes. Do not overcook.

Yield: 30 cupcakes

Carey Vickery Thomasian '87

Carey Thomasian is the daughter of Harry Vickery, a member of the Mississippi College Board of Trustees.

Cheesecake Cupcakes

3 (8-ounce) packages cream cheese
1¼ cups sugar, divided
5 eggs
1¾ teaspoons vanilla, divided
1 (8-ounce) carton sour cream
Strawberry jam

Preheat oven to 300 degrees. Cream the cream cheese; add 1 cup sugar. Add eggs 1 at a time, beating until light and fluffy. Stir in 1½ teaspoons vanilla. Pour mixture into cupcake pan with paper liners, filling each section two-thirds full. Bake for 30 minutes. Mix sour cream, one-fourth cup sugar and one-fourth teaspoon vanilla. After cupcakes are taken from oven, spread 1 teaspoon sour cream mixture on top of each cake while still in the pan. Then place a small amount of strawberry jam on each cupcake. Bake for 5 minutes more. (These may be made in miniature pans or regular cupcake pans.)

Yield: 30 regular cupcakes

Dorothy Boyd Carpenter (Ray W. Carpenter '49)

Light Lemon Cheesecake

3 cups graham cracker crumbs (reserve ½ cup)
1 stick light margarine
1 (3-ounce) box lemon gelatin
1 cup boiling water
1 (8-ounce) package light cream cheese
1 cup sugar
1 (8-ounce) can evaporated milk, chilled
Whipped topping

Mix crumbs and margarine and press in to a 9x13 pan. Dissolve gelatin in boiling water. Combine cream cheese and sugar. Fold in gelatin. Whip evaporated milk until soft peaks form. Fold in gelatin and cheese mixture thoroughly. Pour into crust and sprinkle with reserved crumbs. Serve with whipped topping.

Yield: 16 servings

Mrs. James Newell

New York Cheesecake

Crust:

1¼ cups graham cracker crumbs
¼ cup sugar
2 Tablespoons butter or margarine

Filling:

5 (8-ounce) packages cream cheese, softened
1½ cups sugar
3 Tablespoons all-purpose flour
Dash salt
1½ teaspoons lemon juice
1 teaspoon vanilla
5 eggs
2 egg yolks
¼ cup whipping cream
Fresh fruit (optional)
Strawberry jelly, melted (optional)

Preheat oven to 425 degrees. Crust: Combine crumbs, sugar, and butter or margarine; press into the bottom of a buttered, 10-inch springform pan. Chill. Filling: Beat cream cheese at high speed with electric mixer until light and fluffy. Add sugar, flour, salt, lemon juice, and vanilla; beat for 5 minutes. Add eggs and egg yolks, 1 at a time, beating after each addition. Add cream; mix well. Pour batter over crust. Bake for 10 minutes; reduce temperature to 250 degrees and bake for 1 hour and 15 minutes. Do not open oven door during baking time. Cool for 1 hour; cover and chill for at least 8 hours. Garnish with fresh fruit glazed with melted jelly, if desired.

Yield: 12-14 servings

Jo Turcotte

When whipping cream is sweetened with a small amount of honey, it will stay firm much longer without separating.

Cheesecake Supreme

Crust:

1¼ cups graham crackers, crushed
½ cup sugar
½ cup melted butter
1 teaspoon cinnamon

Cake:

1 pound cream cheese
1 cup light cream or sour cream
¼ cup all-purpose flour
1 cup sugar
4 eggs, separated
1 Tablespoon vanilla

Sour Cream Topping (optional):

1 pint sour cream
2 Tablespoons sugar
½ teaspoon vanilla
Graham cracker crumbs

Crust: Preheat oven to 300 degrees. Mix all ingredients for crust and press into springform pan. Cake: Cream the cream cheese and light cream or sour cream in a large bowl. Mix flour and sugar together and add to cheese mixture. Add beaten egg yolks and vanilla. Fold in stiffly beaten egg whites. Pour batter into crust and bake for 1 hour. If sour cream topping is used, add at this point. Cool cake completely before releasing from springform pan. Sour Cream Topping: Mix sour cream, sugar, and vanilla and pour over cake. Sprinkle with graham cracker crumbs. Bake for 5 minutes at 475 degrees. Chill.

Yield: 10-12 servings

Linda Lytal '61, Faculty
Lynn Wilkie

Fruitcake Filling

2 cups sugar
1 cup butter
1½ cups milk

Boil the ingredients until thick (about 7 minutes). Cool and beat lightly. Spread filling between layers and over cake.

Yield: Filling for a 3-layer cake

Nell Porter Ratliff

Fruitcake Coconut Filling

2 (7-ounce) packages coconut
2½ cups sugar
2-3 Tablespoons all-purpose flour
2 lemons, grated rind and juice
1½ cups hot water

Combine all ingredients and cook for 20 minutes until thickened. Cool and spread between layers of fruitcake.

Yield: Filling for a 3-layer cake

Mrs. (M. D.) Katherine Crouch

Cream Cheese Frosting

1 (8-ounce) package cream cheese, softened
½ cup butter or margarine, softened
1 Tablespoon vanilla
4 cups confectioners' sugar, sifted
1 cup pecans, chopped

Combine cream cheese and butter, beating until light and fluffy. Add vanilla and sugar; beat until smooth. Stir in chopped pecans.

Yield: Frosting for a 3-layer cake

Mrs. Mary Sims

Chocolate-Pecan Frosting

1 stick margarine
4 Tablespoons cocoa
6 Tablespoons buttermilk
1 (1-pound) box confectioners' sugar
1 teaspoon vanilla
1 cup pecans, chopped (optional)

Melt and bring to a boil the margarine, cocoa, and buttermilk. Remove from heat; add confectioners' sugar, vanilla, and pecans. Frost while cake is hot.

Yield: Frosting for an 11x16 cake

Glenna Farmer Pearson '57

Old-Fashioned Caramel Icing

2½ cups sugar, divided
2 cups milk
½ stick butter or margarine
1 teaspoon vanilla

In an iron or heavy skillet carefully melt one-half cup of the sugar. Bring remaining sugar and milk to a boil and add the melted sugar. Cook, stirring, to a soft ball stage (234 degrees). Remove from heat and beat until creamy. Add vanilla and spread on cake.

Yield: Icing for a 2-layer cake

Anise P. McDaniel (Major C. McDaniel, Sr. '21)

Creamy Caramel Icing

2 cups brown sugar
1 Tablespoon shortening
1 Tablespoon light corn syrup
½ cup milk
½ cup shortening
2½ cups confectioners' sugar, sifted
4 Tablespoons hot milk
1 teaspoon vanilla

Boil brown sugar, 1 tablespoon shortening, syrup, and milk until mixture reaches 235 degrees on candy thermometer. Set aside. Beat with an electric mixer one-half cup shortening, confectioners' sugar, milk, and vanilla until smooth. Pour hot caramel mixture over confectioners' sugar mixture. Beat until thick and creamy. Cool before icing cake.

Yield: Icing for a 2 layer (9-inch) cake

Janet Stampley Lee '74, Faculty Wife

Coconut Icing

2 (6-ounce) packages frozen coconut
1 cup sour cream
1 cup sugar

Mix well. This is good with golden butter cake.

Yield: Icing for a 2 layer (9-inch) cake

Dewana Hawkins

Coconut-Pecan Icing

3 egg yolks, beaten
1 cup evaporated milk
1 stick margarine
1 cup sugar
1½ cups canned coconut
1 cup pecans, chopped
Pecan halves for garnish

In a heavy boiler, mix the egg yolks with the milk. Add margarine and sugar. Mix thoroughly. Stirring constantly, let come to a rolling boil for approximately 30 seconds. Remove from heat. Add coconut and chopped pecans. Cool. This is great on German Chocolate cake layers.

Yield: Icing for a 2-layer (9-inch) cake

Mary Ann Graves '72

Clear Lemon Icing

2 Tablespoons lemon peel, grated
1 stick margarine, room temperature
1 cup sugar
2 eggs, beaten
Juice of 2 lemons

Mix lemon peel with grated margarine. Beat together. Add all other ingredients and beat very well. Cook this mixture over medium heat, *stirring constantly*. When it begins to bubble, cook 2 more minutes. Let icing *cool completely*. Spread onto a cooled 3-layer cake, preferably a yellow butter cake. This icing is not fluffy; it must be spooned over the cake until set.

Yield: Icing for a 3-layer cake

Alicia Smith Wilbanks '84

Mocha Butter Cream Frosting

⅔ stick butter
⅔ (1-pound) box confectioners' sugar
1 Tablespoon cocoa
1 teaspoon vanilla
3 Tablespoons hot coffee, regular or instant

Using a mixer, cream butter. Add sugar, cocoa, vanilla, and coffee. Mix well.

Yield: Frosting for 10-inch tube cake

Betty Robinson Oswald '50

Fresh Peach Cobbler

2 cups sugar, divided
2 Tablespoons all-purpose flour
4 cups peaches, sliced
½ stick margarine, melted
2 deep-dish pie crusts, unbaked

Preheat oven to 350 degrees. Mix 1⅔ cups sugar with flour. Combine with sliced peaches. Pour into deep-dish pie crust. Cut the other pastry into narrow strips and cover the top of the pie. Mix remaining sugar and margarine and pour it over top of cobbler. Bake until bubbly and brown, about 45 minutes.

Yield: 6-8 servings

Mary Etta Thompson, Faculty Wife

The Peach Tree Cobbler

1 cup sugar
1 cup self-rising flour
1 cup milk
1 teaspoon vanilla
1 stick butter or margarine
1 can peaches or other canned fruit, undrained

Preheat oven to 400 degrees. Stir sugar and flour into a bowl; stir in milk and vanilla. Melt butter in bottom of a 9x13 Pyrex baking dish. Pour batter into pan over butter, add canned fruit. Bake for 30 minutes.

Variation: *Barbara Y. Wills '62* suggests substituting apple or peach pie filling for canned fruit and adding one-half cup chopped nuts.

Yield: 6 servings

Sharon Mordecai '85

Do not substitute light or extra light margarine for regular margarine in baking.

Classic Pecan Pie

3 eggs
1 cup sugar
½ cup corn syrup
¼ cup butter or margarine, melted
¼ teaspoon vanilla
1 cup pecans, chopped
1 (9-inch) unbaked pie shell

Preheat oven to 375 degrees. Beat eggs slightly in a 2-quart bowl. Stir in sugar, corn syrup, and melted butter or margarine. Add vanilla. Mix. Stir in chopped pecans. Pour into an unbaked 9-inch pie shell. Bake for 40 minutes or until filling is slightly firm.

Variation: Decrease sugar to ¾ cup; increase butter to 6 tablespoons.

Yield: 1 (9-inch) pie

Mrs. A. G. Shepherd, Jr. (Martha)
Mrs. Harry Lane Cole (Harry Lane Cole '41)

English Apple Dessert

½ cup butter or margarine, softened
½ cup brown sugar
1 cup all-purpose flour
2 teaspoons cinnamon, divided
1 cup pecans, chopped
4 large tart cooking apples, peeled and sliced
1 cup granulated sugar
Whipped cream or ice cream (optional)

Preheat oven to 350 degrees. Butter a 9-inch square baking dish. Cream butter and brown sugar. Add flour, 1 teaspoon cinnamon, and pecans and mix well. Place apples into prepared dish; cover with sugar and cinnamon. (For juicier pie sprinkle with 2 Tablespoons water.) Spread butter mixture over apples. Bake for 30-40 minutes until crust is puffy and lightly browned. Recipe may be doubled or tripled and baked in rectangular baking dish. Glass bakeware is preferred. Serve while warm and top with whipped cream or ice cream.

Yield: 6-8 servings

Lisa Williams Hall '84

Sweet Potato Pie

3 small sweet potatoes
1½ cups sugar
1 stick margarine, melted
1 can sweetened condensed milk
3 eggs
1 teaspoon vanilla
½ teaspoon cinnamon
2 (9-inch) pie shells, unbaked

Preheat oven to 350 degrees. Boil potatoes in jackets. Drain and peel. With electric mixer, mix potatoes with sugar, margarine, milk, eggs, vanilla, and cinnamon. Pour into unbaked pie shells. Bake for 30-40 minutes. These may be frozen.

Yield: 2 (9-inch) pies

Jo Acker (Dwain Acker '63)

Fluffy Peanut Butter Pie

1 (8-ounce) package cream cheese, softened
½ cup peanut butter (creamy or crunchy)
1 cup confectioners' sugar
½ cup milk
1 (8-ounce) container whipped topping
1 (9-inch) graham cracker crust
¼ cup peanuts, finely chopped

Whip cream cheese until soft and fluffy. Beat in peanut butter and sugar. Slowly add milk, blending thoroughly into mixture. Fold whipped topping into mixture. Pour into prepared crust. Sprinkle with chopped peanuts. Freeze until firm.

Yield: 1 (9-inch) pie

Betty Tucker Malone '74

This recipe was given to me by J. D. Grey, pastor of First Baptist Church, New Orleans, for many years.

Frozen Banana Split Pie

1 (9-inch) graham cracker deep-dish crust

Chocolate Sauce:

½ cup semisweet chocolate morsels
1 (5⅓-ounce) can evaporated milk
1 cup confectioners' sugar, sifted
¼ cup margarine

Pie Layers:

1 pint vanilla ice cream, softened
1 cup pecans, chopped, divided
½ pint chocolate ice cream, softened
1 (8-ounce) can crushed pineapple, drained
2 bananas, sliced
1 cup whipping cream
¼ cup confectioners' sugar, sifted
1 Tablespoon chocolate, grated

Chocolate Sauce: Combine all ingredients in top of a double boiler; bring water in double boiler to a boil; reduce heat to low; cook sauce ingredients for 15-20 minutes or until slightly thickened, stirring occasionally. Cool completely. Pie: Spread half of vanilla ice cream evenly over graham cracker crust; cover with plastic wrap and freeze until firm. Spread one-third of chocolate sauce over ice cream; sprinkle with one-half cup pecans. Cover and freeze until set. Spread chocolate ice cream over pie; cover and freeze until firm. Spoon half of remaining chocolate sauce over chocolate ice cream; top with drained pineapple. Cover and freeze. Spread remaining vanilla ice cream evenly over pie; cover and freeze. Spread remaining chocolate sauce over ice cream; top with remaining pecans and banana slices. Beat whipping cream until foamy; gradually add confectioners' sugar until soft peaks form. Spread whipped cream over pie; sprinkle with grated chocolate and freeze. Let stand at room temperature for 5 minutes before serving.

Yield: 1 (9-inch) pie

Shea P. Elkins, Staff

Frozen Caramel Pie

50 caramels
⅔ cup water
1 (16-ounce) carton of whipped topping
1 (8-ounce) carton sour cream
1 (9-inch) graham cracker crust
Whipped cream (optional)
Toasted coconut or fresh strawberries or bananas, sliced

Melt caramels in water in saucepan on medium heat, stirring frequently. Cool. Add whipped topping and sour cream and blend together. Spoon into a graham cracker crust and freeze. Cover with whipped cream and toasted coconut or fresh fruit at serving time. Return unused portion to freezer.

Yield: 1 (9-inch) pie

Doris Johnston

Caramel Pie

1 cup dark brown sugar
1 Tablespoon all-purpose flour
2 egg yolks
1 cup evaporated milk
½ cup water
1 Tablespoon margarine
2 teaspoons vanilla, divided
1 (9-inch) pie shell, baked
2 egg whites
4 Tablespoons sugar

Preheat oven to 300 degrees. Combine brown sugar and flour; mix well. Add egg yolks, milk, and water; stir with a wire whisk until lumps are gone. Cook in top of double boiler until thick, stirring constantly. Remove from heat; add margarine and 1 teaspoon vanilla. Pour into baked pie shell. For meringue: mix egg whites and cream of tartar and beat. Gradually add sugar and 1 teaspoon vanilla, beating until stiff peaks form. Spread over top of pie. Bake until lightly browned. Cool before serving.

Variation: To prepare caramel filling in the microwave, mix brown sugar, flour, egg yolks, milk, and water in a microwave-safe bowl. Cook on High for 2 minutes; remove and beat with whisk. Continue this process (microwave, whisk) at 30 second intervals. Mixture is very thick. Follow directions for browning meringue in conventional oven.

Yield: 1 (9-inch) pie

Janie White, Staff

Cream Cheese Pie

2 (8-ounce) packages cream cheese
3 eggs
⅔ cup plus 2 Tablespoons brown sugar, divided
1 teaspoon vanilla
1 (9-inch) graham cracker crust
1 cup sour cream
½ cup pecans, chopped

Preheat oven to 350 degrees. Beat cream cheese with electric mixer until smooth. Add eggs, mixing well. Add two-thirds cup brown sugar and vanilla; mix well. Pour into crust. Bake for 30 minutes; cool for 10 minutes. Beat sour cream and 2 tablespoons brown sugar together. Spread over pie and sprinkle pecans on top. Bake for an additional 10 minutes. Chill.

Yield: 1 (9-inch) pie

Renee' Thaggard Jones '91

Sugar-Free Strawberry Pie

1 (6-ounce) box sugar-free strawberry gelatin
3½ cups water
1 pound fresh or frozen strawberries, sliced
¾ cup cornstarch, lightly packed
9 packets artificial sweetener
2 (9-inch) graham cracker crusts

Mix gelatin, water, cornstarch, and strawberries. Heat until the mixture thickens, stirring constantly. Cool. Add sweetener, stirring thoroughly. Pour into pie crusts. Cover and cool before eating. Each slice of pie has about 200 calories.

Yield: 2 (9-inch) pies

Maurice Stringer '40

Cold ingredients will make flakier pie crusts. Even flour can be chilled.

Surprise Pie

⅔ cup corn syrup
2 eggs, beaten
⅔ cup sugar
⅔ cup uncooked oatmeal
⅓ cup margarine, melted
⅛ teaspoon salt
1 teaspoon vanilla
1 (9-inch) pie shell, unbaked

Preheat oven to 350 degrees. Mix corn syrup, eggs, sugar, oatmeal, margarine, salt, and vanilla. Pour into unbaked pie shell. Bake for 1 hour.

Variation: For a low cholesterol dessert, reduce margarine to 2 tablespoons and substitute 3 egg whites for the eggs. This tastes like pecan pie without the fat of pecans.

Yield: 1 (9-inch) pie

Amy Turner Rowan '85

Chocolate Chess Pie

1½ cups sugar
3 Tablespoons cocoa
¼ cup margarine, melted
2 eggs, slightly beaten
⅛ teaspoon salt
1 (5⅓-ounce) can evaporated milk
1 teaspoon vanilla
1 (9-inch) pie shell, unbaked

Preheat oven to 350 degrees. Mix sugar, cocoa, and margarine in mixing bowl. Mix well. Add eggs and beat with electric mixer for 2½ minutes. Add salt, milk, and vanilla. Pour filling into pie shell. Bake for 35-45 minutes. This may be served chilled or at room temperature.

Yield: 1 (9-inch) pie

Penny Smith Stokes '85

Chocolate-Nut Brownie Pie

1 (9-inch) pie shell, unbaked
1 cup semi-sweet chocolate chips
¼ cup butter or margarine
1 can sweetened condensed milk
½ cup biscuit mix
2 eggs
1 teaspoon vanilla
1 cup nuts, chopped

Preheat oven to 375 degrees. Bake pie shell for 10 minutes; remove from oven. Reduce oven temperature to 325 degrees. In saucepan, over low heat, melt chocolate chips with butter. In mixer bowl, beat chocolate mixture with sweetened condensed milk, biscuit mix, eggs, and vanilla until smooth. Add nuts. Pour into prepared pastry shell. Bake for 35-45 minutes or until center is just set. Do not overbake. Serve warm or at room temperature.

Yield: 1 (9-inch) pie

Julie Ann Bowlin '93

Chocolate Brownie Pie

2 (1-ounce) squares unsweetened chocolate
2 Tablespoons butter or margarine
3 large eggs
½ cup sugar
¾ cup light corn syrup
Pinch of salt
¾ cup nuts, chopped (optional)
1 teaspoon vanilla
1 (8-inch) pie shell, unbaked
Whipped cream

Preheat oven to 375 degrees. Melt chocolate and butter over hot water; remove from heat. Beat in eggs; add sugar, syrup, and salt. Beat again. Add nuts and vanilla. Pour into pie shell and bake for about 40 minutes until puffy and set. This pie will settle when cool. Serve with whipped cream.

Yield: 1 (8-inch) pie

Lucille Gardner Grant '45

Lucille Grant is the widow of David Grant, who served on the Mississippi College Board of Trustees, 1954-60, 1962-68, 1977-83.

Brownie Pie

1 stick margarine
2 eggs, beaten
1 cup sugar
2 Tablespoons cornstarch
¼ cup cocoa
1 teaspoon vanilla
1 (8-inch) pie shell, unbaked

Preheat oven to 325 degrees. Melt margarine and let cool; mix in eggs. Combine dry ingredients and add to margarine and eggs; add vanilla. Pour into unbaked pie shell and bake for about 45 minutes.

Yield: 1 (8-inch) pie

Patti Pittman Gough '86

Margie's Pecan Pie

3 eggs, lightly beaten
1 cup light corn syrup
¾ cup sugar
1 teaspoon vanilla
¼ teaspoon salt
3 drops yellow food coloring
3 drops butter flavoring
1 cup pecans, coarsely chopped
½ cup pecan halves
¼ cup butter-flavored shortening, melted
1 (9-inch) unbaked pie shell

Preheat oven to 350 degrees. Combine eggs, syrup, sugar, vanilla, salt, food coloring and butter flavoring in large bowl. Mix well with spoon. Stir in nuts. Let nuts rise to top. Pour melted shortening over nuts. Stir again. Pour gently into unbaked pie shell. Bake for 45 minutes or until filling is set. Cool to room temperature before serving.

Variation: *Mrs. William Van "Billy" Hardin '64* suggests increasing the sugar to 1 cup, adding 3 tablespoons fine cornmeal, and substituting 1 tablespoon melted butter for shortening. She omits the yellow food coloring and butter flavoring and reduces the pecans to 1 cup. Bake at 325 degrees until done (approximately 1 hour).

Yield: 1 (9-inch) pie

Mrs. V. E. (Margie) Malpass

Strawberry Icebox Pie

1 (8-ounce) can crushed pineapple
1 cup sugar
1 (3-ounce) box strawberry gelatin
1 (12-ounce) can evaporated milk, chilled and whipped
2 (9-inch) graham cracker crusts

Mix pineapple, including juice, and sugar with gelatin in top of double boiler. Heat gelatin mixture over boiling water, stirring constantly, until gelatin is dissolved. Pour hot mixture into bowl and place in refrigerator to chill. When mixture begins to set, fold in whipped evaporated milk. Pour into pie crusts. Chill thoroughly.

Yield: 2 (9-inch) pies

Anne Washburn McWilliams '70

Fudge Sundae Pie

1 cup evaporated milk
1 (6-ounce) package semi-sweet chocolate morsels
1 cup miniature marshmallows
¼ teaspoon salt
1 quart vanilla ice cream
1 (9-inch) pie shell, baked, cooled
½ cup pecans, chopped

Combine milk, chocolate morsels, marshmallows, and salt in a heavy 1-quart saucepan and stir over medium heat until chocolate and marshmallows are completely melted and mixture thickens. Remove from heat and cool to room temperature. Spoon half of the ice cream into the cooled pie shell and cover with half the chocolate mixture. Repeat layers. Top with chopped pecans. Freeze until firm, 3-5 hours.

Yield: 1 (9-inch) pie

Faye Reynolds

Pumpkin Pie

1 cup sugar
1 teaspoon salt
½ teaspoon cinnamon
½ teaspoon nutmeg
¼ teaspoon cloves
2 cups canned pumpkin
3 eggs, beaten
2 cups milk
1 (9-inch) pie shell, unbaked

Preheat oven to 450 degrees. Mix sugar, salt, and spices. Add to pumpkin and stir eggs into mixture. Slowly stir in the milk. Mix well. Pour mixture into pie shell. Bake for 10 minutes. Lower heat to 350 degrees and bake for 30-40 minutes until filling is set.

Yield: 1 (9-inch) pie

Madelyn Folkes Lofton, Faculty Wife (Don Lofton '78)

Million Dollar Pie

1 can sweetened condensed milk
1 (8-ounce) carton whipped topping
1 cup pecans, chopped
1 can flaked coconut
1 (8-ounce) can crushed pineapple, drained
⅓ cup lemon juice
2 (9-inch) graham cracker crusts

Mix together condensed milk, whipped topping, pecans, coconut, and pineapple; add lemon juice and stir well. Place into pie crusts and chill thoroughly.

Yield: 2 (9-inch) pies

Robert Travis Hughes '52

Dreamy Fruit Pie

1 (16-ounce) can dark sweet cherries, drained and chopped
1 (8-ounce) can crushed pineapple, drained
1 cup sugar
3 Tablespoons all-purpose flour
1 (3-ounce) box orange gelatin
4 ripe bananas, chopped
1 cup pecans, chopped
2 (9-inch) pie shells, baked
Whipped topping (optional)

Reserve juice from cherries and crushed pineapple. Add sugar and flour to the juices and bring to a boil. Remove from heat and add orange gelatin. Cool mixture to room temperature and add cherries, crushed pineapple, bananas, and pecans. Pour into pie shells, chill and serve. Whipped topping may be used for garnish.

Yield: 2 (9-inch) pies

Thelma Crick Riley '59

Mother's Angel Pie

4 egg whites
Pinch of salt
1 cup confectioners' sugar
½ cup sugar
⅛ teaspoon cream of tartar
1 teaspoon vanilla
Whipped cream
Unsweetened chocolate, grated

Line a 9-inch pie plate with brown paper. Beat egg whites and salt until stiff. Sift both sugars and cream of tartar together 4 times. Gradually add the sugar mixture to the egg whites, beating until very stiff. Add vanilla. Pour into a prepared pie plate. Bake for at least 50-55 minutes at 350 degrees, starting in a cold oven. Let cool. Invert onto serving plate and completely cover with whipped cream. Grate unsweetened chocolate on top.

Variation: For a healthier dessert, substitute low-fat whipped topping and fruit for whipped cream and chocolate.

Yield: 1 (9-inch) pie

Ann Hall Vickery (Harry E. Vickery '57)

Harry Vickery has served as a member of the Mississippi College Board of Trustees, 1974-80, 1981-87, 1988-91, 1991-.

Refrigerator Fruit Pie

1 (20-ounce) can crushed pineapple, drained
1 (17-ounce) can peaches (cut in bite-size pieces, drained)
1 (16-ounce) carton whipped topping
2 Tablespoons lemon juice
1 can sweetened condensed milk
2 (9-inch) graham cracker crusts

Drain pineapple and peaches well. Mix all ingredients. Pour into crusts. Refrigerate overnight. This is very easy and delicious!

Yield: 2 (9-inch) pies

Shirley Thomas '55

Black Bottom Pie

20-25 chocolate wafers, crushed
5 Tablespoons margarine, melted
4 eggs, separated
1 cup sugar, divided
1 Tablespoon all-purpose flour
2 cups milk
2 (1-ounce) squares unsweetened chocolate
2 teaspoons vanilla, divided
1 envelope unflavored gelatin
¼ cup cold water
¼ teaspoon cream of tartar
½ pint heavy cream, whipped
Grated chocolate

Preheat oven to 275 degrees. Mix crushed chocolate wafers and margarine. Press into a 10-inch pie plate and bake for 10 minutes; cool. Make custard of egg yolks, one-half cup sugar, flour, and milk. Cook in double boiler until thick. Melt chocolate; add 1½ cups custard and 1 teaspoon vanilla. Spread over chocolate crust. Add gelatin dissolved in cold water to remaining warm custard. Cool. Beat egg whites; add one-half cup sugar and cream of tartar. Fold whites into custard and add 1 teaspoon vanilla. Spread over black bottom. Chill. Top with whipped cream and garnish with grated chocolate.

Yield: 1 (10-inch) pie

Blanche Potter Montgomery '26

Chocolate Pie

1½ cups sugar
3 Tablespoons cocoa
2 Tablespoons all-purpose flour
½ teaspoon salt
2 cups milk
4 eggs, separated
1½ teaspoons vanilla
¼ teaspoon cream of tartar
6 Tablespoons sugar
1 (9-inch) pie shell, unbaked

Preheat oven to 350 degrees. Mix sugar, cocoa, flour, salt, and milk in double boiler and cook until it coats the spoon. Remove from heat and, using hand mixer, beat in slightly beaten egg yolks; add vanilla. Pour into pie shell and bake for 35-40 minutes until set in center. For meringue: beat egg whites with teaspoon cream of tartar until soft peaks form. Slowly add 6 tablespoons sugar and continue beating until stiff. Spread over pie and bake until lightly browned.

Yield: 1 (9-inch) pie

From the recipes of Elizabeth Hitt, Faculty Wife

On the original recipe, Mrs. Hitt had noted that her 4 Mississippi College boys liked a few finely chopped pecans sprinkled over the top of the filling just before the pie was done and before the meringue was added.

Fudge Pie

1½ cups sugar
3 Tablespoons cocoa
¼ cup margarine, melted
2 eggs, beaten
½ cup evaporated milk
1 teaspoon vanilla
1 (8-inch) pie shell, unbaked

Preheat oven to 400 degrees. Combine sugar and cocoa; mix well. Add margarine, sugar, and cocoa; stir well. Add beaten eggs; stir but do not beat! Add milk and vanilla; mix well. Pour into pie shell. Bake for 10 minutes; reduce heat to 350 degrees and bake for 20-25 minutes.

Yield: 1 (8-inch) pie

Steve Wilson '83

Dr. Buckner's Lemon Meringue Pie

½ (12-ounce) box vanilla wafers
½ cup fresh lemon juice (no substitutes)
1 can sweetened condensed milk
3 eggs, separated
¼ teaspoon lemon extract
¼ teaspoon cream of tartar
1 Tablespoon sugar

Preheat oven to 325 degrees. Crush enough vanilla wafers to cover the bottom of a 9-inch pie plate about ¼-inch deep. Line the sides of the plate with whole vanilla wafers. Mix the lemon juice, sweetened condensed milk, egg yolks, and lemon extract gently with a rubber spatula. Pour into the vanilla wafer crust. For meringue: beat the egg whites and cream of tartar with an electric mixer until stiff peaks form. Add sugar slowly and mix in thoroughly. Pile on top of pie filling and spread to all edges. Bake for about 15 minutes or until lightly browned. Cool thoroughly before refrigerating or meringue will form sugar droplets and separate. Refrigerate overnight before serving.

Yield: 1 (9-inch) pie

Kari Buckner Norberg, Faculty Wife

When melting chocolate, the container and stirring utensil must be absolutely dry or the chocolate will become very grainy. If the texture does deteriorate, restore it by stirring in one teaspoon of vegetable shortening (not butter or margarine) for each ounce of chocolate.

Buttermilk Lemon Pie

2 cups sugar
½ cup plus 3 Tablespoons cornstarch
5 cups buttermilk
1 (3-ounce) package cream cheese, softened
7 eggs, separated, room temperature
2 teaspoons grated lemon rind
¼ cup lemon juice
2 Tablespoons butter or margarine
1 teaspoon lemon flavoring
2 (10-inch) pie shells, baked
¾ teaspoon cream of tartar
¼ cup plus 3 Tablespoons confectioners' sugar
¼ teaspoon lemon extract

Combine sugar and cornstarch in a heavy saucepan; gradually add buttermilk, stirring until blended. Add cream cheese and cook over medium heat, stirring constantly, until mixture comes to a boil and thickens slightly - about 5 minutes. Beat egg yolks until thick and lemon-colored. Gradually stir about a fourth of the hot mixture into yolks, then add yolks to remaining hot mixture. Continue to cook, stirring constantly for 2-3 minutes until thick. Remove from heat; stir in lemon rind, lemon juice, butter or margarine, and lemon extract. Spoon into pie shells. For Meringue: preheat oven to 350 degrees. Beat egg whites and cream of tartar at high speed of electric mixer for 1 minute. Gradually add confectioners' sugar, 1 tablespoon at a time, continuing to beat until stiff peaks form. Beat in lemon flavoring. Spread meringue over hot filling, sealing to edge. Bake for 12-15 minutes or until browned.

Yield: 2 (10-inch) pies

Mrs. Dan 'Ted' Mobley

Chess Pie

3 eggs
2 cups sugar
½ cup milk
1 teaspoon vanilla
¾ stick butter or margarine, melted
1 teaspoon vinegar
1 (9-inch) pie shell, unbaked

Preheat oven to 325 degrees. Beat eggs with sugar. Add milk and vanilla and mix thoroughly. Add butter or margarine; then add vinegar. Pour into unbaked pie shell and bake for about 1 hour or until set in center.

Yield: 1 (9-inch) pie

From the recipes of Lona Douglas, Faculty Wife

Lemon Chess Pie

1½ cups sugar
1 Tablespoon all-purpose flour
1 Tablespoon cornmeal
4 eggs (3 if large)
¼ cup margarine, melted
¼ cup milk
¼ cup lemon juice
Grated rind of 1 lemon
1 (9-inch) pie shell, unbaked

Preheat oven to 350 degrees. Mix sugar, flour, and cornmeal in bowl. Add eggs and mix well. Add margarine, milk, lemon juice, and rind. Pour into pie shell and bake for 40-45 minutes until set in center.

Yield: 1 (9-inch) pie

Laura Sue Lofton (Widow of W. D. Lofton, Jr. '42)

W. D. Lofton, Jr., served four terms as a member of the Mississippi College Board of Trustees.

Perfect Apple Pie

1 cup sugar
2 Tablespoons all-purpose flour
⅛ teaspoon salt
1 teaspoon cinnamon
¼ teaspoon nutmeg
2 (10-inch) pie shells, unbaked
5-7 large tart apples, cored, peeled, and sliced thin
2 Tablespoons butter or liquid margarine
Milk
Sugar

Preheat oven to 450 degrees. Mix together the sugar, flour, salt, cinnamon, and nutmeg. Sprinkle about a third of the mixture over bottom of pastry-lined pie plate. Pour in about half of prepared apples. Sprinkle with a third of the sugar mixture, add rest of apples, then sprinkle rest of sugar mixture. Dot with butter (cut into small pieces) or squeeze on liquid margarine. Place second crust on top of apples; pinch top and bottom crust together around the edges. Cut several air vents in top crust; brush with milk and sprinkle with sugar. Bake for 10 minutes at 450 degrees, then reduce heat to 350 degrees; bake for 35-40 minutes. Check after 30 minutes.

Yield: 1 (10-inch) pie

Marilyn Morton Joiner '64, Staff

Pecan Tassies

Tart Shells:
1 cup all-purpose flour
1 (3-ounce) package cream cheese, softened
¼ cup plus 3 Tablespoons margarine, softened

Filling:
¾ cup light brown sugar, firmly packed
¾ cup pecans, chopped
1 egg
1 Tablespoon margarine, softened
1 teaspoon vanilla
Dash of salt

Tart Shells: Combine flour, cream cheese, and margarine; stir until blended. Shape dough into 24 balls; chill. Place into greased 1¾-inch tart pans, shaping each ball into a shell. Preheat oven to 350 degrees. Filling: Combine sugar, pecans, eggs, margarine, vanilla, and salt; mix until blended. Spoon mixture into tart shells, filling three-fourths full. Bake for 20 minutes or until browned.

Yield: 2 dozen

Mrs. John McCall, Faculty Wife

John W. McCall served as a member of the Mississippi College Board of Trustees, 1958-64, 1970-76, 1977-83.

Hot Water Pastry

1 cup all-purpose flour
¼ teaspoon baking powder
½ teaspoon salt
⅓ cup shortening
3 Tablespoons boiling water

Preheat oven to 475 degrees for unfilled crust or 425 degrees for filled crust. Mix dry ingredients, then place shortening on top; slowly pour boiling water over shortening. Stir with a fork and then mix by hand. Do not handle more than necessary. Roll out to about ⅛-inch thick and fit into pie pan. Unfilled crusts should be pricked before baking. Bake until lightly browned.

Yield: 1 pie crust

Antonina Canzoneri '40

Basic Pie Crust

1 cup all-purpose flour
½ teaspoon salt
⅓ cup shortening
2-4 Tablespoons cold water

Preheat oven to 425 degrees. Mix flour and salt. Cut in shortening with a pastry blender or fork. While stirring with a fork, sprinkle water on dough 1 tablespoon at a time, using just enough water to hold dough together. Roll dough out onto a floured surface to about ⅛-inch thick (large enough to fit an 8 or 9-inch pie plate). Carefully place dough in pie plate, trim any excess dough, and flute edges. To bake unfilled pie shell, prick the surface with a fork. Bake for 10 minutes or until lightly browned. Recipe may be doubled for a double-crust pie.

Variation: To make a quick pie crust that does not have to be rolled out, bring one-third cup oil and one-fourth water to a boil. Pour into 1 cup self-rising flour. Stir with a fork until blended. Pat dough into pie plate with fingers doing sides first and then center. Bake as above.

Yield: 1 (8 or 9-inch) pie crust

Janet Taylor '67, Faculty

Creme Caramelo

(Flan)

1 cup sugar
1 can sweetened condensed milk
1½ cans milk (use condensed milk can to measure)
3 eggs
2 teaspoons vanilla

Preheat oven to 250 degrees. Caramelize the sugar in heavy saucepan by placing sugar in pan over medium high heat. Stir as it begins to melt. Cook to medium caramel color. Pour immediately into a deep Pyrex dish (round) or 6 individual custard dishes. Spread evenly. Whip or use blender to mix sweetened condensed milk, whole milk, eggs, and vanilla. Pour into baking dish. Place in a larger pan with 1 inch of hot water; bake for 2 hours. Cooking in slow oven for longer time makes a creamier custard.

Yield: 6 servings

Deborah Trott Pierce '77, Faculty

Banana Pudding

2 (3½-ounce) boxes instant vanilla pudding
2 cups milk
1 can sweetened condensed milk
1½ ounces powdered coffee creamer
1 (16-ounce) carton whipped topping, divided
1 large box vanilla wafers
6 bananas, sliced

Completely mix together pudding, milk, condensed milk, coffee creamer and 12 ounces of whipped topping. Reserve 4 ounces of whipped topping for garnish. In a 9x13 Pyrex dish, layer whole vanilla wafers, slices of bananas, and pudding mixture. Repeat layers until all pudding mixture is used. Top with remaining whipped topping and vanilla wafer crumbs. Refrigerate overnight.

Yield: 8-12 servings

Tim Tolleson '86

Low-Fat Banana Pudding

½ cup sugar
3 Tablespoons flour
3 egg whites, slightly beaten
½ cup frozen egg product (not egg substitute)
½ cup skimmed evaporated milk
1¾ cups skim milk
1 teaspoon vanilla
30 vanilla wafers
3 medium bananas
3 Tablespoons lite whipped topping (optional)

Combine sugar and flour. Combine egg whites and thawed egg product; beat together until slightly frothy. Add eggs to sugar-flour mixture, beating until smooth. Add evaporated milk and mix well. Then pour in skim milk. Cook over medium heat, stirring constantly. When custard thickens, remove from heat and cool. Stir in vanilla during cooling stage. Layer vanilla wafers, bananas, and custard alternately, finishing with custard on top. Sprinkle with crushed wafer crumbs if desired. Also, "lite" topping may be layered on the bottom of the pudding dish, with wafer next, to add lightness to pudding.

Yield: 8 servings

Louise H. Griffith '48, Retired Faculty

Bessie's Old-Fashioned Banana Pudding

1 cup sugar
3 Tablespoons flour
¼ teaspoon salt
2 eggs, beaten
2⅓ cups milk
1-2 Tablespoons butter
1 teaspoon vanilla
Vanilla wafers
Bananas
Whipped topping

Mix sugar, flour, and salt in heavy pot or double boiler until lumps disappear. In a large mixing bowl, mix eggs with milk and then add to the dry ingredients. Mix well. Over medium heat, cook and stir until mixture begins to bubble and mixture will coat a metal spoon. Remove from heat and add butter and vanilla. Stir until mixed; cool. Line a serving dish with vanilla wafers. Top with sliced ripe (not overripe) bananas. Top with a layer of cooled custard. Continue alternating layers of wafers, bananas, custard. Top with whipped topping. Chill and serve.

Yield: 10-12 servings

Carolyn Bowman '60

Royal Bread and Butter Pudding

6 Tablespoons butter, softened
1 cup confectioners' sugar
4 slices bread
2 eggs, beaten
2½ cups milk
½ cup raisins (optional)
½ teaspoon nutmeg (freshly ground is better)
1 Tablespoon fresh orange peel, grated
1 cup heavy cream, whipped

Preheat oven to 350 degrees. Cream butter and sugar; then spread onto bread and cut each slice into 4 squares. Place into a 9-inch square baking dish or a loaf pan. Combine eggs with milk, raisins, and nutmeg. Pour over bread and sprinkle with orange peel. Bake for approximately 45 minutes. Serve with whipped cream.

Yield: 6-8 servings

Doug Palmer '58

Mr. Palmer obtained this recipe while stationed in New Zealand from a former chef to the Queen of England.

Fruited Bread Pudding

16 slices day-old bread, torn into 1-inch pieces
2 cups sugar
4 eggs
3 cups milk
2 teaspoons ground cinnamon
½ teaspoon salt
2 Tablespoons vanilla
1 (21-ounce) can apple pie filling, slices cut in half
1 cup golden raisins
¾ cup margarine, melted
Whipped topping (optional)

Combine bread and sugar and set aside. Grease a 9x13 pan. Beat eggs, milk, cinnamon, salt, and vanilla until foamy and pour over bread and sugar. Cover and refrigerate for 2 hours. Preheat oven to 350 degrees. Stir together pie filling, raisins, and margarine and combine with refrigerated ingredients. Pour into prepared pan. Bake uncovered for 45-50 minutes or until firm. Cover with whipped topping to serve.

Yield: 12-15 servings

Odessa Hill '65

Apricot Pudding

1 cup confectioners' sugar
⅔ cup butter or margarine
2 eggs
½ pound sugar wafers, crushed
1 cup nuts, chopped
1 (16-ounce) can apricot halves
½ pint heavy cream, whipped

Mix sugar, butter, and eggs in double boiler. Cook, stirring often, over hot water for 10-12 minutes or until thick. Put two- thirds of the wafer crumbs in the bottom of a 9x13 glass baking dish. Carefully spoon hot custard over crumbs. Let cool for 10-15 minutes. Sprinkle nuts over custard and arrange apricots in rows on top of nuts. Spread whipped cream over this. Top with remainder of wafer crumbs and a few nuts. Refrigerate. Cut so that an apricot half is in each serving. This is very rich.

Yield: 15 servings

Mamie Ruth Stranburg Abernathy

Royal Chocolate Custard

4 Tablespoons butter or margarine
⅓ cup confectioners' sugar
2 (1-ounce) squares semi-sweet chocolate, melted
1 egg, separated
¼ teaspoon vanilla
1 recipe Custard, see recipe below

Butter small square dish or pan. Cream butter and sugar. Beat the egg yolk, add to butter and sugar and mix well. Add the chocolate and beat well. Beat the egg white until stiff and fold it into the chocolate mixture along with the vanilla. Spread in a prepared dish. Refrigerate for several hours. To serve: Fill sherbet dishes two-thirds full of warm custard and place a 1½-inch square of the chocolate into the center of the custard. The cold chocolate melting slowly into the warm custard makes a luscious combination.

Yield: 8 servings

Barbara Parks, Faculty Wife

Custard

4 egg yolks
⅓ cup sugar
1¾ cups light cream
1 teaspoon vanilla

Beat egg yolks; cook in top of double boiler until thick and lemon colored; gradually add sugar, beating well. Stir in cream. Cook over low heat, stirring constantly, until mixture thickens and coats a metal spoon (about 10 minutes). Stir in vanilla; cool. Cover and chill for 8 hours or overnight. Serve with fresh berries (raspberries, strawberries, or blueberries), over cake, or as a pudding.

Yield: 8 servings

Nina R. L. Compton '74

Baked Chocolate Custard

2 (1-ounce) squares unsweetened chocolate
1 quart milk
4 eggs
⅔ cup sugar
¼ teaspoon salt
1 teaspoon vanilla
Whipped cream (optional)

Preheat oven to 350 degrees. Cut chocolate into small pieces. Put chocolate and milk into top of double boiler. Scald over hot water, blending thoroughly. Beat eggs, sugar, salt, and vanilla together. Add chocolate/milk to egg mixture gradually, mixing well. Pour into custard cups which have been rinsed with cold water. Set cups in a pan of warm water. Bake until firm, about 45 minutes. Chill thoroughly. Serve with whipped cream, if desired.

Yield: 10 custard cups

Bobbie M. Gardner

White House Coconut Custard

5 eggs
1½ cups sugar
Grated rind of 1 lemon
2 cups light cream, slightly warmed
Dash of salt
1 medium-size fresh coconut, shelled and drained, coarsely grated
Whipped topping (optional)
Pineapple chunks (optional)

Preheat oven to 350 degrees. Butter a 1½-quart casserole. Beat eggs; add sugar, lemon rind, warm light cream and salt. Blend. Pour into prepared casserole. Sprinkle coarsely grated fresh coconut over the custard. Set casserole into a shallow pan of water. Bake on lower shelf of oven for 35 minutes or until custard is set. It should be just slightly shaky. Cool slightly before serving. If desired, add whipped topping and pineapple chunks.

Yield: 8 servings

Mary S. Parkman

Low-Fat Rice Pudding

2 cups sugar
1 cup skim milk
1 carton egg substitute (equivalent of 4 eggs)
1 teaspoon vanilla
4 cups cooked white rice
Cinnamon or nutmeg

Preheat oven to 375 degrees. Coat a 2-quart glass dish with non-stick cooking spray. Mix sugar, milk, egg substitute, and vanilla. Beat well. Add rice and beat on medium speed until thoroughly mixed. Pour into casserole. Sprinkle top lightly with cinnamon or nutmeg. Bake for 1 hour. Cool slightly before serving.

Yield: 8 servings

Carolyn Callahan (Fletcher L. Callahan '58)

Frosted Pudding

2 (3½-ounce) boxes instant French vanilla pudding
3 cups milk
1 (16-ounce) container whipped topping
1 box graham crackers
1 can caramel pecan frosting

Mix pudding with milk; fold in whipped topping. In a 9x13 dish, layer graham crackers, then pudding mixture; repeat, ending with graham crackers. Top with caramel pecan frosting. Chill 24 hours, then cut into squares. Must be stored in refrigerator.

Yield: 24 servings

Shelia Carpenter '87, Staff

Uncle Mike's Millionaires

1 (10-ounce) package caramels
2 Tablespoons milk
2 cups pecans, chopped
1 (6-ounce) package milk chocolate chips
1 Tablespoon paraffin, shaved

Melt caramels and milk in top of double boiler. Add pecans and drop by tablespoonsful onto wax paper. Melt chocolate chips and shaved paraffin in double boiler. Dip nut mixture 1 piece at a time into chocolate. Take out with toothpick, drawing off excess chocolate. Drop onto wax paper.

Yield: Approximately 36 pieces (half-dollar size)

Elizabeth Lee '91

Pulled Mints

4 cups sugar
2 cups water
1 stick butter (no substitution)
8-10 drops oil of peppermint
Food coloring (optional)

Mix sugar and water together in a large heavy saucepan and bring to a boil. Keep at hard boil until hard crack stage is reached when dropped into cold water or 300 degrees on candy thermometer. Do not stir after it begins to boil. Pour onto buttered marble slab and drop oil of peppermint onto candy as soon as it is poured onto slab. Cool slightly, pull like taffy and cut with scissors. Candy may be tinted by adding a drop of food coloring of your choice to sugar and water mixture. This is especially nice for receptions and teas.

Yield: 6 dozen

Jean Blair, Faculty Wife

Nut Clusters

8 blocks almond bark
1 (12-ounce) package semi-sweet chocolate morsels
1 (16-ounce) jar roasted unsalted peanuts or 2 cups lightly toasted pecans
Raisins (optional)

Melt almond bark and chocolate morsels in a large bowl in microwave oven for 3 minutes. Remove and stir. Add nuts and mix well. Drop by teaspoonsful onto wax paper and cool.

Variation: Additional nuts or raisins may be added, if desired.

Yield: 6 dozen small clusters

N. W. Carpenter '43, Retired Faculty

À la Orleans Style Pralines

(Microwave)

1 (1-pound) box light brown sugar
1 cup whipping cream
2 cups pecan halves (may use broken pieces)
2 Tablespoons margarine, softened
1 teaspoon vanilla (optional)
Dash of salt

In a 4-quart microwave-safe bowl, mix brown sugar and whipping cream. Microwave on High for 13 minutes or until mixture reaches soft-ball stage when tested. It is not necessary to stir mixture while in microwave. Remove bowl and quickly stir in pecans, margarine, vanilla, and salt. Drop by teaspoonsful onto wax paper. Cool.

Yield: 2 dozen

Laura L. Parkman

Tammie's Peanut Butter Balls

2 sticks margarine
1 (1-pound) box confectioners' sugar
1 (1-pound) jar crunchy peanut butter
⅓ (16-ounce) box graham crackers, crushed fine
1 cup pecans, chopped fine
⅔ (4-ounce) block paraffin
1 (16-ounce) package chocolate or butterscotch chips (do not use morsels)

Cream margarine and sugar; beat in peanut butter. Add graham cracker crumbs and pecans. Shape mixture into small balls. Refrigerate overnight or freeze for 1-3 hours. Melt paraffin and chips in double boiler over low heat. Use toothpick to pick up balls and dip in mixture until covered. Place onto wax paper. Remove toothpick when candy is hard. These may be frozen or refrigerated.

Yield: 60 balls

Brenda Castleberry '91

Martha Washington Balls

3 (1-pound) boxes confectioners' sugar
2 cans sweetened condensed milk
2 cups flaked coconut
2 pounds pecans, chopped
2 sticks margarine, melted
1 (12-ounce) package semi-sweet chocolate chips
¾ (4 ounces) block paraffin

Mix sugar, milk and coconut. Add chopped pecans and margarine. Mix well. Chill for 1 hour and then roll into small balls. Freeze for at least 1 hour before dipping. Melt chocolate chips and paraffin (cut into small pieces) in double boiler. Dip balls (on tooth pick) in chocolate; cool on wax paper. Keep chocolate hot while dipping.

Yield: 175 balls

Brenda Castleberry '91

Holiday Apricot Balls

18 ounces dried apricots, chopped fine
7 ounces sweetened flaked coconut
1 can sweetened condensed milk
1 cup pecans, chopped
Confectioners' sugar (approximately 1 cup)

Mix apricots, coconut, milk, and pecans. Put confectioners' sugar on work surface (a cutting board works nicely). Drop the apricot mixture by teaspoonsful onto the confectioners' sugar. Coat with the sugar and shape into balls. (Mixture is gooey to handle.) Chill and serve. These may be frozen.

Yield: 6½ dozen balls

Betty R. Barber '48, Faculty Wife

Make candy on a low-humidity day. If this is not possible, add 2 degrees to the recommended final cooking temperature.

Golden Nugget Fudge

½ cup evaporated milk, undiluted
1½ cups sugar
2 cups miniature marshmallows
1½ cups butterscotch morsels
1 teaspoon vanilla
2 cups walnuts or pecans, chopped

Combine milk and sugar in a heavy saucepan. Heat to boiling. Boil for 5 full minutes, stirring constantly. Remove from heat; add marshmallows, butterscotch morsels, vanilla, and nuts. Stir until marshmallows are melted. Drop the mixture by teaspoonsful onto a piece of wax paper.

Yield: 4 dozen pieces

Anne A. Thames

Old-Fashioned Chocolate Fudge

1½ Tablespoons light corn syrup
3 cups sugar
4 Tablespoons cocoa
1½ cups light cream
2 Tablespoons butter
1 teaspoon vanilla

Combine syrup, sugar, cocoa, and cream in a medium-size, heavy saucepan. Heat, stirring until mixture boils. Cook without stirring to soft ball stage (234 degrees). Remove from heat. Add butter and vanilla but do not stir. Cool to 110 degrees (lukewarm). Butter an 8x8 pan. Beat hard until mixture begins to thicken and loses its gloss. (This may take 15 minutes). Spread into prepared pan. Cut as soon as possible after it cools slightly. Put into a covered container. This gets creamier and better in 1 or 2 days.

Yield: 64 (1-inch) pieces

Mrs. L. L. Harned

Check the accuracy of a candy thermometer by placing it into boiling water. The temperature should be 212 degrees. Add or subtract the number of degrees necessary to compensate.

Chocolate Fudge

¼ pound margarine or butter
1 (6-ounce) package chocolate chips
2 cups sugar
1 (5-ounce) can evaporated milk
10 large marshmallows, cut up
1 cup nuts, chopped

Butter a large platter. Put margarine or butter and chocolate chips in a bowl. Mix sugar, milk, and marshmallows in a 2-quart saucepan. Bring to a rapid boil, stirring frequently, for 6 minutes. Pour into bowl with other ingredients. Stir until chocolate and butter have melted. Add nuts. Pour onto prepared platter and cool.

Yield: 36-40 pieces

Annette Trotter '73, Faculty Wife

Divinity

4 cups sugar, divided
1 cup light corn syrup
1½ cups water
3 egg whites
1 teaspoon vanilla

Mix 3 cups sugar, corn syrup, and water in heavy saucepan. Stir well and cook to hard crack stage (300 degrees). Remove from heat; in a second saucepan mix 1 cup sugar and water and cook to soft ball stage (240 degrees). While second mixture is cooking, beat egg whites until stiff. Mix the syrups and add vanilla. Pour in a very fine stream over egg whites, beating constantly with mixer on candy setting until mixture is thick and will drop from a spoon. Quickly drop by teaspoonsful onto wax paper or lightly greased cookie sheet. When completely cool, store in an airtight container.

Variation: 1 cup chopped pecans may be added before dropping candies.

Yield: 3 dozen small pieces

Dorothy Stevens Rogers '67, Faculty Wife

Old-Fashioned Peanut Brittle

3 cups sugar
1½ cups water
1 cup light corn syrup
1 pound raw, shelled Spanish peanuts
2 Tablespoons soda
½ stick margarine
1 teaspoon vanilla

Boil sugar, water and corn syrup in a non-stick pot until it spins a thread (290 degrees). Add peanuts and stir continuously until syrup is light golden brown. Remove from heat and add soda, followed by margarine, then vanilla; mixture will foam. Stir until margarine melts. Pour onto 2 baking sheets (10x14) with sides. Let cool before breaking into pieces. Candy stores best if wrapped in plastic wrap.

Yield: 3 pounds

Terry Blais Compton '79

Pecan Brittle

1 cup sugar
½ cup light corn syrup
¼ cup water
¼ teaspoon salt
1 cup pecans, coarsely chopped
1 Tablespoon butter or margarine
1 teaspoon soda
1 teaspoon vanilla (optional)

Butter a 15x10x1 jelly roll pan or aluminum foil. Combine sugar, syrup, water, and salt in a large, heavy saucepan; mix well. Cook over medium heat, stirring constantly, until mixture boils and sugar dissolves. Add pecans; return to aboil and cook, stirring frequently, until mixture reaches hard crack stage (300 degrees). Remove from heat; immediately stir in butter and soda. Add vanilla, if desired. Quickly spread mixture thinly onto a buttered jelly roll pan or buttered foil. Let cool. Break into pieces.

Yield: 1 pound

Cynthia B. Foster, Staff

Fudge-Coffee Ice Cream Bars

2½ cups vanilla wafer crumbs, crushed, divided
3 (1-ounce) squares unsweetened chocolate
¼ pound butter or margarine
2 cups confectioners' sugar
4 eggs, separated
1½ cups pecan halves or large pieces
½ gallon coffee ice cream (or chocolate chip)

Sprinkle 1¾ cups crumbs mixed with enough melted margarine to hold the crumbs together over bottom of 9x13 baking dish. In a medium saucepan over low heat, melt chocolate and butter. Remove from heat. Stir in confectioners' sugar. Beat egg yolks; stir into chocolate mixture. Beat egg whites until stiff. Fold into chocolate mixture, blending well. Pour chocolate mixture over crumbs in baking dish. Top with pecans (use additional pecans so that the sides and ends of each pecan are touching). Freeze until solid. Soften ice cream. Spread ice cream over fudge layer and top with remaining ¾ cup crumbs. Cover with foil. Freeze until solid (will keep in freezer up to 6 months). To serve, cut into 2-inch squares.

Yield: 16-20 servings

Betty Sue Wilbanks Campbell '52

Strawberry-Ice Cream Dessert

1 angel food cake
½ gallon vanilla ice cream, softened
2 (10-ounce) packages sliced frozen strawberries, thawed
1 cup pecans, broken (optional)
1 (12-ounce) carton whipped topping

Break cake into pieces and mix with ice cream, fruit, pecans, and whipped topping. Place into pan and freeze. (May use free-form angel food cake pan which as been sprayed with non-stick vegetable spray.) When unmolding, dip briefly in hot water.

Yield: 12-15 servings

Mrs. W. C. Applewhite

Ice cream picks up freezer odors quickly. Store in a zipper plastic freezer bag to maintain flavor.

Peach Ice Cream

2 cups fresh peaches, chopped
1 cup sugar
1 Tablespoon lemon juice
1 (8-ounce) can evaporated milk
3 Tablespoons water
1-2 teaspoons almond flavoring

Mix all ingredients and place mixture in a freezer container in the freezer; stir occasionally. Mixture will be icy. Recipe may be doubled.

Yield: 1 quart

Mamie Ruth Stranburg Abernathy

Basic Vanilla Ice Cream

4 eggs
2 cups sugar
4 cups milk
4 cups light cream
4 teaspoons vanilla
½ teaspoon salt

Beat eggs and sugar together until thick. Add milk, light cream, vanilla, and salt; mix well. Pour mixture into 1-gallon freezer container. Follow manufacturer's directions for freezing.

Variation: If cooked eggs are preferred to raw, cook egg mixture until slightly thickened. Cool before adding other ingredients.

Yield: 3 quarts

F. L. Lummus '56

Toby's Vanilla Ice Cream

4 eggs, pasteurized, or equivalent egg substitute
1 can sweetened condensed milk
1 cup sugar
1 Tablespoon vanilla
½ gallon milk

Beat eggs. Add condensed milk, sugar, vanilla, and other milk to the eggs and stir well. Place mixture in ice cream freezer and freeze according to manufacturer's instructions.

Yield: 3 quarts

Becky Jones Rodgers '92

Easy Fruit Ice Cream

2 quarts milk
2 cans sweetened condensed milk
4 pasteurized eggs or egg substitutes
1¼ cups sugar
½ teaspoon vanilla
½ teaspoon almond flavoring
2 (10-ounce) packages of favorite frozen fruit, (peaches or strawberries)

In a blender, blend 2 cups milk, 1 egg and about one-half cup condensed milk, eggs, sugar, flavorings, and fruit. Fruit will be pureéd. Pour into freezer canister. Repeat process until all is blended. Fill canister as needed with some of remaining milk. Freeze in electric or hand-crank freezer according to manufacturer's instructions. Uneaten ice cream can be re-frozen and kept in plastic containers. When cream is ready to eat, it may be softened in microwave for 20 seconds or so. For 5-quart freezer, increase recipe ingredients by one-fourth.

Variations: Use 1 (20-ounce) can pineapple, or equivalent fresh fruit - bananas, berries, etc. - or 1 cup chocolate syrup.

Yield: 4 quarts

Norman S. Deaton '54

Easy Chocolate Ice Cream

½ gallon chocolate milk
1 can sweetened condensed milk
1 (8-ounce) container whipped topping

Mix all ingredients thoroughly on low speed of electric mixer. Pour into container and place in freezer, stirring occasionally until well frozen. Add an extra pint of chocolate milk to mixture if recipe is used in an ice cream freezer.

Variation: For Doc's Famous Chocolate Ice Cream, omit whipped topping and add 1 pint of whipping cream and 2 cups sugar; if necessary, add whole milk to the fill line. (The chocolate flavor is more distinct if chocolate syrup is added.)

Yield: 3-4 quarts

Theresa P. Lambert
Ted Snazelle, Faculty

ALUMNI HALL

ALUMNI HALL

Alumni Hall was built in 1926 — at a cost of $3.00 per square foot! It is special in that it was financed, not by the College, but by the Alumni Association. At the time of construction, its amenities included offices, classrooms, dormitory rooms, a basketball court, a swimming pool, and other athletic facilities; it was reported to have been one of the finest athletic centers in the South. When alumni from the 1950's visit the dusty gym today, they can almost hear ghostly echoes from frenzied crowds as Coach "Stute" Allen's Choctaws set national scoring records that remain unbroken. The building awaits major renovation as funds become available.

MISCELLANEOUS

Roosevelt Hotel Rémoulade Sauce

1 cup mayonnaise
1 teaspoon onion, chopped
1 teaspoon parsley, chopped
1 teaspoon celery, chopped
1 teaspoon horseradish
1 teaspoon paprika
2 teaspoons Creole mustard
½ teaspoon salt
1 Tablespoon vinegar
½ teaspoon water
Dash Tabasco sauce

Mix all ingredients well; chill. Serve with boiled shrimp.

Yield: 1 cup sauce

Rosa Taylor Russell '63

This recipe came from the old Roosevelt Hotel in New Orleans, now the Fairmount.

Steak Shoyu

½ cup soy sauce
3 Tablespoons sugar
3 Tablespoons Italian salad dressing

Combine ingredients. Use as a marinade for steak, chicken, or any kind of shish kebab. The sauce may be refrigerated for several weeks.

Yield: ½ cup sauce

Kay Miller

Bouligny Glaze

1 (10-12-ounce) jar plum jam
Teriyaki sauce
Ground ginger

Mix the plum jam with enough teriyaki sauce to make a paste-like consistency. Add ground ginger to taste. Use on chicken, duck, pork roast, or fish, before and after cooking. This glaze will keep indefinitely in the refrigerator.

Yield: 2 cups sauce

Jane Clover Alexander, Faculty

The chef at Bouligny Restaurant in New Orleans shared this with me.

Cajun Seasoning Mix

1 Tablespoon salt
2 teaspoons paprika
1½ teaspoons onion powder
1½ teaspoons garlic powder
1½ teaspoons basil leaves (dried)
1 teaspoon dry mustard
1 teaspoon cumin (ground)
1 teaspoon black pepper
¾ teaspoon white pepper
½ teaspoon thyme leaves (dried)
½ teaspoon ground savory
½ teaspoon cayenne pepper

Combine all ingredients. Use to flavor roasted chicken.

Yield: ⅓ cup seasoning mixture

Teresa Cockerham '90

Hog Dog/Hamburger Sauce

2 Tablespoons margarine
1 medium onion, chopped
1 bell pepper, chopped
2 Tablespoons brown sugar
2 Tablespoons prepared mustard
1 Tablespoon Worcestershire sauce
½ teaspoon salt
¾ cup catsup

Combine all the ingredients and simmer for 15 minutes; cool. Serve as a sauce for hot dogs, hamburgers, or barbecued meats.

Yield: 8 servings

Sarah Fortenberry Talley '61

Nick's Barbecue Sauce

1½ cups sugar
¾ cup vinegar
1 (10-ounce) bottle steak sauce
½ cup Worcestershire sauce
1 gallon catsup
1 Tablespoon chili powder
1 Tablespoon garlic salt
1 teaspoon pepper
¾ Tablespoon celery salt
1 teaspoon salt
1½ Tablespoons bacon drippings

Mix all ingredients in a stock pot. Simmer for 20-30 minutes. Cool; store in refrigerator in glass jars.

Yield: Approximately 4½ quarts

Rosa Taylor Russell '63

Big Mama's Tomato Chili Sauce

1 gallon tomatoes
2 cups onions, chopped
2 cups green pepper, chopped
3 hot peppers, chopped
2 Tablespoons salt
2 cups sugar
1 cup cider vinegar

Peel tomatoes and cut into quarters. Mix all ingredients together except vinegar. Bring to a boil, then reduce heat to medium and cook for 45 minutes, stirring to prevent sticking. Add vinegar and cook for 1½ hours or until mixture reaches desired consistency. Pour hot chili sauce into hot sterilized jars; adjust lids and seal. Jars should seal without processing in boiling-water bath. This sauce is good with black-eyed peas.

Yield: 6 pints

Mary Eleanor Cade '62

Hot Mustard

1 (4-ounce) can dry mustard
1 cup white wine vinegar
1 cup sugar
2 eggs, beaten

Mix dry mustard and wine vinegar. Refrigerate overnight. Add sugar and eggs; stir until smooth. Microwave on Medium, stirring every 4-5 minutes until mustard thickens; texture should resemble custard. This recipe is wonderful with egg rolls, cold cuts, ham, or turkey. It keeps indefinitely in refrigerator.

Yield: 1 pint

Ann Grundfest Gerache '91

Picante Sauce

6 quarts tomatoes, chopped
6 cups green peppers, chopped
6 cups onions, chopped
4 Tablespoons salt
1½ Tablespoons garlic, chopped
Jalapeño peppers, chopped (3-4, mild; 8-10, medium hot)

Put all ingredients into a large pan and bring to boil. Cook on low heat for about 1½ hours or until mixture reaches desired thickness, stirring often. Pour into hot sterilized jars, seal, and process in boiling-water bath for 10 minutes.

Yield: 8-9 pints

Frances Ivey (George D. Ivey '47)

Mamaw's Squash Pickles

8 cups squash, sliced
2 cups onions, chopped
2 cups green pepper, chopped
2 Tablespoons salt
2 Tablespoons mustard seed
2 cups vinegar
3 cups sugar
2 Tablespoons celery seed
1 (4-ounce) jar pimientos

Mix squash, onions, green pepper, and salt together. Let stand for 2 hours. Drain. Mix mustard seed, vinegar, sugar, and celery seed; add pimientos for color. Bring vinegar mixture to a boil. Add squash mixture and bring to a boil again. Seal in hot sterilized jars.

Yield: 8 pints

Florence "Tubby" Blough Pickering '58

This is an old family recipe. My 91-year-old mother uses it in potato salad, tuna salad, and stuffed eggs.

Bread and Butter Pickles

1 gallon medium cucumbers, thinly sliced
2 bell peppers, thinly sliced
2 medium onions, thinly sliced
1 quart crushed ice
½ cup salt
5 cups sugar
5 cups vinegar
1 teaspoon celery seed
1½ teaspoons turmeric
½ teaspoon ground cloves
2 teaspoons mustard seed

Layer cucumbers, peppers, onions, ice, and salt in a large bowl. Cover with weighted lid and place into refrigerator for 3 hours or longer. Drain; rinse in cold water and drain again thoroughly. Combine sugar, vinegar, celery seed, turmeric, cloves, and mustard seed in a large pan; bring just to the boiling point. Add vegetables gradually and heat slowly with very little stirring. Bring to a scald, but do not boil. Place the pickles in hot sterilized jars and seal at once. Before opening jars to serve, refrigerate. These pickles are better cold.

Yield: About 12 pints

Jean Horn Ross '45

Quince Jam

3 yellow quince
2 apples
3 cups sugar
¼ cup cinnamon red hot candies
Water to cover

Peel quince and apples; cut into small pieces. Cover with water and boil until fruit is soft. Press through a sieve or food processor to remove all lumps. Add sugar and bring to a boil, stirring constantly. Reduce heat to prevent spattering. Add cinnamon red hot candies and cook until candies have melted. When the jam is thick, test for doneness by pouring a small quantity on a cold plate. Jam is done when no rim of liquid separates around the jam on the plate. Pour hot jam into hot sterilized ½-pint jars and seal.

Yield: 4-5 half-pint jars

Arie Farr, Retired Staff (Eugene I. Farr '26)

Seasoned Oyster Crackers

1½ cups oil
2 Tablespoons dill weed
1 teaspoon lemon pepper
1 (1-ounce) package ranch dressing mix, dry
¼ teaspoon garlic powder
¼ teaspoon onion powder
2 (11-ounce) packages dry oyster crackers

Mix oil, dill weed, lemon pepper, dressing mix, garlic powder and onion powder. Pour over crackers. Bake at 225-250 degrees for 1¼-1½ hours, stirring every 15 minutes.

Carol J. Garrett, Staff

Almond Bark Scramble

4 cups square graham cereal
4 cups chex-type cereal
2 cups pecans
2 cups pretzels (optional)
1 (16-ounce) package almond bark

Mix cereals, nuts, and pretzels in a large container. Melt almond bark in the microwave according to package instructions. Pour over the dry mixture and stir until thoroughly covered. Pour onto wax paper or foil and spread evenly. When mixture is set, break into small pieces and store in an airtight container.

Yield: 10-12 servings

Tracy Brannon '93

Parched Peanuts

1 pound peanuts, dried, unshelled

Preheat oven to 500 degrees. Put unshelled peanuts 1½ inches deep in a light metal skillet (not cast iron or other heavy metals). Set container of peanuts on the middle shelf of oven. Close oven door and cut off heat. Do not open door for any reason until oven has completely cooled; this takes about 3 hours.

Yield: 1 pound

Mary Lane Burkes Wheatley '54

My grandmother, who began keeping house in 1873, used this method for parching peanuts in her wood stove.

Puppy Chow

1 (12-ounce) package chocolate chips
1 stick margarine
1 cup smooth peanut butter
1 large box chex-type cereal (15-ounce or larger)
1 (1-pound) box confectioners' sugar

Melt chips, margarine, and butter in a large plastic bowl (can be done in microwave). Add cereal and mix until cereal is coated with chocolate. Next transfer mixture to large plastic bag containing the powdered sugar and shake until cereal mix is coated. Chill. Individual cereal biscuits will not stick to each other when coated with powdered sugar.

Yield: 6-8 servings

Lisa Leavell '80
Julie Fussell '84

In preparing pickles, the best results are achieved by using a high-grade apple cider vinegar for all but light pickles. Those need white vinegar.

Food Guide Pyramid

A Guide to Daily Food Choices

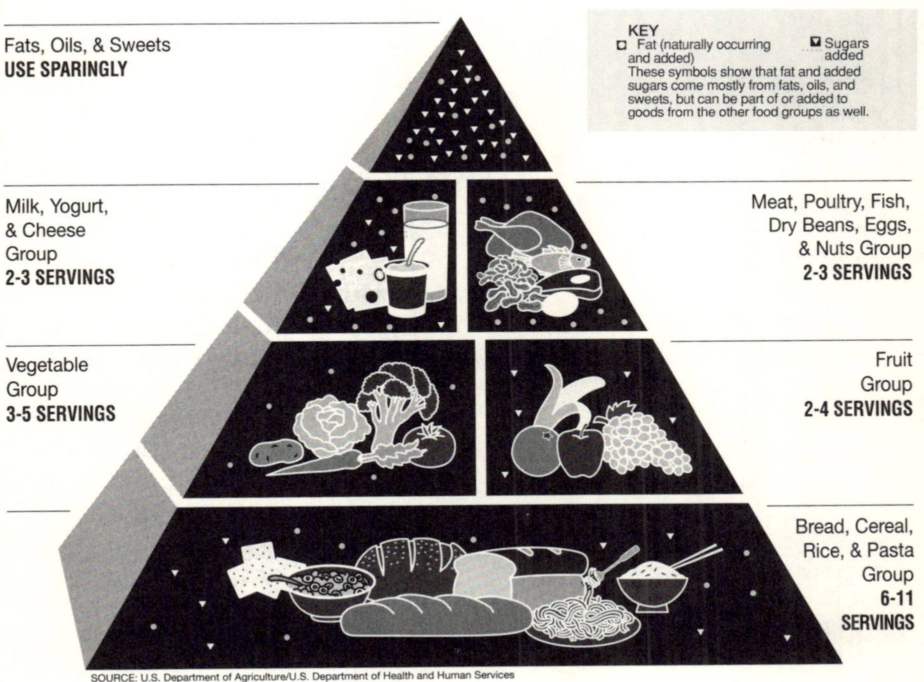

SOURCE: U.S. Department of Agriculture/U.S. Department of Health and Human Services

Use the Food Guide Pyramid to help you eat better every day. . .the Dietary Guidelines way. Start with plenty of Breads, Cereals, Rice, and Pasta; Vegetables; and Fruits. Add two to three servings from the Milk group and two to three servings from the Meat group.

Each of these food groups provides some, but not all, of the nutrients you need. No one food group is more important than another — for good health you need them all. Go easy on fats, oils, and sweets, the foods in the small tip of the Pyramid.

To order a copy of "The Food Guide Pyramid" booklet, send a $1.00 check or money order made out to the Superintendent of Documents to: Comsumer Infromation Center, Department 159-Y, Pueblo, Colorado 81009

U.S. Department of Agriculture, Human Nutrition Information Service, August 1992, Leaflet No. 572

Substitutions

Ingredient Called For:	Substitute:
1 cup self-rising flour	1 cup all-purpose flour plus 1 teaspoon baking powder and ½ teaspoon salt
1 cup cake flour	1 cup sifted all-purpose flour minus 2 tablespoons
1 cup all-purpose flour	1 cup cake flour plus 2 tablespoons
1 teaspoon baking powder	½ teaspoon cream of tartar plus ¼ teaspoon soda
1 tablespoon cornstarch or arrowroot	2 tablespoons all-purpose flour
1 tablespoon tapioca	1½ tablespoons all-purpose flour
2 large eggs	3 small eggs
1 egg	2 egg yolks (for custard)
1 egg	2 egg yolks plus 1 tablespoon water (for cookies)
1 (8-ounce) carton commercial sour cream	1 tablespoon lemon juice plus evaporated milk to equal 1 cup; or 3 tablespoons butter plus ⅞ cup sour milk
1 cup yogurt	1 cup buttermilk or sour milk
1 cup sour milk or buttermilk	1 tablespoon vinegar or lemon juice plus sweet milk to equal 1 cup
1 cup fresh milk	½ cup evaporated milk plus ½ cup water
1 cup fresh milk	3 to 5 tablespoons nonfat dry milk solids in 1 cup water
1 cup honey	1¼ cups sugar plus ¼ cup water
1 (1-ounce) square unsweetened chocolate	3 tablespoons cocoa plus 1 tablespoon butter or margarine
1 tablespoon fresh herbs	1 teaspoon dried herbs or ¼ teaspoon powdered herbs
¼ cup chopped fresh parsley	1 tablespoon dried parsley flakes
1 teaspoon dry mustard	1 tablespoon prepared mustard
1 pound fresh mushrooms	6 ounces canned mushrooms

Tables of Weights and Measures

Dash = less than 1/8 teaspoon

1 teaspoon = 60 drops

3 teaspoons = 1 Tablespoon

2 Tablespoons = 1 fluid ounce

4 Tablespoons = 1/4 cup

8 Tablespoons = 1/2 cup

12 Tablespoons = 3/4 cup

16 Tablespoons = 1 cup

1 cup = 8 fluid ounces or 1/2 pint

1 pint = 16 fluid ounces or 2 cups

2 pints = 1 quart

1 quart = 4 cups

2 quarts = 1/2 gallon

4 quarts = 1 gallon

1 pound = 16 ounces or 2 cups liquid

1 pound of butter or margarine = 2 cups

1 stick of butter or margarine = 1/2 cup

1 pound of flour = 4 cups sifted

1 pound of cheese = 4 cups shredded

1 pound of granulated sugar = 2 cups

1 pound of brown sugar = 2-1/4 cups

1 pound of confectioners sugar = 3-1/2 cups

Modifications

IF THE RECIPE CALLS FOR	"NEAR EQUAL"	"HEALTHIER CHOICE"
Milk Group		
Buttermilk (made from skim milk) 1 cup = 99 calories, 2.2 grams fat	1 cup whole milk plus 1 tablespoon lemon juice or vinegar. Allow to stand 5 or 10 minutes.	1 cup skim milk plus 1 tablespoon lemon juice or vinegar
Cream Cheese 1 ounce = 100 calories, 10 grams fat	"Light" cream cheese 1 ounce = 80 calories or Cottage cheese, creamed in food processor	Neufchatel 1 ounce = 74 calories, 6.6 grams fat. Low-fat cottage cheese creamed in food processor.
Cottage cheese 1 cup = 217 calories, 9.5 grams fat	Ricotta, part skim 1 cup = 171 calories, 10 grams fat	Low-fat 1% cottage cheese 1 cup = 164 calories, 2.3 grams fat
Heavy cream or whipping cream 1 cup = 832 calories, 45 grams fat	¾ cup milk plus ⅓ cup margarine	¾ cup skim milk plus ¼ cup margarine
Milk, whole 1 cup = 170 calories, 9 grams fat 1 cup 2% = 120 calories, 4.7 grams fat	2% milk plus 2 tablespoons margarine or ¼ cup non-fat dry milk powder plus 1 cup water plus 3 teaspoons margarine.	Skim milk or evaporated skim milk plus ½ cup water
Sweetened condensed milk 1 ounce = 123 calories, 3.3 grams fat	1 cup non-fat dry milk solids plus ⅔ cup sugar plus ⅓ cup boiling water plus 3 tablespoons margarine. Process and refrigerate.	1 cup non-fat dry milk solids plus 4 packs artificial sweetener plus ½ cup boiling water plus 1 tablespoon margarine. Process and refrigerate.
Sour cream 1 cup = 208 calories, 20 grams fat	Plain yogurt plus drop of lemon juice or vinegar to sour. Or ⅞ cup sour milk plus ⅓ cup butter	Low-fat yogurt plus drop of lemon juice or vinegar to sour. 1 cup = 127 calories, 0.4 grams fat
Yogurt 1 cup = 140 calories, 7.5 grams fat	⅞ cup buttermilk plus 3 tablespoons margarine or 1 cup low-fat cottage cheese pureed	1 cup buttermilk, cultured with heat
Half and half 1 ounce = 40 calories, 4 grams fat	⅞ cup whole milk plus 3 tablespoons margarine	
Fats & Oils		
Butter - 1 cup 1 tablespoon = 108 calories, 12.2 grams fat	⅞ - 1 cup hydrogenated fat plus 1 teaspoon salt. 1 tablespoon = 106 calories, 12 grams fat	⅞ cup vegetable oil or corn, safflower, peanut or canola
Margarine - 1 cup 1 tablespoon = 100 calories, 11 grams fat	⅞ to 1 cup oil plus ½ teaspoon salt	⅞ cup vegetable oil or corn, safflower, peanut or canola
Oil 1 tablespoon = 120 calories, 14 grams fat		Use as for margarine, with the exception of tropical oils (palm and coconut).

IF THE RECIPE CALLS FOR	"NEAR EQUAL"	"HEALTHIER CHOICE"
Other		
Baking powder 1 teaspoon	¼ teaspoon baking soda plus ½ teaspoon cream of tartar	
Breadcrumbs	Crushed corn flakes	Unsweetened bran cereal
Broth	Bouillon cube or 1 teaspoon powder plus 1 cup boiling water	
Chocolate 1 square	3 tablespoons cocoa plus 1 tablespoon shortening	
Semi-sweet chocolate 6 ounces	2 ounces unsweetened chocolate plus 7 tablespoons sugar plus 2 tablespoons shortening	
Corn syrup 1 cup	¾ cup sugar plus ¼ cup water or 1 cup honey	
Flour		
1 tablespoon all-purpose for thickening	½ tablespoon cornstarch or 1 tablespoon quick cooking tapioca	
1 cup, sifted	1 cup unsifted all-purpose flour minus 2 tablespoons	
Cake Flour 1 cup, sifted	1 cup sifted all-purpose flour minus 2 tablespoons	
Self-Rising 1 cup, sifted	Combine 1 cup sifted all-purpose flour, 1 teaspoon baking powder, and ½ teaspoon salt	
Graham cracker crust	1½ cups ground almonds plus 2 teaspoons butter	1½ cups ground almonds plus 1 teaspoon vegetable margarine
Herbs	1 tablespoon fresh = 1 teaspoon dried, ground or crushed	½ teaspoon, fresh or powdered
Honey 1 cup	1¼ cups sugar plus ¼ cup liquid or 1 cup molasses	
Ketchup	1 cup tomato sauce plus ½ cup sugar plus 2 tablespoons vinegar	1 cup tomato sauce plus 2 packages artificial sweetener plus 2 tablespoons vinegar
Lemon peel	1 teaspoon grated = ½ teaspoon lemon extract	
Prepared mustard 1 tablespoon	1 teaspoon dried mustard	
Onion 2 teaspoons minced	1 teaspoon onion powder	
Canned tomatoes 1 cup	1⅓ fresh tomatoes, simmer 10 minutes	
Tomato juice 1 cup	½ cup tomato sauce plus ½ cup water	
Tomato sauce 2 cups	¾ cup tomato paste plus 1 cup water	
Vinegar 1 tablespoon	2 teaspoons lemon juice	

For Your Information

Food	Weight or Count	Measure or Yield
Apples	1 pound (3 medium)	3 cups sliced
Bacon	8 slices cooked	½ cup crumbled
Bananas	1 pound (3 medium)	2½ cups sliced, or about 2 cups mashed
Bread	1 pound	12 to 16 slices
	About 1½ slices	1 cup soft crumbs
Butter or margarine	1 pound	2 cups
	¼ pound stick	½ cup
Cabbage	1 pound head	4½ cups shredded
Candied fruit or peels	½ pound	1¼ cups chopped
Carrots	1 pound	3 cups shredded
Cheese		
American or Cheddar	1 pound	About 4 cups shredded
cottage	1 pound	2 cups
cream	3-ounce package	6 tablespoons
Chocolate morsels	6-ounce package	1 cup
Cocoa	1 pound	4 cups
Coconut, flaked or shredded	1 pound	5 cups
Coffee	1 pound	80 tablespoons (40 cups perked)
Corn	2 medium ears	1 cup kernels
Cornmeal	1 pound	3 cups
Crab, in shell	1 pound	¾ to 1 cup flaked
Crackers		
chocolate wafers	19 wafers	1 cup crumbs
graham crackers	14 squares	1 cup fine crumbs
saltine crackers	28 crackers	1 cup finely crushed
vanilla wafers	22 wafers	1 cup finely crushed
Cream, whipping	1 cup (½ pint)	2 cups whipped
Dates, pitted	1 pound	3 cups chopped
	8-ounce package	1½ cups chopped
Eggs	5 large	1 cup
whites	8 to 11	1 cup
yolks	12 to 14	1 cup
Flour		
all-purpose	1 pound	3½ cups
cake	1 pound	4¾ to 5 cups sifted
whole wheat	1 pound	3½ cups unsifted
Green pepper	1 large	1 cup diced
Lemon	1 medium	2 to 3 tablespoons juice; 2 teaspoons grated rind
Lettuce	1 pound head	6¼ cups torn
Lime	1 medium	1½ to 2 tablespoons juice; 1½ teaspoons grated rind
Macaroni	4 ounces (1 cup)	2¼ cups cooked
Marshmallows	11 large	1 cup
	10 miniature	1 large marshmallow
Marshmallows, miniature	½ pound	4½ cups
Milk		
evaporated	5.33-ounce can	⅔ cup
evaporated	13-ounce can	1 5⁄8 cups
sweetened condensed	14-ounce can	1¼ cups
Mushrooms	3 cups raw (8 ounces)	1 cup sliced cooked

Food	Weight or Count	Measure or Yield
Nuts		
almonds	1 pound	1 to 1¾ cups nutmeats
	1 pound shelled	3½ cups nutmeats
peanuts	1 pound	2¼ cups nutmeats
	1 pound shelled	3 cups
pecans	1 pound	2¼ cups nutmeats
	1 pound shelled	4 cups
walnuts	1 pound	1⅔ cups nutmeats
	1 pound shelled	4 cups
Oats, quick-cooking	1 cup	1¾ cups cooked
Onion	1 medium	½ cup chopped
Orange	1 medium	⅓ cup juice; 2 tablespoons grated rind
Peaches	2 medium	1 cup sliced
Pears	2 medium	1 cup sliced
Potatoes		
white	3 medium	2 cups cubed cooked or 1¾ cups mashed
sweet	3 medium	3 cups sliced
Raisins, seedless	1 pound	3 cups
Rice		
long-grain	1 cup	3 to 4 cups cooked
pre-cooked	1 cup	2 cups cooked
Shrimp, raw in shell	1½ pounds	2 cups (¾ pound) cleaned, cooked
Spaghetti	7 ounces	About 4 cups cooked
Strawberries	1 quart	4 cups sliced
Sugar		
brown	1 pound	2⅓ cups firmly packed
powdered	1 pound	3½ cups unsifted
granulated	1 pound	2 cups

Terms Used in Cookery

AL DENTE

The point in the cooking of pasta at which it is still fairly firm to the tooth; slightly undercooked.

À LA MODE

Served with ice cream.

ALMONDINE

Shredded blanched almonds toasted in butter.

ASPIC

A well-seasoned jelly made from stock, broth, or tomato juice held together with gelatin.

AU GRATIN

With a browned crumb crust mixed with cheese. Usually applied to a scalloped dish.

BAKE

To cook in an oven.

BARBECUE

To roast meat over coals or on a spit, usually basting with a highly seasoned sauce. Also applies to meats cooked indoors with a barbecue sauce.

BASTE

To brush or spoon liquids over food while cooking, especially over roasting meats.

BEAT

To whip by lifting mixture rapidly up and over with fork, spoon, wire whisk, rotary or electric mixer.

BLANCH

To dip in boiling water, generally in order to loosen skin or to set color.

BLEND

To combine thoroughly.

BOIL

To cook in a liquid which should bubble actively during the time indicated. Just enough heat should be applied to keep the liquid in this state, unless rapid boiling is designated in the recipe.

BOUILLON

Soup stock clarified by straining.

BRAISE

To brown meat or vegetables in oil and then to cook covered, sometimes adding a small amount of liquid.

BREAD

To dip food into an egg-milk mixture and then into fine dry crumbs.

BROIL

To cook under or over direct heat.

BROTH

Liquid in which meat has been simmered.

CANAPÉ

Usually a small round of toasted bread spread with an appetizing mixture.

CANDY

To cook in sugar or syrup.

CARMELIZE

To heat sugar or food containing a high percentage of sugar until a brown color and characteristic flavor develop.

CHOP

To cut into small pieces with a sharp knife or chopper.

COMPOTE

Fruit stewed in a sugar syrup.

CONDIMENT

A seasoning.

CREAM

To mix softened shortening or cream with sugar by beating with a spoon or electric mixer.

CREOLE

A well-seasoned tomato sauce containing green pepper and chopped onion.

CROUTON

A small piece of crisply toasted bread used in soups, garnishes, etc.

CUBE
To cut into small square pieces.

CUT IN SHORTENING
To mix cold shortening with flour as in pastry and biscuits.

DICE
To cut into very small pieces.

DISSOLVE
To mix a dry substance with liquid until it is in solution.

DREDGE
To cover with a thin coating of dry ingredient, such as sugar or flour.

DRIPPINGS
The fat and juices which cook out of meat or poultry.

DUST
To sprinkle lightly, usually with flour or sugar.

EN BROCHETTE
Food cooked or served on a skewer.

ENTREE
Applied to an informal meal, means the main dish of the main course—meat, vegetable, poultry, fish or meat substitute; applied to a formal dinner, means a light savory course served between two courses, usually between the soup and the meat course.

FILÉ
Powder made of sassafras leaves used to season and thicken foods.

FILLET
A boneless piece of fish or lean meat.

FLAKE
To break lightly into small pieces with a fork.

FLAN
In France, a filled pastry; in Spain, a custard.

FLORENTINE
A food containing or placed upon spinach.

FOLD

To combine ingredients with a cutting and folding motion.

FRAPPÉ

A liquid mixture frozen to a mush.

FRY

To cook in hot oil. When food is surrounded with hot oil, process is known as deep frying.

GARNISH

To add something for sake of appearance or flavor.

GLACÉ

To coat with a sugar syrup cooked to the crack stage. It may also refer to a less concentrated mixture, containing thickening and used for coating certain types of rolls or pastries.

GLAZE

A coating produced by cooking with sugar or syrup and fat.

GRATE

To rub on a grater until finely divided.

GRILL

To broil.

GRIND

To put through food chopper using fine, medium, or coarse blade.

GUMBO

Soup or stew made with okra.

JULIENNE

To cut into lengthwise strips.

KNEAD

To fold and press dough firmly with palms of hands, turning between foldings.

LEAVENING

Ingredients needed to make mixture rise, such as baking powder, soda, yeast.

MARINATE

To let stand in a liquid for the purpose of tendering and/or enhancing flavor.

MASH

To reduce to a soft, pulpy state.

MELT

To change a solid into liquid form by heating.

MINCE

To cut or chop fine.

MOCHA

A flavor combination of coffee and chocolate.

PAN-BOIL

To cook in dry, hot frying pan, pouring off fat as it cooks out of meat.

PAN-FRY

To fry in small amount of oil.

PARBOIL

To boil in water until food is partially cooked.

PARCH

To brown by the application of dry heat.

PARE

To remove skin or rind by cutting off with a knife.

PEEL

To remove skin by pulling or rubbing off.

PICKLING

Preserving foods by means of salt and vinegar. Sugar and spices are often added.

POACH

To cook in hot liquid below boiling point.

PREHEAT

To heat oven to desired temperature before putting in food to bake or roast.

PUREE
To press food through a coarse sieve.

REDUCE
To boil down evaporating liquid from a cooked dish.

ROAST
To cook by dry heat in an oven.

ROUX
A mixture of fat and flour used to thicken a liquid.

SAUTÉ
To cook in a small amount of fat.

SCALD
To heat liquid, usually milk, until just below boiling point.

SCALLOP
To bake food in a casserole in layers with sauce.

SCORE
To make shallow lengthwise and crosswise slits across surface with a sharp knife.

SEAR
To brown surface quickly with high heat, then reducing heat to cook.

SHRED
To cut or tear in thin strips or pieces.

SIFT
To put dry ingredients through a sieve.

SIMMER
To cook in liquid just at or below the boiling point.

SKEWER
To fasten meat with a thin wooden or metal pin. Sometimes small bits of meat, fish, or vegetables are broiled on a metal skewer.

STEAM
To cook over or surrounded by steam.

STEEP
To let stand in hot liquid below the boiling point.

STERILIZE

To destroy micro-organisms by boiling in water, by dry heat, or by steam.

STEW

To cook slowly in liquid held below the boiling point.

STIR-FRY

To cook quickly in a small amount of oil over high heat, using light tossing and stirring motions to preserve shape of food.

STOCK

Liquid in which meat, fish and/or vegetables have been cooked. Used as a base for soups and gravies.

STUFFING

A mixture of materials having as its base cereals, bread, crackers, etc. Used with meat, poultry, fish, and vegetables.

TOAST

To brown by direct heat.

TOSS

To mix by lifting lightly and repeatedly, usually with a fork or a fork and spoon.

WHIP

To beat rapidly in order to incorporate air.

Kitchen Hints

Avocado To ripen, place into a brown paper bag and store in a warm place. To peel an avocado, pull the skin off by hand carefully so as not to break the inner green surface. This prevents the flesh from discoloring.

Brown Sugar An apple placed in the container prevents sugar from hardening.

Egg Whites They will have more volume if they are beaten in a small, deep bowl so the beaters are immersed, and the mixture is thoroughly aerated.

Separate whites from yolks as soon as eggs are removed from the refrigerator. Cold yolks are firmer and less likely to break.

Adding a teaspoon of cold water to egg whites while beating increases the volume.

When beating egg whites, avoid tapping the egg beater on the bowl since this will cause the whites to lose much of their fluffiness.

Flour When recipe calls for sifted flour, the flour should be sifted, then measured.

Frying When deep-fat frying, add a tablespoon of vinegar to the fat while it is still cold. This prevents the food from absorbing an excessive amount of fat and eliminates a greasy taste.

Garlic A clove of garlic is a piece of garlic —the bulb or pod is the whole garlic.

Grating Before grating lemon rind, cheese, carrots, onions, etc., coat the grater with non-stick cooking spray to make cleanup easier.

Marshmallows Dip knife or cooking shears in hot water frequently when chopping marshmallows, raisins, and other sticky foods.

Measuring To measure dry ingredients use measuring cups and spoons with a flat rim so ingredients can be leveled off with a spatula.

Liquids should be measured in cups with pouring spouts.

Olive Oil Prevent olive oil from becoming rancid by adding one lump of sugar per pint of oil.

The greener the olive oil, the better the quality.

Oranges Place oranges into a hot oven for two to three minutes before peeling. This prevents the white fiber from being left on the orange.

Red Stains To prevent red stains on plastic containers, spray the inside with non-stick cooking spray before storing spaghetti sauce and other foods cooked with tomatoes.

Tomatoes Dip tomatoes in boiling water for thirty seconds for easy peeling.

Ripen tomatoes stem up. The rounded top of a tomato is the most tender part and bruises easily.

Storing tomatoes in the refrigerator kills both flavor and the ripening process.

Microwave Ideas

Breadcrumbs Cut six slices of bread into half-inch cubes. Microwave in a three-quart casserole for six to seven minutes, or until dry, stirring after three minutes. Let stand for one minute and crust in blender.

Brown Sugar To soften a box of hardened brown sugar, place box in microwave beside one cup of hot water for one and one-half to two minutes. If you store brown sugar in the freezer, remove it thirty minutes before using and the sugar will always be soft.

Butter or Margarine will soften in one minute when microwaved at 20% power.

Cakes or Potatoes If not quite done on the bottom, cakes or potatoes can be placed in another dish or on a roasting rack and microwaved for one to two minutes.

Chicken When microwaving chicken, place meaty pieces around the edges of the dish and bony pieces in the center.

Fat To drain fat from hamburger while it is cooking in the microwave, cook it in a plastic colander placed inside a casserole dish.

Gelatin To dissolve gelatin in the microwave, measure liquid into a measuring cup, add gelatin.

Ice Cream To soften hard ice cream, microwave at 30% power. One pint will take twenty-five seconds; one quart thirty to forty-five seconds; and one-half gallon forty-five seconds to one minute.

Lemons/Limes To squeeze more juice, cut fruit in half and heat in the microwave for about thirty seconds.

Nuts Nuts will be easier to shell if you microwave two cups of nuts in a casserole with one cup of water for four to five minutes.

Potato Chips Refresh stale potato chips, crackers, or other similar snacks by placing a plateful in the microwave for thirty to forty-five seconds. Let stand for one minute to crisp. This also works with cereals.

Avoid using any paper or plastic product in the microwave which is not labeled as microwaveable. Any color or bleach in the product can contaminate the food.

Usage of Herbs

Basil Eggs, meats, salads, sauces, casseroles

Chives Appetizers, eggs, cream soups, salads

Cilantro Mexican, Chinese and Italian dishes and as a garnish (also known as ***Chinese*** or ***Italian Parsley***)

Dill Weed Fish, vegetables, sauces, salads

Marjoram Fish, poultry, lamb, sausages, stews

Mint Beverages, desserts, fish, lamb, sauces, soups

Oregano Italian dishes, meats, vegetables, soups

Rosemary Pork, fish, lamb, casseroles, seafood

Sage Stuffings, poultry, fish, sausages

Savory Vegetables, sauces, poultry, soups

Tarragon Eggs, meats, fish, poultry, tomatoes

Thyme Chowders, fish, meats, poultry, stews, tomatoes

Add fresh herbs at the last minute. Once they are cut, herbs lose about 50% of their flavor.

HENDRICK HOUSE

Hendrick House, the President's Home at Mississippi College, was built in 1966 through the generosity of Mr. Roger Hendrick, Class of 1922. The style is modified Georgian with white columns reminiscent of the Old Chapel. It was first occupied during the last two years of Dr. R. A. McLemore's tenure as President. The two women who have resided there as First Lady have made Hendrick House a campus landmark and a symbol of gracious hospitality for students, faculty, staff, members of the community, and guests of the College.

Special Foods and Special People

The final section of this cookbook has been reserved for individuals who have a unique relationship with Mississippi College. "Special Foods and Special People" describes two distinct groups: (1) descendants of those individuals who have served as President of Mississippi College, and (2) celebrities who at some time have appeared on campus.

Included in this section are a menu from the Mississippi Governor's Mansion; charming and unusually worded recipes from earlier, less-hurried times; interesting historic information about Presidential families; and favorite food preparations from entertainers, sports figures, scientists, and authors.

But the terms "menu" and "recipe" cannot always be neatly defined. When asked to submit a favorite recipe, Dr. Elton Trueblood, author, teacher, and renowned theologian, wrote, "Living alone, I have the same breakfast every day: 1 cup of orange juice, 1 cup of hot coffee, 1 bowl of Quaker® Oats (I cook the Quick Quaker® Oats for at least one minute)."

Efforts to identify a favorite recipe of the beloved Dr. Chester Swor '19, for whom the Swor Auditorium is named, yielded interesting information. The long-time English professor and inspirational speaker was a true son of the South — his favorite dinner consisted of fried chicken, mashed potatoes and gravy, turnip greens, cornbread, and plenty of coffee.

We hope the reader will find "Special Foods and Special People" a fascinating perspective on some of the individuals who have made Mississippi College a place of special distinction.

In 1976 the College was privileged to present Van Cliburn in a special concert celebrating the sesquicentennial of the institution. Following the concert in Jackson's City Auditorium, Carroll Waller, First Lady of the State and a Mississippi College alumna who supervised the restoration of the historic Governor's Mansion, opened that residence for a gala reception. The menu from Mrs. Waller includes the recipes which were used on that occasion.

Mansion Reception
Honoring Van Cliburn

Cheese Straws, p. 32

Meringues, p. 255

Sausage Balls, p. 29

Parsley-Cream Cheese Sandwiches, p. 376

Crabmeat Shrimp Dip, p. 21

Tuna Sandwiches, p. 376

Pecan Tassies, p. 310

Slush Punch, p. 13

Faculty Wives Brunch

Fresh fruit with dip, p. 19

Miniature Cheese Quiche, p. 226

Banana Nut Bread with Cream Cheese, p. 39

Strawberry Jam Coffeecake, p. 66

Breakfast Casserole, p. 224

Ham Biscuits, p. 55

Coffee Russian Tea, p. 15

Luncheon for Board of Trustees

Beef Stroganoff with Rice, p. 364

Carrot Soufflé, p. 116

Sweet and Sour Green Beans, p. 133

Orange-Pineapple Salad, p. 84

Yeast Rolls, p. 51

Apple-Date Cake, Deluxe Pound Cake, pp. 260, 285

Coffee Tea

New Faculty Reception

Crabmeat Hors d'oeuvres, p. 35

Choctaw Cheese Ball, p. 18

Elegant Orange Muffins, p. 64

Apricot Balls, p. 320

Buttermilk Fudge, p. 373

Chicken Salad Sandwiches, p. 93

Pulled Mints, p. 318

Coconut Bars, p. 254

White Nut Loaf, p. 46

Punch, p. 12

Mam-Ma's Dumplings

½ cup shortening
5 cups self-rising flour, sifted
1½ cups hot water (not boiling)
1 hen, boiled and boned (reserve broth)

Cut shortening into flour. Add water and stir, using a spoon until mixture is cool enough to mix by hand. The mixture must be stiff enough to roll out. Divide into 4 separate sections; place on wax paper to cool. When cool, roll out very thin; cut into small squares, drop into boiling chicken broth. Dumplings will cook instantly. Add chicken.

Yield: 8-10 servings

Mary Elinor Moore Comfort '77 (A. J. Comfort, Jr. '53)

A. J. Comfort, Jr., is a descendant of Daniel Comfort, Principal of Hampton Academy (1828-1834), and President of Mississippi College (1837-1841; 1845-1846).

Cranberry Salad

2 envelopes unflavored gelatin
1 cup orange juice
1 quart fresh cranberries, ground
1½ cups sugar
1 (8-ounce) can crushed pineapple
1 cup nuts, chopped

Combine gelatin and orange juice. Heat to dissolve gelatin. Add remaining ingredients and chill until set.

Yield: 12-14 servings

Jerry M. Comfort '82

Jerry is a descendant of the Reverend Daniel Comfort, Principal of Hampton Academy (1828-1834) and President of Mississippi College (1837-1841; 1845-1846).

Watermelon Rind Preserves

1 pound rind from 1 watermelon
2 gallons water
1 Tablespoon lime
1½ pounds sugar
1 or 2 lemons
Slivers of ginger root
1 teaspoon vanilla

Cut prepared rind into strips 1-inch wide and 4-inches long and place in lime water overnight; drain and weigh. Soak in clear water to cover until a little tender. Add 1½ pounds of sugar to each pound of rind. Add lemon and ginger. Cook in this solution until syrup is amber colored and a little thick. Cool a little before adding vanilla; then place into hot sterilized jars.

Yield: 8 quart jars or 16 pints

Christine Buntin Britten

Christine Buntin Britten is the daughter of Effie Granberry Buntin, the granddaughter of Hattie R. Granberry, and great-granddaughter of President W. S. Webb and Mary McMath Webb. The Reverend W. S. Webb was President of Mississippi College (1873-1891). This recipe is from the collection of Effie Granberry Buntin.

Cranberry-Apple Casserole

1½ pounds fresh cranberries
2 large apples, sliced (unpeeled)
1½ cups sugar
Dash of salt
2 sticks butter, melted
1 cup brown sugar
1 cup pecans, chopped
⅔ cup flour
1 cup oatmeal (may use 2 packages instant)

Preheat oven to 350 degrees. Wash cranberries. Line the bottom of a 3-quart casserole with sliced apples and cranberries. Sprinkle sugar and salt over fruit. Mix other ingredients together and crumble mixture over fruit. Bake for 1 hour. This dish may be served as a side dish with turkey and dressing.

Yield: 10-12 servings

Martha Rogers Elliot '63

Martha Rogers Elliot is a great-great niece of President Robert Venable, Sr., (1891-1895).

Sponge Cake with Foam Sauce

Cake:
3 eggs
1½ cups sugar
½ cup water
2 cups all-purpose flour
2 scant teaspoons baking powder

Foam Sauce:
1 cup sugar
⅔ cup butter
1 teaspoon all-purpose flour
3 gills* boiling water (1½ cups)

Preheat oven to 325 degrees. Beat eggs 2 minutes; add sugar and beat 5 minutes more. Add water, flour, and baking powder. Bake for about 1 hour in a 10-inch ungreased tube pan. To prepare sauce, beat sugar, butter, and flour until smooth. Place over heat and stir in boiling water. A little lemon, vanilla, or orange adds much to the sauce.

*gill = ¼ of a pint or ½ cup

Yield: 14-16 servings

From the recipes of Margaret Sherman Webb

Margaret Sherman Webb, deceased, was a wife of President W. S. Webb (1873-1891). This cake and sauce recipe appeared in Godey, 1870.

Buttermilk Flapjacks

2 cups sifted all-purpose flour
1 teaspoon soda
½ teaspoon salt
1 Tablespoon sugar
1 egg
2 cups buttermilk
1½ Tablespoons melted butter

Mix flour, soda, salt, and sugar. Beat egg and mix into buttermilk. Add dry ingredients, then melted butter. Cook on a heated griddle; turn when surface of each pancake is bubbly. Brown the opposite side of each pancake until done.

Yield: 16-20 pancakes

Catherine Latimer Monroe '30

Catherine Latimer Monroe is the granddaughter of Dr. W. S. Webb, President (1873-1891). This recipe is taken from the recipe collection of Mrs. Mariah Johnson Latimer, deceased, wife of Dr. Murray Latimer.

Cream-Style Corn

6 ears corn
2 cups water
1½ teaspoons salt
1 Tablespoon margarine
1 Tablespoon cornstarch
¼ cup water

Shuck and clean corn. Be sure to brush away silks. Cut corn off the cob into an iron skillet or other heavy skillet. Add water and salt. Cook at medium boil, stirring frequently, for 25 minutes. Add margarine. Dissolve cornstarch in water and add to the corn. Corn varies in starch content and sometimes thickens without the cornstarch. Additional cornstarch and water may be added if needed. When the corn thickens, remove from heat and serve hot. This may be prepared ahead and refrigerated or frozen.

Yield: 8 servings

This was a favorite recipe of Dr. M.P.L. Berry, President of Hillman College (1918-1942).

Kisses

4 egg whites
Pinch of salt
1 cup sugar
1 teaspoon baking powder
1 teaspoon vanilla
1 cup pecans, chopped

Preheat oven to 225 degrees. Grease cookie sheet. Have egg whites at room temperature. Mix egg whites with pinch of salt and beat in mixer until thick. Mix sugar and baking powder and gradually add to egg whites, continually beating until very thick and holding peaks. Add nuts and vanilla and mix well. Drop by teaspoonsful on cookie sheet and bake about 1 hour.

Yield: 2 dozen

Dorothy Provine

Dorothy Provine is the daughter-in-law of Dr. J. W. Provine who served as President of Mississippi College (1895-1898 and 1911-1932).

Mrs. Nelson's Punch

4 juice oranges, thinly sliced
2 ounces citric acid
5 cups sugar
1 quart cold water
4 (46-ounce) cans pineapple juice

Mix oranges, citric acid, sugar, and water in a large container until sugar dissolves. Refrigerate overnight. Strain and divide equally between 4 (1-gallon) glass containers. Pour 1 can of pineapple juice into each container and fill with water. Serve over finely crushed ice.

Yield: 4 gallons

From the recipes of Mary White Nelson '10, Hillman

Mary White Nelson, deceased, was the wife of Dr. Dotson McGinnis (D.M.) Nelson, President (1932-1957).

Chicken and Spaghetti Casserole

1½ cups celery, chopped
1 cup green pepper, chopped
1 small onion, chopped
1 clove garlic, minced
2 pimientos, chopped
1 Tablespoon butter
1 quart chicken stock, divided
1 (4-5 pound) hen, cooked and cut into bite-size pieces
1 Tablespoon Worcestershire sauce
Salt and pepper
1 (8-ounce) package spaghetti, cooked in salted water

Cook celery, pepper, onion, garlic and pimiento in 1 tablespoon butter and about half of chicken stock until tender. Sprinkle chicken over top of cooked vegetables, Worcestershire sauce, salt, and pepper. Add remaining stock. Spread spaghetti on top. Do not stir but press spaghetti down into other ingredients; let stand for 30 minutes before serving.

Yield: 10-12 servings

From the recipes of Mary White Nelson '10, Hillman

Mary White Nelson, deceased, was the wife of Dr. Dotson McGinnis (D.M.) Nelson, President (1932-1957).

Jeff Davis Pie

2 cups sugar
1/8 teaspoon salt
1 Tablespoon flour
1 cup butter
1 cup cream or milk
6 eggs, separated
2 teaspoons vanilla
1 (10-inch) pie shell, unbaked
1/2 cup sugar

Preheat oven to 400 degrees. Mix 2 cups sugar, salt, and flour. Cream with butter until light and frothy. Add cream, beaten egg yolks and vanilla. Pour into for pie shell. Bake as for a custard pie about 15 minutes to set the pastry. Reduce temperature to 350 degrees for the remainder of baking time, 20-30 minutes or until center is nearly set. To prepare the meringue, beat the 6 egg whites until stiff. Gradually add one-half cup sugar. Cover pie with meringue and brown in a slow oven at 325 degrees.

Variation: Fold the beaten egg whites into pie mixture before cooking.

Yield: 8 servings

D. M. Nelson, Jr. '35

This recipe was a favorite of Jefferson Davis and was given to the Nelsons by the church cook in their church in Kansas City, Missouri. She "declared" it was 100 years old.

Green Chili Soup

1 can cream of chicken soup
1 can chicken broth or 2 cups chicken bouillon
1 (4-ounce) can chopped green chilies
1 (16-ounce) can stewed tomatoes, diced
1/2-1 pound Cheddar or Monterey Jack cheese, shredded

Combine all ingredients. Heat slowly, stirring until the cheese melts. Serve hot with cornbread and green salad for a hearty supper.

Yield: 3-4 servings

Mary Nelson Sweet '46

Mary White Nelson Sweet is the daughter of Dr. and Mrs. D. M. Nelson, Sr., President (1932-1957).

Virginia Spoon Bread

1 scant cup cornmeal
3 cups milk, divided
Butter size of walnut
1 teaspoon salt
3 level teaspoons baking powder
3 eggs, beaten

Stir meal into 2 cups milk. Bring to a boil, making a mush. Take off stove; add butter, salt, and baking powder. Add the remaining milk and eggs. Place into a greased casserole. Bake in preheated 450 degree oven until done, approximately 20-25 minutes.

Yield: 8 servings

Mrs. D. M. Nelson, Jr. (D. M. Nelson, Jr. '35)

This recipe was given to the Nelson family during Dr. D. M. Nelson, Jr.'s first pastorate in Vinton, Virginia. It is dated 1943.

Mrs. McLemore's Coconut Cake

1¼ cups butter
1½ cups sugar
5 eggs
3 cups cake flour
½ teaspoon salt
4 teaspoons baking powder
½ cup milk
1 teaspoon vanilla

Coconut Icing:
4 cups sugar
2 cups milk
2 fresh coconuts, grated

Preheat oven to 350 degrees. Grease and flour a 9x13 pan or 3 (9-inch) cake pans. Cream butter and sugar until fluffy. Add eggs one at a time, beating well after each. Sift dry ingredients and add alternately with milk to butter mixture, beginning and ending with flour. Add vanilla. Pour into prepared pans and bake for about 25 minutes. Prepare the icing by bringing sugar and milk to a boil and adding coconut. Cook until thick enough to spread; pour slowly over warm 9x13 cake or stack layers, with icing between layers and on top of cake. Stacked cake should be cold before cutting. Cake should be refrigerated for storing.

Yield: 12-15 servings

From the recipes of Nannie Pitts McLemore (R. A. McLemore '23)

Nannie Pitts McLemore, deceased, was the wife of President Richard Aubrey McLemore (1957-1968).

Beef Stroganoff

2 large onions, chopped
2 Tablespoons shortening
2 pounds lean round steak, slivered
1½ cups tomato juice
2 bay leaves, broken
2 teaspoons soy sauce
2 Tablespoons Worcestershire sauce
Dash of Tabasco sauce
Salt, pepper, and paprika (to taste)
2 cloves garlic, minced
5 Tablespoons flour
2 (4½-ounce) cans mushrooms (reserve juice)
1 pint sour cream

In skillet, sauté onions in shortening. Place onions into deep pot. To sliver meat, slice partially frozen steak into thin pieces; sauté in skillet. Place into pot with onions. Add tomato juice, seasonings and sauces. Cook slowly for about 30 minutes until meat is tender but not falling apart. Set aside until ready to serve. (This may be prepared the day before.) When ready to serve, heat tomato-meat mixture and thicken with flour mixed with 1 tablespoon juice from the mushrooms. Add mushrooms and sour cream. Serve over rice.

Yield: 8-10 servings

Joy Nobles

Joy Nobles is the wife of Dr. Lewis Nobles, President of Mississippi College (1968-1993).

Cakie Pie

½ pound butter
1 cup sugar
½ cup flour
2 eggs, slightly beaten
1 (6-ounce) package chocolate chips
1 teaspoon vanilla
1 (9-inch) frozen pie shell

Preheat oven to 325 degrees. Melt the butter and cool slightly. Set aside. Mix sugar and flour. Add beaten eggs, butter, chocolate chips, and vanilla. Pour into frozen pie shell and bake for 1 hour.

Yield: 6-8 servings

Sandra Nobles Nash '73

Sandra is the daughter of Dr. Lewis Nobles, President, (1968-1993).

Eggplant Spaghetti Sauce

1 eggplant, peeled or unpeeled, cut into cubes
3 Tablespoons oil
1 small onion, sliced
1 garlic clove, minced
1 green pepper, sliced
1 cup plum tomatoes
1 cup tomato juice
1 teaspoon oregano
2 teaspoons basil
Hot cooked spaghetti

Sauté eggplant in oil for about 7 minutes, add onion, garlic, and pepper; cook for 7-8 additional minutes, or until tender. Combine tomatoes, tomato juice, and herbs. Add to the eggplant mixture; cover and simmer for half an hour. Serve over hot, cooked spaghetti.

Yield: 4-6 servings

Jimmy and Rosalyn Carter

Jimmy Carter spoke at Mississippi College in the summer of 1976 before becoming the 39th President of the United States. Since his retirement from the political scene, Jimmy and Rosalyn Carter have been very involved in hands-on housing construction through Habitat for Humanity.

Extra Inning Pasta

1 pound pasta, cooked and drained
1 quart thick pasta sauce
1 pound ricotta cheese
½ cup Parmesan cheese
1 pound mozzarella cheese, grated
1 teaspoon dried basil
1 teaspoon dried oregano
Salt and pepper
2 cloves garlic, minced
1 pound Italian sausage, cooked

Mix above ingredients. Bake in a covered 9x13 pan 1 hour at 300 degrees.

Yield: 8-10 servings

Don Sutton '68

Don Sutton was a professional baseball player with the Los Angeles Dodgers, Houston Astros, Milwaukee Brewers, and California Angels. As a pitcher he tallied over 300 major league wins; he is now associated with the Atlanta Braves organization as a broadcaster.

Smoked Pheasant Breasts in Pepper Jelly

2 pheasant breasts
2 cups milk
4 strips bacon
½ teaspoon seasoned salt
½ pint pepper jelly
5 pounds charcoal
4 beef bouillon cubes
Wet hickory chips

Marinate pheasant breasts in milk. Fry bacon and reserve drippings. Rub each breast with drippings. Sprinkle with seasoned salt and coat with pepper jelly. Start charcoal fire in water smoker. Add water to water pan according to smoker instructions. Add bouillon cubes to water. Place wet chips on fire. Place meat on racks and cook for 2 hours; baste twice with pepper jelly. Remove the breasts from cooker, slice and serve.

Yield: 4 servings

Billy Joe Cross '54

Billy Joe Cross is a well-known wild game cook. He has authored six cookbooks and edited three for Ducks Unlimited. He is the food editor for the national organization of Ducks Unlimited.

Poor Man's Steak

1-1½ pounds ground beef
1 cup milk
1-1½ teaspoons salt
Pepper
1 can cream of mushroom soup

Mix all ingredients except soup and pat onto cookie sheet. Refrigerate overnight. Cut in serving size pieces. Flour and brown. Place into a baking dish, cover with soup. Bake in a preheated 350 degree oven for about 20-25 minutes or until bubbly.

Yield: 6 servings

Steven Curtis Chapman

Steven Curtis Chapman is a composer and singer who has been named Artist of the Year six times by the Gospel Music Association. He performed at Mississippi College in April, 1991.

Cappiello's Meatballs

3 slices stale bread
1 pound beef, chopped
3 eggs, beaten
3 Tablespoons Romano cheese, grated
1 clove garlic, chopped
2 Tablespoons parsley, chopped
Salt and pepper
½-¾ cup flour
6 Tablespoons olive oil

Soak bread in water for 5 minutes; squeeze dry. Mix thoroughly with meat, eggs, cheese, garlic, and parsley. Add salt and pepper to taste. Shape into balls about size of small egg; roll in flour; fry in hot oil for about 10 minutes or until golden brown. Serve very hot with vegetables and salad. It may also be served with spaghetti and Plain Tomato Sauce.

Yield: 4-6 servings

Cappiello's Plain Tomato Sauce:
2 large onions, sliced
3 Tablespoons olive oil
1 can tomato paste
½ teaspoon oregano
Salt and pepper
2½ cups water

Fry onion in oil for about 5 minutes or until medium brown. Add paste; cook for 3 minutes, stirring constantly. Add oregano, salt, pepper, and water; cover. Simmer over low heat for 25 minutes. This is easily and quickly prepared and is sufficient for 1 pound any type macaroni. Serve very hot.

Yield: 6 servings

Frank A. Cappiello

Frank Cappiello, a well-known Wall Street personality, author, and economic panelist, spoke on campus in 1984. A note included with the recipe states, "When I was a lieutenant in the Marine Corps, word got out about my cooking and my platoon was known as Cappiello's Meatballs!"

Carruth Crawfish Fettucine

1½ sticks butter
1½ cups onions, chopped
1 green pepper, chopped
2 cloves garlic, minced
2 Tablespoons flour
1 pound crawfish tails
½ pound pasteurized processed cheese spread, cubed
1 pint light cream
1 Tablespoon jalapeño peppers, chopped
½ Tablespoon lemon pepper
Salt and pepper
1 (12-ounce) package fettucine
Parmesan cheese

Sauté onions, green pepper, and garlic in butter for 15 minutes. Add flour, cover, and cook on low for 15 minutes, stirring frequently. Add crawfish tails. Stir well; cover and cook for 20 minutes stirring often. Add cheese, cream, jalapeño pepper, lemon pepper, pepper, and salt. Cover and cook for 20 minutes. Cook fettucine noodles according to package directions. Drain noodles and gently blend with sauce. Pour into buttered casserole and sprinkle with Parmesan cheese. Bake in preheated 350 degree oven for 15-20 minutes. It may be made ahead, refrigerated, and baked at a later time.

Yield: 6-8 servings

Paul Ott

Paul Ott is a musician, humorist, and outdoorsman. He composed a special ballad commemorating Lewis Nobles' 25th anniversary as President of Mississippi College and performed it in chapel in October, 1992.

Lasagna

1 pound Italian sausage
1 clove garlic, minced
1 Tablespoon whole basil
1½ teaspoons salt
1 (16-ounce) can tomatoes
2 (6-ounce) cans tomato paste
8 ounces lasagna or wide noodles
3 cups fresh ricotta
½ cup grated Parmesan cheese
2 Tablespoons parsley flakes
2 eggs, beaten
2 teaspoons salt
½ teaspoon pepper
1 pound mozzarella cheese, sliced very thin

Brown meat slowly. Spoon off excess fat and add garlic, basil, salt, tomatoes, and tomato paste. Simmer uncovered for 30 minutes, stirring occasionally. Cook noodles according to package instructions; drain and rinse. Combine remaining ingredients except mozzarella cheese. Place half the noodles in 13x9x2 baking dish; spread with half the ricotta cheese filling, half the mozzarella cheese, and half the meat sauce. Repeat layers. Bake at 375 degrees for 30 minutes. Let stand for 10 minutes before cutting.

Yield: 10 servings

Landrum Shettles '33

Landrum Shettles is a research physician and pioneer in the field of in vitro fertilization and gender determination studies. He received an honorary doctorate from Mississippi College in 1966.

Baked Rice

1 stick butter or margarine
1 large onion, chopped
2 (10-ounce) cans consommé
1 cup uncooked rice
1 (8-ounce) can mushrooms, drained (optional)

Melt butter or margarine in frying pan, add chopped onion and cook until softened. Add consommé and uncooked rice. Stir, then pour into buttered casserole and bake at 350 degrees for about 1 hour. If you like, about 20 minutes before rice is done, stir in a small can of mushrooms. Remove from oven and serve from casserole.

Yield: 6-8 servings

Willard Scott

Willard Scott is the immediately recognizable weather forecaster and humorist for NBC's Today show. He spoke on campus in April, 1989, and established The Common Sense Scholarship.

Red Raspberry Cake and Icing

Cake:

1 white cake mix
3 Tablespoons flour
1 (3-ounce) package raspberry gelatin
1 cup oil
½ cup cold water
4 eggs
1 (10-ounce) package frozen red raspberries, divided

Mix dry ingredients. Add oil, water, and eggs one at a time, beating after each. Don't overbeat. Break up half the package of frozen raspberries and add to batter. Bake in a preheated 350 degree oven for 20-25 minutes or until golden. For best results use 3 (8-inch) cake pans.

Icing:

1 stick butter
1 box confectioners' sugar
½ package frozen red raspberries

Mix together until creamy and spread on top of layers.

Gloria Gaither

Gloria Gaither is a contemporary religious singer, lyricist, author, and speaker. She has written six books, recorded forty albums, and won two Grammy Awards and ten Dove Awards. She appeared at Mississippi College in October, 1989.

Best-Ever Lemon Pie

1¼ cups sugar
6 Tablespoons cornstarch
2 cups water
3 egg yolks
⅓ cup lemon juice
1½ teaspoons lemon flavoring
2 teaspoons vinegar
3 Tablespoons butter
1 (9-inch) pastry shell, baked

Mix sugar and cornstarch together in top of double boiler; add water. Combine egg yolks with juice and beat; add to sugar mixture. Cook until thickened over boiling water for 25 minutes, stirring frequently. Add lemon flavoring, vinegar, and butter, and stir thoroughly. Pour into deep pastry shell and cool. Cover with meringue.

Never-Fail Meringue:
1 Tablespoon cornstarch
2 Tablespoons cold water
½ cup boiling water
3 egg whites
6 Tablespoons sugar
Pinch of salt
1 teaspoon vanilla

Blend cornstarch and cold water in saucepan. Add boiling water and cook, stirring until clear and thickened. Completely cool at room temperature. With electric beater at high speed, beat egg whites until foamy. Gradually add sugar and beat until stiff, but not dry. Turn mixer to low speed, add salt and vanilla. Gradually beat in cold cornstarch mixture. Change mixer to high speed and beat well. Spread meringue over cooled pie filling. Bake in a preheated 350 degree oven for about 10 minutes.

Yield: 8 servings

Ann Landers

An internationally syndicated writer, Ann Landers' folk-wise, common sense advice column is read by millions on a daily basis. She spoke on campus in 1974.

Joan's Pound Cake

½ pound butter
3 cups sugar
1 Tablespoon vanilla
1 teaspoon almond flavoring
5 egg yolks
3 cups bread flour
½ teaspoon salt
½ teaspoon soda
1 Tablespoon hot water
1 cup buttermilk
5 egg whites

Grease and flour tube pan. Cream butter and sugar together. Add vanilla and almond flavorings. Add egg yolks one at a time, beating after each addition. Sift flour and salt together. Dissolve soda in hot water, then add buttermilk to it; let it froth about 5 minutes. Add flour mixture and buttermilk mixture alternately. Beat egg whites to soft peaks and fold into batter. Pour into tube pan. Bake in a preheated 350 degree oven for 1 hour and 10 minutes or until golden. This keeps for weeks if well-wrapped. This is delicious sliced into 7 layers and put together again with lemon filling.

Yield: 16-20 servings

Joan Myers Bayer '69

Joan Myers Bayer represented the College in the state pageant and was named Miss Mississippi in 1967. She was first alternate to Miss America. The Joan Myers Art Scholarship was established in her honor in 1971.

Iced Pecan Halves

1 cup pecan halves
½ cup sugar
2 Tablespoons butter or margarine, melted
½ teaspoon vanilla
¾ teaspoon salt

Heat nuts, sugar, and butter or margarine in heavy skillet over medium heat, stirring constantly for about 15 minutes or until nuts are toasted and sugar is golden brown. Remove the mixture from heat and add the vanilla. Now quickly spread the mixture over aluminum foil. Sprinkle with salt. Cool the pecans for about 5 minutes and then break the mixture into small clusters. Do not double recipe.

Yield: Variable

Amy Grant

Big Mama's Tea Cakes

1 cup butter
1 cup sugar, heaping
2 eggs
½ teaspoon salt
1 teaspoon soda
3 cups plus 3 Tablespoons all-purpose flour, divided
3 Tablespoons buttermilk
1 teaspoon vanilla
Dash sugar

Preheat oven to 350 degrees. Cream butter and sugar; add eggs. To sugar and butter mixture, add dry ingredients alternately with buttermilk and vanilla mixture. Drop batter by tablespoonful on lightly greased cookie sheet and sprinkle with a dash of sugar. Bake for 8-13 minutes depending on size of the cakes.

Yield: 5-6 dozen

Jerry Clower

Jerry Clower, probably the most famous native of Amite County, Mississippi, is a humorist who has built a career on side-splitting, down-home experiences. He has served as a commencement speaker and was awarded an honorary degree in May, 1988.

Buttermilk Fudge

2 cups sugar
1 cup buttermilk
1 teaspoon soda
2 Tablespoons butter
1 teaspoon vanilla
1 cup nuts, chopped

Cook sugar, buttermilk, and soda in a large, heavy saucepan until the mixture reaches the soft ball stage. Remove the mixture from heat. Add butter and vanilla and beat until thickened. Stir nuts into thickened fudge and pour mixture onto a greased platter or 8x8 pan. Cool and cut into pieces.

Yield: 25 pieces

Amy Grant

Amy Grant is an enormously popular contemporary religious singer and composer. In recent years she has "crossed over" to the pop charts to become an equally successful entertainer in that realm. She appeared at Mississippi College in the early 1980's. She contributed two of her favorite "sweets."

Prayer Bars

First Layer:

½ cup butter, melted
¼ cup sugar
¼ cup cocoa
1 teaspoon vanilla
1 egg, beaten
2 cups graham crackers, crushed
1 cup coconut flakes
1 cup nuts, chopped (optional)

To melted butter, add sugar, cocoa, vanilla, and egg; cook over low heat for 2 minutes until thickened. Stir constantly. Mix with crumbs, coconut, and nuts. Press into a buttered 9x7 pan. Cool.

Second Layer:

½ cup butter
3 Tablespoons milk
2 Tablespoons instant vanilla pudding mix
2 cups confectioner's sugar

Cream butter, add milk and pudding mix. Beat in sugar until creamy. Spread over first layer. Chill.

Icing:

1 (12-ounce) package chocolate chips or 1 large plain chocolate bar
1 Tablespoon butter

Melt ingredients over low heat. Spread on second layer and let set until chocolate cools and is firm enough to cut into bars.

Yield: 10-12 servings

Dallas Holm

Dallas Holm is a Christian contemporary entertainer who performed at Mississippi College in 1980 and 1985. This recipe originated with his mother and was used at a bridal shower for his wife.

Florida Orange Cake

Juice Mixture:
2 cups orange juice, strained
2 cups sugar
1 teaspoon orange peel, grated

Cake:
1 cup butter
2 cups sugar
2 teaspoons vanilla
½ teaspoon salt
6 eggs
3 cups flour, sifted
2 teaspoons baking powder
1 cup milk

Preheat oven to 325 degrees. Grease and flour a 9x13 pan. Stir juice, sugar, and orange peel until sugar is dissolved and set aside. Cream butter, sugar, vanilla, and salt. Add eggs to creamed mixture and continue to beat. Sift flour and baking powder together and add to creamed mixture alternately with milk. Beat only on low speed. Pour mixture into prepared pan. Bake for 25-35 minutes. While cake is still hot, puncture with toothpick and pour on the juice mixture; use back of wooden spoon to spread.

Yield: 12-16 servings

Patrick D. Smith

Patrick D. Smith, a native Mississippian, is the author of six novels. He has been nominated three times for the Pulitzer Prize and was nominated for the 1985 Nobel Prize for Literature.

He has received five additional Nobel nominations for the complete body of his literary works. His chosen recipe "is based on the original pioneer recipe for a Florida orange cake."

Boiled Custard

3 Tablespoons flour
1 cup sugar
¼ teaspoon salt
1 quart milk
3 eggs, beaten
Rind of 1 orange

Sift flour with sugar and salt. Gradually add the milk to the sugar mixture. Cook in a double boiler until mixture steams. Add a little of the hot mixture to beaten eggs, then combine the two liquids in the double boiler. Stir the rind of an orange around in the mixture to flavor the custard as it thickens. Remove from heat when it reaches desired consistency. Remove orange rind and cool the custard.

Yield: 6 servings

Arthur Guyton

Arthur Guyton is a physician and author whose textbook on human physiology is used in medical schools throughout the world. He delivered the address at the annual Faculty-Staff Dinner for the beginning of the 1992-93 academic year.

Tuna Sandwiches

1 (6½-ounce) can tuna, drained
½ cup cucumber, chopped
1 Tablespoon onion, grated
2 teaspoons lemon juice
½ cup bell pepper, chopped
½ cup celery, chopped
Salt
Pepper
Paprika
¼ cup mayonnaise
1 loaf sandwich bread

Combine all filling ingredients and chill. Spread tuna mixture thinly between slices of bread. Trim crusts.

Yield: 24 party sandwiches

Carroll Waller '48

Parsley Cream Cheese Sandwich Filling

1 (8-ounce) package cream cheese
1½ cups parsley, chopped
2 Tablespoons milk

Soften cream cheese in medium-size bowl. Blend in milk and parsley.

Yield: 1 cup filling

Carroll Waller '48

Recipe Testers

Jane Alexander
Libby Allen
Laverne Applewhite
Barbara Barber
Betty Barber
Rebekah Barber
Lucy Barnett
Linda Bass
Ernestine Baxter
Julia Blalock
Ann Boone
Amy Brand
Debbie Brewer
Tommie Broome
Thelma Bush
Carolyn Cannon
Dorothy Carpenter
Shelia Carpenter
Sadie Carroll
Edith Cassibry
Ruth Churchill
Jo Ellen Clark
Joy Cliburn
Fleda Collins
Bettye Coward
Alice Cox
Cheryl Cox
Nancy Davis
Dolly Dawkins
Vicki Derrick
Anne Dial
Joyce Dotson
Ann Eaves
Charlotte Evans
Connie Evans
Teresa Floyd
Sarah Folkes
Cynthia Foster
Melinda Gann
Mary Catherine Gentry
Ruth Ann Gibson
Robin Goodwin
Margie Gore
Marleen Gough
Mary Beth Graves
Louise Griffith
Janelle Hamilton
Sonia Hancock
Carolyn Hand
Mildred Harden
Johnnie Harper
Hyacinth Hayman
Lisa Headley
Rosalind Headley
Marion Hewett
Bess Holladay
Glenda Holleyman
Brenda Holloway
Jan Hurt
Diane Hutto
Katty Ireland
Gena Jackson
Mary Jenkins
Jane Johnson
Terrie Johnson
Marilyn Joiner
Janice Jones
Penny Jones
Sandra Jones
Marva Nell King
Carol Kirk
Ann Kolb
Jeannie Lane
Cynthia Leavell
Janet Lee
Peggy Lee
Betty Legg
Madelyn Lofton
Marian Lyons
Billy Lytal
Anne Martin
Dixie Martin
Vicki McCall
Hazel McCarty
Maellen McIntire
Charlotte McMath
Carnette McMillan
Lana McNeece
Annie Ruth McPhail
Susan Meadors
Vicki Moore
Wanda Mosley
Lynn Myers
Alice Nettles
Susan Newman
Dorothy Nixon
Joy Nobles
Karrie Norberg
Lynn O'Dell
Audra O'Neal
Mary Jean Padgett
Donna Palmertree
Rochelle Park
Dot Parkman
Betty Parks
Libby Patterson
Alicia Pittman
Vicki Prather
Donna Purvis
Pat Quisenberry
Jean Ramsey
Jennifer Ray
Donna Reed
Danie Robbins
Rowland Roberts
Elizabeth Robertson
Jane Rochester
Amy Rowan
Mamie Sage
Jennifer Salers
Marion Sessums
Martha Shepherd
Nita Skinner
Alice Smith
Mittie Kay Smith
Bea Snazelle
Ruby Rae Stampley
Bettye Stewart
Beverly Taylor
Janet Taylor
Mary Etta Thompson
Ann Townsend
Jean Triplett
Annette Trotter
Pat Turner
Barbara Wade
Beth Walsh
Carol West
Eloise Western
Melissa Wiggins
Tee Willis
Deborah Woodall
Debbie Wright

INDEX

A

APPETIZERS
DIPS AND SPREADS
Almond Fruited Cheese Ball 17
Cheese Ring 19
Cheesecake Dip 20
Choctaw Cheese Ball 18
Crabmeat-Shrimp Dip 21
Date Sandwich Spread 27
Delicious Cheese Ball 18
Hot Artichoke Dip 20
Hot Broccoli Dip 21
Jezebel Dip 20
Layered Nacho Dip 22
Nacho Delight 23
Party Dip for Fruit 19
Shrimp or Smoked Oyster Mousse 28
Shrimp Party Dip 22
Tangy Mild Salsa 23
HORS D'OEUVRES
Almond Bark Scramble 333
Asparagus Foldovers 24
Barbecued Shrimp 34
Chipped Beef Hors d'oeuvres 36
Cocktail Meatballs 35
Crabmeat Hors d'oeuvres 35
Cucumber Sandwiches 24
Curried Chicken Balls 31
Date Sandwich Spread 27
Ham and Cheese Bites 29
Hot Cheese Toasties 27
Marinated Carrot Strips 29
Marinated New Potatoes 30
Mari's English Horse Drawers 36
MC Bacon-Wrapped Chicken Livers 33
Meatlover's Delight 26
Mississippi Sin 26
Mushroom Puffs 33
Nannie McLemore's Cheese Straws 32
Oysters Point Clear 34
Parched Peanuts 334
Pickled Mushrooms 30
Puppy Chow 334
Sausage Balls 29
Seasoned Oyster Crackers 333
Shrimp Sandwiches 25
Shrimp Wheels 25
Texas Tortilla Pinwheels 28
Tortilla Roll-Ups 32
Vegetable Appetizers 31
APPLES
Apfel Kuchen (Apple Cake) 285
Apple Meat Loaf 192
Apple-Date Cake 285
Apple-Pineapple Slaw 88
Cranberry-Apple Casserole 358
Crustless Sausage-Apple Quiche 226
English Apple Dessert 294
Fresh Apple Cake 279
Fresh Apple Spice Cake 283
Frozen Waldorf Salad 86
Fruit Salad with Pineapple Pecan Whip Topping 82
Healthy Apple Muffins 62
Holiday Cranberry Casserole 143
Norwegian Apple Dessert 236
Perfect Apple Pie 309
Pineapple-Apple Salad 80
Scalloped Apples 142
Yuma Dump Cake 283
APRICOTS
Apricot Nectar Cake 282
Apricot Pudding 314
Apricot Squares 247
Holiday Apricot Balls 320
ARTICHOKES
Artichoke Soup 102
Green Beans and Artichokes 133
Hot Artichoke Dip 20
ASPARAGUS
Asparagus Crab Soufflé 170
Asparagus Foldovers 24
Classic Asparagus Casserole 130
Easy Asparagus Casserole 131
Natchez Chicken Casserole 173
Souped-Up Asparagus 130

B

BANANAS
Banana Bread 39
Banana Pudding 312
Bessie's Old-Fashioned Banana Pudding 313
Chocolate Chip Banana Bread 39
Classic Strawberry Salad 83
Frozen Strawberry Fruit Salad 85
Fruit Salad with Pineapple Pecan Whip Topping 82
Jeweled Fruit Salad 80
Low-Fat Banana Pudding 312
Orange Fruit Mélange 82
Winter Fruit Salad 81
BEANS *(See Green Beans also)*
Black Bean and Zucchini Chilaquiles 230
Burrito Bake 197
Deluxe Baked Bean Casserole 127
Lima Bean-Broccoli Casserole 138
Red Beans and Rice 223
Spanish Mama's Red Hot Chili 107
Spicy Lima Beans 139
Ten Bean Soup 103
Western Style Beans 126
White Chili 197

BEEF
Apple Meat Loaf ... 192
Bar-B-Q Brisket ... 205
Beef and Noodle Skillet ... 212
Beef Patties ... 210
Beef Stroganoff ... 364
Beef-Vegetable Pie ... 196
Best Eggplant Casserole ... 195
Burrito Bake ... 197
Cabbage Beef Soup ... 100
Cappiello's Meatballs ... 367
Carne Mechada ... 209
Casa Myers Lasagna ... 200
Chinese Ground Beef Casserole ... 201
Chipped Beef Hors d'oeuvres ... 36
Classic Meat Sauce ... 199
Cocktail Meatballs ... 35
Corned Beef Salad ... 93
Cowboy Stew ... 105
Deluxe Baked Bean Casserole ... 127
Easy Autumn Pot Roast ... 203
Easy Spaghetti ... 202
Eggplant Parmesan ... 213
English Beef Short Ribs ... 205
Eye of Round Roast ... 203
Favorite Fiesta Casserole ... 210
Fiesta Stack Ups ... 194
Five-Hour Stew ... 104
Grilled Sirloin Tip Roast ... 204
Hamburger Pie ... 213
Hot French Bread Sandwiches ... 150
Italian Meat Loaf ... 193
Lady Astor's Plush Steak ... 207
Lemon Lover's Meat Loaf ... 192
Meat Loaf Man ... 193
Meatlover's Delight ... 26
Mexican Casserole ... 208
Mexican Steaks ... 206
Nacho Delight ... 23
Natchitoches Meat Pies ... 147
No-Peep Stew ... 106
One-Dish Meal ... 211
Pizza Squares ... 212
Poor Man's Steak ... 366
Pop Earley's Marinated Steaks ... 207
Potato Puff Casserole ... 196
Reuben Pie ... 195
Sauerbraten ... 202
Shish Kebab ... 149
Sirloin Vegetable Soup ... 101
Spanish Mama's Red Hot Chili ... 107
Spiced Orange Pot Roast ... 206
Spicy Italian Roast ... 204
Stuffed Cabbage Rolls ... 152
Stuffed Zucchini ... 199
Supper Sandwich ... 151
Sweet and Sour Beef Balls ... 198
Taco Casserole ... 209
Teacher's Soup ... 100
Western Style Beans ... 126
Zucchini and Cheese Casserole ... 201

BEETS
Harvard Beets ... 114

BELL PEPPERS
Buckwheat with Roasted Eggplant and Pepper ... 116

BEVERAGES
50's Open-House Homecoming Punch 11
Blackberry Punch or Punch Base ... 12
Fireside Coffee ... 16
First Baptist Punch ... 13
Fruited Mint Julep ... 14
Hot Cherry Punch ... 15
Hot Chocolate Mix ... 17
Hot Spiced Wassail ... 16
Kissimee Punch Slush ... 13
Lemon-Pineapple Slush Punch ... 14
Lemonade Base Punch ... 12
Lemonade Tea ... 14
Mississippi Punch ... 12
Mrs. Nelson's Punch ... 361
Russian Tea ... 15
Spiced Tea Mix ... 17
Wedding and Shower Punch ... 11

BLUEBERRIES
Blueberry Cake ... 263
Blueberry Salad ... 85
Favorite Blueberry Muffins ... 61
Quick Blueberry Dessert ... 238

BREADS
BREADS
Banana Bread ... 39
Bread Sticks ... 48
Buttermilk-Nut Bread ... 41
Chocolate Chip Banana Bread ... 39
Cinnamon Bread ... 42
Date Nut Loaf ... 45
Easy Supper Bread ... 46
Easy Sweet Monkey Bread ... 41
Glazed Raisin Loaf ... 43
Holiday Bread ... 44
Holiday Fruit Bread ... 45
Pluckin' Bread ... 40
Red's Garlic Bread ... 50
Savory French Bread ... 45
Sweet Potato Bread ... 48
Tribesman Pumpkin-Nut Bread ... 42
White Nut Loaf ... 46
CORNBREAD
1-2-3 Spoon Bread ... 56
Aunt Maggie's Cornbread Dressing ... 60
Broccoli Cornbread ... 58
Broccoli-Cheese Cornbread ... 58
Calhoun Cornbread ... 59
Company Cornbread ... 59
Healthy Cornbread ... 60
Mexican Cornbread ... 55

Mississippi College Hushpuppies 61
Onion Cornbread 57
Sausage Cornbread 57
Virginia Spoon Bread 363
MUFFINS AND BREAKFAST BAKING
Bran Muffins 62
Breakfast Casserole 224
Breakfast Pizza 214
Breakfast Quiche 227
Buttermilk Flapjacks 359
Butter Pecan Muffins 65
Butterscotch Breakfast Ring 68
Cinnamon Roll-Ups 69
Cranberry Crunch Muffins 64
Easy Cinnamon-Jelly Rolls 68
Easy Mexican Omelette 228
Egg and Sausage Bake 224
Elegant Orange Muffins 64
Favorite Blueberry Muffins 61
Glazed Doughnuts 70
Healthy Apple Muffins 62
Honey Bran Muffins 63
Morning Glory Muffins 66
Pancakes 69
Sour Cream Coffeecake 67
Sour Cream Muffins 65
Strawberry Jam Coffeecake 66
Stuffed French Toast Casserole 225
Sweet Potato Muffins 63
Whole Wheat Muffins 65
ROLLS AND BISCUITS
All-Bran Rolls 54
Buttermilk Biscuits 55
Easy Cinnamon-Jelly Rolls 68
Easy Sweet Monkey Bread 41
Graham Scones 56
Ice Box Rolls 52
Mashed Potato Rolls 54
Mayonnaise Biscuits 55
Never-Fail Rolls 52
Old-Fashioned Yeast Rolls 51
Quick Yeast Rolls 53
Rebecca's Easy Yeast Rolls 53
YEAST
All-Bran Rolls 54
Dilly Bread 47
Glazed Doughnuts 70
Glazed Raisin Loaf 43
Holiday Bread 44
Honey Whole Wheat Bread 50
Ice Box Rolls 52
Mashed Potato Rolls 54
Never-Fail Rolls 52
Old-Fashioned Yeast Rolls 51
Pluckin' Bread 40
Quick Yeast Rolls 53
Rebecca's Easy Yeast Rolls 53
Sourdough Bread 49
Zucchini Bread 47
BROCCOLI
Broccoli and Cauliflower Casserole 138
Broccoli Cornbread 58
Broccoli, Ham, and Macaroni Bake 222
Broccoli Salad 90
Broccoli with Cream Cheese and Chives 137
Broccoli-Cheese Cornbread 58
Broccoli-Cheese Strata 229
Broccoli-Rice Casserole 125
Chicken Divan 189
Crunchy Broccoli Salad 91
Hot Broccoli Dip 21
Jade Green Broccoli 137
Lima Bean-Broccoli Casserole 138
Norm's Broccoli-Cheese Soup 101

C

CABBAGE
Apple-Pineapple Slaw 88
Bohemian Creamed Cabbage 115
Cabbage Beef Soup 100
Stuffed Cabbage Rolls 152
CAKES
Amalgamation Cake 266
Apfel Kuchen (Apple Cake) 285
Apple-Date Cake 285
Apricot Nectar Cake 282
Blackberry Jam Cake 282
Blueberry Cake 263
Byrds' Fruitcake, The 268
Carrot Cake 279
Chocolate Chip Cake 266
Chocolate Chip Oatmeal Cake 272
Chocolate Icebox Cake 270
Chocolate Sheet Cake 265
Christmas Date Loaf 271
Coconut Cake 264
Cranberry Cake 284
Cream Cheese Pound Cake 261
Date Cake 263
Delicious Plum Cake 273
Deluxe Pound Cake 260
Devil's Food Cake 270
Elegant Chocolate Party Roll 242
Florida Orange Cake 375
Flower Pot Surprise 271
Fresh Apple Cake 279
Fresh Apple Spice Cake 283
Fudge Pudding Cake 269
Gingerbread 281
Gold and Silver Coconut Cake 278
Heavenly Hash Cake 276
Holiday Cake 264
ICINGS
Chocolate-Pecan Frosting 290
Clear Lemon Icing 292

Coconut Icing 291, 363
Coconut-Pecan Icing 292
Cream Cheese Frosting 290
Creamy Caramel Icing 291
Fruitcake Coconut Filling 290
Fruitcake Filling 289
Mocha Butter Cream Frosting 292
Old-Fashioned Caramel Icing 291
Irene's Sour Cream Cake 275
Italian Cream Cake 284
Japanese Fruitcake 267
Jello Cake 280
Joan's Pound Cake 372
Lemon Cream Cake 263
Lemon Poppy Seed Cake 262
Mama Griffis' No-Bake Fruitcake 268
Miss Esther's Squaw Valley Cake 274
Mrs. McLemore's Coconut Cake 363
My Favorite Cake 277
Nut Cake 275
Old Tyme Pineapple Upside Down Cake 276
Peach Pound Cake 261
Pumpkin Cake 274
Quick Sour Cream Pound Cake 260
Red Raspberry Cake and Icing 370
Red Velvet Cake 272
Rich Layer Fruitcake 267
St. Louie Gooie Butter Cake 280
Sponge Cake with Foam Sauce 359
Strawberry Cake Supreme 262
Turtle Cake 269
Vanilla Wafer Cake 273
Yuma Dump Cake 283

CANDY

À la Orleans Style Pralines (Microwave) 319
Buttermilk Fudge 373
Chocolate Fudge 322
Divinity 322
Golden Nugget Fudge 321
Holiday Apricot Balls 320
Iced Pecan Halves 372
Martha Washington Balls 320
Nut Clusters 318
Old-Fashioned Chocolate Fudge 321
Old-Fashioned Peanut Brittle 323
Pecan Brittle 323
Pulled Mints 318
Tammie's Peanut Butter Balls 319
Uncle Mike's Millionaires 317

Cantaloupe/Chicken Salad 95

CARROTS

Carrot Cake 279
Carrot Soufflé 116
Horseradish Carrot Casserole 117
Marinated Carrot Strips 29
Morning Glory Muffins 66
Sunshine Veggie-Fruit Salad 78
Vitamin A & C Congealed Salad 77

Cauliflower Casserole, Broccoli and 138
Celery, Baked 117

CHEESE

Almond Fruited Cheese Ball 17
Blue Cheese Dressing 97
Broccoli-Cheese Cornbread 58
Broccoli-Cheese Strata 229
Cheese and Potato Chowder 104
Cheese Ring 19
Cheesecake Dip 20
Cheesy Chicken Skillet 173
Cheesy Enchilada Casserole 172
Choctaw Cheese Ball 18
Delicious Cheese Ball 18
Easy Cheesy Peas 140
Eggplant Parmesan 213
Garlic Cheese Grits 230
Ham and Cheese Bites 29
Hot Artichoke Dip 20
Hot Broccoli Dip 21
Hot Cheese Toasties 27
Macaroni and Cheese 229
Nacho Delight 23
Nannie McLemore's Cheese Straws 32
Norm's Broccoli-Cheese Soup 101
Parmesan Vegetable Casserole 119
Spinach-Cheese Casserole 132
Texas Tortilla Pinwheels 28
Tortilla Roll-Ups 32
Zucchini and Cheese Casserole 201

CHEESECAKES

Cheesecake Cupcakes 287
Cheesecake Dip 20
Cheesecake Supreme 289
Light Lemon Cheesecake 287
New York Cheesecake 288

CHERRIES

24-Hour Fruit Salad 81
Pink Fluff Salad 76

CHICKEN *(See Poultry)*

COBBLERS

Cranberry-Apple Casserole 358
English Apple Dessert 294
Fresh Peach Cobbler 293
Peach Tree Cobbler, The 293

COFFEECAKES

Sour Cream Coffeecake 67
Strawberry Jam Coffeecake 66

COOKIES AND BARS

7-Layer Bars 245
Almond Bark and Cherry Drop Cookies 253
Almond-Brown Sugar Bars 248
Apricot Squares 247
Best Ever Sugar Cookies 256
Big Mama's Tea Cakes 373
BROWNIES
Easy Brownies 249

Incredible Disappearing Brownies 251
The Ultimate Chocolate Bar 250
Turtle Brownies 249
Chewy Coconut Bars 254
Chewy Walnut Squares 245
Chocolate Raisin Cookies 256
Chocolate-Caramel Squares 246
Chocolate-Oatmeal Cookies 252
Cream Cheese Cookies 257
Crescent Cream Cheese Bars 254
Date Squares 247
Easy Dropped Tea Cakes 245
Holiday Hunks 253
Honey Ozark Oatmeal Cookies 257
Kisses 360
Lemon Squares 246
Meringues 255
Miss Nelly Magee's Honeyballs 243
Molasses Cookies 255
No-Bake Cookies 259
Nutty Fingers 259
Old-Fashioned Tea Cakes 244
Orange Slice Bars 248
Outstanding Oatmeal Cookies 252
Peanut Butter-Chocolate Kiss Cookies 258
Prayer Bars 374
Sara's Teacakes 244
Secret Kiss Cookies 258

CORN
Company Cornbread 59
Corn Pudding 136
Cornbread Salad 86
Cream-Style Corn 360
Crusty Corn Casserole 136
Green Bean and Corn Casserole 135
Mexican Cornbread 55
Onion Cornbread 57
Sweet Corn Casserole 136

CRABMEAT
Asparagus Crab Soufflé 170
Best Gumbo Ever 109
Cajun Fettuccine 171
Crabmeat Casserole 163
Crabmeat Hors d'oeuvres 35
Crabmeat Soup 99
Crabmeat-Shrimp Dip 21

CRANBERRIES
Cranberry Cake 284
Cranberry Crunch Muffins 64
Cranberry Salad 357
Cranberry-Apple Casserole 358
Fresh Cranberry Salad 75
Holiday Cranberry Casserole 143

CRAWFISH
Cajun Fettuccine 171
Carruth Crawfish Fettucine 368
Easy Crawfish Etouffeé 159
Shrimp or Crawfish Casserole 161
Thibaut Crawfish Etouffeé 158

CUCUMBERS
Cool-As-A-Cucumber Dressing 96
Cucumber Sandwiches 24

CUPCAKES
Cheesecake Cupcakes 287
Chocolate Cupcakes 286
Chocolate Surprise Cupcakes 286

D

DATES
Apple-Date Cake 285
Christmas Date Loaf 271
Date Cake 263
Date Nut Loaf 45
Date Squares 247
Holiday Hunks 253

DESSERTS *(See also Cakes, Candy, Cheesecakes, Cobblers, Coffeecakes, Cookies and Bars, Cupcakes, Ice Cream and Frozen Desserts, Pies, Puddings and Custards)*
Birchermuesli 236
Caramel Nougat Dessert 237
Norwegian Apple Dessert 236
Puppy Chow 334
Quick Blueberry Dessert 238
Strawberry Pizza 241

DIPS AND SPREADS *(See Appetizers)*

DRESSINGS
Aunt Maggie's Cornbread Dressing 60
Squash Dressing 129

E

EGGPLANT
Best Eggplant Casserole 195
Buckwheat with Roasted Eggplant and Pepper 116
Eggplant Parmesan 213
Eggplant Pyramids 115
Eggplant Spaghetti Sauce 365

EGGS
Breakfast Casserole 224
Breakfast Pizza 214
Breakfast Quiche 227
Broccoli-Cheese Strata 229
Easy Mexican Omelette 228
Egg and Sausage Bake 224
Eggs McMurff 223
Quick Quiche 226
Stuffed French Toast Casserole 225

F

FISH
Best Ever Catfish 156
Brazilian Coconut Fish 157
Catfish Margurey 154

Crunchy Onion Catfish 154
Crusty Tuna Pie 165
Delta Baked Catfish 155
Easy Seafood Au Gratin 162
Fish Soufflé 160
Granna's Tuna Croquettes 166
Herbed Fish Fillets 156
Hot Tuna Sandwiches 151
Lemon Catfish with Parmesan 155
Low-Fat Grilled Catfish 153
Pat's Catfish Fillets 153
Shish Kebab 149
Tuna Noodle Casserole 165
Tuna Sandwiches 376

FRUIT *(See individual listings also)*
Birchermuesli 236
Byrds' Fruitcake, The 268
Easy Fruit Ice Cream 326
Frozen Banana Split Pie 296
Fruited Bread Pudding 314
Fruited Chicken 179
Fruited Mint Julep 14
Gooseberry Salad 76
Holiday Bread 44
Holiday Fruit Bread 45
Hot Curried Fruit 141
Mama Griffis' No-Bake Fruitcake 268
My Favorite Cake 277
Quince Jam 333

G

GRAPEFRUIT
Congealed Grapefruit Salad 84
Fruit Salad with Pineapple Pecan Whip Topping 82

GREEN BEANS
Chicken and Green Bean Casserole 191
Green Bean and Corn Casserole 135
Green Beans and Artichokes 133
Green Beans Au Gratin 134
Green Beans with Horseradish Dressing 135
Green Bean Wraps 132
Stir-Fried Green Beans 132
Sweet and Sour Green Beans 133
Swiss Green Beans 134

H

HAM
Baked Ham 220
Broccoli, Ham, and Macaroni Bake 222
Broccoli-Cheese Strata 229
Go Chocs Pre-Game Sandwich 152
Ham and Cheese Bites 29
Ham Loaf 221
Ham Rolls 222
Quick Quiche 226
Red Beans and Rice 223
Sweet and Sour Ham Loaf 220
Tortilla Roll-Ups 32

HUSHPUPPIES
Mississippi College Hushpuppies 61

I

ICE CREAM AND FROZEN DESSERTS
Basic Vanilla Ice Cream 325
Easy Chocolate Ice Cream 326
Easy Fruit Ice Cream 326
Frozen Banana Split Pie 296
Frozen Caramel Pie 297
Fudge Sundae Pie 302
Fudge-Coffee Ice Cream Bars 324
Peach Ice Cream 325
Raspberry Chocolate Delight 239
Strawberry-Ice Cream Dessert 324
Toby's Vanilla Ice Cream 325

J

JAMS AND JELLIES
Quince Jam 333
Watermelon Rind Preserves 358

L

LEMON
Best-Ever Lemon Pie 371
Buttermilk Lemon Pie 308
Clear Lemon Icing 292
Dr. Buckner's Lemon Meringue Pie 307
Lemonade Base Punch 12
Lemonade Tea 14
Lemon Catfish with Parmesan 155
Lemon Chess Pie 309
Lemon Cream Cake 263
Lemon Lover's Meat Loaf 192
Lemon-Pineapple Slush Punch 14
Lemon Poppy Seed Cake 262
Lemon Sauce 281
Lemon Squares 246
Light Lemon Cheesecake 287

M

MEAT *(See individual listings also)*
Bobotee 211

MUFFINS *(See Breads)*

MUSHROOMS
Mushroom Marinade 140
Mushroom Puffs 33
Pickled Mushrooms 30

O

OKRA
Chicken Okra Palau Over Rice 179

Fried Okra 114
Stewed Okra and Tomatoes 113
ONIONS
Onion Cornbread 57
Vidalia Onion Casserole 141
ORANGES
24-Hour Fruit Salad 81
Ambrosia Salad 79
Citrus Salad Dressing 97
Congealed Grapefruit Salad 84
Elegant Orange Muffins 64
Five Cup Salad 80
Florida Orange Cake 375
Fruit Salad with Pineapple Pecan Whip Topping 82
Jeweled Fruit Salad 80
Orange Fruit Mélange 82
Orange Pineapple Salad 84
Orange Slice Bars 248
Spiced Orange Pot Roast 206
OYSTERS
Oysters Mosca 161
Oysters Point Clear 34
Shrimp or Smoked Oyster Mousse 28

P

PANCAKES
Pancakes 69
Buttermilk Flapjacks 359
PASTA
Beef and Noodle Skillet 212
Broccoli, Ham, and Macaroni Bake 222
Cajun Fettuccine 171
Carruth Crawfish Fettucine 368
Casa Myers Lasagna 200
Chicken and Spaghetti Casserole 361
Chicken and Spinach Noodle Casserole 190
Chicken Spaghetti 181
Chinese Ground Beef Casserole 201
Easy Spaghetti 202
Eggplant Spaghetti Sauce 365
Extra Inning Pasta 365
Lasagna 369
Macaroni and Cheese 229
Pasta Salad 73
Shrimp and Pasta 162
Shrimp in Angel Hair Pasta Casserole 167
Spaghetti Pie 228
Spinach Lasagna 231
Tuna Noodle Casserole 165
PEACHES
Chunky Fruit Salad 79
Fresh Peach Cobbler 293
Jeweled Fruit Salad 80
Orange Fruit Mélange 82
Peach Ice Cream 325
Peach Pound Cake 261
Peach Tree Cobbler, The 293
PEAS
Black-eyed Peas with Rice 125
Creole Black-Eyed Peas 214
Easy Cheesy Peas 140
English Pea Casserole 139
PICKLES AND PRESERVES
Bread and Butter Pickles 332
Mamaw's Squash Pickles 332
Watermelon Rind Preserves 358
PIES
Basic Pie Crust 311
Best-Ever Lemon Pie 371
Black Bottom Pie 305
Brownie Pie 301
Buttermilk Lemon Pie 308
Cakie Pie 364
Caramel Pie 297
Chess Pie 308
Chocolate Brownie Pie 300
Chocolate Chess Pie 299
Chocolate Pie 306
Chocolate-Nut Brownie Pie 300
Classic Pecan Pie 294
Cream Cheese Pie 298
Dr. Buckner's Lemon Meringue Pie 307
Dreamy Fruit Pie 304
English Apple Dessert 294
Fluffy Peanut Butter Pie 295
Frozen Banana Split Pie 296
Frozen Caramel Pie 297
Fudge Pie 306
Fudge Sundae Pie 302
Hot Water Pastry 310
Jeff Davis Pie 362
Lemon Chess Pie 309
Margie's Pecan Pie 301
Million Dollar Pie 303
Mother's Angel Pie 304
Pecan Tassies 310
Perfect Apple Pie 309
Pumpkin Pie 303
Refrigerator Fruit Pie 305
Strawberry Icebox Pie 302
Sugar-Free Strawberry Pie 298
Surprise Pie 299
Sweet Potato Pie 295
MEAT PIES
Beef-Vegetable Pie 196
Chicken-Vegetable Pot Pie 174
Crusty Tuna Pie 165
Easy Chicken Pie 182
Hamburger Pie 213
Natchitoches Meat Pies 147
Reuben Pie 195
PIE CRUSTS
Basic Pie Crust 311

Hot Water Pastry ... 310

PINEAPPLE

24-Hour Fruit Salad ... 81
Ambrosia Salad ... 79
Blueberry Salad ... 85
Chunky Fruit Salad ... 79
Congealed Grapefruit Salad ... 84
Dieters' Congealed Salad ... 77
Five Cup Salad ... 80
Frozen Strawberry Fruit Salad ... 85
Frozen Waldorf Salad ... 86
Fruit Salad with Pineapple Pecan Whip Topping ... 82
Fruited Chicken ... 179
Jeweled Fruit Salad ... 80
Million Dollar Pie ... 303
Old Tyme Pineapple Upside Down Cake ... 276
Orange Pineapple Salad ... 84
Papa's Pineapple Casserole ... 143
Pineapple-Apple Salad ... 80
Pink Fluff Salad ... 76
Scalloped Pineapple ... 142
Strawberry Icebox Pie ... 302
Strawberry Pretzel Salad ... 83
Strawberry Supreme ... 75
Sunshine Veggie-Fruit Salad ... 78
Sweet and Sour Chicken ... 180
Vitamin A & C Congealed Salad ... 77
Winter Fruit Salad ... 81

PLUMS

Delicious Plum Cake ... 273

PORK

Bacon-Wrapped Pork Tenderloin ... 219
Casa Myers Lasagna ... 200
Creole Black-Eyed Peas ... 214
Easy and Delicious Pork Chops ... 218
Ham Loaf ... 221
Khao Phat Mu Kung Sai Khai (Thai Fried Rice with Pork, Shrimp and Egg) ... 218
Maggie's Easy Gumbo ... 107
Natchitoches Meat Pies ... 147
Pork Chop Casserole ... 217
Red Beans and Rice ... 223
Stuffed Pork Loin ... 217
Sweet and Sour Ham Loaf ... 220
Sweet and Sour Pork Chops ... 219

POTATOES

Big Mom's Potato Salad ... 74
Cheese and Potato Chowder ... 104
Crispy "Tater" Chicken ... 186
Giant's Potato Fingers ... 123
Hash Brown Potato Casserole ... 123
Hot Potato Salad ... 74
Mackinac Island Potato Soup ... 105
Marinated New Potatoes ... 30
Mashed Potato Rolls ... 54
Potato Casserole ... 122
Potato Puff Casserole ... 196
Quick Potato Salad ... 73
Skewered Grilled Potatoes ... 121
Venetian Potatoes ... 122

POULTRY

CHICKEN

Baked Chicken Parmesan ... 191
Barrentine's Chicken ... 182
Bill's Chicken Breasts Florentine for Two ... 190
Brunswick Stew ... 106
Cantaloupe/Chicken Salad ... 95
Caquela De Ave (Chicken Soup) ... 99
Cheesy Chicken Skillet ... 173
Cheesy Enchilada Casserole ... 172
Chicken and Green Bean Casserole ... 191
Chicken And Rice Casserole ... 177
Chicken and Sausage Gumbo ... 108
Chicken and Spaghetti Casserole 361
Chicken and Spinach Noodle Casserole ... 190
Chicken Cashew ... 184
Chicken Divan ... 189
Chicken Las Vegas ... 186
Chicken Okra Palau Over Rice ... 179
Chicken Parmigiana ... 189
Chicken Spaghetti ... 181
Chicken Tenders ... 175
Chicken-To-Go Biscuits ... 178
Chicken-Vegetable Pot Pie ... 174
Chinese Chicken ... 177
Country Captain ... 175
Crispy "Tater" Chicken ... 186
Curried Chicken and Pecan Salad . 94
Curried Chicken Balls ... 31
Darlene's Glazed Chicken ... 184
Easy Chicken and Dumplings ... 187
Easy Chicken Pie ... 182
Exotic Salad ... 94
Family Reunion Chicken ... 181
Fruited Chicken ... 179
Groundnut Stew ... 185
Honey Curry Chicken ... 187
Hot or Cold Chicken Salad ... 93
Italian Chicken ... 183
Ladies' Luncheon Chicken Sandwich ... 150
Mam-Ma's Dumplings ... 357
Marinated, Grilled Chicken ... 180
MC Bacon-Wrapped Chicken Livers ... 33
Mexican Chicken ... 183
Natchez Chicken Casserole ... 173
Poppy Seed Chicken ... 185
Russian Chicken ... 188
Sadie's Baked Chicken Breasts ... 188
Shish Kebab ... 149
Special Creamy Chicken ... 176

Stir-Fried Jambalaya ... 172
Sweet and Sour Chicken ... 180
White Chili ... 197
Smoked Pheasant Breasts in Pepper Jelly ... 366
TURKEY
Low-Fat Taco Salad ... 92
Pizza Squares ... 212

PUDDINGS AND CUSTARDS
Apricot Pudding ... 314
Baked Chocolate Custard ... 316
Banana Pudding ... 312
Bessie's Old-Fashioned Banana Pudding ... 313
Boiled Custard ... 376
Chess Squares ... 240
Creme Caramelo (Flan) ... 311
Custard ... 315
Death By Chocolate ... 235
Four-Layer Chocolate Delight ... 237
Frosted Pudding ... 317
Fruited Bread Pudding ... 314
Low-Fat Banana Pudding ... 312
Low-Fat Rice Pudding ... 317
Party Trifle ... 240
Quick Chocolate Mousse ... 235
Royal Bread and Butter Pudding ... 313
Royal Chocolate Custard ... 315
White House Coconut Custard ... 316

PUMPKIN
Pumpkin Cake ... 274
Pumpkin Pie ... 303
Tribesman Pumpkin-Nut Bread ... 42

R

RAISINS
Amalgamation Cake ... 266
Holiday Hunks ... 253
Japanese Fruitcake ... 267
Rich Layer Fruitcake ... 267

RASPBERRIES
Raspberry Chocolate Delight ... 239
Raspberry Delight ... 238
Red Raspberry Cake and Icing ... 370

RICE
Baked Rice ... 369
Black-eyed Peas with Rice ... 125
Broccoli-Rice Casserole ... 125
Chicken And Rice Casserole ... 177
Chicken Okra Palau Over Rice ... 179
Fiesta Stack Ups ... 194
Fried Rice with Almonds ... 126
Granny's Rice Casserole ... 124
Green Rice ... 124
Hampton Plantation Shrimp Pilau ... 164
Khao Phat Mu Kung Sai Khai (Thai Fried Rice with Pork, Shrimp and Egg) ... 218
Low-Fat Rice Pudding ... 317
Mexican Chicken ... 183
Red Beans and Rice ... 223
Sausage and Rice Casserole ... 215
Sausage Jambalaya ... 215
Shrimp Creole ... 170
Spanish Shrimp ... 169
Stir-Fried Jambalaya ... 172
Taco Casserole ... 209
Tamale Casserole ... 209

ROLLS AND BISCUITS (See Breads)

S

SALADS AND SALAD DRESSINGS
CONGEALED SALADS
Blueberry Salad ... 85
Classic Strawberry Salad ... 83
Congealed Grapefruit Salad ... 84
Corned Beef Salad ... 93
Cranberry Salad ... 357
Deluxe Tomato Aspic ... 78
Dieters' Congealed Salad ... 77
Gooseberry Salad ... 76
Orange Pineapple Salad ... 84
Strawberry Pretzel Salad ... 83
Sunshine Veggie-Fruit Salad ... 78
Vitamin A & C Congealed Salad ... 77
FRUIT SALADS
24-Hour Fruit Salad ... 81
Ambrosia Salad ... 79
Apple-Pineapple Slaw ... 88
Blueberry Salad ... 85
Chunky Fruit Salad ... 79
Classic Strawberry Salad ... 83
Congealed Grapefruit Salad ... 84
Dieters' Congealed Salad ... 77
Five Cup Salad ... 80
Fresh Cranberry Salad ... 75
Frozen Strawberry Fruit Salad ... 85
Frozen Waldorf Salad ... 86
Fruit Salad with Pineapple Pecan Whip Topping ... 82
Gooseberry Salad ... 76
Jeweled Fruit Salad ... 80
Orange Fruit Mélange ... 82
Orange Pineapple Salad ... 84
Pineapple-Apple Salad ... 80
Pink Fluff Salad ... 76
Strawberry Pretzel Salad ... 83
Strawberry Supreme ... 75
Sunshine Veggie-Fruit Salad ... 78
Vitamin A & C Congealed Salad ... 77
Winter Fruit Salad ... 81
MEAT SALADS
Cantaloupe/Chicken Salad ... 95
Corned Beef Salad ... 93
Curried Chicken and Pecan Salad ... 94
Exotic Salad ... 94

Hot or Cold Chicken Salad 93
Low-Fat Taco Salad 92
Pasta Salad 73
SALAD DRESSINGS
Blue Cheese Dressing 97
Citrus Salad Dressing 97
Cool-As-A-Cucumber Dressing 96
French Country Dressing 96
French Vinaigrette 96
Poppy Seed Dressing 95
Thousand Island Salad Dressing 95
VEGETABLE SALADS
Big Mom's Potato Salad 74
Broccoli Salad 90
Cornbread Salad 86
Crunchy Broccoli Salad 91
Deluxe Tomato Aspic 78
Don't-Stop-At-Seven Layer Salad! 90
Easy Layered Salad 89
Fresh Spinach Salad 92
Easy Tossed Salad 92
Garden Salad with Almonds and Oranges 91
Grace's Tomatoes 89
Green Wonder Salad in Marinade 87
Hot Potato Salad 74
Marinated Vegetable Salad 87
Quick Potato Salad 73
Sunshine Veggie-Fruit Salad 78
Vegetable Bouquet 88

SAUCES AND GRAVIES
Big Mama's Tomato Chili Sauce 331
Bouligny Glaze 329
Cajun Seasoning Mix 330
Cappiello's Plain Tomato Sauce 367
Classic Meat Sauce 199
Eggplant Spaghetti Sauce 365
Hog Dog/Hamburger Sauce 330
Hot Mustard 331
Lemon Sauce 281
Nick's Barbecue Sauce 330
Picante Sauce 331
Roosevelt Hotel Rémoulade Sauce 329
Steak Shoyu 329

SAUSAGE
Breakfast Casserole 224
Breakfast Pizza 214
Breakfast Quiche 227
Chicken and Sausage Gumbo 108
Creole Black-Eyed Peas 214
Crustless Sausage-Apple Quiche 226
Egg and Sausage Bake 224
Extra Inning Pasta 365
Lasagna 369
Meatlover's Delight 26
Quick Quiche 226
Ratatouille 216
Sausage and Rice Casserole 215
Sausage Balls 29
Sausage Casserole 216
Sausage Cornbread 57
Sausage Jambalaya 215
Stir-Fried Jambalaya 172
Stuffed Cabbage Rolls 152
Vidalia Onion Casserole 141

SEAFOOD *(See Crabmeat, Crawfish, Fish, Oysters and Shrimp)*

SHRIMP
Barbecued Shrimp 34
Best Gumbo Ever 109
Cajun Fettuccine 171
Carolyn's Shrimp Etouffeé 159
Crabmeat-Shrimp Dip 21
Easy Crawfish Etouffeé 159
Easy Seafood Au Gratin 162
Easy Shrimp Creole 167
French (White) Shrimp Etouffeé 158
Hampton Plantation Shrimp Pilau 164
Khao Phat Mu Kung Sai Khai (Thai Fried Rice with Pork, Shrimp and Egg) 218
Low Country Boil 163
Maggie's Easy Gumbo 107
Mrs. Mayfield's Shrimp 168
New Orleans Barbecued Shrimp 166
Shrimp and Pasta 162
Shrimp Creole 170
Shrimp in Angel Hair Pasta Casserole 167
Shrimp or Crawfish Casserole 161
Shrimp or Smoked Oyster Mousse 28
Shrimp Party Dip 22
Shrimp Quiche 225
Shrimp Sandwiches 25
Shrimp Scampi 168
Shrimp Stroganoff 169
Shrimp Wheels 25
Shrimp-N-Squash Stir-Fry 164
Spanish Shrimp 169

SOUPS
COLD
Quick Gazpacho 98
Spicy Gazpacho 98
HOT
Artichoke Soup 102
Best Gumbo Ever 109
Brunswick Stew 106
Cabbage Beef Soup 100
Caquela De Ave (Chicken Soup) 99
Cheese and Potato Chowder 104
Chicken and Sausage Gumbo 108
Cowboy Stew 105
Crabmeat Soup 99
Five-Hour Stew 104
Green Chili Soup 362
Groundnut Stew 185
Light Zucchini Soup 103
Mackinac Island Potato Soup 105

Maggie's Easy Gumbo ... 107
No-Peep Stew ... 106
Norm's Broccoli-Cheese Soup ... 101
Oaty Vegetable Soup ... 102
Sirloin Vegetable Soup ... 101
Spanish Mama's Red Hot Chili ... 107
Teacher's Soup ... 100
Ten Bean Soup ... 103
White Chili ... 197

SPINACH
Bill's Chicken Breasts Florentine for Two ... 190
Fresh Spinach Salad ... 92
Spinach and Bacon Soufflé ... 227
Spinach Casserole with Crumb Topping ... 131
Spinach Lasagna ... 231
Spinach-Cheese Casserole ... 132

SQUASH
Butternut Squash Casserole with Crunchy Topping ... 128
Creamy Squash Casserole ... 129
Mamaw's Squash Pickles ... 332
Shrimp-N-Squash Stir-Fry ... 164
Squash Delight ... 128
Squash Dressing ... 129

STRAWBERRIES
Chunky Fruit Salad ... 79
Classic Strawberry Salad ... 83
Frozen Strawberry Fruit Salad ... 85
Jeweled Fruit Salad ... 80
Party Trifle ... 240
Strawberry Cake Supreme ... 262
Strawberry Icebox Pie ... 302
Strawberry Jam Coffeecake ... 66
Strawberry Pizza ... 241
Strawberry Pretzel Salad ... 83
Strawberry Supreme ... 75
Strawberry-Ice Cream Dessert ... 324
Sugar-Free Strawberry Pie ... 298
Winter Fruit Salad ... 81

SWEET POTATOES
Mother's Holiday Sweet Potato Bake ... 120
Sweet Potato Bread ... 48
Sweet Potato Casserole ... 121
Sweet Potato Muffins ... 63
Sweet Potato Pie ... 295

T

TOMATOES
Brazilian Coconut Fish ... 157
Cappiello's Plain Tomato Sauce ... 367
Chicken Spaghetti ... 181
Cornbread Salad ... 86
Deluxe Tomato Aspic ... 78
Easy Shrimp Creole ... 167
Fried Green Tomatoes ... 113
Grace's Tomatoes ... 89
Granny's Baked Tomatoes ... 113
Spanish Shrimp ... 169
Stewed Okra and Tomatoes ... 113
Tangy Mild Salsa ... 23
Tofu Pesto ... 149

TUNA
Crusty Tuna Pie ... 165
Easy Seafood Au Gratin ... 162
Granna's Tuna Croquettes ... 166
Tuna Noodle Casserole ... 165

TURKEY *(See Poultry)*

V

VEAL
Italian Scaloppine ... 148

VEGETABLES *(See individual listings also)*
Beef-Vegetable Pie ... 196
Chicken-Vegetable Pot Pie ... 174
Low Country Boil ... 163
Mama Bell's Mixed Vegetable Casserole ... 118
Marinated Vegetable Salad ... 87
Oaty Vegetable Soup ... 102
Parmesan Vegetable Casserole ... 119
Quick Gazpacho ... 98
Ratatouille ... 216
Sirloin Vegetable Soup ... 101
Spicy Gazpacho ... 98
Vegetable Appetizers ... 31
Vegetable Bouquet ... 88
Vegetable Garden Casserole ... 118
Viva Veggie Casserole ... 119

Venison Crockpot Steak ... 208

W

Watermelon Rind Preserves ... 358

Z

ZUCCHINI
Black Bean and Zucchini Chilaquiles ... 230
Light Zucchini Soup ... 103
Stuffed Zucchini ... 199
Zucchini and Cheese Casserole ... 201
Zucchini Bread ... 47
Zucchini Casserole ... 127

Mississippi College
P. O. Box 4041
Clinton, MS 39058

Please send ____ copy(ies) @ $19.95 each ________
Mississippi residents add 7% sales tax @ $1.40 each ________
Postage and Handling @ $2.50 each ________
TOTAL $ ________

Name: ______________________________
(Please print)
Address: ______________________________
City: ______________ State: ________ Zip: ________

Make checks payable to Mississippi College

☐ Check or money order enclosed
☐ Visa/Mastercard

Number ______________ Expiration Date ________

Signature ______________________________

Mississippi College
P. O. Box 4041
Clinton, MS 39058

Please send ____ copy(ies) @ $19.95 each ________
Mississippi residents add 7% sales tax @ $1.40 each ________
Postage and Handling @ $2.50 each ________
TOTAL $ ________

Name: ______________________________
(Please print)
Address: ______________________________
City: ______________ State: ________ Zip: ________

Make checks payable to Mississippi College

☐ Check or money order enclosed
☐ Visa/Mastercard

Number ______________ Expiration Date ________

Signature ______________________________